MORE ADVANCE PRAISE

"*Rebel Code* is an amazing and exciting in-depth view of the Linux movement. Glyn Moody explores the spirit of the movement and chronicles its history, not forgetting some of the more outrageous aspects and the egos of the programmers involved. This is a thoroughly investigated and absorbing story."

—MATTHIAS ETTRICH,
Senior Software Engineer, Trolltech, and KDE project founder

"This book is an entertaining tapestry that weaves together the people, technologies, and companies of the open source software movement."

—JOHN OUSTERHOUT,
Creator of the Tcl scripting language

"If you've read about 'open source' and 'free software' and been puzzled about what it is and where is comes from, Glyn Moody's *Rebel Code* is for you. If you know who rms and Linus, Eric Raymond and Larry Wall, Bob Young and Eric Allman are, you'll love the history and anecdotes, too."

—PETER H. SALUS,
Chief Knowledge Officer, Matrix.Net,
and author of <u>A Quarter Century of Unix</u>

REBEL CODE

REBEL CODE

[The Inside Story of Linux and the Open Source Revolution]

GLYN MOODY

PERSEUS PUBLISHING
Cambridge, Massachusetts

To My Family

A CIP catalog record for this book is available from the Library of Congress
ISBN 0-7382-0333-5

Perseus Publishing is a member of the Perseus Books Group.

Find us on the World Wide Web at http://www.perseuspublishing.com

Perseus Publishing books are available at special discounts for bulk purchases in the U.S. by corporations, institutions, and other organizations. For more information, please contact the Special Markets Department at HarperCollins Publishers, 10 East 53rd Street, New York, NY 10022, or call 1-212-207-7528.

Text design by Jeffrey P. Williams
Set in 11-point Berkeley by Perseus Publishing Services

First printing, January 2001

1 2 3 4 5 6 7 8 9 10—03 02 01

CONTENTS

Prologue   *1*

1   The Coolest Year   *5*

2   The New GNU Thing   *13*

3   A Minor Rebellion   *31*

4   Factor X   *55*

5   Patching Up   *71*

6   Root then Boot   *87*

7   Linus 2.0   *106*

8   Learning from Berkeley   *120*

9   The Art of Code   *140*

10   Low-Down in the Valley   *162*

11   Free the Lizard   *182*

12   A Foothold   *205*

13   Alliances and IPOs   *220*

14   Open for Business   *237*

15   Trolls Versus Gnomes   *252*

16   Lies, Damned Lies, and Benchmarks   *269*

17   Tomorrow's Hothouse   *289*

18   Beyond the Market   *305*

Index   *324*

ACKNOWLEDGMENTS

Unless otherwise noted, the vast majority of quotations in this book are drawn from interviews conducted between September 1999 and September 2000 in person, by telephone, or by e-mail. These have been supplemented by extensive material taken from an interview with Linus Torvalds at a critical juncture in his life, in December 1996, as well as other interviews with key players from the last three years.

I am particularly grateful to all these people, who somehow managed to take time from their important work and hectic schedules to talk to me, often at great length. My only regret is that because of space constraints I was not able to introduce more of their memories, thoughts, and comments.

Despite this generous help, I am conscious that there will be mistakes and omissions in this book, for which I alone am responsible. I would be happy to receive corrections as well as general comments on the text at glynmoody@rebelcode.net.

The 1996 interview with Linus Torvalds was carried out for a feature commissioned by Sean Geer, editor of the UK edition of *Wired* magazine. The feature eventually appeared as "The Greatest OS That (N)ever Was" in the August 1997 issue of the U.S. edition of *Wired*, where it was shepherded through by Jim Daly, a features editor at the time. Jim kindly suggested my name to Jacqueline Murphy of Perseus Books when, in 1999, she was looking for someone to write a book about GNU/Linux and open source. My thanks go to him, and even more to Jacqueline, my editor, who not only followed up the suggestion but also persuaded me that I should undertake this project. I am also grateful to Jacqueline's assistant, Arlinda Shtuni, for her constant help; Marco Pavia for steering the book through production and to Jennifer Blakebrough-Raeburn for her sensitive copyediting.

Others who have provided key assistance along the way are David Croom, who offered valuable advice early on, and two people who kindly read draft versions of the text and made helpful comments, Anna O'Donovan and Sean Geer.

Finally, I must record my deep gratitude to my wife and family, without whose constant support this book would not have been possible.

—Glyn Moody

PROLOGUE

Outside, a lowering Seattle sky broods over the clumps of squat white buildings scattered around an extensive campus in constant expansion. Neat lawns, assiduously tended flowerbeds, and the tidy ornamental ponds create a mood of cloistered reflection and tranquillity.

Inside, a similar calm reigns in the cubicles where young men and women toil diligently. The silence is broken only by bursts of clattering keys; hardly a word is exchanged, as if a stern vow were in force. And yet despite a conducive environment and comforting faith, there is unease among the cubicles' inhabitants, a rising tide of something close to fear. They know that a terrible ghost is abroad in the cloisters of Microsoft.

The ghost has a name: open source. Its characteristics have been meticulously detailed by two of the company's expert ghost-watchers in a pair of lengthy memos. Though marked "Microsoft confidential," they surfaced outside the company and were published on the Web, suitably enough during Halloween 1998. Forced to concede that the memos did indeed originate from within the company, Microsoft dismissed them as the private speculations of a couple of engineers.

As he read the memos describing this crazy phenomenon, Bill Gates must have shuddered in recognition; it was as if a spirit from the past had tapped him on the shoulder. Gates had sought to exorcise the ghost of free software over twenty years before.

In 1976, Gates had published what he called—with what would prove deep irony—an Open Letter to Hobbyists, addressed to users of the first personal computer, the MITS Altair. Gates and Paul Allen, the other founder of Microsoft, had written a version of the Basic (Beginner's All-Purpose Symbolic Instruction Code) language that would run on this

1

rudimentary machine—a considerable feat given its limited memory. Gates wrote his Open Letter to condemn what he saw as software piracy—making illegal copies of the program he and Allen had written— but which many users then regarded as part of computer community's long tradition of sharing useful tools.

In his tirade against the practice of passing around software, Gates thundered, "As the majority of hobbyists must be aware, most of you steal your software. Hardware must be paid for, but software is something to share. Who cares if the people who worked on it get paid?" He went on to claim that the result of such piracy is the prevention of "good software from being written." After all, he asked rhetorically, "Who can afford to do professional work for nothing? What hobbyist can put three man-years into programming, finding all bugs, documenting his product, and distribute for free?"

As he penned these lines, Gates probably thought these were unanswerable arguments. And yet the Halloween memos, written by his own engineers, document in great detail the incontrovertible fact: There was now not just one hobbyist out there, but several thousand of them. Collectively, they were putting thousands of man-years into programming, finding bugs, documenting products, and then distributing them free, complete with the source code—that holy text that Microsoft and other software companies had withheld from profane eyes for the last twenty years.

In the light of his Open Letter to Hobbyists, the open source movement emerges as Bill Gates' worst nightmare magnified a thousand times. Not just a few hobbyists who "steal," but a thriving community that writes its own—excellent—code, and then gives it away. Because their actions patently do not "prevent good software from being written," they implicitly call into question the very basis of the Microsoft Empire: If good software can be written and given away like this, who needs Microsoft or companies like it?

The appearance of the Halloween Documents, and the fundamental issues they raise, could not have come at a worse time for the company. The antitrust lawsuit brought by the U.S. Department of Justice in 1998 had, for perhaps the first time, called Microsoft's aura of invincibility into question. The lawsuit's existence meant that people began considering, if only theoretically, the possibility of a computing world not dominated by the Redmond giant.

That looked more plausible thanks to the continuing delays in the delivery of what Microsoft had no hesitation in branding its key enterprise product. This had formerly been known as Windows NT 5, but when the

Halloween documents were leaked it had just been renamed Windows 2000. If Windows NT 5 had arrived in 1998, companies would doubtless have been too busy adopting it to contemplate alternatives; but coupled with the antitrust lawsuit, the resulting vacuum allowed other options to be considered.

Moreover, when the company found itself faced by a public relations disaster during the antitrust trial as well as grave technical problems in delivering Windows 2000, there was an unprecedented loss of some half-a-dozen top executives—the people Microsoft most needed to resolve these problems. Even Bill Gates seemed fatally distracted by the Department of Justice's lawsuit. His woeful videotaped testimony for the trial, in which he appeared unable to recall his own e-mail or even his key business decisions, destroyed once and for all his image as the infallible high-priest of high-tech.

At this moment, when Microsoft was at its most vulnerable, and its boss at his least admired, there appeared on the computing scene not only an alternative but a rival.

Alongside the Internet, the Halloween documents had identified the free operating system kernel Linux—pronounced "Lih-nooks"—as among the most successful examples of the open source philosophy: "Linux has been deployed in mission critical, commercial environments with an excellent pool of public testimonials," Vinod Valloppillil, one of the memos' authors, had noted. It also formed the nucleus of a free-software project that directly attacked Microsoft's core product line, notably the troubled Windows 2000.

Linux had been started by a twenty-one-year-old Finnish student, Linus Torvalds, who distributed it freely, including the source code—the underlying programming instructions, which form a kind of blueprint for software. In Linus ("Lee-noose"), as he was universally known within his community, the open source movement had not only a gifted leader but an invaluable icon. Although complex but important issues of software development methodology might leave the mass media outlets cold, this modest and photogenic young man proved an immediate hit. Linus seemed to embody everything Bill Gates was not, just as open source was the antithesis of Microsoft. Linus also belied the traditional image of those who made up the open source movement.

These self-described hackers—not to be confused with the malevolent crackers who break into computer systems—have traditionally been caricatured as maladjusted youths who turn to hacking because they lack social skills and feel marginalized. And yet here was Linus Torvalds, one of the hacker princes, who not only washed regularly, kept his hair short, and wore neat, clean clothes, but had a respectable job, was married, and was a father.

There could be no better symbol for the new generation of hackers who are turning open source into a powerful force in today's computing world. They are the heirs of an earlier hacking culture that thrived in the 1960s and 1970s when computers were still new, a community that believed software should be shared, and that all would benefit as a result. This was the ethic that Bill Gates had lambasted in his Open Letter to Hobbyists. Microsoft and a few other key companies at the time, notably AT&T, are largely responsible for nearly extinguishing the old hacker spirit and replacing it with a view that redefined sharing software as piracy.

Thanks to the advent of relatively low-cost but powerful PCs and the global wiring of the Net, the new hackers are immeasurably more numerous, more productive, and more united than their forebears. They are linked by a common goal—writing great software—and a common code: that such software should be freely available to all. Hackers rebel against the idea that the underlying source code should be withheld. For them, these special texts are a new kind of literature that forms part of the common heritage of humanity: to be published, read, studied and even added to, not chained to desks in inaccessible monastic libraries for a few authorized adepts to handle reverently.

As a result, the open source movement poses a challenge not just to Microsoft but to the entire software industry. And perhaps beyond. For as the Internet moves ever closer to heart of the modern world, it inevitably carries with it the free programs that drive it, and seeds the values that led to their creation. Its basic code of openness, sharing, and cooperation is starting to spread outside the confines of one or two high-tech industries. Many now believe that this potent combination of the Net with open source has more than a ghost of a chance of thriving in the current post-Microsoft era.

1

The Coolest Year

IF 1998 AND 1999 WERE THE WORST YEARS in Microsoft's history, 1991, by contrast, must have been a period when Bill Gates was feeling good. Windows 3.0, launched in May 1990, was a growing success; in the first year alone, 4 million copies had been shipped, a huge number for the time. In May 1991, Microsoft launched Visual Basic, a radically new way of programming that employs visual design methods rather than traditional ones based on editing text files.

Even better, Windows 3.1 was close. Despite the point upgrade, version 3.1 represented a major advance over 3.0 in almost every way. Microsoft claimed that it contained over 1,000 enhancements. Its cool new user interface seduced almost everyone that saw it.

When Windows 3.1 shipped in June 1992, it cemented Microsoft's dominance on the desktop. It also created a discontinuity in the software world as companies switched from DOS-based programs to those running under Windows. Microsoft was able to exploit this crossover to wrest leadership in the spreadsheet and word-processor sectors by quickly launching programs such as Excel and Word.

Windows 3.1 was not the only major operating system nearing completion in 1991. Microsoft Windows New Technology, better known as Windows NT, had been started back in 1988 in a drive to create an enterprise-level operating system that would be as widely deployed in companies' back offices as MS-DOS and then Windows were in the front offices.

The Windows NT project was headed by Dave Cutler, who had built the operating system VMS for the computer giant Digital, formerly known as DEC. VMS was a rival to Unix, another robust operating system, but was an official corporate product, unlike Unix, which had always been regarded as software for hackers. Windows NT, too, was unashamedly meant as a Unix-killer when, against expectations, Unix—not VMS— emerged as the leading enterprise operating system.

NT's chances looked good. By the late 1980s, Unix was highly fragmented, each vendor offering a slightly different version; this meant that application software had to be rewritten many times, and that users were locked into the software of one supplier. Because Unix had also failed to embrace fully the new wave of graphical interfaces, its solutions in this area were crude when compared with the Apple Macintosh or Microsoft Windows. Windows NT, by contrast, was designed to marry the power of a VMS-like operating system with the elegance and usability of Windows 3.1.

But plenty was happening outside Microsoft's immediate sphere of interest. In 1991, Tim Berners-Lee, a British physicist at CERN, the European Centre for Nuclear Research, released for public use a hypertext system that he had been developing over the past two years. The system, which he called the World Wide Web, ran across the Internet, then still small-scale and used mostly by academics.

Also in 1991, a new programming language called Java was being drawn up by a team at Sun Microsystems. Born originally as part of an attempt to develop an interactive set-top box for the cable TV industry, Java was later adapted for use on the Internet. An important feature of Java was portability: The same program could run without modification on a wide range of hardware, a novelty at the time.

Although the threats these developments represented at the time were negligible compared to their later impact, it is possible that Microsoft was tracking them in 1991. The Internet was well known enough, the Web was in the public domain, and Sun was a competitor whose moves were certainly watched with interest. But surely it is impossible that, in the same year, Microsoft could have had even the merest whisper of a suspicion that a key element of an equally potent challenge was about to take shape in the bedroom of a second-year computer science student in Helsinki, the capital of Finland.

As one of the most northerly capitals in the world, Helsinki is a city of seasonal extremes: dark, cold winters with only a few hours of daylight, and bright summers where the days never seem to end. Geographically, Helinski is close to Russia's St Petersburg, and parts of it are visually similar; culturally, it has closest ties with Sweden, of which for centuries Finland formed a province. When Russia invaded and annexed Finland as part of its empire in 1809, it separated from Sweden. Finland only won full independence in 1917.

Two cathedrals form important landmarks on the eastern side of the city center. The Lutheran church possesses an elegant neo-classical exterior, but takes the form within of a huge stone shell almost devoid of ornament; the Russian Orthodox Uspensky Cathedral is a typical concoction of onion domed towers outside, and icons inside. Helsinki is compact; its low buildings and broad streets are mostly laid out on two grid systems that abut at a slight angle. Green spaces abound, and the sight and smell of the sea, which surrounds Helsinki on three sides, is never far away.

Into this ordered but individual world, Linus Benedict Torvalds was born on 28 December 1969. Linus explains the significance of this day in his culture: "It's special in the same way most days are special—many days have some traditional meaning. December 28th is 'menlösa barns dag,' which means roughly 'day of children without defects' although 'menlös' is fairly old Swedish and a lot more poetic than 'without defect.'"

The name *Linus* was an unusual choice: "not unheard of," Linus explains, "but not exactly common" in Finland either. The name itself has a history that stretches back to the roots of Western civilization. It is mentioned in Homer's *Iliad* in the original Greek form *Linos,* where it is associated with a song of mourning. There is also a St. Linus, who is traditionally listed as the second pope after St. Peter. Another famous Linus—though better-known for his last name—is the American inventor Linus Yale.

But rather than any of these, Linus was named in part after the U.S. scientist Linus Pauling, who received two Nobel Prizes: one for chemistry, and one for peace. "I think I was named equally for Linus the peanut-cartoon character," Linus adds, and notes that this makes him "a mix of 50 percent Nobel-prize-winning chemist and blanket-carrying cartoon character."

Torvalds is a rare surname: "There are probably something like twenty-five people in the world with that last name," Linus says. "Torvald" is "a rather old-fashioned Nordic name," Linus explains. "You'll find it in Sweden and Norway. The genitive 's' is unusual, an old way of turning a regular name into the name of a farmstead—and from there into a surname." Linus explains that it was his paternal grandfather "who took the name for personal reasons, namely, that he didn't like his family." As a result, he says, "to my knowledge, all Torvalds in the whole world are [his] descendants." In other words, one of the most famous names in computing is "completely made up, and not more than two generations ago."

The Torvalds clan is notable not just for its unusually small size: A surprising number of them are journalists. Linus runs down the list: "My dad, Nils Torvalds: reporter for Finnish radio. His brother, my uncle, Jan Torvalds: Finnish TV. My paternal grandfather—the founder of the Torvalds clan, deceased—used to be a newspaper reporter, writer, and poet. My mom: Mikke (Anna) Torvalds: working at the Finnish News Agency. Used to do translations, does news graphics these days. My sister, Sara Torvalds: used to do translations for the Finnish News Agency too, but is moving more towards books and films."

The Torvalds family formed part of the Swedish-speaking community in Finland, about 300,000 strong in a total population of 5 million. That their mother tongue has nothing in common linguistically with the Finnish language that surrounds them has doubtless helped them become a very close-knit group. Reflecting this, Swedish speakers themselves call this society within a society "Ankdammen"—the Duck Pond. One of Linus's friends from Helsinki, future fellow hacker Lars Wirzenius, says, "Almost all Swedish-speaking people know lots of other Swedish-speaking people, who know lots of other Swedish-speaking people, and the end result is that everyone either knows everyone, or knows someone who knows someone."

Growing up as a member of the Duck Pond, Linus spoke Swedish at home and with family friends, and only started learning Finnish when he was five. Contact with English, which would become a crucially important factor in his work, came a few years later.

It was around the same time that he first encountered a computer. Linus explains that his maternal grandfather was a statistician at Helsinki University; he bought a Commodore Vic-20 microcomputer, "one of the first ones to get on the market, at least in Finland." He adds, "It wasn't exactly what you'd call a number-cruncher today, but it was certainly faster than any calculator." The speed of the processor was just 1 Megahertz (MHz), a thousandth of that of modern PCs.

Linus recalls that his grandfather "bought the Vic-20 for his own needs to do math," but soon asked his young grandson to help. "I think my grandfather wanted me to learn, so he made me help him," he explains. "So I started off helping him with the computer, and then I did my own stuff on the side."

Linus recalls, "I had the Vic for five years because I couldn't afford to upgrade. I programmed in Basic, maybe the first two years." But Linus soon moved on from this popular beginner's programming language to something more demanding: assembly language.

Assembly language commands are easier for the computer to act on but harder for programmers to think in. "I kind of got used to doing stuff myself by reading books about assembly language," he says. "I didn't know about assemblers," programs that make writing assembly language code easier, "so I had to do it by hand; after a few years I essentially had to upgrade because everybody else had better machines."

Linus goes on to add another reason for buying a new computer: "I was getting to know the Vic too well." Throughout his computing life, Linus would search for new programming challenges, but it is interesting to see this trait emerge so early.

His next machine, and the reasons for that choice, are also highly characteristic of the later Linus. "I was looking at different machines—I didn't want a PC because I really disliked the Z80 [chip] architecture and in the PC, the chip was essentially the same," he says. That is, he decided not to buy a PC because he disliked the design of the Intel chip family that lay at its heart—an unusual way of looking at things.

"Back then I was doing just assembly language, and I didn't want to have anything to do with that [particular processor]." Because Linus was writing "low-level" code, which interacted directly with the chip, he was more conscious of the merits and demerits of the various chip families. Most programmers write in "high-level" languages like Basic, which effectively shield them from the details of the hardware.

As Linus himself says, he has always been a "low-level" person. There are probably two reasons for his early interest in this aspect. One was his emerging love of programming at the most fundamental level. The other is more pragmatic: "I had been a performance junkie since forever. When you had to write games for a slow 1 MHz [processor]," Linus explains, "you have to be kind of crazy and tweak cycles." "Tweaking cycles"—getting every last drop of performance out of code—would later mean that Linux was far faster and leaner than comparable programs.

In the end, Linus chose an unusual micro for his next machine, the Sinclair QL ("Quantum Leap"). This was a typically quirky product from the British inventor Sir Clive Sinclair.

Linus had been content to put up with Sinclair's QL—although it had some fairly obvious shortcomings—for a simple reason. The main thing he wanted, he explained, was "a machine at home that does multitasking." Even though the Sinclair QL was in many ways a toy, it had one very powerful feature, thanks to its choice of chip: it could run several programs simultaneously, just like commercial minicomputers.

This area of computing—multitasking—led him to start coding the simple program that would eventually turn into Linux. But this was still some years off from the time when Linus was hacking on his Sinclair QL. First, in the fall of 1988, he entered Helsinki University to study computer science, which by now already looked likely to turn from a passion into a profession.

At university, Linus found the same tendency for the two language communities in Finland to keep to themselves. His fellow student in computer science, Lars Wirzenius, comments that "at that time there weren't very many Swedish-speaking computer science students, and those that were, were at least a couple of years older than we were." It was therefore only natural that a pair of Swedish speakers isolated among the Finnish majority of the new intake for computer studies should gravitate towards each other.

Wirzenius recalls that the first time he met Linus, "it was one of the introductory lectures for new students.," Wirzenius didn't notice much of his friend that day except that "the end of his big nose tends to twitch up and down when he speaks, and it is fun to look at." Aside from the nose, which, in truth, is not that big, little in Linus's appearance is out of the ordinary: He is of medium height, with brown hair; his blue eyes gaze steadily from behind his glasses. Only the eyebrows, which are remarkably dark and bushy, jar slightly with the otherwise boyish face.

In an effort to meet more student members of the Duck Pond, Wirzenius and Linus joined one of the many societies that form an important element of Helsinki University's student scene. "The club that Linus and I joined was called the Spektrum," Wirzenius recalls, "which is the Swedish-speaking club for people who study math, computer science, physics, or chemistry." As far as the teaching at the university was concerned, Wirzenius explains that "there isn't actually a curriculum which says that during the first year you have to take this course and that course. The so-called academic freedom in Finland is interpreted so that students can take any course they want, mostly in whichever order they want.

"The nominal study length is five years, but most people study for six or seven years," he continues. Alongside the main courses there were various ancillary subjects. "To get a computer science degree, you have to study a certain amount of math, and also some other subjects. Each week we got some exercises to do, and then we had small groups of people and a teacher who asked each one of us to demonstrate some of the problems we were supposed to have solved. And if you hadn't solved all the problems, that was OK, but you had to solve a certain amount to pass the course.

"One of these weeks, Linus—for some reason, I don't remember—hadn't done all his homework. So he just claimed that he had done one of the exercises that he hadn't done—and the teacher asked him to demonstrate his solution. [Linus] walked up to the blackboard . . . and faced the problem that he claimed he had solved. Linus decides this is a simple problem, draws a couple of diagrams, and waves his hand a lot. It takes a long time for the teacher to understand that yes, this is actually a correct solution."

According to Wirzenius, this incident was atypical in one respect: "[Linus] didn't usually try to cheat, because he didn't have to. He knew math well from high school, and had a sort of mathematical brain, so he didn't have to spend much time on homework to get it done." Wirzenius believes there is something characteristic of his friend in the way Linus handled the situation—"the attitude, the arrogance that he displayed—most people would just have acknowledged that they didn't actually have a solution," but Linus hates having to admit that he doesn't know the answer.

Wirzenius says that "the arrogance he showed then is still visible" in how Linus handles challenges within the Linux community. "These days, he might claim that a certain kind of approach to a problem is the correct one, even though he hasn't necessarily thought about all the other approaches or solutions, and then the rest of the Internet either agrees with him or tries to convince him otherwise."

This approach works because Linus is "careful enough to not do it all the time. Most of the time when he says something, he has been thinking about it," Wirzenius notes, and concludes: "I wouldn't like to play poker against him. He can bluff." Just as important, if after all the bluffing Linus is caught out and shown to be wrong, Wirzenius says, he will accept corrections with good grace, a trait that would prove crucial in managing the community of equally opinionated and able hackers that would later coalesce around him.

After the first year's introductory course, there followed a major hiatus in their university studies. "All Finnish men are required to do either military or civil service," Wirzenius says. "Civil service is sort of you get an ordinary job but you don't get paid for it." In 1989, when he and Linus were required to choose, "the shortest time to do military service was eight months [and] all civil service was sixteen months. So I figured that's eight months too much, so let's do the shortest possible. Actually, the totally shortest possible way would be to refuse to do either kind of service, and then it would be six months in jail."

Like Wirzenius, Linus, too, decided that he'd rather not spend half a year in prison. But instead of choosing the next shortest option—eight months as a simple army private—he opted for one that lasted eleven months, which was training to become a noncommissioned officer.

Of this training, Wirzenius says, "It's sort of useful as an exercise in leadership, but a certain kind of leadership. . . what the army needs is group leaders who can teach their group to act almost on reflex, which was sort of scary. It's the same kind of stuff that all armies teach." He adds, "It's not just a way to learn how to make reflexes, but also a way to keep a group together as a working unit even if they don't like each other, and stuff like that." It is hard to imagine a better description of what would be involved in coordinating the global movement of volunteers that develop Linux.

Wirzenius recalls that he and Linus didn't see much of each other during that time even though they were both stationed in the same area of east Finland towards the end of their service; however, they made up for lost time when they were back at the university and had resumed their exploration of the computer world.

They began with a course that would have an effect not only on them—Wirzenius said that it felt "sort of like falling in love for the first time"—but on the entire history of computing. In the fall of 1990, they started using the university's recently acquired MicroVAX system, designed by none other than Dave Cutler, at that moment busily at work on Windows NT. Wirzenius and Linus were about to discover Unix.

2

The New GNU Thing

THE PROGRAM THAT CAUSED LINUS'S HEART to beat a little faster in the fall of 1991 was Digital's Ultrix, one of the many commercial variants of the Unix operating system. Others included Sun's Solaris, IBM's AIX and Hewlett-Packard's HP-UX. Despite the confusion of versions, they all derived from the original Unix system created by Ken Thompson and Dennis Ritchie at AT&T's Bell Labs in 1969–the year Linus was born.

Peter Salus, author of *A Quarter Century of Unix*, generally regarded as the standard history of the operating system, explains how Unix came about: "At the beginning of 1969, there was a group of people working on a project that was MIT, AT&T Bell Labs and General Electric. The project was called Multics. In February 1969, they were several millions behind budget, they were months and months behind schedule, and the powers that be at Bell Labs decided this is never going to go anywhere, and they pulled out of the arrangement.

"And that left the not-quite half-dozen Bell employees who had been involved in the project without anything to do," Salus continues, "but with a large number of ideas they had picked up from the cross-fertilization with GE and with MIT." Among them were Ken Thompson and Dennis Ritchie; they decided that a "cut-down version of this incredible project could be doable for a much smaller machine" than the original project used. "The machine that the project was working on was a GE 645, and it was what you would call a large piece of iron," Salus says.

13

"Dennis and Ken began plotting down some ideas on a blackboard," he continues. "In August of '69, Ken Thompson and his spouse had a new son and it was now almost a year old, and none of their relatives, all of whom were on the West Coast of the U.S., had seen them. So [Ken's wife] Bonnie took their not quite one-year-old and flew to the West Coast for the month of August 1969."

During this time, Salus says, "Ken just sat down and wrote the Unix operating system in four weeks, in assembler"–the low-level programming language that is only slightly easier to use than entering binary digits of machine code directly. "He told me it wasn't so bad; all I could say is that was truly what Brooks would call the Mythical Man-Month–it was a real, single man-month by a man [whom] I consider probably the [greatest] master programmer I've ever encountered. It was quite amazing," Salus concludes. Fred Brooks's classic 1974 book of essays, *The Mythical Man-Month,* was an early and perceptive analysis of the problems of managing large software projects.

With the new Unix came a new way of thinking about operating systems. "The Unix philosophy is really very easy," Salus says, "and consists of maybe two or three notions. The first one, which is perhaps the most innovative thing that Thompson ever thought of, is that everything is a file. Second is the notion that when you build something, no matter whether it's an editor or whether it's a way of attaching one file to another file, you write things that are for a single purpose but do that purpose well."

Although the first of these would have some amusing personal consequences for Linus, it was the second element that proved key for the success of Linux. It meant that a Unix-like operating system could be built piecemeal, and that others could help with the task by working independently on some of the various components. It was even conceivable that one person alone–if exceptional enough–could put together the entire operating system if given enough time.

One such exceptional person was Richard Stallman, who labored for years to create a Unix-like system, written from scratch, that would be free. He worked alone at first; then he gradually received contributions from others, including–though neither of them knew it in 1991–Linus, whose Linux program would provide the last major piece still missing from Stallman's huge software jigsaw puzzle.

Richard Matthew Stallman was born in New York in 1953, an only child. His father owned a printing company and his mother was a teacher. He grew up on New York's West Side, and he thrived on the stimulation of living in a big city.

Evidence of Stallman's self-assurance in computing matters and of his broad intellectual skills was evident from his view when he went to Harvard in 1970 that it would have been "redundant" to study computing there. "I could learn programming by doing it, and so I decided I would use my classes to learn something else. I wanted to learn as much as possible," he says, and he chose mathematics and physics as his subjects. "I loved math," he notes, "I used to tell people 'Math You' is my middle name."

But "the joy that I had from being able to do programming and actually produce something" soon became too strong, he says. "In physics and math I could only learn things, so the pleasure of accomplishing something with the computer gradually won my interest away." Despite this, Stallman graduated magna cum laude in physics in 1974.

Stallman was tremendously proud that the programs he wrote were "useful to some people, much more than I could feel pride in merely learning something." This desire to do something that helped others, perhaps deriving in part from his mother's strongly held liberal convictions, soon became one of the driving forces of his life; it would have unexpected knock-on effects in the world of software that he was only just entering.

One of the key events during his time at Harvard occurred in 1971, at the end of his freshman year, when he wandered over to the famous AI Lab. The AI Lab had become one of the world's greatest centers for research into Artificial Intelligence (AI), which endowed computers with human-like capabilities. Dealing with the magnitude of this task required the most advanced computer technology of the time, and the AI Lab attracted some of the world's best programmers.

Although this visit in 1971 to one of the Meccas of computing appears surprisingly delayed, Stallman didn't find out about its existence until then. Moreover, he says, "I was sort of timid, I didn't know anybody there, I didn't know how they would respond to somebody like me. But eventually I summoned up the courage to go there and see what there was."

It all proved pleasantly easy. "I went around to people, said I'd like some documentation [about their computer], and someone suggested to me, 'Well, maybe you'd like a summer job, too.' And they brought me over to somebody else who was a manager, who talked with me, and said, 'OK, we'll hire you.'" Little did he suspect it at the time, but Stallman was about to enter a kind of hacker's paradise.

The hot-house environment created by a tightly knit bunch of great programmers inventing and exploring the new worlds opened up by computing is vividly evoked in Steven Levy's 1984 book *Hackers*. Levy describes the classic hacker life: feats of virtuoso coding that ignored minor irritations like times of the day or night; sleeping on the floor of the AI Lab when exhaustion finally won out over inspiration; the countless Chinese meals, the heated conversations, the love of word-play, the pranks. "Fun" was central to what might be considered the golden age of hacking: "We had fun writing programs, we had fun playing hacks on each other," Stallman says. He defines the hacker spirit as "playful cleverness."

This haven of playful cleverness lasted nearly ten years after Stallman took his summer job at the AI Lab. His work consisted of adding capabilities to the operating system for the AI Lab's Digital PDP-10 minicomputer. The software was called ITS, the Incompatible Time-Sharing System—a conscious dig at the earlier Compatible Time-Sharing System, CTSS, which had been used to develop Multics, the progenitor of Unix. Although there was no real plan to his work—"I was just going along doing my usual 'think up a feature and add it' type stuff," Stallman says—the result was one of the most famous and powerful pieces of software ever written, even if today it is little known outside programming circles. It is an editor program called Emacs, which stands for "Editing MACroS."

In the text-based pre-graphical world that existed before the Apple Macintosh and Microsoft Windows, the editor was a fundamental program for creating and manipulating text, as central to the way people worked then as the Web browser is for the Internet age.

The previous editor on ITS was called TECO, which stood for TExt Editor and COrrector, and also referred to a language of the same name. "People no longer edited by typing TECO commands," Stallman explains. "Instead, people wrote large collections of TECO programs called macros, and users invoked the macros." The move to macros provided users with more immediate onscreen feedback. "Emacs was designed to synthesize the best ideas of the other editors written in TECO, and make one that would replace them and have all the best characteristics and features of all of them."

The first Emacs was created in 1975. Initially, it was used only at MIT—"not just within the AI Lab; there were a couple of neighboring labs that used ITS also"—and Emacs ran only on ITS. A year or two later, however, "somebody ported TECO so it would work on another time-sharing system," Stallman recalls.

"Porting" refers to the process of translating a program to work on new hardware; once TECO could run elsewhere, so could Emacs.

As well as starting the spread of Emacs throughout the wider world, this move later had other important consequences. When he sent out copies, Stallman established an "informal rule that anyone making improvements had to send them back" to him. This "informal rule," once crystallized, would become the basis of the entire free software movement and one of the crucial factors for its success.

The reason for the informal requirement was that Stallman was sending copies to those outside the immediate hacker community at the AI Lab who "didn't have experience of it at all; so I didn't take for granted that they would want to share," he says. And it had become increasingly obvious to him how important this sharing was to the very existence of the world he was so happy to be part of. "I'd thought about our way of life," Stallman recalls. "I wasn't the only one to think about it, but I thought more about this aspect of it than other people."

The question of sharing, apparently incidental to the business of writing computer programs, proved central to events that ocurred in the early 1980s. These events not only ended the unique community that had flourished for so long at the AI Lab but drove Stallman to feats of programming probably never matched before or since. They also led directly to Stallman's resolve to write a free Unix clone from scratch–single-handedly if need be.

At the center of these events was something called the Lisp Machine. The programming language Lisp (short for List Processing) is, like Emacs, little known today outside programming circles; as with Stallman's editor, Lisp enjoys a near-mythical status within that group. Stallman describes Lisp simply as "a more powerful and elegant language than any of the others." If Emacs was the editor of the hackers, Lisp was their language.

Because Lisp was so central to the computing research at the AI Lab, one of the key projects there had been the design of the Lisp Machine, a hardware system that was optimized for running Lisp programs. By allying the power of Lisp with the speed of dedicated hardware, a new generation of computing tasks could be tackled.

The person who had designed the Lisp Machine, Richard Greenblatt— described by Levy as "the hacker's hacker"—wanted to found a new venture. Stallman recalls that "he wanted to make what he called a 'hacker company,' which would mean that it would be less controlled by management which was unfriendly to hackers than most companies, and it would have nicer policies in some way.

"One of the ideas was that they wouldn't get outside investors," Stallman continues, "because outside investors would insist on imposing all the usual ways of doing things that would make it ugly. And another idea was that they wouldn't just hire away the hackers from the [AI] Lab, but would hire them part-time, so the Lab would still have its hacker culture, and the community that we belonged to wouldn't be wiped out." But this vision was never realized.

"The other people [in the AI Lab] said that they didn't trust Greenblatt to run a business," Stallman says. As a result, a company called Symbolics was formed without Greenblatt, who, undaunted, went on to set up his own, called Lisp Machine Incorporated (LMI). But as Stallman recalls, "Symbolics had more money and hired several of the best hackers away from the Lab, and a year later they hired the rest of the hackers except for me and Greenblatt. And the result was that my community was wiped out." Stallman is still moved when he recalls these events. His beloved Lab "felt like a ghost town," he says. "It was desolate, and I was grief-stricken."

Not only were his friends and colleagues leaving but he was losing ITS as a result. "At that time, the AI Lab was buying a new computer," he says, "and there were no hackers to port ITS to it" because all the hackers had been hired away. "Everything was dying."

This turn of events might have left Stallman in despair, but he channeled his pain into an anger that would spur him on to undertake a crusade that continues to this day. He decided to fight back in the only way he knew how: by coding. As the Symbolics development team–largely the former hackers of the AI Lab–made additions to their version of the software for the Lisp Machine, Stallman set about reproducing those same features in the version of the software that the AI Lab used.

"I had myself taken off of all mailing lists, because I wanted nothing to distract me. I knew I had to compete with a much larger army and that I would have to do the work of several people; I'd have to work in the most focused way I possibly could," he says.

Because LMI and Symbolics both had the right to use features from the AI Lab's software for the Lisp machine—and Symbolics already had the new features—Stallman enabled LMI to match every move of Symbolics, and so denied Symbolics any advantage from its larger team of developers.

Looking back, Stallman says that this period beginning March 1982 saw "absolutely" the most intense coding he had ever done; it probably represents one of the most sustained bouts of one-person programming in history.

"In some ways it was very comfortable because I was doing almost nothing else," he says, "and I would go to sleep whenever I felt sleepy;

when I woke up I would go back to coding; and when I felt sleepy again I'd go to sleep again. I had nothing like a daily schedule. I'd sleep probably for a few hours one and half times a day, and it was wonderful; I felt more awake than I've ever felt. And I got a tremendous amount of work done [and] I did it tremendously efficiently." Although "it was exhilarating sometimes, sometimes it was terribly wearying. It was in some ways terribly lonesome, but I kept doing it [and] I wouldn't let anything stop me," he says.

Stallman kept up this unprecedented feat for nearly two years. But by 1983, the situation was beginning to change. On the plus side, "LMI was getting bigger and was able to hire some programmers," he remembers, "so I could see that LMI was going to be able to do this work for itself." But more negatively, Symbolics had designed a new kind of Lisp machine, so "there was no hope and not much point, either, in making the MIT version of the system [software] run on those machines," he acknowledges.

In hindsight, this situation provided an important demonstration of one of the key factors of the new way of developing programs that free software in general and Linux in particular would build on in the coming years. As Stallman explains, "I could write code, but I couldn't test everything myself. Users had to find the bugs." Consequently, "as the AI Lab switched over to [Symbolics' new] machines, I would lose my ability to do the job" of producing good code for the LMI machine because nobody could test it at the Lab. "I would have been unable to continue," he says.

This development proved a blessing in disguise. "I decided I didn't want to just continue punishing Symbolics forever. They destroyed my community; now I [wanted] to build something to replace it," he says. "I decided I would develop a free operating system, and in this way lay the foundation for a new community like the one that had been wiped out."

Another important consideration in all this, he recalls, was that "the MIT Lisp Machine system was proprietary software. It was licensed by MIT to Symbolics and LMI, and I wasn't happy with that" because the essence of proprietary software is that it cannot be shared; this stifled the formation of the kind of software community that Stallman now wished to create. Working on the MIT Lisp Machine software had in some ways revealed itself to have been a wrong turn.

Once Stallman had decided on this new course of action—creating a free operating system—he soon made "the major design decision–that we would follow Unix," he says. In retrospect, it might have seemed the obvious choice, but at the time this was by no means the case because

Stallman knew little about the system. "I'd never used it," he says, "I'd only read a little about it, but it seemed like it was a good, clean design [that had some] nice clean and powerful ideas."

But the main impetus for his choice grew once again out of his experiences during the diaspora of the hacker community at the AI Lab. "Digital had discontinued the PDP-10"–the last machine on which ITS had run–"which meant that ITS was now completely unusable on any modern computer," Stallman says. "And I didn't want that kind of thing to happen again. The only way to prevent it from happening again was to write a portable system."

Stallman wanted an operating system that could be easily transferred from one type of hardware to another. Because most operating systems had been conceived as the housekeeping software for one type of computer, portability was the exception rather than the rule. "Unix was, at least as far as I knew, the only portable system that really had users on different kinds of computers. So it was portable not just in theory but in actual practice," Stallman says.

Another important reason why Stallman chose Unix as his model, he explains, was that he "decided to make the system compatible with Unix so people who had already written programs for Unix would be able to run them on this system. People who knew how to use Unix would know how to use this system without being required to learn something new." Once again, as he had with Emacs, he was building on something that already existed, but making it better–in this case, by creating a Unix-like system that could be shared freely.

Although the project was born at this most unhappy time for Stallman, the name he chose for his new project showed a typical hacker humor. His Unix work-alike would be called GNU, an acronym that stood for "GNU's Not Unix," and which thus explained itself self referentially. This kind of recursion is often used as a programming technique, and applying it to words is highly popular amongst hackers.

The name GNU also proved a fruitful source of inspiration for similarly self-referential names for many of the programs that went to make up the overall GNU project. Another important virtue of Unix was that its design "consists of a lot of small pieces, often fairly small pieces," Stallman explains; to create a Unix-like system, "what you do is you just have to write each piece. So I sat down and started writing small pieces."

Although this makes the entire process sound disarmingly simple, writing these "small pieces" involved reproducing work that had taken hundreds of people fifteen years–an even harder task than when Stallman matched the team of programmers at Symbolics. In his fight against that company, he was able to look at the source code–the underlying lines of programming–to help him write his own versions; but with Unix this was not an option.

"I certainly never looked at the source code of Unix," Stallman says. "Never. I once accidentally saw a file, and when I realized it was part of Unix source code, I stopped looking at it." The reason was simple: The source code "was a trade secret, and I didn't want to be accused of stealing that trade secret," he says. "I condemn trade secrecy, I think it's an immoral practice, but for the project to succeed, I had to work within the immoral laws that existed."

Once again Stallman had set himself an almost impossible task that would require an exhaustive dedication and sacrifice–which was perhaps part of the attraction. "I wasn't certain I could finish the job," he recalls, "but it wasn't important for me to know whether I could finish the job; the point was I was going to start it."

The GNU project formally began, in January 1984, when Stallman started working on a replacement for an obscure programmer's tool called Yacc. One reason he chose this was "because there was a similar program available called Bison"–another typical hacker pun–"but it wasn't compatible with Yacc; it was missing some features." Stallman obtained permission from the author to make Bison compatible with Yacc, and in doing so, he put in place the first small stone of the GNU edifice.

Having limbered up with this relatively minor task, Stallman moved on to one of the most important. One of the key elements of a Unix system is the C compiler. Programs written in C are text files whose contents are lines of instructions following the rules of the language. Before a computer can obey the instructions contained in the source code, they must be converted into binaries–the sequence of 0s and 1s that the processor chip can understand.

This is the job of the C compiler—a kind of mediator between the source code and binaries, which is therefore an indispensable tool for every C programmer. As such, it held a particular importance for Stallman in his endeavor to create a new, freely available version of Unix. A poor C compiler might seriously damage the chances of GNU's being taken seriously; equally, a great C compiler that was free would immediately make people sit up and take notice of the project.

Once more, Stallman tried to build on an existing program to minimize the amount of work that needed doing, and something he had heard about seemed to be perfect for the job. The Amsterdam Compiler Kit was a powerful compiler that ran on Unix and could compile not just C but most of the languages then in use. It had been written by the U.S.

academic Andrew Tanenbaum at the Free University of Amsterdam. Perhaps slightly misled by another name for the software–the Free University Compiler Kit–Stallman wrote to Tanenbaum to ask whether he could use it for his GNU project.

As Stallman recalls, "[Tanenbaum] said, 'The university is free; the compiler isn't. Why don't you give up that silly idea of a free system? I'd like to have some utilities to distribute with the compiler to boost sales. Contribute some utilities to me and I'll give you a share of the profits.'" What seemed eminently reasonable–generous even–to Tanenbaum, was an insult to Stallman, for whom proprietary software of the kind represented by the Amsterdam Compiler Kit was precisely what he was hoping to combat with his GNU project.

Tanenbaum doesn't recall what he said exactly, but he explains why he was unable to give permission for the Amsterdam Compiler Kit (ACK) to be used by Stallman as part of GNU: "I think we may have already signed a contract to sell ACK commercially via a company in the U.S. and one in Europe," he says. "Our research group needed that money to support graduate students, etc., and as I recall, we were already committed when he came around."

Despite these laudable aims, Stallman saw only Tanenbaum's refusal to aid him in his free software crusade. His response was identical to that he had made to Symbolics a few years earlier: He determined to write his own rival software that would match or beat the offending code.

In September 1984, after an unsuccessful attempt to adapt yet another compiler, Stallman returned to his most successful program so far, Emacs. The code for this new Emacs, which became known as GNU Emacs, had "nothing in common with the original Emacs, which was written in TECO," Stallman says. And in another symbolic act of return to his AI Lab roots, he decided to rewrite most of GNU Emacs in Lisp, that "powerful and elegant language" Stallman prized so highly.

By early 1985, GNU Emacs was able to edit files, and Stallman made it available publicly. This was an important step because it represented the first time people could use and judge GNU software. Even though the free GNU operating system was almost nonexistent, people could still use Emacs: The Unix compatibility that was Stallman's constant guide meant that GNU Emacs could run on any Unix and provide him with a huge potential constituency of users.

First, "people started asking for and writing improvements, and the result was I kept working on Emacs a lot, much longer that I'd expected to, and it ended up much better than I'd originally planned on its being," recalls Stallman. This approach of releasing code and encouraging feedback and modifications from users, although not new–it had formed an implicit part of the entire Unix culture for years–became central to the rapid improvement of free software over the next fifteen years. Its adoption in an extreme form for the development of Linux was one of the key factors in its rapid growth and robustness.

The second consequence of making Emacs available was that Stallman could sell it on tape, the standard distribution medium before floppies; this was alongside free distribution on the Internet because at that time few people had access to this fledgling medium. As well as serving users who might otherwise find it difficult to obtain copies, selling tapes had the even more beneficial effect of giving Stallman an income. "See," he says, "I had quit my job at MIT to start the GNU project. And the reason is I wanted to make sure that MIT would not be in a position to interfere with making GNU software free in the way I wanted to do it. I didn't want to have to beg the MIT administration for permission to do this and then maybe they would insist on spoiling it in some way."

To its credit, the AI Lab allowed Stallman to continue to use its computers, and to sleep in his former office at 545 Tech Square for twelve years. He was even registered to vote at that address. Stallman did retain one significant momento of those happy times: his log-in ID. To this day he signs himself "rms," his original username for the ITS machine, and most of the hacker world knows him by these initials.

Although Stallman says that he "lived cheaply–I would have done so for the sake of this project, but I'd always lived cheaply," money was an obvious concern in those early days of GNU. "I didn't know at the beginning whether I would have any sources of income," he recalls, though "for the first year I think I was paid by LMI to update some manuals from MIT." In any case, "the point is," he says, "I was utterly determined to do this; nothing could have intimidated me at that point."

Fortunately, selling GNU Emacs for $150 a tape–"I just thought it would be a good price," he explains–soon provided him with a steady income. "By the middle of the year, I was getting some eight to ten orders a month and that was enough for me to live on [although] I couldn't have saved any money from that alone."

With GNU Emacs out of the way, and perhaps encouraged by its reception and the money he was starting to receive from it, Stallman turned his thoughts to the other projects, including that problematic C compiler. This time, he decided he would not try to adapt a pre-existing program, but would write it all himself. It proved a hugely complex project. "It was the most challenging program I've ever written," he says simply. "It's one that required me to write plans down on paper rather than just code."

Stallman's general approach to coding is quite different. "I start with a sort of vague idea in my head," he says, "and I find some part of the job I can write, and then having written one part will enable me to envision neighboring parts enough that I can write them; and then I basically go through and end up having written the whole thing." This probably explains in part why Unix was so attractive as a model for his GNU project: Its use of many small elements meant that Stallman could "find some part of the job" he could write–a utility here, a program there–and then "basically go through and end up having written the whole thing."

Stallman called his compiler GCC–for GNU C Compiler. Even more than GNU Emacs, it helped spread the word about the GNU project because GCC proved to be top-class software. "There was a period of a few years when GCC was pretty much the best compiler available for most of the systems it supported," he recalls. "But that wasn't immediate, it took a while of working on optimization before it got to be the best." As with Emacs, this optimization was helped enormously by the comments Stallman received from users once the program was released.

The new GCC also boosted his income further. It "opened up the possibilities of commissions a lot more. People were more interested in commissioning changes in GCC, and in commissioning classes about GCC, than they were doing similar things for Emacs," Stallman says. "I was very glad to have that source of income, especially when the Free Software Foundation was formed. I think it was October 1985; it took over from me the business of selling Emacs tapes, so I didn't have that income any more."

The Free Software Foundation (FSF) represented an important step forward for GNU. "When I started it out, it didn't have the money to hire anyone. Then it had money to hire one person, and it hired one person," he explains. "The point is just that that enabled us to do more work at the same time because there were lots and lots of programs that were missing." Gradually, more of these programs were written, either by Stallman himself or by the growing band of FSF staff and volunteers. "In the earliest years [there were just] two or three people [helping]," he remembers; "by the later 80s, I'd expect there were somewhere between thirty and fifty people."

Two of the other big projects were to create a shell program and a C library. A shell provides the basic interface to the operating system: "If you want to be able to type any commands, you need a shell," says Stallman. GNU's program is called Bash, which is short for Bourne Again Shell, a play on the Unix shell called the Bourne shell.

The C library is a chunk of auxiliary code that other programs can call. By separating out an entire set of commonly used functions in this way, user programs can be much smaller. Creating a C library for GNU was therefore a key prerequisite before the GNU operating system could run such user programs and do something useful.

Both the C library and Bash were finished around 1990, along with many other elements of the Unix operating system. Still missing, though, was in many ways the single most important program of all: the kernel. As its name suggests, the kernel sits at the very heart of the operating system. It acts as housekeeper (handling tasks such as the screen and keyboard) and judge (ensuring that all the competing calls for attention from user programs are handled correctly). Although many other programs are indispensable for a fully functional operating system—for example a C library and a shell—it is the kernel that defines its essence.

That Stallman had left the kernel until last might seem strange given its central nature. In part it was because he had been distracted by his feud with Tanenbaum and his vow that a C compiler would be one of the first programs that he wrote for his GNU system. In addition, it made sense to develop all the programming tools first so that they could then be used in the creation of the kernel.

There was another reason, however. "I was trying to bypass the hardest part of the job," Stallman says. Debugging kernels is difficult because the standard programming tools depend on a functioning kernel. To get round this, Stallman had been on the lookout once more for suitable software that could be adapted—and he had something particular in mind: "I was looking for a microkernel," he says.

A microkernel is a kernel that takes the idea of a small, central adjudicating piece of software to its logical conclusion; it makes all the other housekeeping tasks normally found in a kernel into programs that are controlled just like end-user applications such as word processing and spreadsheets. The pros and cons of this approach with respect to the classic all-in-one kernel—known as a monolithic kernel—form the subject of what hackers call a "religious war" between their respective adherents that rages to this day.

Stallman was interested in microkernels not for reasons of doctrine but because, he says, "that way we could avoid the job of debugging the part of the software that runs on the bare machine"—the underlying hardware. As usual, he was sensibly trying to save time and effort by taking existing code that had tackled one of the harder parts and building on it. He also thought the design provided some "nice features."

Stallman was lucky—or so he thought at the time. "Eventually we found a microkernel that at least was supposedly already developed and working," he says, "and we just had to write the user programs [that] do the jobs . . . normally done by parts of the kernel" to create that missing heart of the GNU operating system, which was dubbed the GNU Hurd.

Unfortunately, the microkernel he found "wasn't already working totally reliably," as he had believed. Moreover, eliminating all the errors from this code proved much more difficult than expected. "It turns out that the debugging environment we had was hard," he explains. "In effect, the problem with this was it was a research project, and in general my policy was to avoid research projects [and] use tried-and-true designs, because a research project is risky. You may try out an idea and find that it doesn't work very well. Anyway, we tried out this design, and found out that it was hard to get it finished."

In fact, "in retrospect, it seems that developing a monolithic kernel would have been maybe faster and easier and might have been the right thing to do"—the first working version of the Hurd wasn't released until 1996. But Stallman is philosophical about the matter: "You see," he says, "any individual software project is just a piece of the GNU project; the GNU project isn't fundamentally about developing this piece of software or that piece of software. GNU, like any operating system, is a collection of many programs. We wrote some, and we obtained some from elsewhere; in the end, we achieved the overall goal of a complete free system."

As Stallman began writing the components of his GNU operating system and released them to the public, one of his primary concerns was to ensure that the programs he and his fellow coders were creating would remain free and open as they were passed on from user to user; simply putting them in the public domain would not achieve this because someone could easily come along and sell the GNU programs as proprietary products. Stallman needed to do something new and radical, namely, to draw up a software license that did not restrict the user's rights, as most did, but that protected them.

He did this first with the GNU Emacs General Public Licence, in 1985. "I worked with a lawyer to draw it up," he says; he had to make sure that the freedoms he was trying to perpetuate were watertight legally. Under this new "copyleft"—as opposed to copyright—users could copy the program, modify it, and sell the original or the modified versions. They could not modify the rights granted by the copyleft to any user, however; for example, software based on the program they sold had also to be freely available. Similarly, modifications they made to a copylefted program had to be copylefted—and so freely available. Furthermore, if software released under the GNU General Public Licence (GPL) were combined with proprietary (nonfree) code, the resultant combination had to be released under the GPL. In other words, the GNU GPL "converted" software it was used with to its own license, an extraordinarily clever approach to propagating freedom.

This first GNU Emacs General Public License (GPL) was followed later by a GCC GPL and a similar license for several other GNU programs. But Stallman realized that this piecemeal approach was not only inelegant (a cardinal sin among hackers) but also inconvenient because it blocked certain uses. For example, "you couldn't take code from one [program released under a GPL license] and put it in another," Stallman explains, "so I decided that we had better have a single license that could be used for all of them." This was the GNU General Public License—what Stallman calls "the subroutinised license" because "you could drop it verbatim into any program and it would apply," just as programming subroutines can be dropped into other code to save time—and boost their elegance.

Stallman's intent in crafting the GNU GPL was to protect the newly forged liberties that his GNU software embodied. But the GNU GPL had another consequence that would prove key to the success of later free software projects such as Linux.

The freedom to modify a GNU GPL program means that the source code for copylefted software must be available: If the binaries only—the sequence of 0s and 1s—are supplied, modifying the program is impractical and therefore breaches the license. Part of the GNU GPL's effect is therefore to ensure that the source is always available for a program; this is vital if others are to adapt and—especially—improve the program. Moreover, the GNU GPL also ensures that such improvements must be freely available, along with their source code, to enable the community as a whole to benefit from the collective advances of all users.

It also minimizes duplication of effort. Once a program carrying out a certain function is released under copyleft, others can then take this work for granted when they write similar software. There is no need to reinvent the wheel every time a particular type of program is written as is the case with commercial software.

Stallman created in the GNU GPL a kind of written constitution for the hacker world that enshrined basic assumptions about how their community should function. In doing so, he enabled that world to progress far more efficiently than it had in the past when all these "laws" were unwritten. As the use of the GNU GPL became more common, so its power grew, because the more copylefted programs there are the greater the pool for future such programs to draw on; this eases their creation and the pool of GPL'd software grows yet further.

This enormous efficiency acted as one of the main engines in driving the free software projects on to their extraordinary successes during the 1990s. For this alone, and for his work in putting together the GNU system, the computer community's debt to Stallman is immense.

Yet for Stallman, this emphasis on inherent efficiency misses the point about the GNU project and about the GNU GPL. His essential concern is freedom, and the GNU project a means to an end rather than an end in itself.

"The overall purpose," Stallman explains, "is to give the users freedom by giving them free software they can use and to extend the boundaries of what you can do with entirely free software as far as possible. Because the idea of GNU is to make it possible for people to do things with their computers without accepting [the] domination of somebody else. Without letting some owner of software say, 'I won't let you understand how this works; I'm going to keep you helplessly dependent on me and if you share with your friends, I'll call you a pirate and put you in jail.'

"I consider that immoral," Stallman continues, "and I'm working to put an end to that way of life, because it's a way of life nobody should have to be part of, and the only way you can do that is by writing a lot of software and saying to people, 'Come, use it, share it with your friends, change it to do whatever you want it do. Join us, have fun.' And that's what GNU is for, it's to give people the alternative of living in freedom, and the individual software packages like GNU Emacs and GCC or the GNU Hurd, they're important because they're parts of getting that larger job done."

Stallman has not only devoted much of his time and energy to this cause, he has given his money, too. In 1990, he won a McArthur Foundation fellowship, worth somewhere in the neighborhood of $230,000, divided into quarterly installments over five years. "That was a lot more money than I need to live on, and more income than I had ever had before. Rather than spending it, I decided to invest most of it in mutual funds so that I can live on it for the rest of my life while working on free software or another worthy cause."

He has no car: "I live in a city where you don't need to have a car." He rents a room: "I don't want to own a house, I don't want to spend a lot of money. If you spend a lot of money then you're the slave of having to make money. The money then jerks you around, controls your life." Stallman has never married or had children. "That takes a lot of money.

There's only one way I could have made that money, and that is by doing what I'd be ashamed of"–writing nonfree software. "If I had been developing proprietary software, I would have been spending my life building walls to imprison people," he believes.

Deadly serious intensity aside, Stallman also has a lively sense of humor that manifests itself in a constant stream of ideas, puns, and hacker-type plays on words that courses through his conversations. His personal Web site carries a picture of him dressed as the outrageous be-toga'd Saint IGNUcius–a character he is happy to re-create in his travels around the world with his music CDs and a battered Toshiba portable as he gives talks whenever and wherever he can to spread his message.

And yet many have a different image of Stallman: It is not so much playful mock saint as implacable Old Testament prophet–a kind of geek Moses bearing the GNU GPL commandments and trying to drag his hacker tribe to the promised land of freedom whether they want to go or not. His long hair, which falls thickly to his shoulders, full beard, and intense gaze doubtless contribute to the effect.

This impression arises largely from Stallman's ability to offend even supporters through his constant refusal to compromise. "The only reason we have a wholly free operating system is because of the movement that said we want an operating system that's wholly free, not 90 percent free," he says. "If you don't have freedom as a principle, you can never see a reason not to make an exception. There are constantly going to be times when for one reason or another there's some practical convenience in making an exception."

He admits that sometimes he gets tired of hammering home this message over and over again, but believes he must keep on doing it, even beyond the tolerance of most of his audiences if need be. "I'm never optimistic," he says, "I'm never sanguine. I've achieved a lot, but it's not the whole job. The job is not finished."

When will it be finished? "Well, maybe never," he acknowledges. "In what sense is freedom ever assured for the future? People are always going to have to work to keep a free society."

This is the real point of the self-referential GNU's Not Unix, and of ideas like "copyleft." For Stallman, free software matters not because software is special and deserves a special freedom; indeed, he acknowledges that "there are more important issues of freedom–the issues of freedom that everybody's heard of are much more important than this: freedom of speech, freedom of the press, free assembly."

Free software matters because all freedoms matter, and software happens to be the domain in which Stallman can contribute most. "I don't see how I could do something more important in some other area," he says.

Stallman's work is significant not only because it engendered many of the key elements and pioneered many of the processes that made the success of what came to be the combined GNU/Linux operating system possible but because it provides an ethical backdrop against which the entire free software and open source story is unfolding.

Stallman, too, should be seen as more than just the greatest hacker who has ever lived—which he almost certainly is. His example of unswerving dedication to lofty ideals may be too idealistic and daunting for most to follow, but it provides a yardstick of integrity against which the actions of his fellow coders, both great and not-so-great, may be judged.

3

A Minor Rebellion

WHEN LINUS ENCOUNTERED UNIX in the fall of 1991, Richard Stall-man's great GNU project, begun seven years before, was almost complete. The one crucial element that was still lacking, the kernel, was under development in the form of the GNU Hurd—the heart of Stallman's operating system. For Stallman, this delay was regrettable but not serious; it was more important that most elements of his free Unix-like system were now available and that the missing piece of the puzzle was on its way. This was cold comfort for Linus, who wanted to run his own copy of Unix immediately, not in a few years' time when the GNU Hurd was finished. The more he and Lars Wirzenius learned about Unix, the more they liked it.

Wirzenius recalls the excitement he and Linus shared as they explored this new world: "We spent a number of evenings while we talked about the exercises for the course during that fall, and we had marvelous simple contests for stuff like implementing a certain exercise in the most elegant possible way, or in some cases the shortest possible way"–classic coder games.

But their growing frustration with having to wait in line for the Unix (the only computer that ran Unix at Helsinki University supported just sixteen users at a time) led them to contemplate desperate measures. "One of the things that we discussed [was that] we might need to actually write the Unix ourselves because the commercial ones were really expensive," Wirzenius says, but adds, "that was a joke, especially from my side; I'm not quite as good a programmer as Linus is. It's not something you decide–'this week I will write an operating system.'" The jest proved truer than either could have imagined.

Fortunately, in addition to whetting his appetite for Unix, Linus's studies that fall provided him with a way to acquire it. He recalls that "one of the course books was *Operating Systems: Design and Implementation.*" The book came with its own illustrative software, which was unusual. Called Minix, it had been written to teach students how an operating system worked through examining its source code. Linus found that Minix was essentially a Unix-like system that ran on a PC. He could not know then that not only would it provide him with the scaffolding for building his own PC-based Unix kernel, Linux, but it would also foreshadow many of the techniques and even much of the development history of that system.

Minix was written by the same Andrew Tanenbaum who had rebuffed Richard Stallman's overtures in 1984 when Stallman was searching for a compiler and who provoked Stallman into writing GCC. Despite this inauspicious start, Tanenbaum says Stallman had later suggested to him that Minix could provide the missing kernel of the otherwise complete GNU system. "He approached me a couple of times," Tanenbaum says, "but he had all these conditions; it's got to be this, and it's got to be that. I said 'whoa, whoa, whoa.' He's kind of an abrasive person [and] it didn't really turn me on."

Stallman, for his part, says he has no recollection of the idea because it was so long ago, but acknowledges that that the discussions could have taken place.

Had Tanenbaum said yes to Stallman's proposal, the history of computing would have been very different. Linus emphasized later that "if the GNU kernel had been ready"–for example, through a form of Minix–when he was casting around for his own copy of Unix, "I'd not have bothered to even start my [Linux] project." But Tanenbaum said no, and instead of nipping Linux in the bud, Minix played a fundamental role in helping it germinate and flower.

After his studies at MIT as an undergraduate, and at the University of California at Berkeley as a graduate student, Tanenbaum joined the computer science faculty at the Free University of Amsterdam in 1971; he became a professor there in 1980.

In 1979, ten years after Unix was first created, Version 7 of the system was released by AT&T. Version 7 was of note for several reasons; for example, it was the first Unix to be ported to (translated for use on) an Intel processor, the 8086, a slightly more powerful version of the 8088 chip later used in the first IBM PC. Xenix, as it was called, was the joint project of two companies. One was The Santa Cruz Operation, better known today as SCO (and later the owner of Unix). The other was Microsoft. It is little known today that one year before Microsoft had launched MS-DOS in 1981, it had already brought out a PC version of Unix. But the existence of Xenix, never a popular product, makes the current challenge from systems based around Linux piquant, to say the least.

Tanenbaum was more affected by another significant change from Version 6. "The license said fairly clearly [that] the source code shall not be made available to students," Tanenbaum recalls. "Period. Nothing. None. Zero." Version 7 represented the symbolic closing of Unix inside the black box of proprietary software—a sad end to what had long been the ultimate student hacker's system.

From an educational viewpoint, the ban on discussing Unix's source code was unsatisfactory. "Between 1979 and 1984 I stopped teaching practical Unix at all and went back to theory," Tanenbaum says. He realized that the only way to make something comparable available to his students "was to write an operating system on my own that would be system-call compatible with Unix"—that is, working in exactly the same way—"but which was my own code, not using any AT&T code at all."

When Tanenbaum began Minix in 1984—just as Stallman started work on GNU—he decided that it would be compatible with Unix, but also that, as he puts it, "while I was at it, let's design it right." This offers an interesting contrast to Stallman's approach, where the emphasis was on the free availability of what he wrote, not on how he wrote it. Tanenbaum's "designing it right" in this context meant in part using a micro-kernel–although as Tanenbaum is quick to point out, "I decided to make a microkernel long before anybody had heard of microkernels." In fact, he says, "I think Minix may have been the first."

As a result, "the basic kernel is very, very simple," although this did not mean that completing Minix was easy: "It was thousands and thousands of hours [to get it working]; it's not a trivial matter," Tanenbaum explains. He wrote Minix at home in the evenings.

Writing a new operating system is difficult, one reason Stallman searched for an existing microkernel system that he could use. Tanenbaum recalls that "debugging any kernel on flaky hardware which you don't really understand well is horrible. I almost gave up the project a couple of times. I had bugs that I just couldn't find." The difficulty was caused in part because the hardware he was working with had undocumented features and strange bugs that depended on the temperature of some of the chips. Tanenbaum would have definitively abandoned the entire effort had not a chance remark by one of his students explained the problem.

Eventually, in 1986, after two years' hard work, he had a system that was ready for others to use. "I put out a note on the Net saying I was doing this, and then I got some people to help me." Things really changed when Tanenbaum created a new Usenet newsgroup to go with the software, which was released with the book he had written to explain his system to students. "The book and the software came out together, it was '87," Tanenbaum recalls. "At that point, the newsgroup started and went crazy–it was like 40,000 people within a month. It had at least the same enthusiasm that Linux has now," he notes.

What had begun as a personal project "to make it possible to teach students how operating systems work, and to illustrate it by a simple and straightforward example," as Tanenbaum puts it, had tapped into something much bigger and hitherto unsuspected in the computer community.

Minix was an instant success, Tanenbaum says, because it was "Unix with source code for the PC, which required minimal hardware and had a book describing how it worked. Nobody had done anything like that before. It wasn't free, but almost–$59, $69–but that was like fourteen discs or something, which was almost the manufacturing cost."

There was another reason the hacker community took up Minix with such alacrity: "Although I said it 10,000 times, 'this is an educational system,' many people saw it as the answer to their [programming] prayers."

From the beginning, Tanenbaum says, "in the newsgroup I was getting two hundred messages a day, and there were two hundred emails a day asking for adjustments, saying 'I want this, I need that.'"

Tanenbaum refused to give in to their demands. "I was afraid the system code would get hairier and hairier and bigger and bigger," he says. "It wouldn't run on this minimal hardware, which I wanted for the students, and it would be too hard to explain. I didn't want a 10,000-page listing at the back [of the accompanying book]."

Tanenbaum did make some changes, however. "The basic criteria were [that] if there was a huge amount of yelling for it, and [it] was relatively simple to do and didn't muck up the structure of the system much, then to do it," he explains. "If there wasn't much demand, or it was really hairy, and it changed the system radically, don't do it."

As a result, Minix did evolve, although more slowly than many of its users wanted. "There was a whole bunch of new releases," Tanenbaum says. "There wasn't a calendar in the sense that it must be every six months; there was certain new stuff and at some point I said, 'Gee, there's enough new stuff that warrants a new version. It's stable and it's been tested by a lot of people on the Net; it's a working version.' Then at that point it was worth putting up a new version on the floppy disk." Minix was also ported to chips other than the 8088 found in the original PC, including the Intel 80386 processor.

The arrival of the 80386 chip, and the gradual fall in price of systems using it, proved a key development for Linus. "The 386 was a lot better than any of the previous chips," he recalled later. Moreover, Linus says, "from the Tanenbaum book I knew that you could get Unix for a PC. So that's when I actually broke down and got a PC,"–something he had been loath to do before.

Because of the way the Finnish university education system is funded, Linus was in luck. Says Wirzenius, "The Finnish government gives money to students and also backs student loans that the students take from banks. The money is supposed to be used for food and housing, but also for stuff needed for studies. Linus managed to get a student loan, which he could use for buying the computer since he was living with his mother–so he didn't have to spend as much money on living." The debt was finally paid off in November 1992.

Linus added other recently acquired funds. "I had Christmas money," he says. "I remember the first nonholiday day of the New Year I went to buy a PC." That was 5 January 1991. In 1996, he still recalled the machine's specification: "386, DX33, 4 Megs of RAM, no co-processor; 40 Megs hard disk." This is unbelievably puny by today's standards, but aside from the hard disk, which Linus acknowledged was "not very large," these specs were respectable for the time—especially for running Minix.

In his first published interview, with *Linux News*, "a summary of the goings-on of the Linux community" put together initially by Wirzenius, and which ran for six months from the fall of 1992, Linus explained what happened next. "While I got my machine on January 5th 1991, I was forced to run DOS on it for a couple of months while waiting for the Minix disks." He passed the time in an unusual way: "Jan-Feb was spent about 70–30 playing [the computer game] 'Prince of Persia' and getting acquainted with the machine."

In retrospect, it seems extraordinary that Linus's main activity before writing Linux was playing "Prince of Persia" for two months, even if it had been named Best Computer Game, Action Game of the Year and Game of the Decade.

Whatever the reason, Linus was not completely lost in the blocky if effective graphics of the sultan's dungeons as he fought off the minions of the evil Grand Vizier Jaffar. By his own calculation, during this period Linus was spending around a third of his time "getting acquainted with the machine," presumably in a typically thorough manner.

Wirzenius says that at this time Linus "started playing around with programming tools for MS-DOS on a PC. At some point he had an assembler for writing assembly language programs" just as he had done on his grandfather's Vic-20. The benefits of assembly language programming include faster programs and direct control of the hardware. Doubtless the ability to explore the 386 chip in this way was the main reason Linus employed it, not as a demonstration of hacker prowess; he had been programming in assembly language since his early teens and had nothing to prove there.

Wirzenius recalls one of those first DOS assembler programs. "I remember him being very proud over a short piece of code that implements a subroutine that did nothing except calculate the length of a sequence of characters. It wasn't the task that was complicated, it was the fact that he had written everything for himself" that made Linus so pleased.

But as Wirzenius said in a speech he made at the 1998 Linux Expo, "when Linus decides to learn something, he really learns it, and very quickly." Just because these first steps were small certainly did not mean that they were doomed to stay that way. Already his next assembly language program was more sophisticated than the earlier subroutine; it investigated one of the key features of the 386: task-switching.

The ability of the Intel 80386 chip to switch between tasks meant that it could handle more than one task, or user, than once (by jumping quickly between them). Task-switching lay at the heart of multitasking, which in turn was one of the key capabilities of Unix. Linus may not have been aware then that almost imperceptibly his experiments were moving in the direction of creating the kernel of a Unix-like system.

Linus describes his first experiments in this area on the 386 this way: "I was testing the task-switching capabilities, so what I did was I just made two processes and made them write to the screen and had a timer that switched tasks. One process wrote 'A,' the other wrote 'B,' so I saw 'AAAABBBB' and so on." Later, Linus would write of this task-switcher, "Gods I was proud over that"; but this was still hardly an operating system kernel, let alone one that was Unix-compatible. Linus was, however, getting closer—at least to the realization of what might be possible. The final leap forward came after Minix turned up.

That historic moment is memorialized in his first posting to the newsgroup comp.os.minix, which had been set up at the time of

Minix's launch. Linus had doubtless been reading this for some while before—"I read a lot of newsgroups then"—but not until Friday, 29 March 1991, did he summon up the courage to make his first posting there. It begins:

Hello everybody,

I've had minix for a week now, and have upgraded to 386-minix (nice), and duly downloaded gcc for minix. Yes, it works—but . . . optimizing isn't working, giving an error message of "floating point stack exceeded" or something. Is this normal?

and concludes with the curious signature

advTHANKSance, Linus Torvalds
torvalds@cc.helsinki.fi

Several interesting points stand out in this posting. First, Linus had installed 386-Minix. This was a series of patches (changes and additions) to the original Minix code "to make it usable on a 386 so that you could actually take advantage of 32 bits, because the original Minix was 16 bits," as Linus explains. These patches constituted the port written by the Australian, Bruce Evans; he remembers that he had to fight to get them accepted, so conservative was Tanenbaum when it came to enlarging his teaching system. Evans was soon to become the first person to provide Linus with help and advice as he wrote Linux.

Linus was already using the C compiler GCC, which shows that he was writing or about to write in C—the computer language most widely used by professional programmers and, like assembler, requiring considerable skill. These C programs, combined with the simple assembly language experiments he had been conducting, would eventually become the basis of Linux.

Linus's first posting to comp.os.minix is interesting, but his second is extraordinary. By his own admission he had had Minix for just a week; and yet two days later—on 1 April 1991—in response to a polite question from someone having problems with 386-Minix, Linus replies as if he were some kind of Minix wizard for whom such questions are so trivial as to be almost insulting. He wrote:

RTFSC (Read the F**ing Source Code :-)—It is heavily commented and the solution should be obvious but then mitigates this brusqueness by adding

(take that with a grain of salt, it certainly stumped me for a while :-).

Even though the first part is meant presumably as a joke, its tone of exaggerated self-confidence is characteristic; in public Linus frequently deflates some expression of apparent arrogance with a self-deprecating and honest humility.

The explanation for this confusing behavior is not hard to find. Like many gifted intellectuals, Linus as a young man lacked self-confidence; for example, at university, he says, "I was really so shy I didn't want to speak in classes. Even just as a student I didn't want to raise my hand and say anything." Perhaps as a Minix newbie, posting for just the second time to comp.os.minix, Linus was similarly overcompensating with his coarse reply. Whatever the reason, it is interesting to see displayed here a behavior that in various and often more subtle forms would be repeated in other public forums, though less as time went on; as Linux grew more obviously successful, Linus grew more self-confident.

His third posting to the Minix newsgroup, another reply to a fellow Minix user's query written a week after the 1 April outburst was more moderate: "I'm rather new to 386-Minix myself," he begins modestly, "but have tried porting some stuff and have a few comments."

The demands of his university studies may have been responsible for the nearly three months that pass until Linus's next major posting to the newsgroup. As Wirzenius recalls, despite the growing fascination his programming project held for him, "Linus did actually spend enough time at the university to pass his courses." This was not because of what his teachers might otherwise have done: "The university itself doesn't penalize you if you don't pass your courses," Wirzenius explains. "It just means if you want to graduate then you have to take those courses later."

Linus needed to pass his exams because of the student loan he had taken out to buy his PC. As Wirzenius notes, "If you don't get enough [academic] credits for a year then you won't get support from the government for the next year. If you don't get enough credits during two years or so then you have to start paying back the loan, which is quite a bit of money if you aren't working."

Fortunately, Linus had enough natural ability to pass the required exams and still have time for serious hacking. In April, at the same time he began exploring Minix, he decided to turn his simple task-switching program, where one process wrote "A" and another wrote "B," into a terminal emulator that would allow him to read Usenet newsgroups on the university system from his bedroom when he used his PC hooked up to a modem.

Linus's description of his work makes it sound disarmingly simple: "I changed those two processes to work like a terminal emulation package. You have one process that is reading from the keyboard and sending to the modem, and the other is reading from the modem and sending to the screen." To do this, he had to write various drivers. These are small software programs that act as mediators between peripherals such as keyboards and screens and the central software that is doing most of the calculation.

As Linus said in the October 1992 interview, "Linux stopped for quite a while at the terminal emulator stage; I played around with Minix, and used my program to read news from the university machine." But later on, he decided to extend it further. "I wanted to download stuff," he says. This meant interfacing his modified task-switching software to a disk drive: "So I had to write a disk driver," Linus recalls. Theoretically, this maneuver was straightforward, but, just as they had when Tanenbaum was writing Minix, "problems with bad documentation started to crop up," Linus said later.

Linus noted in a Usenet posting in 1992, "The PC may be the most used architecture in the world right now, but that doesn't mean the docs are any better." It was the Minix hacker Bruce Evans who helped him out at this critical time by explaining some undocumented feature of the hardware that Linus was using. "He was really one of the people who I talked a lot with," Linus says.

When he had sorted out the disk driver, Linus needed a way of reading and writing files on the disk that was now accessible. This required what is called a file system, a set of rules about how data is organized on the disk. Linus sat down and wrote one, basing it on the Minix file system he had been using for several months. This was "in order to be able to write files and read files to upload them," he explains.

"I started out trying to make a file system, and used the Minix [file system] for simple practical reasons; that way I already had a file layout I could test things on," he noted in the *Linux News* interview. The "file layout" referred to the pre-existing Minix installation on his PC: He could test his new file system code by trying to read and write to it. Linus may have used the Minix file system "for simple practical reasons," but being able to learn from the Minix source code in Tanenbaum's book was obviously another major benefit of adopting this approach.

As Linus remembered in the 1992 posting, just as "the worst part is starting off," so the more basic features he added to his system the easier it got: "Hairy coding still, but I had some devices, and debugging was easier. I started using C at this stage, and it certainly speeds up development." Moreover, "this is also when I start to get serious about my megalomaniac ideas to make 'a better Minix than Minix.'"

Linus was using Minix as a kind of scaffolding for his work on what became Linux. But there was a drawback to this approach. As Linus recalls, "I essentially had to reboot the machine just to read news with my fancy newsreader, and that was very inconvenient" because it took time and meant that Linus lost Minix's other capabilities. He continues, "I decided hey, I could try to make all the other features of Minix available" from within the "fancy newsreader" he had written. Linus says this evolution "was really very gradual. At some point I just noticed that hey, this is very close to being potentially useful instead of [needing] Minix."

It was much more than just "potentially useful": "Essentially when you have task-switching, you have a file system, you have device drivers—that's Unix," he explains. Linux—or rather some distant ancestor of Linux—had been born.

When university holidays began, Linus was able to devote himself fully to his project, which doubtless aided the subsequent rapid development of Linux. As Wirzenius explains, the holidays ran "in theory June, July, August, and in practice from the middle of May to the middle of September." Linus recalls that "the first summer I was doing [coding] full-time. I did nothing else, seven days a week, ten hours a day."

As Linus wrote later in a short history of Linux he put together in 1992, the consequence of these sustained bouts of programming was that "by July 3rd I had started to think about actual user-level things: Some of the device drivers were ready, and the hard disk actually worked. Not too much else." The shift of interest is evident from his next posting to the comp.os.minix newsgroup, on 3 July, where he asked about something called Posix for "a project"—Linux, in other words. He wrote

Hello netlanders,

Due to a project I'm working on (in minix), I'm interested in the posix standard definition. Could somebody please point me to a (preferably) machine-readable format of the latest posix rules?

Posix is a standard that defines how programs run on Unix—what Linus referred to as "actual user-level things," rather than system-level—and defines a kind of general Unix compatibility. Posix was drawn up to address the problem of the highly fragmented Unix market that existed at that time where programs running on one flavor of Unix could not run on another. When an operating system follows the Posix specifications it can run any Posix-compliant application.

Linus explains, "I wanted to know what the standards said about all the interfaces"–the ways programs interact with the kernel–"because I didn't want to port all the programs. Every time that I had a problem porting a program to Linux, I changed Linux so that it would port. I never ported programs, but I ported the kernel to work with the programs." This was the approach that Richard Stallman had adopted for his GNU project, and with the same benefit of ready access to a large base of existing Unix applications.

Unfortunately, as Linus recalls, "One of the people who responded to my original query about the Posix standards said 'Sorry, they aren't available electronically, you have to buy them.' That essentially meant that OK, I couldn't afford them." But Linus had another idea: "We had SunOS at the University." SunOS was an early version of Sun's variety of Unix that later became Solaris. "So I used SunOS manual pages to find out the interfaces for stuff."

What began as a second best "actually turned out to be a lucky move," Linus says, "because the SunOS interface was kind of what Unix became a year or two later." This would not be the first time that a move dictated more by chance or circumstances proved to be a blessing in disguise for the future growth of Linux.

But Linus's request for information about Posix turned out to have even more important consequences. "The same person who told me that the standards weren't available also told me his area of interest was kernels and operating systems," Linus says of a member of the Helsinki University staff called Ari Lemmke. "[Lemmke] had this small area on ftp.funet.fi"–an Internet server at the university where files were stored for visitors to download using the standard File Transfer Protocol (FTP). "It was called nic.funet.fi at that point, and he said that 'hey, I'm putting a directory aside for you.' So he created the /pub/os/linux directory," Linus recalls.

"Linux was my working name," Linus continues, "so in that sense he didn't really name it, but I never wanted to release it as Linux." He says he was afraid that "if I actually used it as the official one people would think that I am egomaniac, and wouldn't take it seriously."

Linus had originally planned to call his slowly evolving software something else. In moments of depression, he sometimes felt like calling it "Buggix" to reflect what seemed its hopelessly buggy nature, he revealed in a 1995 FAQ entry. But most of the time he had another name for it. "I chose this very bad name: Freax–free + freak + x. Sick, I know," Linus acknowledges. "Luckily, this Ari Lemmke didn't like it at all, so he used this working name instead. And after that he never changed it." Linux had now been christened as well as born.

At first, there was nothing in this Linux subdirectory on the university server; Linus wasn't willing to release his young and fragile kernel to the public for a while. In the 1992 interview with Wirzenius, he said, "I wasn't really ready for a release yet, so the directory contained just a README for about a month ('this directory is for the freely distributable Minix clone' or something like that)," he said. At this stage, Linus is still thinking of Linux as a Minix clone, nothing grand like Unix.

Though unwilling to release Linux, he was ready to mention its existence. On Sunday, 25 August 1991, under the subject line "What would you most like to see in minix?" he wrote in the comp.os.minix newsgroup:

Hello everybody out there using minix —

I'm doing a (free) operating system (just a hobby, won't be big and professional like gnu) for 386(486) AT clones. This has been brewing since April, and is starting to get ready. I'd like any feedback on things people like/dislike in minix, as my OS resembles it somewhat (same physical layout of the file-system (due to practical reasons) among other things).

. . . I'll get something practical within a few months, and I'd like to know what features most people would want. Any suggestions are welcome, but I won't promise I'll implement them :-)

Linus (torvalds@kruuna.helsinki.fi)

Response to this posting was immediate. A fellow Finn wrote less than four hours later, "Tell us more!" and asked: "What difficulties will there be in porting?" A Minix user from Austria said: "I am very interested in this OS. I have already thought of writing my own OS, but decided I wouldn't have the time to write everything from scratch. But I guess I could find the time to help raising a baby OS :-)"–a portent of the huge wave of hacker talent that Linux would soon ride.

In reply to the question about porting, Linus was pessimistic: "Simply, I'd say that porting is impossible. It's mostly in C, but most people wouldn't call what I write C. It uses every conceivable feature of the 386 I could find, as it was also a project to teach me about the 386."

In conclusion, Linus detailed the current state of his project: "To make things really clear—yes, I can run gcc on it, and bash, and most of the gnu utilities, but it's not very debugged. It doesn't even support floppy disks yet. It won't be ready for distribution for a couple of months. Even then it probably won't be able to do much more than minix, and much less in some respects. It will be free though."

In his 1992 history, Linus recalls that from this first mention of his "hobby" he got "a few mails asking to be beta-testers for Linux." A couple of weeks later, in September 1991, he had pulled together the first official Linux, which he dubbed version 0.01. Nonetheless, Linus was still not happy with the product of this sustained bout of coding. "It wasn't pretty; I wasn't too proud of it," he said, and decided not to announce it in comp.os.minix.

Instead, he recalls, "I put together a list of all the people who had reacted to my [25 August] posting by e-mail." And then as soon as he had uploaded Linux 0.01 to the /pub/os/linux directory that had been created by Ari Lemmke, "I sent them an e-mail and said that 'hey, now you can go and look at this.' I don't think that this list was more than maybe ten to fifteen" people.

The only reason he posted this first, unsatisfactory version he says, was that "I felt that because I had this site, I had to upload something to it." He uploaded just the source code.

Token gesture or not, the sources came with surprisingly full release notes—some 1,800 words. These emphasized that "this version is meant mostly for reading"—hacker's fare, that is, building on a tradition of code legibility that had largely begun with the creation of C, as Dennis Ritchie had noted in his 1979 history of Unix.

And highly readable the code is, too. As well as being well laid out with ample use of space and indentation to delineate the underlying structure, it is also fully commented, something that many otherwise fine hackers omit. Some of the annotations are remarkably chirpy, and they convey well the growing excitement that Linus obviously felt as the kernel began to take shape beneath his fingers:

This is GOOD CODE!
    Yeah, yeah, it's ugly, but I cannot find how to do this correctly and this seems to work . . . Most of this was trial and error . . . Urghh.
    Let's hope this is bug-free, 'cause this one I don't want to debug :-)
    I'm grumpy.
    I just love not having a manual.

Well, that certainly wasn't fun :-(. Hopefully it works . . . This is how
REAL programmers do it.
For those with more memory than 8 Mb–tough luck. I've not got it, why
should you :-) The source is here. Change it. (Seriously–it shouldn't be too
difficult. Mostly change some constants etc. I left it at 8Mb, as my machine
even cannot be extended past that (ok, but it was cheap :-)

In the accompanying notes Linus warned: "Though I will help in any
way I can to get it working on your machine (mail me), it isn't really supported. Changes are frequent, and the first 'production' version will
probably differ wildly from this pre-alpha-release." Frequent changes
would be a hallmark of Linux throughout its history.

Linus also pointed out something that would have been obvious to any
hacker of the time, but which has become obscured as Linux has become
more widely known. "Sadly," he writes, "a kernel"–which is what Linux
is and always has been–"by itself gets you nowhere. To get a working system you need a shell, compilers, a library, etc." He then pointed out that
"most of the tools used with linux are GNU software and are under the
GNU copyleft," an early indication of the symbiosis of the two systems.

And yet it is strange that Linus did not adopt Stallman's General Public
License, copyleft, for his own kernel. Instead, he wrote

This kernel is © 1991 Linus Torvalds, but all or part of it may be redistrib-
uted provided you do the following:
— Full source must be available (and free), if not with the distribution
then at least on asking for it.
— Copyright notices must be intact. (In fact, if you distribute only
parts of it you may have to add copyrights, as there aren't ©'s in all
files.) Small partial excerpts may be copied without bothering with
copyrights.
— You may not distribute this for a fee, not even "handling" costs.

The last clause meant that people could not charge for the work involved in making floppies with the kernel (just 72K when compressed)
on them, a clear brake on Linux's wider distribution.

In the 1992 interview with *Linux News*, Linus explained why he had
chosen this license. Shareware, where the software is distributed free but
you must pay if you decide to use the program, was never an option for
him: "I generally dislike shareware. I feel guilty about not paying, so I
don't use it, but on the other hand it is irritating to know that it's there.

Illogical, but that's how I feel." The first form of the license, he said, "was probably an overreaction to the dislike I felt against the way Minix had been set up; I thought (and still do) that Minix would have been better off had it been freely available by FTP or similar."

The rest of the release notes for 0.01 are mainly technical, but contain two interesting statements. "The guiding line when implementing linux was: get it working fast." "Get it working fast" would become one of the fundamental principles of Linux development and would distinguish it from other, more careful, slower approaches.

Linus also noted that "this isn't yet the 'mother of all operating systems,' and anyone who hoped for that will have to wait for the first real release (1.0), and even then you might not want to change from minix." Little did Linus suspect that Linux 1.0 would be another two and a half years away, but that by then few would hesitate about making the switch.

Linus signed off his release notes for 0.01 with a phrase that had become Richard Stallman's trademark farewell: "Happy hacking." The results of Linus's own happy hacking soon showed themselves in Linux 0.02. This time Linus had no qualms about telling the world. On Saturday, 5 October 1991, he sent a posting to comp.os.minix that began

Do you pine for the nice days of minix-1.1, when men were men and wrote their own device drivers? Are you without a nice project and just dying to cut your teeth on a OS you can try to modify for your needs? Are you finding it frustrating when everything works on minix? No more all-nighters to get a nifty program working? Then this post might be just for you :-)

As I mentioned a month(?) ago, I'm working on a free version of a minix-look-alike for AT–386 computers. It has finally reached the stage where it's even usable (though may not be depending on what you want), and I am willing to put out the sources for wider distribution.

A later paragraph in the same posting gives us some insight into how Linus regarded Linux in the context of the other, better-established Unix kernels, the GNU Hurd and Minix:

I can (well, almost) hear you asking yourselves "Why?". Hurd will be out in a year (or two, or next month, who knows), and I've already got minix. This is a program for hackers by a hacker. I've enjoyed doing it, and somebody might enjoy looking at it and even modifying it for their own needs. It is still small enough to understand, use and modify, and I'm looking forward to any comments you might have.

Linus was beginning to see that between the finished but essentially frozen Minix program, and the promising but still incomplete GNU, there was a niche for his "program for hackers by a hacker." Linux might be crude now, but it worked–just–which meant that it could be improved, whereas the Hurd remained a tantalizing promise. Just as important, Linus, unlike Tanenbaum, was soliciting ideas for improvement and welcomed other people's own efforts in this direction.

Linus says that "the second version was much closer to what I really wanted. I don't know how many people got it–probably ten, twenty, this kind of size. There was some discussion on the newsgroup about design, goals, and what the kernel should support." Things were still pretty small-scale, but growing. In the 1992 *Linux News* interview, Linus said of the preceding version (0.01): "I don't think more than about five [to] ten people ever looked at it."

As a result, he told *Linux News*, "Heady with my unexpected success, I called the next version 0.10." Linus recalls that "things actually started to work pretty well." Version 0.11 came out some time in early December. "It's still not as comprehensive as 386-minix," Linus wrote in a posting to comp.os.minix on 19 December 1991, "but better in some respect." This posting included some interesting comments from him on the present state of Linux and its future development: "/I/ think it's better than minix, but I'm a bit prejudiced. It will never be the kind of professional OS that Hurd will be (in the next century or so :), but it's a nice learning tool (even more so than minix, IMHO), and it was/is fun working on it."

The launch date of the GNU Hurd is now receding fast into the "next century or so," and Linux is even a better learning tool than Minix. But the main thing is that Linux "was/is fun," the ultimate hacker justification for any kind of project.

The 19 December posting also included a copy of Linus's "plan." This is a file that is sent when a user is "fingered" over the network (using a program called "finger"), and was an important way for people to obtain information about Linux without needing to sort through hundreds of newsgroup postings. Linus's plan at that time was headed "Free UNIX for the 386–coming up 4QR 91 or 1QR 92". It begins: "The current version of linux is 0.11–it has most things a unix kernel needs"–probably the first time Linus had publicly pitched Linux as a project to create a Unix-like kernel rather than just a development from Minix.

The plan also noted that two other sites were now carrying the Linux software, one in Germany, and one in Richard Stallman's home town, Boston, at MIT. This was run by Ted Ts'o (pronounced "cho"), whose name appears at the bottom of the same information page (using his e-mail name tytso) as someone who was working on new features for the imminent Linux 0.12.

Although barely visible, this was an extremely significant development; it meant that already other hackers were contributing to the Linux project. This same 19 December posting to comp.os.minix also spoke of "people" who were working on drivers for SCSI to allow another kind of hard disk system to be accessed by Linux. "People" meant not Linus, another indication that others were involved.

This is confirmed by a message posted the next day from Drew Eckhardt, who was the person writing those SCSI drivers, and who had already contributed to version 0.11. His posting was in response to a general enquiry about Linux, which said in part,

> Could someone please inform me about [Linux]? It's maybe best to follow up to this article, as I think that there are a lot of potential interested people reading this group.

It is striking that Eckhardt answers rather than Linus, and in great detail, an indication that at least one other person already knew enough to act in this capacity, and that he uses the pronoun "we" when talking about Linux. What had once been one hacker's "hobby" was turning into a community. Moreover, even at this early stage, Linus was prepared to listen to that community's needs.

Some of the first users of Linux wanted something called Virtual Memory (VM), which is the ability to use hard disk space as if it were ordinary RAM; this was a standard feature of Unix, and a big help at a time when memory chips were expensive. Linus wasn't interested in this feature, probably because he had just about enough RAM, and his own hard disk was so small. But over that Christmas he nonetheless sat down and wrote the code to add Virtual Memory to the Linux kernel and released it as version 0.11+VM. Wirzenius recalls that Linus "just decided, now it's Christmas, it's boring, it's family and I need to hack."

In the early history of Linux, which he wrote in 1992, Linus recalled that 0.11+VM "was available only to a small number of people that wanted to test it out; I'm still surprised it worked as well as it did," and modestly omitted to mention that he had written this code in just a couple of days. Virtual Memory then became a standard part of the kernel from the next version. What had begun as a small private request had turned into a public benefit.

It seems both appropriate and yet astonishing that version 0.12 of Linux should appear on 5 January 1992, one year to the day from that pivotal moment when, as Linus put it, "I actually broke down and got a PC." Appropriate, because the PC thus celebrated its first birthday with what Linus later called "the kernel that 'made it': that's when linux started to spread a lot faster." Astonishing, because in that time Linus had gone from a student who knew little about C programming, and nothing about writing for the Intel architecture, to the leader of a rapidly growing group of hackers who were constructing a fully functional Unix kernel for the PC from the ground up.

The release notes for 0.12 display well Linus's growing sense of achievement; they are full of a kind of exhilaration, a sense that maybe, just maybe, he was on the brink of something big.

They begin with a plea, written entirely in capitals, not to install Linux unless the user knows what he or she is doing: "If you are sure you know what you are doing, continue. Otherwise, panic. Or write me for explanations. Or do anything but install Linux.–It's very simple, but if you don't know what you are doing you'll probably be sorry. I'd rather answer a few unnecessary mails than get mail saying, 'you killed my hard disk, bastard. I'm going to find you, and you'll be sorry when I do.'"

Linus has said that "earlier releases were very much only for hackers," implying that version 0.12 was suitable for a wider audience. This may well be true, but the installation instructions still include such steps as the following: "Boot up linux again, fdisk to make sure you now have the new partition, and use mkfs to make a filesystem on one of the partitions fdisk reports. Write 'mkfs -c /dev/hdX nnn' where X is the device number reported by linux fdisk, and nnn is the size–also reported by fdisk. nnn is the size in /blocks/, ie kilobytes. You should be able to use the size info to determine which partition is represented by which device name."

This indicates the gulf that separated Linux from Windows 3.1, say, released just a couple of months later.

As well as important improvements to its code, Version 0.12 brought with it a revised license. Linus explains why:

Fairly early, there were people who happened to live in the same area and wanted to make Linux available to others who were interested. But the original license didn't even allow copying fees. So you couldn't even just sell the diskettes for more than the price of the diskette. So it didn't make sense, somebody obviously had to do a lot of work because copying diskettes is boring, it takes time, and very few people have access to these automated copiers. So there were people asking me to allow some kind of copying fee–even just a small one. Not because they wanted to make money, but because they didn't want to lose money on making Linux available to others, and helping others.

In the end he decided to adopt Richard Stallman's GNU General Public License (GPL).

In 1996, Linus admitted that "I wasn't really a GPL fan. It was too much lawyerese, and it's a bit too strict in my opinion." But he also conceded that "on the other hand, the GPL has worked very well. I can't say I'm unhappy." In retrospect, the change to the GPL proved to be a key move, particularly concerning the later commercialization of Linux.

The release of version 0.12 was perhaps the turning point for Linux. Before that, it was something of a curiosity: interesting, but neither particularly useful nor obviously important. With 0.12, many more people started to take note. A new mailing list, Linux-activists, already had 196 members by 13 January. Linus had already noticed a difference in the comp.os.minix newsgroup: "Within two weeks [of the release of Linux 0.12] there was a lot more discussion [about it]," he says. "There were obviously people who were really using Linux for what they had used Minix for before, mostly Minix people because that was where all the discussion had been, on the Minix newsgroups."

Obviously, many Minix users were trying Linux and talking about it, but not everyone was delighted by the growing volume of Linux discussions on comp.os.minix. One wrote

> I really don't wish to flame, but it's starting to annoy me that 50% of the articles I read in this newsgroup are about Linux.

On the same day that this not unjustified plaint was posted, Linus was reporting an amusing accident on his machine. He had been trying to connect with the university's computer, but by mistake instructed his terminal emulator program to dial his hard disk. Contrary to appearances, this was an easy thing to do, thanks to what Peter Salus had called "perhaps the most innovative thing that [Unix's creator] ever thought of," which was that everything is a file for Unix and hence for Linux. This means no conceptual difference exists between sending data to a modem or to a disk drive.

This slip wiped out the Minix system that Linus had kept alongside the steadily growing Linux. Initially, Minix had formed an indispensable scaffolding for the development of Linux; but since Linux could now function without the crutch of Minix, there was no reason to re-install Minix after this mishap. Perhaps that command to dial his hard disk had been not so much an accident as a Freudian slip on Linus's part, a symbolic cutting free from an older-generation program.

By a remarkable coincidence, the final rupture between the worlds of Minix and Linux was brought about just two weeks later, when Andrew

Tanenbaum posted to comp.os.minix what would become one of the
most famous messages in Usenet history.

It bore the provocative subject line "Linux is obsolete," and began

I was in the U.S. for a couple of weeks, so I haven't commented much on
LINUX (not that I would have said much had I been around), but for what
it is worth, I have a couple of comments now.

   As most of you know, for me MINIX is a hobby, something that I do in the
evening when I get bored writing books and there are no major wars, revolutions, or senate hearings being televised live on CNN. My real job is a professor and researcher in the area of operating systems.

   As a result of my occupation, I think I know a bit about where operating
[systems] are going in the next decade or so. Two aspects stand out.

Tanenbaum went on to focus on two areas, the issue of microkernels
versus monolithic kernels and portability, in a typically polished and
well-argued prose that betrays its academic roots.

On the issue of kernel design, Tanenbaum said

While I could go into a long story here about the relative merits of the two
designs, suffice it to say that among the people who actually design operating systems, the debate is essentially over. Microkernels have won."

He then took a rather more pointed jab at Linus's creation:

"LINUX is a monolithic style system. This is a giant step back into the 1970s.
That is like taking an existing, working C program and rewriting it in BASIC.

This was a real insult to any hacker, as Tanenbaum must have known.

As far as portability is concerned, Tanenbaum began with a witty compressed history of chip design, and concluded:

I think it is a gross error to design an OS for any specific architecture, since
that is not going to be around all that long. MINIX was designed to be reasonably portable, and has been ported from the Intel line to the 680x0
(Atari, Amiga, Macintosh), SPARC, and NS32016. LINUX is tied fairly
closely to the 80x86. Not the way to go.

Contrary to his expectations, the Intel family of chips is currently going so strongly that most others have dwindled in importance; but apart
from this, Tanenbaum was correct that Linux at the time was "fairly
closely tied" to the Intel architecture, but simply because it had grown

out of experiments to understand a chip from that family. As later events would show, Linux was by no means doomed to be an Intel-only system.

Linus could not ignore Tanenbaum's comments. Linus had devoted an increasing proportion of his life to Linux over the last nine months, and the rapidly growing community of Linux users and coders was doubtless a cause of justifiable pride. Now here was some fusty old academic coming along and trashing it all.

Wirzenius notes that "Linus has this big ego; if someone says something that hurts his pride then he will retaliate." In this case it took Linus just eleven hours to retaliate, his words positively bubbling with rage. You can almost see him rolling up his metaphorical shirt-sleeves in preparation for the fight:

> Well, with a subject like this, I'm afraid I'll have to reply. Apologies to minix-users who have heard enough about linux anyway. I'd like to be able to just 'ignore the bait,' but . . . Time for some serious flamefesting!

He begins with a general sideswipe at the quality of Minix: "linux beats the pants off minix in almost all areas," and adds a rather low blow by adding, "not to mention the fact that most of the good code for PC minix seems to have been written by Bruce Evans."

He is incensed by Tanenbaum's comments that Minix is a hobby and throws some interesting light on the initial motivation for writing Linux in the first place:

> Look at who makes money off minix, and who gives linux out for free. Then talk about hobbies. Make minix freely available, and one of my biggest gripes with it will disappear.

Linus then returns to knocking Minix. Referring to Tanenbaum's comments that his real job is being a professor and researcher, Linus comments,

> That's one hell of a good excuse for some of the brain damages of minix. I can only hope (and assume) that Amoeba doesn't suck like minix does.

(The operating system Amoeba is Tanenbaum's main research project and hence his "real job.")

Aside from the venom, it is surprising that somebody who started using Minix only nine months previously now has no qualms about calling it "brain-damaged" to its creator, a man, moreover, who is not only a highly respected professor in the area of operating systems but author of

Operating Systems: Design and Implementation, which, by his own admission, Linus had studied intensively.

Just as he had done nine months before the April Fool's Day letter, Linus almost immediately starts to backtrack on his attack: "PS. I apologize for sometimes sounding too harsh: minix is nice enough if you have nothing else. Amoeba might be nice if you have 5–10 spare 386's lying around, but I certainly don't. I don't usually get into flames, but I'm touchy when it comes to linux :)"

The next day, perhaps having slept on it, he is even more contrite:

I wrote:

Well, with a subject like this, I'm afraid I'll have to reply.

And reply I did, with complete abandon, and no thought for good taste and netiquette. Apologies to [Andrew Tanenbaum], and thanks to John Nall for a friendy "that's not how it's done" letter. I overreacted, and am now composing a (much less acerbic) personal letter to [Andrew Tanenbaum]. Hope nobody was turned away from linux due to it being (a) possibly obsolete (I still think that's not the case, although some of the criticisms are valid) and (b) written by a hothead :-)

Linus "my first, and hopefully last flamefest" Torvalds

It was by no means his "last flamefest," but the tone of the discussion was now more moderate as he and Tanenbaum argued some of the more technical points at stake. This drew in several other people and called forth the following wise words that neatly summarize the situation from an independent standpoint:

Many if not most of the software we use is probably obsolete according to the latest design criteria. Most users could probably care less if the internals of the operating system they use is obsolete. They are rightly more interested in its performance and capabilities at the user level.

I would generally agree that microkernels are probably the wave of the future. However, it is in my opinion easier to implement a monolithic kernel. It is also easier for it to turn into a mess in a hurry as it is modified.

Regards,

Ken

"Ken" is Ken Thompson, the inventor of Unix.

Between Linus and Tanenbaum, the tone became almost playful. Picking up again on the two main themes, kernel design and portability, Tanenbaum wrote, "I still maintain the point that designing a monolithic kernel in 1991 is a fundamental error. Be thankful you are not my student. You would not get a high grade for such a design :-)" As for portability, he said, "Writing a new OS only for the 386 in 1991 gets you your second 'F' for this term. But if you do real well on the final exam, you can still pass the course."

To which Linus replied in good humor

> Well, I probably won't get too good grades even without you: I had an argument (completely unrelated—not even pertaining to OS's) with the person here at the university that teaches OS design. I wonder when I'll learn :)

Shortly after the "Linux is obsolete" flamefest, Linus stopped posting almost altogether in the comp.os.minix newsgroup, not because he might have felt it inappropriate to continue to peddle Linux there, and not even because he was offended by Tanenbaum. It was simply that he had his own newsgroup now: alt.os.linux. This was in the "unofficial" alt Usenet hierarchy, but in due course it would turn into the "official" comp.os.linux, fully the equal of Tanenbaum's comp.os.minix. Nothing could symbolize more neatly the sense that, having rebelled against the old lion, as all young lions must, Linus had left to form his own pride.

Later, in his 1992 *Linux News* interview, he said: "I have to admit to a very unbecoming (but understandable, I hope) feeling of glee when I saw that [comp.os.]linux had finally more readers than [comp.os.]minix." More readers, that is, than a newsgroup that had once been read avidly by 40,000 people.

And yet Linus retains a soft spot for Minix and the comp.os.minix newsgroup. As late as July 1999, he was still reading and even posting there. Somebody was asking about GCC for Minix, which was where it had all begun in that first message of 29 March 1991: "How did Linus get the GCC library to work with MINIX, and add support to his own system calls and the like?" the writer asked.

It seems Linus couldn't resist responding to this siren call from the past. His answer spools back time as he describes in a few sentences how it all began. He concludes:

> Much of this work has to be available still. I made my 1.40 port [of GCC] available, but I have to admit that I don't know where it ended up. It's been eight years . . .

It is hard not to detect in these words a hint of a nostalgia for those far-off, heady days of youth when, starting alone and working from nothing, he built, bit by bit, the program that bears his name; when he planted the seed of what would grow into the kernel of a complete operating system used by tens of millions of people, and began a movement whose ramifications continue to spread.

4

Factor X

ALMOST IMMEDIATELY AFTER HE AND TANENBAUM had argued over the relative merits of Linux and Minix, Linus bumped up the version number of his operating system kernel from 0.12 to 0.95, which came out on 7 March 1992. In part this promotion was probably made in the honest if ultimately over-optimistic belief that the first "real" version of Linux might be near (it was still two years away); it probably also reflected a psychological need to emphasize to the world, and maybe even to himself, the almost-finished nature of the code.

Many Minix users remained skeptical. For example, when Tim Murphy, director of computing at an Irish university, had asked in comp.os.minix in January 1991 whether "any independent person [is] actually running Linux, and can give an opinion on its merits vis-à-vis 386-Minix?" he went on to say, "It seems to me pretty unlikely on the face of it that anyone could really write a reliable operating system from scratch in a short time." Murphy now explains, "I did think that Minix was beautifully written. In fact, it was far better written, in my view, than Linux is today."

Murphy was not alone in his opinion. Another Minix user of the time, Derek Lieber, a systems programmer at a large computer company, says he found the Minix code "clearly written and organized into comprehensible subsystems. Of course, Minix was written that way deliberately," he adds, "because it was intended as a tool for teaching. As for the code

55

quality [of early Linux], I guess I thought it was mediocre." But mediocre or not, he adds, "I was amazed that it worked. I'd expected that I'd get it installed, watch it crash, and move on. But the damn thing actually ran. I don't think I pushed it too hard, but I don't remember ever crashing it. Even in the early days."

Not only that, but Linux was eminently usable: "I was running on a dinky 386 laptop with 5 Mbyte of memory and a 40 Mbyte disk," Lieber recalls. "But I could fit all of the [kernel], its source code, and the source code for all the GNU tools and still have 10 Mbyte for my own stuff; it was programmer heaven."

Not surprisingly, this "programmer heaven" soon attracted a growing band of enthusiastic and able coders. Some, including Ted Ts'o and Drew Eckhardt, were already adding to Linux back in 1991. For example, Ts'o had "made some heavy changes even to 0.10," as Linus put in one of his exchanges with Tanenbaum during the "Linux is obsolete" flamefest. Similarly, Eckhardt remembers that he had "pulled down" version 0.10 and found that it didn't work properly. "So I figured out what would [work]," he says, and sent Linus a patch, or corrected version, of the part of the Linux source code that caused the problem. Soon afterwards, Linus "released 0.11 and 0.12 with my changes included," Eckhardt recalls.

Many more people began using Linux after the 0.95 release, and some started sending their own contributions to the kernel code. A mailing list for these contributors was set up to allow them to keep up-to-date with developments there and swap ideas. One of these early kernel hackers was Rich Sladkey. "My first installed kernel was 0.95b"–a minor upgrade to version 0.95 that came out in spring 1992–"but I was tracking Linux for several months before that," he recalls, "basically waiting for a 200 MByte disk so I could multiboot Windows 3.1, which I needed for [applications] with Linux."

Multibooting meant being able to choose between running Windows and Linux when the PC was fired up, and its mention here is significant. Although Sladkey used Unix at work, it demonstrates that he was also familiar with the world of Microsoft and wanted to run Linux and Windows on the same machine.

This was to be the case with increasing numbers of Linux hackers; they were able to choose between Windows and Linux because of a design decision that Linus had made early on, inspired in part by the presence of the "Prince of Persia" game he had played on his PC before commencing his Linux project. So that he could play this game while working on Linux he needed to keep part of his hard disk formatted for

MS-DOS. As Linus said in his interview with *Linux News* in 1992, "When Minix finally arrived, I had solved PoP [Prince of Persia]. So I installed Minix, (leaving some room for PoP on a DOS partition)"–a separate area of his hard disc–"and started hacking."

Linus wrote Linux so that it could work alongside the Microsoft operating system, just as Minix could, rather than as an all-or-nothing replacement for it. The knock-on effect of this personal requirement was that, later on, those curious about Linux could try it without needing to throw out DOS completely, a much bigger step that would have throttled the early take-up of Linux considerably.

Matt Welsh, later author of one of the first books on GNU/Linux, *Running Linux*, and then an undergraduate at Cornell University, was typical of these hesitant PC users. He says, "Early on, I was very skeptical about Linux. I had a nice setup with MS-DOS with most of the GNU DOS utilities installed"–versions of Stallman's GNU programs that had been ported to run on MS-DOS–"so my DOS machine acted much like a Unix system. Why would I want to throw that out and struggle with this bleeding-edge, barely working Unix clone?"

The reason Sladkey had taken the plunge was simple. "The idea of a free compiler with the quality of GCC, already well established at the time, and a free hosting OS [operating system] supporting a full multitasking Unix environment was very attractive. So attractive, it had to be tried to see if it could be real," he says. Despite this attraction, Sladkey chose to leave MS-DOS on his machine, just as Linus had. Sladkey couldn't help noticing that "from my very first installation, Linux was dramatically more stable than my co-resident installation of Windows 3.1 on top of MS-DOS 5."

Once again Stallman's GCC had played a key role in driving the uptake of Linux. Less apparent is that the "free hosting OS" Sladkey refers to consisted of Linux plus several other indispensable GNU programs. In effect, Linux was able to drop into the hole left in the GNU project by the long-delayed Hurd kernel and realize Stallman's dream of a complete and free Unix clone. Rather than being called just "Linux," the resulting operating system is more correctly described as "GNU/Linux" to reflect its two major components.

Welsh remembers that when he eventually installed GNU/Linux, he, too, "got the fever. It was all about doing things yourself," he explains, "adding new features, and constantly learning more about how computers and operating systems work."

Sladkey provides a good example of what the practical benefits of "doing things yourself" were, and why even at this early stage GNU/Linux had crucial advantages over Windows. "There were in fact bugs," he recalls, "But the essential difference was in the obviousness of bugs, the repeatability of bugs, and potential for fixing bugs oneself. In this environment, bugs were only temporary delays on a steady road towards excellence and stability."

"Windows, on the other hand," he continues, "was miserably unreliable with mysterious crashes, inexplicable hangs, and a pervasive fragility that taught you to avoid doing anything fancy with even advertised features of the OS because it could not take the stress. The only way to make things more stable on Windows was to avoid doing things or to fiddle ad nauseam with the configuration and then just wait and see if things improved."

Sladkey recalls the first time he found and sent a bug to Linus: "My first contribution was in porting some program, probably one of my smaller personal projects. I discovered a bug. Since Linux came with source, my first inclination as a hacker was to take a look under the hood and see if I could fix the problem. I found that although I had never done any kernel work, that I was able to navigate around the code pretty easily and provide a small patch to correct the problem.

"With my heart beating and my palms sweating, I composed the most professional message I could muster and sent it off to linus.torvalds@cs. helsinki.fi describing the bug and including my proposed fix. Minutes later he replied something like, 'Yup, that's a bug. Nice investigation. Thanks. Fixed,' and I was hooked."

These events are emblematic of the entire Linux development. Users running a program—perhaps something unusual that reveals hitherto unsuspected problems—find bugs; operating system code can be made to work well with all the most common programs and yet still contain more subtle bugs that are thrown up only in the course of time.

Because Linux comes with the source code (unlike MS-DOS or Windows, which are sold only as "black boxes" that cannot be opened), a hacker is able to poke around inside the program. Whatever reservations some Minix users might have had about the quality of the Linux code, it was written in such a way that hackers could find and fix the cause of the problems they encountered.

Thanks to the Internet, the solutions to these problems could be sent directly to Linus, who could similarly use the medium to reply, sometimes within minutes. Linus's own openness to bug-fixes, and his lack of protectiveness regarding his code, is key in making the process work.

Linus explains his viewpoint on these early bug fixes. "They started out so small, that I never got the feeling that, hey, how dare they impose on my system. Instead, I just said, OK, that's right, obviously correct, and so in it went [to the kernel]. The next time it was much easier, because at that time there weren't many people who did this, so I got to know the people who sent in changes. And again they grew gradually, and so at no point I felt, hey, I'm losing control."

This sensible attitude speaks volumes about how much Linus had matured since his early and somewhat adolescent outbursts to the Minix newsgroup; his accepting implicit criticism with such good grace shows that not just Linux had made progress by 1992.

Sladkey's experience is also a good example of the benefits to Linux and its users that this openness to suggestions and willingness to act on them engendered. As he explains, "Initially I just fixed bugs everywhere I found them. I would spot a problem, research the problem, determine the expected behavior, fix the problem, test my fix," and then send off a description of the bug with the resultant patch to the kernel code.

Although finding and fixing bugs was an extremely useful activity, Sladkey was soon doing more: "I was becoming more loyal to Linux, and so any negative publicity about a bug or missing feature was enough motivation for me to hunt down a problem and fix it, even though it didn't affect me personally because I didn't use that feature of the OS."

The culmination of this altruism was his work on the Network File System (NFS). Even though Sladkey describes NFS as "a dated and brain-damaged protocol"–a protocol is just a set of rules–"and useful mostly for connecting with legacy Unix systems," it was an important networking capability for a Unix-like operating system to offer.

He continues, "I wrote the NFS client"–the software that runs on a user's machine so that he or she can access a Unix system running the NFS server–"partly as a challenge for myself." What is more remarkable, he says he wrote it "partly because people who were critical of Linux were using the absence of NFS as a fault" that could be laid against what had become his system of choice.

"When I initially announced my NFS client on the kernel mailing list, there was a great deal of interest," Sladkey recalls. "Many people were willing to try early alpha code because they wanted this feature so badly."

Being able to draw on many users "was a whole model that was worked out and debugged in the Minix world," as Tanenbaum points out. That Linus himself was aware of this early on is shown by his posting to the Minix newsgroup on 19 December 1991. In it, commenting on the pros and cons of Minix and Linux, he noted that the "minix still has a lot more users," and that this meant Minix had "better support" than

Linux. Linus noted that his kernel "hasn't got years of testing by thousands of people, so there are probably quite a few bugs yet."

Similarly, eighteen months later, when Linus introduced yet another version of the kernel, he made what he called a by now "standard request":

"Please try it all out, give it a real shakedown, and send comments/bug-reports to the appropriate place. The changes are somewhat bigger than I'd prefer, so the more testers that try it out, the faster we can try to fix any possible problems."

As Linux increased in age and stature, so did the number of people who had used it and found bugs. The better Linux became, the more people used it; and the more people debugged it, the faster it improved: a virtuous circle that continues to drive Linux development at a vertiginous rate. Linux exploited what might be called the "Minix method" better than Minix employed it because Tanenbaum allowed his operating system to grow slowly and only in certain ways. Linus was happy to accept improvements to his kernel, and even to make them the basis of more far-reaching changes, as Sladkey's experience with NFS was to show.

"The NFS client patch quickly stabilized to a useful if not too speedy addition to the Linux kernel," Sladkey says. "I was too shy to submit the patch to Linus directly, but someone else requested that Linus incorporate it and so Linus approached me about inclusion of my patch into the main kernel." Linus has always been open to requests from users; he later said, "I never really liked [the] 'for hackers, by hackers' mentality," even though this was how he had billed Linux to begin with, perhaps to win over the Minix community. "I always wanted Linux to be for users."

Sladkey notes that when Linus asked for the NFS code, it "could have just been integrated [into the kernel] blind since many people were using it successfully," and so had winkled out most of the bugs. "But Linus evaluated my patches and suggested that some things be done differently before he integrated it into his sources. I had made some tentative changes to other parts of the kernel which were just enough to get what I needed to work to work," Sladkey says, "and I had, purposely, minimized the size and extent of those changes. In the opinion of Linus, there were better, more invasive ways of supporting the new features—the right way—and were to be preferred to simple change-avoidance—the easiest way.

"So in my case, Linus improved the kernel in a way that made more work for himself and for me in the short term, but made the kernel clearer, cleaner, and more maintainable in the long run. This lesson by example of taking the high road and doing things right, instead of taking the path of least resistance, made a very big impression on me at the time and became an essential part of my programming philosophy."

What Linus chose to do in this case was significant and typical. Upon being presented with code that added major new functions to the kernel, he did not bolt it on in the simplest way possible; instead, he used lessons learned from the new code to extend and strengthen the existing kernel for possible future developments. Although this meant more work, not only did it provide a sounder base to work from but it helped to ensure that (unlike many commercial software programs that become increasingly spaghetti-like and convoluted as new features are added) the structure of Linux would improve the more such functions were added.

Linus adopted the same approach for Sladkey's port of GNU Emacs to GNU/Linux, an important addition to the collection of applications. Sladkey describes this as "a classic example of how a port showed up weaknesses or incompatibilities in Linux that were addressed not so much by porting the program to the host but by adapting the host so that the program required fewer changes."

Linus had chosen this approach early on. "I even fetched GNU sources off the Net and compiled them under Linux, and checked that they worked just like they should work even though I didn't use them personally," he recalls. "Just to make sure that, yeah, I got that part right." In doing so, he was building once more on many years' work by Richard Stallman.

Stallman had decided to create a Unix-like system that was not based on AT&T's source code in any way; instead, it used the features of Unix as a template and implemented them independently. Because he succeeded so well, the GNU suite of programs provided a bench test of Unix kernel compatibility against which Linux could be measured without the need to run or, just as important, to buy expensive commercial Unix software.

This approach of adapting the kernel to fit the applications paid off handsomely when it came to porting what would prove to be one of the strategically most important additions to the portfolio of GNU/Linux programs: the X Window System.

Drew Eckhardt, who has followed Linux from the very earliest days, rates the arrival of X as one of the three milestones in the history of

Linux. The other two are the virtual memory (VM) capabilities, which Linus had added in December 1991, and networking.

At first, Linux had been controlled through a bare shell like GNU's Bash, one of the reasons for calling the overall operating system GNU/Linux. This shell works rather like MS-DOS: Users type in commands that cause the kernel to respond in certain ways. Such command-line interaction was standard for the Unix world at the time; as a result, most Unix hackers were completely at home entering these opaque commands on a keyboard.

The world of the Apple Macintosh or Microsoft Windows, then at version 3.1, was a complete contrast. Here, control was effected by selecting options from pull-down menus available from various overlapping windows present on the screen, or, even more directly, by clicking on-screen graphical icons.

For many years Unix had possessed the foundation of a similar graphical approach; this was called X because it was the successor to a windowing system called W, and it was a standard component on commercial Unixes. Unlike the Macintosh or Microsoft Windows systems, its principal use was not to make control easier (X on its own lacked menus and icons) but to enable viewing and control of multiple programs simultaneously through several X windows open at once.

As soon as GNU/Linux began to offer more than the most basic Unix functions, X climbed high on the wish list of many users. Because Linus was busy improving the kernel, and windowing systems are not part of that in Unix systems (unlike Microsoft Windows, where the graphical interface is tightly integrated with the basic operating system code), somebody else needed to step forward to start things moving.

The Linux movement did not and still does not have a formal hierarchy whereby important tasks like these can be handed out, an apparent weakness that has proved a strength. A kind of self-selection takes place instead: Anyone who cares enough about developing a particular program is welcome to try. Because those most interested in an area are often the most skillful, they produce high-quality code. If they succeed, their work is taken up. Even if they fail, someone else can build on their work or simply start again.

And so it was that in early 1992, Orest Zborowski started to port X to GNU/Linux. Dirk Hohndel, who later took over responsibility for the entire area of X for Linux explains that "getting X ported wasn't all that hard, since X is already rather portable. The majority of the work [Zborowski] did was actually adding features to the Linux kernel." So that he could obtain this important feature for systems running the

Linux kernel, Linus was once more prepared to accept changes. But un-like other ports for Linux, X soon became part of a major independent free software project that had interesting parallels to Linux in its origins and subsequent development.

The X Window standard was managed by the X Consortium, a body put together with the aim that whatever other splits there were in the Unix world, at least windowing would be unified. To ensure that no manufacturer could gain an unfair advantage from this work, the X Win-dow standards were made freely available under the MIT X licence, which essentially allows you to do anything with the code.

This was good news for those outside the consortium because it meant that they could take the code for X and port it to other plat-forms. For example, at the end of 1990, Thomas Roell had created X386, which was designed for Unix running on the Intel 80386, the chip Linus had in his PC. "Everybody said the Intel-Unix PCs would be just toys," Roell recalls, "but I wanted to have graphics." Roell gener-ously contributed the updated version of his code, X386 1.2, to the X Consortium for inclusion in its next release of X Window, X11R5, which came out in October 1991.

One user of X386 1.2 was David Wexelblatt. He remembers how "the X11R5 server itself was basically buggy as hell, a huge step backwards from the X11R4 stuff." Even more unfortunately, Wexelblatt explains, Roell "had taken the [X386 server] stuff commercial [so] there weren't going to be any free enhancements" from him to fix these problems. As a result, Wexelblatt and a group of other people started putting together their own patches to the X386 server.

Two of them, "Glenn Lai and Jim Tsillas," Wexelblatt remembers, "each independently were working on the performance problems," one of the main areas that needed fixing through patches to the X386 code. "David Dawes, down in Australia," Wexelblatt continues, "had started working on some of the various other bugs in the R5 server, and he was also distributing patches." Meanwhile, Wexelblatt was working on his own solution.

"And we were all out there, all doing these things and distributing lit-tle bits and pieces out through Net news," he says, referring to the Usenet newsgroups that were commonly used at the time for passing around code. "And after I had been doing that for a couple of weeks, I got the brilliant idea, you know, this is really stupid, there are four peo-ple doing this work and some of it's at cross-purposes, and we're dupli-cating effort—why don't we all get together and just produce one package?

"We first started this in April '92," Wexelblatt recalls. A month or two later, they started distributing their combined patches. "We called what we were distributing simply X386 1.2e," an enhanced version of the current X386 1.2. Afterward, Wexelblatt and his fellow hackers renamed their software:

> These days most people don't get the pun [Wexelblatt notes], but this thing came out of X386 which had gone commercial, and since we were doing freeware, ours was XFree86. We really had no grand plans at that time, but basically once we had gotten past this first bug-fixing thing, we started getting requests for other stuff. Like, oh, we need a driver for this video card, and oh, there's this operating system out there, we need to support it. And at that time, about June or July of '92, we first started seeing the Linux people coming to talk to us. There seemed to be from the start a philosophy in the Linux community of well, we're defining this from scratch, we might as well define this to what's as close to a standard as is out there.

Changing the kernel to follow standards in this way made it much easier for the XFree86 group to support GNU/Linux, and was a continuation of the approach Linus had adopted when modifying his early kernel to ensure better compatibility with GNU software.

The relationship between the XFree86 and GNU/Linux movements became positively symbiotic: XFree86 for GNU/Linux made the latter more attractive and brought it more users; and the spread of GNU/Linux-based systems gave XFree86 the perfect, free platform. Dirk Hohndel remembers discussing this with Linus: "We talked about the synergy between the two. XFree86 wouldn't be anywhere close to where it is without Linux. And vice versa."

That XFree86 came into being and flourished at just the time Linux too was created and growing is no coincidence. Both arose then thanks to the fall in cost of PCs based around Intel's 386 chip. In a reply to a posting in comp.os.minix in December 1992 in which the writer had said, "I've never used a 386. I'll never use one, unless you put a gun on my head," Linus wrote,

> You are missing out on something. I programmed a 68k machine [his Sinclair QL, which had Motorola's 68008 chip] before getting a PC, and yes, I was a bit worried about the intel architecture. It turned out to be ok, and more importantly: it's the cheapest thing around.

Minix had successfully created a Unix clone on the earlier 8086 chip, but it lacked such crucial features as virtual memory, the feature that Linus had written in a few days before Christmas 1991, or any X Window port. And although 386-Minix existed, Tanenbaum was unwilling for it to be developed too far lest it lose its value as an educational tool, the original impetus behind writing Minix. This left many Minix users frustrated and only too ready to switch to a faster-moving and more ambitious project such as GNU/Linux when it came along.

Some of the success of GNU/Linux can therefore be attributed to hardware that was powerful enough to allow full Unix-like features to be adopted, and yet cheap enough for many people to own it. The arrival of the 386 chip by itself was by no means enough to drive the GNU/Linux revolution; this was shown by the history of 386BSD, another free Unix operating system created to exploit the power of the Intel chip at the time Linux came into being.

The project had been begun by Bill and Lynne Jolitz. The idea was to port the highly popular Berkeley Systems Distribution (BSD) variant of Unix created at the University of California at Berkeley to the PC and thus satisfy the needs of die-hard Berkeley fans who had bombarded Tanenbaum with hundreds of e-mails every day in an effort to convince him to turn Minix into something similar.

The early Linux hacker Richard Sladkey says of the time he was trying to gauge which one he should install, "I was reading both the Linux and 386BSD [news]groups. Most anyone who was familiar with Unix knew that [the widely used editor] vi and networking came from Berkeley, not AT&T, so the acronym BSD automatically commanded some respect. A lot of people just assumed 386BSD would get there first [ahead of GNU/Linux]."

Linus says, "I knew about the 386BSD project by Jolitz because he wrote about it in *Dr Dobb's* [*Journal*]," a major series of articles that ran from January 1991 in that magazine, the leading programmer's title of the time. Linus told *Linux News* in 1992 that "386BSD was helpful in giving me some ideas," but acknowledges, "if 386BSD [had] come out a year earlier, I probably wouldn't have started Linux. But it was delayed, and delayed some more. By the time it actually came out, I already had a system that worked for me. And by that time I was so proud of [its] being mine that I didn't want to switch." Moreover, "I already had a few users, maybe a few hundred users," he says. This was in early 1992.

In addition to the delay, there were a couple of other factors that gave GNU/Linux important advantages in its competition for users. Sladkey recalls that "Linux could multiboot with another OSes, while 386BSD required a whole disk [formatted in such a way] that wasn't compatible with [MS-]DOS. So for just that one reason alone I chose Linux because I couldn't afford a whole 'nother computer."

Given the huge installed base of MS-DOS, Sladkey was certainly not alone in wanting to be able to run DOS programs too, and 386BSD's approach doubtless lost it users, especially as Microsoft Windows became more popular after the release of version 3.1. It is ironic to see Microsoft's success on the desktop emerging as a factor that helped GNU/Linux gain a crucial early foothold.

Others were put off because 386BSD required a more powerful PC than did GNU/Linux. Lars Wirzenius recalls that 386BSD needed "a 387 coprocessor, which I didn't have, and so there was no chance that I would actually look at that one." The Intel 80387 was a math coprocessor used alongside the 80386 to speed up numerical routines. Linus, by contrast, had chosen to emulate the 387 in software (or some of it at least; full 387 compatibility was added by the Australian, Bill Metzenthen). This meant that Linux users did not need to add the then-costly 387 chip. Once again, whether by luck or judgement, Linus was making all the right decisions.

Last, there was a legal cloud hanging over 386BSD. Sladkey explains that "at the time, the AT&T versus Berkeley lawsuit was going on" over whether the BSD Unix included proprietary material from AT&T's Unix. "And even though everyone on Usenet was in favor of UCB [the University of California at Berkeley, which owned BSD]," there was a concern that maybe some shady stuff had happened, "and even if it hadn't," as Sladkey says, "AT&T would probably win, which would throw anything derived from BSD into question," and that included 386BSD. "So this legal doubt over the outcome of the lawsuit played favorably towards Linux, which was a clean room implementation," he adds.

Sladkey reckons that Linux needed all the advantages it could get at this time "because BSD was a complete OS that just needed to be ported [to the 386], whereas Linux was a kernel looking for a few good utilities that could make it look like a real OS"; these were utilities that would generally be obtained from the GNU project. Linus confirmed this view in the *Linux News* interview. Referring to 386BSD, he said, "It's bit scary to have big and well-known Unix that fills a similar niche as Linux."

Potentially, then, 386BSD might still have won out against GNU/Linux once the port was finished, and the price of 387 chips fell. But as Sladkey notes, "After getting involved with Linux, I continued to read both of the newsgroups and it became clear that I had made the right decision. Releases [of 386BSD] were infrequent, patches didn't make it into releases when they did happen, etc." Drew Eckhardt confirms this view: "Bill Jolitz didn't accommodate users' needs. He said, 'ours is a research system,' meaning we're not going to accept patches, and it doesn't have to work on everyone's hardware, and Linus did [accept patches]. I sent in patches and had a release in hours."

Much of the success of Linux can be directly attributed to Linus's character and the way he ran the project. Key factors were the encouragement he gave to people submitting patches and his readiness to accept them as well as his flexible attitude to such projects as XFree86. Wexelblatt notes that "it was really the right kind of philosophy. At the time, these free operating systems were basically irrelevant in the marketplace," and so needed all the friends they could get.

Together with this openness, Linus had also adopted a new style of releasing updates that became a hallmark of Linux and that contributed to its rapid improvement. As a contrast to the "infrequent" releases of 386BSD, Linus started to speed up the revision cycle until he was producing several releases a month, and sometimes more than one a week. The gradual acceleration is evident from the comprehensive and meticulous Linux Kernel Version History, put together by Riley Williams. This history shows the time and date of the latest file found within the many components that make up a given kernel version, a good guide to when it was available on public sites because Linus had probably uploaded new versions as soon as he had finished updating the last subcomponent.

The Linux Kernel Version History also indicates the compressed size of all the files within that version. For example, according to figures found there, the latest date stamp within version 0.01 of the kernel was 17.30 on Tuesday, 17 September 1991; the compressed kernel size was about 63K bytes (for comparison, Windows 2000's code runs to many tens of millions of bytes). The version of the kernel that "made it," in Linus's own words, 0.12, appeared in early January 1992, and has nearly doubled to 108K.

Despite the big jump in version number, Linux 0.95 is not much larger at 116K, but there is a noticeable gap in the time stamp: The last file is from 8 March 1992. The reason is not difficult to guess: In this period the "Linux is obsolete" flamefest took place, and the hiatus probably represents a moment's pause on Linus's part as he took stock of the situation and prepared for the evolution towards Linux 1.0.

Gradually, the pace quickens. After version 0.95, there are some minor updates, with amusing notational attempts to indicate the size of the gradations. After 0.95 comes 0.95a and then 0.95a.1. Between 0.95c and 0.96a comes 0.95c+ and pre0.96. Version 0.96a, whose last date stamp is 25 May 1992, is notable for being the first to include kernel support for X, a major leap forward and one matched by the increase of the compressed kernel from 131K to 174K. In a posting to comp.os.minix on 27 April, Linus had mentioned that X was "already working, but not available for 'the masses.'" A month later it was out.

After this, Linus has begun his summer holidays; he is now in full hacker mode, as he had been twelve months before during the initial coding of Linux. Five releases bear some form of 0.96 numbering, issued between the end of May and the end of June. Version 0.96b appears at the end of June, followed two days later by 0.96b.1, and this in turn by 0.96b.2 after just two more days. July and August both see three releases, and in September no less than five appear; these culminate in version 0.98, which has a compressed size of 320K, over four times the size of version 0.01, released almost a year before.

These figures give some idea of the coding effort that was being put into Linux development at this time, the rate of its progress, and, above all, the furious pace of updates. Issuing new public versions every few days in this way was without precedent in the software industry. Even the other free software projects, also able to ignore commercial constraints, adopted a more leisurely pace for upgrades.

This coding frenzy was doubtless born in part from Linus's growing determination to make Linux the equal not just of Minix but also of commercial Unix kernels; it was also probably fed by the many fellow hackers who were sending him suggestions and code. Whatever the cause, it had the practical consequence of speeding development yet further.

The release of constantly updated kernels meant that hackers could always work on the latest code rather than struggle with problems already fixed; this helped avoid duplication of effort. Making the latest kernel available also had the effect of enfranchising coders, who felt that they were part of the core development team with access to almost daily "snapshots" of the source code. As Sladkey's development of NFS shows, the more committed hackers felt the more likely they were to contribute in important ways.

None of this rapid-fire development and distribution would have been possible without the Internet. The rise and success of Linux is bound up with the Internet at every stage. Linus's location in Finland, home of the mobile 'phone giant Nokia and a pioneer in early Net connectivity, is probably a key ingredient in Linux's success.

Even before Linux existed, Linus recalls that "e-mail was very practical to talk with [such] people [as] Bruce Evans," who, as the author of 386-Minix, was probably ideal as a guide for Linus's first faltering steps in his exploration of the subtleties of the Intel 386 chip. Evans was based in Australia, but the Net's ability to cancel distance meant that Linus could turn to him for help whenever he needed it, and often receive a response within an hour. E-mail also played a key role in overcoming Linus's early awkwardness with people. "One of the reasons I liked [e-mail] so much at first," he says, "[is that] you don't see anybody, so you don't have to be shy."

The Linux code grew out of the basic terminal emulator program Linus had written so that he could access Usenet newsgroups held on the university computer. Although he read a lot of news in those early days of Linux, he notes that he "wasn't really writing a lot of news." When he did post, it often had a major effect on Linux; for example, in asking about the Posix specifications in the comp.os.minix newsgroup, Linus had come into contact with Ari Lemmke, who offered him space on his FTP site, a critically important step.

"I made a lot of good design issues with Linux," Linus said in 1996, "but the best design decision I ever made was making it available by FTP." This implies that making it available in that way was by no means a foregone conclusion, as it might be today when everything is routinely uploaded to a Net server. Linus explains that "what happened was not so much that people began sending me patches, because that didn't happen at first. It takes a while before people get so used to the system that they start making their own changes and sending them back. But what happened immediately was all the feedback."

Lars Wirzenius has no doubts that this was critically important for his friend at this point. He says, "Without the Internet, Linus would have created 0.01 and maybe 0.02, then he would have become bored [and moved on to something else]"; one of Linus's key character traits is a constant need for new challenges. Linus confirms this view: "Without Usenet, I'd probably have stopped doing Linux after a year or something . . . it was a fun project, but at some point I'd have felt that hey, it's done, I've proved it, I did this thing, it was fun. What's the next project in life?

"But because people started using it, motivation went up, there was a sense of responsibility, and it got a lot more motivating to do it. And so thanks to Usenet I just continued doing it."

Just as the Net motivated Linus, so it would motivate the hackers who started working alongside him. Users who found bugs in software and perhaps had suggestions for their resolution (because the source code was available) could contact the relevant author directly using the Internet. The user benefited by responses that often came in hours or even minutes, and the hacker received instant feedback and kudos.

The Net allowed hackers almost anywhere in the world, starting with Linus in a country that found itself off the beaten track geographically, culturally, and economically but a leader in advanced comms technologies, to take part in the Linux project and forge a new kind of distributed development model.

How ironic, then, that the last major feature to be added to the Linux kernel was support for TCP/IP, the communication protocols that underlie the Internet–the third of Eckhardt's Linux milestones. And how more ironic that, in the process of adding this ability to connect, the hitherto tight-knit Linux community showed signs of unraveling.

5

Patching Up

IT MIGHT SEEM STRANGE THAT LINUX, a system that was born and grew up across the Internet, lacked the ability to connect to it for the first eighteen months of its life. The explanation is that Linux was born on the cusp of the current Internet era, just as it moved out of academe into the mainstream; this is reflected by a comment Andrew Tanenbaum made during the "Linux is obsolete" episode. On the 3 February 1992 he wrote, "A point which I don't think everyone appreciates is that making something available by FTP is not necessarily the way to provide the widest distribution. The Internet is still a highly elite group. Most computer users are NOT on it." Linus, by contrast, said, "the best design decision I ever made was making it available by FTP" for downloading from a Helsinki-based server connected to the Internet.

In effect, Linux came out at the right time to ride the growing wave of interest in the Internet. The reason early computers running GNU/Linux had not needed to connect to the network is explained by Olaf Kirch, author of *Linux Network Administrator's Guide*, and one of the key figures in the Linux networking world. "The point is that everyone was on the Internet" already, he says, "otherwise they wouldn't have been able to participate in Linux development. I think most people were at universities and therefore had decent connectivity."

This comment throws an interesting light on where and how GNU/Linux was used in those early days. In Kirch's view, most people were working on computers at universities that had good connectivity to the Internet. Their GNU/Linux machines, by contrast, were probably at home, where they had no Internet connections, and therefore did not miss the TCP/IP functions absent from the kernel, which acted as a kind of software bridge between the operating system and the Net.

This picture is confirmed by anecdotal information. For example, the early Linux hacker Alan Cox remembers obtaining updated versions of Linux by "walking into [the university] with a pile of floppy disks" to download GNU/Linux by way of the Internet connection there. Then "you took forty floppies home, you fed it in" to the PC and typically found "like three of them didn't work," which meant returning and downloading those files again. Downloading directly would have been far more convenient.

In a posting to the comp.os.minix newsgroup on 21 September 1992, in answer to a query about Linux, Linus had given a rundown on its current state. Three important features were being added, but were available only as patches at the time of writing; these were a driver for the Sound-Blaster soundcard, which made multimedia possible under Linux; a way of reading CD-ROMs, crucially important to ease the installation of the growing range of Linux software; and TCP/IP support, which Linus said would be "in the next major release, probably next week."

The next kernel release was version 0.98, which came out 29 September. On 18 October 18 1992, Linus released a minor upgrade to this, numbered 0.98.2. This included "some TCP/IP patches," but Linus warned, "TCP/IP is still in alpha"—an early stage of development—"has not been extensively tested, and is probably not up to real use yet."

In a further posting to the comp.os.minix newsgroup dated 12 December 1992, replying to yet another question about whether Minix was "much better than Linux," Linus wrote, "The simple answer is a resounding NO," and then went on to give some reasons; but at the end, he had to confess that "on the other hand, 386bsd has a more mature networking setup, as well as having the advantage of being 'the real Mc-Coy,'" since it derived from the original TCP/IP networking code written at Berkeley. As a result, 386BSD still posed a competitive threat to GNU/Linux, partly because of its superior TCP/IP capabilities.

Details of how these came to be included in Linux are contained in the Linux Networking-Howto, one of the many semiofficial Linux texts that are widely available; it is part of a vast corpus of free but high-quality written material created by an analogous co-operative effort of volunteers around the world. Collectively, this material is known as the Linux Documentation Project.

In the Networking-Howto, its original authors, Terry Dawson and Alessandro Rubini, write, "The original volunteer to lead development of the kernel network code was Ross Biro. Ross produced a simple and incomplete but mostly usable implementation set of routines. . . . This was enough to get many people testing and experimenting with the software and some people even managed to connect machines in this configuration to live internet connections" via local area networks with links to the Net.

Olaf Kirch comments that "the reason why Linux hackers decided to roll their own networking" rather than adapt code that was freely available in BSD Unix was the AT&T lawsuit against BSD. "The outcome of that lawsuit was totally uncertain," Kirch recalls. "The common sentiment on the Linux mailing lists at that time was that the only way to avoid anything like this was to stay clear of any code we didn't write ourselves."

Kirch also has some interesting views on why networking was added at this time: "As far as I can remember, the driving force behind this was that people wanted to run X," rather than because they were trying to connect directly to the Internet. Certainly, work on networking began around the same time that X Window was being ported; and surprisingly, perhaps, the X Window system and networking were intimately related.

In one respect, X was much more powerful than the Apple Macintosh or Microsoft Windows systems. The contents of an X window were not limited to programs running on the machine displaying them; X had been designed as a networked window system and allowed output from programs on other machines, connected via a network, to be displayed and operated.

The X Window approach required some kind of networking in the operating system. Consequently, part of Orest Zborowski's task when porting X to GNU/Linux was to write some simple networking code. Linus accepted these additions because, in addition to allowing X to run, the inclusion of this code brought other major benefits. As the Networking-Howto says, Zborowski's work "was a big step forward as it allowed many of the existing network applications to be ported to linux without serious modification."

As a result of this glimpse of the possibilities, Linux users started pushing for improvements to the networking code. As Kirch recalls, "Ross's initial work was quite OK, and it kind of worked. Of course much of it was crude—things are necessarily crude when you rewrite TCP/IP from scratch." The Networking-Howto document explains, "The pressure within the Linux community driving development for networking support was building and eventually the cost of a combination of some unfair pressure applied to Ross and his own personal commitments outweighed the benefit he was deriving and he stepped down as lead developer."

Kirch recalls that things turned nasty. "What happened next was that a bunch of people started to flame Ross quite heavily—I don't recall for what reason. As a result, Ross stopped doing Linux development. It's sad to say this—many old-time Linux hackers tend to paint the early days on the mailing lists in fairly rosy colors. There was a lot more intimacy, but probably that made insults hurt a lot more as well," he says. Alan Cox believes that Biro "quit for various reasons, some of which included the fact that his PhD advisor thought he really ought to be finishing his thesis."

Someone else observing developments was Fred van Kempen. Kirch remembers the time: "After Ross quit," he says, "Fred, or FvK, as many called him, stepped into the breach. In fact, he kind of took over the network development. I recall a message from him where he wrote that he'd had a long phone conversation with Linus, and had convinced him that he was the right person to do the job. To be honest," Kirch continues, "judging by his coding skills, FvK was indeed a good candidate for that job. He had been writing network applications for Minix before."

FvK had ambitious plans. "Fred started out with a great vision," Kirch says. "He tried to implement a layered architecture where you could stack network protocols on top of each other." Such a layered approach would allow networks other than those based on the Net's TCP/IP to be accessed, a good idea at the time when it was by no means clear that TCP/IP would dominate networking.

"He also improved Ross's code quite a bit," Kirch notes. "In order to distinguish his code from Ross's, he started to call his network patches Net-2. Then came Net-2b. Around Net-2b, the code actually became quite usable."

Despite this, things started to unravel. Kirch remembers that "there were several problems with FvK. He didn't want to discuss much of what he was doing with anybody else. Then, he was living behind a very, very slow network link, which made it close to impossible to download the network patches he released. At times, his link was so flaky that he didn't receive any mail for days." More serious, perhaps, was that "sometimes he [created] patches against a modified kernel" rather than against the standard one. As a result, Kirch says, "people had a hard time getting them to apply" to their systems—even Linus.

The Networking-Howto identifies the fundamental problem with van Kempen's work: "Fred's focus was on developing innovations to the standard network implementations and this was taking time. The community of users was growing impatient for something that worked reliably and satisfied the 80 percent of users and, as with Ross, the pressure on Fred as lead developer rose."

The continuing problems in the networking area were becoming a major headache for Linus. Rich Sladkey, who made a number of important contributions to kernel code in the early days, believes that "unreliable networking prior to Net-2 almost killed confidence in Linux"; now problems with Net-2 were further sowing seeds of doubt about GNU/Linux's ability to grow into a serious operating system.

Extreme situations require extreme remedies, and Linus took the unusual step of sanctioning a parallel development of networking code by Alan Cox. As the Networking-Howto document explains, Cox "proposed that he would take Fred's Net-2 code and debug it, making it reliable and stable so that it would satisfy the impatient user base while relieving that pressure from Fred, allowing him to continue his work" in developing the more advanced code with its layered architecture.

This approach was dangerous because it might have led to what is called code-forking, which is the evolution of two separate strands of development whereby some Linux developers would use and improve one networking approach while others worked on the rival, both being convinced that "their" method was best. Such duplication of effort confuses users and divides developers into warring factions, which in turn slows progress. This is the kind of fragmentation that had bedeviled the Unix world and drove the rapid uptake of Microsoft's Windows NT 3.5 when it appeared in 1993.

In the end, the gamble proved more than justified: Stable and usable networking was at last made a standard part of the kernel; and the Net wars that resulted briefly from this two-track effort brought about an important and necessary refinement of the entire Linux development model. The wars also led to the anointing of Alan Cox as Linus's de facto Number 2 and marked his rise as one of the Linux community's most talented and productive figures.

Alan Cox was born a year before Linus, in 1968, in Solihull, just outside Birmingham, England's second largest city, in the heart of the Midlands. Cox was the elder of two boys; his father was a researcher for British Gas, the national company supplying gas to households, and his mother was a teacher.

Cox studied computing at two universities in Wales, first at Aberystwyth, in the north, and then in Swansea, on the south coast. Cox says he learned most of the important things despite rather than because of his computing studies. "I didn't read most of the official course books; they were boring," he says. "Most of those were not written by people who actually sat down and wrote production operating systems," an area he was already interested in.

Alongside his official studies, Cox learned Unix and TCP/IP; he also hacked on an Amiga microcomputer that he kept in his student accommodation. "I only had a small room," he says. "There were certain solid piles of books you could stand [on] to get to the computer or the bed." He contemplated writing an entirely new operating system for the Amiga, but says he wasn't quite bold enough to take the plunge: "I thought writing file system stuff was too hard for one person to do."

Cox came across Linux through Linus's early postings in comp.os.minix. He was reading this newsgroup, he says, because he "was interested in the work people were doing in Minix [and] because . . . a lot of very good operating system discussion went on [in] that newsgroup. It was one of the few newsgroups were people where actually discussing it, arguing over implementation of actual operating system code." Not that he had Minix. "No," he explains, "Minix was then £100 [$150] and I was a tight bastard."

Alan Cox recalls the time, at the end of 1991. "[Linux] 0.11 came out," he says, "[and] shortly after that the alt.os.linux group was formed initially and the Minix newsgroup basically went dead because every single person who'd been trying to do stuff on Minix was grabbing Linux," a clear indication of the huge pent-up demand that Linux unleashed.

Initially Cox was tempted more by 386BSD than GNU/Linux. "I wasn't particularly thinking of Linux because the BSD one looked a lot more complete. Just before Linus announced 0.11, the very initial 386BSD announcement came out." Stimulated by all this operating system activity, he decided to buy a PC with a 386: "The next thing was, what am I going to put on it?" In the end, he chose GNU/Linux; his evaluation at the time of the two rivals confirms that the critical factors weighing against 386BSD were its need for a 387 math co-processor and its inability to share a hard disk with DOS or Windows.

Although he had left the university in Swansea some time before, Cox stayed in touch with his friends there and helped them out with the machine used by the university's computer society. They decided to try out Ross Biro's recently released networking code. "We put [the PC] in the campus [network]" he says, "and we plugged it in and we booted the new wondrous TCP/IP code—and it fell over.

"So we started putting newer versions on it, and the machine would fall over more or less regularly each time" despite the updated code, Cox recalls. The reason was significant: "We were actually one of the few people who, it turned out, had a Linux box on a very busy multiprotocol network." That is, they were testing the code in a new and extreme situation.

"The thing about busy networks is you get very large amounts of data and you also get interesting timings," Cox explains. "One of the big problems of debugging a networking setup is a lot of timing-related bugs only show up on busy networks. So people were seeing that code as being not stable, but it would fall over every few days. Whereas we were in a position where the same bug would fall over every few minutes."

Cox appreciated that what seemed to be bad luck (that their busy network caused the networking code to fall over quickly) was a stroke of fortune for Linux because "we had a great testing ground for it." As a result, he says, "I started sending Ross fixes." Ross Biro stopped then working on the networking code, and Fred van Kempen took over.

Cox does not hide his skepticism about Fred van Kempen's plans: "Fred decided that he was going to rewrite it all, grand wondrous vision, everything out of Fred Brooks [of *The Mythical Man-Month* fame] you shouldn't do. In the meantime, while he was doing that, I started releasing patches which were basically just a collection of fixes."

As the Networking-Howto document puts it, he did this with "some good success and his first version of Linux networking code was called 'Net-2D(ebugged).' The code worked reliably in many typical configurations and the user base was happy. Alan clearly had ideas and skills of his own to contribute to the project and many discussions relating to the direction the Net-2 code was heading ensued." These discussions sharpened until "there developed two distinct schools within the Linux networking community, one that had the philosophy of 'make it work first, then make it better' and the other of 'make it better first,'" as the Networking-Howto puts it.

This was no minor difference of opinion over obscure technical issues; it was a fundamental ideological battle that involved not only networking but the entire Linux development process. The heart of the debate questioned how Linux should go forward; which mechanisms should be employed to add significant new features to the kernel; and, most critical, how the growing development team should be run.

Andrew Tanenbaum had implicitly raised most of these issues in one of the points he made during the "Linux is obsolete" exchanges. On 3 February 1992, he had written,

An interesting question is whether Linus is willing to let LINUX become 'free' of his control. May people modify it (ruin it?) and sell it?

He had then gone on to pose a hypothetical question that shows astonishing perspicacity because it was written months before Linus's problems with networking and Fred van Kempen had blown up:

Suppose Fred van Kempen ... wants to take over, creating Fred's LINUX and Linus' LINUX, both useful but different. Is that ok? The test comes when a sizable group of people want to evolve LINUX in a way Linus does not want.

Tanenbaum expanded on his thoughts a couple of days later:

The problem is coordinating things. Projects like GNU, MINIX, or LINUX only hold together if one person is in charge. During the 1970s, when structured programming was introduced, Harlan Mills pointed out that the programming team should be organized like a surgical team — one surgeon and his or her assistants, not like a hog butchering team — give everybody an axe and let them chop away.

Tanenbaum offered a graphic image for the distributed software development process Linux employed:

I think coordinating 1,000 [software] prima donnas living all over the world will be as easy as herding cats.

Linus posted his reply to the newsgroup the next day, 6 February 1992:

Here's my standing on "keeping control", in 2 words (three?):
  I won't.
  The only control I've effectively been keeping on linux is that I know it better than anybody else, and I've made my changes available to ftp-sites etc. Those have become effectively official releases, and I don't expect this to change for some time: not because I feel I have some moral right to it, but because I haven't heard too many complaints, and it will be a couple of

months before I expect to find people who have the same "feel" for what happens in the kernel. (Well, maybe people are getting there: [Ted Ts'o] certainly made some heavy changes even to 0.10, and others have hacked it as well.)

In fact I have sent out feelers about some "linux-kernel" mailing list which would make the decisions about releases, as I expect I cannot fully support all the features that will /have/ to be added: SCSI etc, that I don't have the hardware for. The response has been nonexistent: People don't seem to be that eager to change yet . . . if Fred van Kempen wanted to make a super-linux, he's quite welcome.

He concluded with an important point:

Yes, coordination is a big problem, and I don't think linux will move away from me as "head surgeon" for some time, partly because most people understand about these problems. But copyright /is/ an issue: if people feel I do a bad job, they can do it themselves.

As Linus explained in the same comp.os.minix posting, he had chosen the GNU General Public License (GPL) because

the only thing the copyright forbids (and I feel this is eminently reasonable) is that other people start making money off it, and don't make source available etc. . . . This may not be a question of logic, but I'd feel very bad if someone could just sell my work for money, when I made it available expressly so that people could play around with a personal project.

The GNU GPL allows others to take the Linux source code and modify it provided they make the modifications available; that is, if someone else makes a "super-Linux," there is nothing even Linus can do to stop that person if the source code is provided. The advantage of this approach is that Linus could then take changes he approved of from such a "super-Linux" and fold them back into "his" Linux. The downside was that the GNU GPL made such divergences possible in the first place.

Linus's answer to the growing split in the networking code between Fred van Kempen's work and Alan Cox's code proved to be the same as the one he gave in February when he replied to Tanenbaum's posting. Although he could not forbid anyone to develop in a certain way, he could use his authority (built, as he had rightly said, on his knowing it "better than anybody else" and on his proven ability in managing the kernel development) to approve one branch of the code, thus making it part of the "effectively official releases." Provided enough people in the Linux user community agreed with this decision, as manifested by their actions in using these "effectively official releases," the code base he chose would flourish and rivals would languish for want of support.

The Networking-Howto document explains how this applied in the case of networking in the kernel. "Linus ultimately arbitrated and offered his support to Alan's development efforts and included Alan's code in the standard kernel source distribution. This placed Fred in a difficult position. Any continued development would lack the large user base actively using and testing the code and this would mean progress would be slow and difficult. Fred continued to work for a short time and eventually stood down and Alan came to be the new leader of the Linux networking kernel development effort."

Kirch says, "I don't know if there ever was a public statement by Linus about him preferring Alan over Fred. What happened was that at some point, Linus stopped accepting patches from Fred and instead accepted those from Alan. That's when Alan effectively took over maintenance of the network code." Alan Cox emphasizes that "it was completely accidental. I just wanted the networking code to work." This is doubtless true, but on Linus's side the move represented a statement of intent.

Linus later said, "I've never been all that concerned with design. I have a very pragmatic approach: What works and what people want to use is good. And who cares about design unless people want to use it?" By choosing Alan Cox, very much a fellow pragmatist, over Fred van Kempen's "great vision," as Kirch calls it, he was sending a signal to all Linux developers about the kind of code he would favor, and the general philosophy he would adopt henceforth: that of "make it work first, then make it better," as the Linux Networking-Howto puts it.

This was, after all, the method Linus had adopted when writing Linux. The first Linux he posted, 0.02, was barely usable, but it worked. More important, it was a starting point that others could then use for adding refinements, which Linus proved perfectly ready to accept.

Alan Cox's subsequent work on the networking code followed the same path. Kirch recalls that "quite unlike his predecessor, Alan did not throw away everything at once. Even though he always said that his eventual goal was to get rid of FvK's layering, because it was making things complicated and slow, and didn't add much in the way of functionality. He started by just making it work." Alan Cox recalls, "The first thing I was doing in many cases was cleaning it up . . . there was actually very little I fixed at the protocol level" in terms of the basic TCP/IP standards. "The protocol stuff was mostly right, it was just everything under-lying was a bit flaky or had holes in it."

Fixing code that "was a bit flaky or had holes in it" was one of Cox's fortes. "Cleaning horrible code up was one thing I appeared to be good at," he says, and he soon emerged as Linux's bug-fixer par excellence. "I often figure bugs out in my sleep," he confesses.

As well as debugging and writing new code, Cox also began to assume the important additional role of one of what are often called Linus's "trusted lieutenants." These are senior hackers who are responsible for certain areas of the kernel. Their job is to filter patches from other hack-ers, check them, and then pass them on to Linus. Alan Cox recalls, "Fairly early on, people started sending me things" for the networking code. "If there's anything they're not sure about, someone would say, 'I think this is a fix but I'm not sure, what do you think?'"

Linus had never planned the addition of this crucially important de-velopment infrastructure; it arose in response to the situation. As he said in 1996,

> I've never made any conscious decisions that this is how I want it to work in the future. All the changes have been automatic responses to different circumstances. At first, people just sent me patches directly, and what hap-pened was I got to trust some people because I'd been e-mailing with them; I knew they were technically sound, and did the right thing [a key hacker concept]. Other people started sending patches to these people I trusted because that offloaded some of my work because the people I trusted checked the patches.
>
> It's worked pretty well. In some cases I tell people who e-mail me di-rectly, 'Can you send it to this other person just to check?' because I don't have the hardware, for example. The other person's the guy in charge of that part. And then after that, it kind of automatically goes the right way. So there's maybe ten or twenty who are in charge of certain parts of the kernel like networking, SCSI drivers subsystem, whatever. And then there are a lot of people who have one specific driver that they are in charge of. Usually the original authors of that driver, but in some cases they may have gotten a new machine and somebody else has taken over that driver. Stuff like that I generally apply directly, because I can't test it and I just have to trust the person who wrote it originally.

One reason this gradual apportionment of the kernel "worked pretty well," Linus said, was because "the way the whole [Linux] system is set up, which also happened kind of by itself, is that if you change one driver it's really so localized that it should never impact anything else." In other words, the kernel design is highly modular, with clean interfaces between the parts. "It has to be so, when there's people all over the world doing this," Linus noted. "There's no weekly brainstorming session where everybody gets together and discusses things."

This model had been evolving even before Cox had taken over responsibility for the networking code. Generally, though, the kind of showdown between rival strands of development that had taken place there had been avoided. The case of another trusted lieutenant, Ted Ts'o, is typical.

Like Cox, Ts'o was born in 1968, but a third of the world away, in California. His father was a doctor, and his mother helped run the family practice. It was through his father's research work that Ts'o first came into contact with computers: "I got started at a relatively early age, playing with my father's [Digital] PDP-8, and PDP-15," Ts'o recalls. "In fact, those were the only computers I really had to play with until high school." He programmed these Digital machines not in a high-level language such as Basic, but in "raw assembler." When Ts'o went to MIT, in 1986, he studied computer science and graduated in 1990.

Soon afterwards, in the fall of 1991, he came across GNU/Linux. This would have been version 0.02 or 0.03, because Ts'o had contributed to the kernel as early as 0.10, which came out in December 1991. He added new code that gave users extra ways of controlling programs that were running. The motivation for sending this code to Linus is interesting. "Part of the reasons why I did it," Ts'o says, "was just simply that it needed to be done, and it would make it a whole lot more useful for myself." But also, he says, "the thought did occur to me, gee, if I did this, I bet a lot more people would find Linux useful.

"I think a number of people instinctively knew that there was such a thing a critical mass, and if you could get enough people working on [Linux], then you might get something very interesting out." Moreover, Ts'o and others had already put this theory into practice elsewhere: "There were a lot of folks who really understood that you could contribute changes back to [free programs], and they would get accepted or not, but that the end result was a much better product."

As well as continuing to feed through patches, Ts'o made another important contribution to the GNU/Linux movement in the early days by setting up the first site in the United States that carried the Linux kernel and related software. Ts'o explains the background to this move. "I noticed that the only place you could get Linux in those days was on ftp.funet.fi"—the main site in Finland, which had been set up by Ari Lemmke—"and that was often very, very slow. Again, it was one of these, gee, I bet it would help people use Linux if I set up an FTP site." The site soon became well known as the TSX-11 repository. Ts'o explains that "tsx-11 just simply happened to be the workstation that was sitting on my desk." Creating a U.S. site for GNU/Linux provided a major boost to its availability on that side of the Atlantic; once again this important step was taken by someone out of sense that it would be a good thing for the entire community.

Gradually, Ts'o started putting more of his effort into just one or two areas. "What generally happened was most people were concentrating on all parts of the kernel, but over time, they would handle less of the questions or bug fixes in parts of the kernel they weren't really concentrating on, because they didn't have the time, or the kernel was getting big enough that you didn't have time to look at all parts of it." As the kernel grew in features and size, resulting specialization meant that it was no longer possible for every hacker to contribute everywhere. When certain people became known for their work on particular areas, they started to take on some of the tasks originally handled exclusively by Linus.

Another important factor helped drive this change. "What gradually started happening was more people were sending bug reports and or requests for help as opposed to actual patches," Ts'o explains. That is, GNU/Linux had become easy enough to use that it was no longer purely for hackers. These nonhacker users sent not code but bug-reports, a vital contribution, nonetheless. As a consequence, some of the main hackers started to reply to the bug reports or requests for help, instead of coming up with patches independently. As Ts'o recalls, "I would just simply be the one to handle the replies."

Things then started to snowball. "This all happened on a public mailing list, so people would see that when so-and-so asked for help, I would be the one who sent in the reply with the bug-fix and patch," he says. "And so what generally ended up happening was other people would start deferring things to me, and start sending patches to me because they knew I was working actively in that area anyway."

The final stage in this evolutionary process, Ts'o explains, was that "after a certain point, people would send patches to Linus, and he would send the patch to me and say, 'What do you think of it?'" As a result, Ts'o took control of certain parts of the kernel and fed through revised patches to Linus for his consideration.

Responsibility for one major area, that of the Linux file system ext2, is shared with another of the most senior Linux hackers, Stephen Tweedie. Tweedie was born in Edinburgh, Scotland in 1969. Both his parents worked in the computer industry, and Tweedie says, "I can't ever remember not having been in the presence of computers."

When he was fourteen, he was already creating operating system extensions for his Sinclair ZX-81 micro, a machine Alan Cox had also used as a boy. Tweedie studied computer science at Cambridge University; after graduating, he returned to Edinburgh to do research at the Scottish capital's university, where he discovered GNU/Linux, around the beginning of 1992. "I didn't specifically get into it for the single purpose of hacking on it," he says, "but I did do that from very early on."

Tweedie echoes the explanation of Ts'o as to how people came to be assigned areas of responsibility. "It's very simply a case of who's actually working on something," Tweedie says, "and who has got a track record of making good choices. And if you are working on something and you've got credibility in the eyes of other people who are doing that, then other patches tend to come through you.

"There are people who are generally recognized as being not owners but simply experts in particular areas. The community takes advantage of that and works through those people to get work done in those areas." In other words, "it's very, very much a meritocracy," he says, and represents a kind of natural selection by the community.

Linus's willingness to defer to his lieutenants and to hand off responsibility for major chunks of the kernel has had another important effect. As the continuing contributions of Alan Cox, Ted Ts'o, and Stephen Tweedie over the last decade indicate, they have all remained deeply committed to the Linux movement for many years, even though any one of them could easily have started up and led his own rival group—as Linux's license permitted.

This fierce loyalty to a single strand of development stands in stark contrast to other free Unix-like kernel projects. For example, after 386BSD lost momentum, NetBSD was started. As the announcement by the founder, Chris Demetriou, of NetBSD 0.8 in April 1993 explained, NetBSD was "based heavily on 386BSD 0.1," with various patches applied and new programs added. Similarly, FreeBSD, "had its genesis in the early part of 1993, partially as an outgrowth of the 'Unofficial 386BSD Patchkit,'" as Jordan Hubbard, one of its instigators, writes in his history of the software. Yet another offshoot of 386BSD is the OpenBSD project, led by Theo de Raadt, which places particularly strong emphasis on security.

The existence of three highly similar projects has led to a division of coding effort and a smaller user base for each than would be the case were there only one such 386BSD descendant. The weaknesses in the split world of the free BSD derivatives highlight the corresponding strengths of the unified Linux development.

When Linux was organized into a patchwork of areas handled by Linus's lieutenants, this evolution's important collateral effects on Linux's growth and development were felt only gradually. Linus's decision to back Alan Cox, however, produced a more immediate consequence. Cox's intense hacking style meant that Linus could push out revised kernels more rapidly to debug the TCP/IP code that had proved so problematic. Olaf Kirch says, "I think Alan's work on making the network layer stable was one of the main points why Linus kept delaying the release of 1.0. He wanted a working TCP/IP [module] before calling it 1.0."

Details from the Linux Kernel Version History reflect this change. Version 0.98 of the code, when TCP/IP was available in the form of Ross Biro's initial patches to the kernel, is dated 29 September 1992. Version 0.99—tantalizingly close to the long-desired Linux 1.0, in numbering at least—came out on 13 December 1992. Kernel releases in 1993 were slow—for Linux, anyway: three in January, two each in February, March, and April, one in May, and none in June. In July and August, Linus managed to squeeze out just one release–that year's summer holidays were not proving very productive. It looked as though the battles within the fledgling Linux group were sapping the movement's progress.

Then suddenly, around the end of September 1993, there is a gear change. Version 0.99.13 is released on 20 September, followed by eleven releases in just over a month, culminating in 0.99.13k on 25 October. The compressed size of the kernel was climbing too: from 320K for 0.98, 420K for 0.99, and nearly 800K for 0.99.13k.

Linus and his fellow coders go into overdrive. In December 1993, there were ten releases; in January 1994, no less than fourteen releases, one every two days, on average. February 1994 saw eleven new versions. At last, with a final date-stamp of 22:38 on March 13 1994, a Sunday, one megabyte of compressed code was officially consigned to the world as Linux 1.0.

Almost three years to the day from when Linus received his copy of Minix, the first officially complete version of Linux, one that could begin to bear serious comparison with other Unix kernels, had at last been finished. Along the way, the GNU/Linux user base had grown from one hacker to hundreds of thousands of people around the world.

It had weathered a highly damaging period of internal dissension to emerge stronger and better-equipped for future growth thanks to its increasingly well-defined development methodology and a core group of gifted senior coders who could second Linus's efforts. The community's new resilience would put it in a good position not only to withstand but even to benefit from another major shift now fully underway: the commercialization of GNU/Linux.

6

Boot Then Root

THE FIRST RELEASE OF LINUX was for "reading" only. But because there was little point in producing a new kernel if no one could use it, Linus started offering binaries—compiled versions that would run on a PC—alongside the source code.

Getting a system up and running was a complicated business, and only for the most dedicated hacker. To aid people, Linus created two floppy disks, called boot and root. Lars Wirzenius explains the procedure. "The boot disk had the kernel." You placed this in your PC and switched it on. "When that booted, it asked you to insert the other disk, and that one had the whole file system for the Linux system," Wirzenius says. "All the stuff that these days would be put on a hard disk was that one floppy. But it was a very, very small file system, very few programs, just enough to be called an independent Unix system," he says.

Once you had this system running, you could get more ambitious. "If you knew what you were doing," Wirzenius continues, "you could format a hard disk or a partition on a hard disk, and copy the programs over to the hard disk and then modify the boot disk to load the kernel from the hard disk instead," much faster than loading it from the boot floppy. Then users could begin to explore the system and try out some of the few programs that had been ported to it—things like Stallman's GCC—which were available separately.

Linus placed copies of the boot and root disks on the Helsinki server, where he also placed the source code. Because both the source and binaries were freely distributable, several other sites around the world started "mirroring," or copying, them. One of these was the Manchester Computing Centre (MCC), part of the University of Manchester, in the United Kingdom.

After simply mirroring Linus's early boot and root disks, MCC decided to make its own distribution, or collection of files that could be used to install GNU/Linux. The first MCC Interim version, using the 0.12 kernel, appeared in February 1992. The Readme file that accompanies it gives a fascinating insight into what was involved in getting GNU/Linux running in those pioneer days.

The Readme explains, "The MCC Interim versions of Linux are designed to allow people who are not Unix experts to install a version of the Linux operating system on a PC. The installed system should be self-contained, but easy to extend." This indicates that there was already demand from people who were not Unix experts for a distribution that would allow them to install GNU/Linux on their PCs.

The Readme goes on, "Our versions are called 'interim' because they are not intended to be final or official. They are small, harmonious, and moderately tested." The last point was important: Not only was it necessary to debug the Linux kernel; as extra components were added to a distribution, it was vital to check that they would all work together, that they were "harmonious." This kind of large-scale debugging became one of the key tasks of people putting together distributions.

As the MCC Readme notes, "Very shortly after the first MCC Interim version of Linux appeared, other people released similar versions: Dave Safford's TAMU [Texas A&M University] releases, and Martin Junius's MJ versions were eventually followed by Peter MacDonald's massive, comprehensive SLS releases and H. J. Lu's small base systems."

Peter MacDonald was one of the first Linux hackers to submit patches to Linus, but he became better known for putting together the Softlanding Linux System (SLS) releases. As the MCC Readme says, these were "massive" and "comprehensive." That is, they tried to provide not just the kernel and basic utilities, but many of the GNU/Linux ports that were starting to appear; this included such major new elements as X Window and TCP/IP.

The drawback of this approach is that as the Linux kernel grew more complex, and the choice of applications richer, the task of keeping up-to-date with everything and making it all work harmoniously grew ever harder. This meant that the SLS distribution, admirable as it was in its intentions of providing a complete solution, did not ultimately meet the pressing need for something stable that newcomers to the Linux world could install easily.

One person increasingly impatient with SLS was Ian Murdock, who was studying accounting at Purdue University at the time. He later wrote an article for the first issue of the then-new *Linux Journal*, dated May 1994, in which he said that SLS was "possibly the most bug-ridden and badly maintained Linux distribution available; unfortunately, it also quite possibly the most popular."

These are typical young man's words; Murdock was in his early twenties at the time. "I regret how harsh I was," he says now, "because the guy was just trying to do something good." Nonetheless, "there were a lot of problems with SLS, and I really wasn't the only one to feel that way. In fact, what I wrote is largely a kind of community view at the time."

Murdock realized that SLS's problems "came out of the fact the fellow who was doing it was trying to do everything by himself. And so I looked on that and I thought, well, you know, if Linux has taught us anything it's that that kind of model is suboptimal," he recalls. "What we really ought to do is we ought try to take the model that Linux has pioneered, intentionally or not, and try to get the same benefits from that for building the system around it."

This was an important insight for late 1993, when Murdock first had the idea. It shows that even at this early stage, some people, at least, were aware that Linux was not just a piece of software but an entire development methodology. The "model" that Murdock mentions involves using a distributed team, connected by the Internet, to feed through smaller elements that together make up the whole—in this case a distribution— and to let users debug the system.

Murdock decided to call his new distribution Debian. "The story behind the name is pretty simple, actually," he says. "My wife's name is Deb and my name is Ian. So it's simply a concatenation of that." He goes on, "My first mention of [Debian] in a public forum was in August 1993. Basically, I had started to do a bit of work on it and I posted a message that said, 'Hey, I'm doing this, does anyone want to help me?' I had no idea what kind of response I would get."

He soon found out. "I got an overwhelming response," Murdock explains. He believes there were two main reasons for this. "Linux clearly had a lot to offer, and the tools that were built around it had a lot to offer, but the presentation [the way it was distributed] was something that was lacking," he says. "Also, the idea of building a system that people could be involved with turned out to be a very popular idea," he adds, just as the idea that anyone could help build a kernel had been when Linus opened up his project.

The parallels between the Linux and Debian go deeper. Just as Linux arose in part from a frustration with Minix, so Debian grew out of dissatisfaction with SLS. Both projects used the Internet as a medium for collaboration, and both were emphatically open, whereas Minix and SLS had been more controlled and closed. Moreover, the Debian project also adopted Linus's idea of parceling out areas to his "lieutenants." As Murdock explains, "Debian would be based on the idea of a package, and all these people who wanted to work on it could then take responsibility for all these different packages." He notes, "Other people taking on subtaskings is very much how Linux worked."

To make this approach function, he says, "We would define standards and rules that would allow a package from any source to be able to fit into the system well. So that when you take all these packages and you install them, you get an entire system that looks like it's been handcrafted by a single closely knit team. And in fact that's not at all how it was put together."

Even the decisionmaking process of Debian was modeled on Linux. "Essentially what would happen is, we would be presented with a decision point," Murdock explains. "And I would ask people who were working on Debian, 'What do you think we should do?' And that would spark some conversation, some discussion, and possibly some disagreement. And then I'd make a decision," he says. "A lot of the time my decision reflected what the group wanted, and some of the time it didn't. This is really the way Linux works, too."

Together with a huge response from those interested in helping with the Debian project, in the fall of 1993 Murdock received an e-mail from Richard Stallman on the subject. "He said, 'We're learning more about Linux and we've been thinking about distributing it ourselves,' because at the time their GNU kernel was taking longer than expected," Murdock explains. "They saw Linux appear on the scene and use pretty much the rest of the system they'd been putting together." That is, the new distributions put together the Linux kernel with many elements of the GNU project to form a complete operating system. "He basically said, 'I'm interested,'" Murdock recalls.

Stallman's approach proved important for Debian. "His early interest was critical in not only giving me the confidence to do it, but also giving it an air of legitimacy," Murdock says. "I really think that, more than anything else in those early days, is what caused people to take notice and get involved." But Debian was also important for the GNU project and

Stallman: "He basically got to know Linux through his involvement with Debian," Murdock believes.

There were two consequences. First, the Linux kernel became a candidate to complete the GNU project begun ten years before and held up at that time by delays in finishing the Hurd kernel. In a sense, the Debian project led to the formal completion of Stallman's dream of a Unix-like operating system that was freely available. The other consequence was that Stallman's Free Software Foundation sponsored the development of Debian in the early days. Murdock explains why: "We took a while to come out with our first releases. Part of the problem had to do with the fact that we were entirely reliant on volunteers, [and] we had such a big job to do. So in a large sense I needed to get paid to keep working on Debian because my attention to it when I had the free time simply wasn't cutting it."

Fortunately, Stallman recognized this need and offered to pay Murdock to work on Debian through the Free Software Foundation (FSF), another example of Stallman's generosity in funding others and his growing recognition of the importance of Linux-based distributions.

But relations with the idealistic and uncompromising Stallman were not easy. Murdock explains the situation: "By this time, Debian was much larger than myself," he says, "and while I had certain ideas about what Debian should be, I was no longer the single opinion. There were a lot of people who didn't agree with the FSF's goals." As a result, "the FSF was sponsoring Debian, so they had certain expectations of me; and at the same time, I was asking people to do work in their free time and they had certain expectations of me. Sometimes those expectations did not match up very well. There turned out to be some conflicting goals," he concludes.

Partly because of these conflicts, Murdock decided to stand down as Debian leader in March 1996. There were other important factors in his decision. "I wanted to finish my degree," he says, "and I had recently been married and I wanted to spend more time with my family. I'd been doing it for three years, and I think I was ready for something new as well." His successor was Bruce Perens. "Bruce was a natural choice, actually," Murdock says. "He had been involved with Debian for a long time, and he had shown a large amount of assertiveness and ability to deal with people."

Perens gives some more details on the problems with Stallman. "Richard wanted to have a part in the technical direction, and the developers on the project didn't really want a boss," he says, "they were all volunteers. If they wanted to take any direction it would be from someone who was working with them on the project." Moreover, Perens says, "We took issue with some of his technical direction because we felt it would lower the performance of the system and make it take up more disk space. We decided that we just could not live with FSF having a right to tell us what to do, and so we split off our own organization. We figured we could make as much money as we needed just from donations, which was the case."

But the dispute did not end there. One of the early Debian developers was Linus's friend and fellow student Lars Wirzenius. He explains what happened: "When Richard Stallman started to notice Linux a lot, he started to make a lot of noise about the relationship between the Free Software Foundation and the GNU project on the one hand, and the Linux community on the other hand.

"His point was mostly that the Linux community would not exist without all the free software that the Free Software Foundation was producing," Wirzenius says. "And he was right about that, so his point was a good one." But from this good point, according to Wirzenius, Stallman made an unfortunate deduction: "He decided that Linux should be renamed LiGNUx," pronounced "LIG-NUX." Stallman doubtless found this wordplay irresistible in its combination of both cleverness and, as he saw it, justice.

"And that was a very terrible thing to try to do," Wirzenius notes, "because one of the things that people get very attached to is the right for them to decide on the name of the thing they have created. And the GNU project didn't have very direct input into the kernel itself, they just made the tools for it, and the tools necessary to add to the kernel. The way that Stallman tried to push his views made it very distasteful and it almost felt like he was betraying everyone in his community." It felt like betrayal, Wirzenius says, "because up until that time it had been all the free software people against the evil people who did not give source code away. But then Stallman started to fight, or at least it looked like he was starting to fight the Linux community [because of] the fact that he wanted Linux to be renamed.

"My reaction was fuelled somewhat by the fact that initially Debian had been partly funded by FSF," he says, "which was a very good thing of them to do." Perhaps because of this earlier help, and despite this ugly incident, the Debian team agreed to call their distribution Debian GNU/Linux. "And that is precisely because the Debian people agree with Stallman that GNU is such a big part in the operating system," Wirzenius says. Perens explains: "Richard asked me to do that, when I was still De-

bian project leader, and it sounded fair to me. In fact, I don't believe anyone [in Debian] objected to it at the time."

Linus tended to remain aloof from such squabbles. "I don't get too
involved," he said in 1996, but added, "personally I don't think GNU/
Linux flies as a name; it should be catchy." And he pointed out that "it's
not just GNU programs we are using"—the X Window software, for example, comes from the XFree86 group—"so personally I prefer to have it
called just Linux and then give credit where credit is due, and that's certainly with the GNU project, too. Most of the Linux [software] literature
has the GNU copyleft and I try to make it very clear that there is more
than just the kernel, and a lot of it is GNU stuff." Nonetheless, it is certainly true that GNU software represents the lion's share of most distributions, and there is a strong argument that GNU/Linux, even if it does
not "fly" as a name, is a fairer description.

Like the Debian team, Ian Murdock harbors no ill-will against Stallman for his attempts to influence the development process, or even to rename Linux. "We wouldn't have our current idea of free software
without him, and without his uncompromising stand, which has not wa-
vered an inch the past fifteen years," Murdock says, "and I think that's
very important." But he recognizes that "some people disagree with
me"—Stallman tends to polarize opinions.

That Murdock views Stallman so positively is not surprising; one of
the main motives for creating the Debian distribution in the first place
was to create a foil to what he viewed as an irresponsible commercialization of GNU/Linux: "I saw that Linux was one day going to be a commercial product," he says, "and I was concerned at the way it might
become a commercial product.

"One of the problems with SLS was it was starting to be commercial-
ized a bit," he continues. "You were seeing advertisements in magazines
talking about Linux, and some of the features they were advertising were
just simply false." He emphasizes that "it wasn't the guy who was doing
SLS, it was people who were just appearing and selling diskettes." This
was an important new development; it represented the first signs that
people outside the GNU/Linux movement had seen a business opportunity in this fast-growing market. And it was from these modest and not
entirely praiseworthy beginnings that the huge GNU/Linux and open-
source industry of today came into being.

Although Murdock was concerned about new distributions based on
SLS, it was Slackware, SLS's successor as the most widely used distribution, that really helped to create the commercial Linux world. Murdock

recalls, "Slackware and Debian had essentially the same origins in that we were both dissatisfied with SLS. We both got started without knowing about the other, and once we found out about each other we started deciding well, maybe we ought to combine our efforts here. Nothing ever really came out of that, partly because we had different goals. I wanted to take the distributed development path, and [the person behind Slackware] wasn't as interested in that; he thought that that would be a disaster waiting to happen, trying to get dozens of hundreds of people pointed in the same direction is a fairly difficult task"—obviously sharing Tanenbaum's view that it would be like trying to herd cats.

While Debian evolved into the purest distribution, created in the same way that the Linux kernel was built, Slackware first of all took over from SLS, which Peter MacDonald had stopped supporting, as the leading distribution, and then spawned a variety of new distributions itself. In the June 1994 issue of *Linux Journal,* in what was only the second interview this new magazine had conducted (the first was with Linus), Slackware's creator, Patrick Volkerding, said, "It would be nice to make money as a result of [Slackware], but not from selling the actual package." This indicates that Slackware was very much part of the earlier, noncommercial tradition of GNU/Linux distributions that existed mainly to serve the community. The official Slackware was sold not by Volkerding but by Walnut Creek, which produced many popular CD-ROMs containing free software.

The arrival of cheap CD-ROM technology in the early 1990s probably played as crucial a role in the commercialization of GNU/Linux distributions as the arrival of cheaper PCs using the 80386 did in the original genesis of Linux itself. Had this new medium not been available at the right price, there would not have been the sudden flowering of companies selling low-cost CD-ROM-based distributions. Some of the credit for ushering in the CD-ROM as a viable distribution medium must go to Microsoft. As early as 1987, it had shipped the Microsoft Bookshelf in this form, which the company described as "the first general purpose application to bring the benefits of CD-ROM technology to personal computers."

The availability of CD-ROMs as a distribution medium for GNU/Linux was important not just because they were cheap (typically a few tens of dollars) and convenient. As more and more programs were ported to GNU/Linux and placed as a matter of course on these CDs, they provided a huge boost to the nascent GNU/Linux community. They not only provided much needed tools and applications but allowed the same distributed development of software to occur beyond the Linux kernel, where it had been perfected. Already, then, the desirability of GNU/Linux was starting to kick-start an aftermarket of applications that would in turn make the operating system even more desirable.

The credit for moving from floppies to CDs must be given to another company that, like Slackware, was once on everyone's lips in the world of Linux, but which has since fallen out of view: Yggdrasil Computing, named after the world tree in Norse mythology. A straw in the wind was the fact that Yggdrasil's creator, Adam Richter, sent out a formal press release about the first beta release of his CD-ROM, dated 18 February 1993, barely a year after the crucial version 0.12 of Linux. The first alpha release had appeared two months earlier, on 8 December 1992. The name for the distribution was LGX, which derived from Linux/GNU/X, its three main components.

The press release announced, "The Yggdrasil beta release is the first PC UNIX(R) clone to include multimedia facilities as part of its base configuration. The beta release also includes X-windows, networking, . . . an easy installation mechanism, and the ability to run directly from the CD-ROM." As the press release noted, the inclusion of multimedia, audio and video, as part of the base configuration was one novelty, as was the ability to run directly from the CD-ROM. That is, it was not necessary to install GNU/Linux first; it could be run, although slowly, directly from the CD-ROM, which functioned as a kind of removable, read-only disk. An "easy installation mechanism" was also a welcome innovation.

Even though Yggdrasil Computing was a commercial operation (the beta release cost $60 and the final production version price was $99), it did not ignore the free software community as many companies were doing. As the press release explained, "Yggdrasil is greatly indebted to the many free software developers whose efforts have made this release possible. As a token of appreciation, anyone who has made a major contribution to the LGX beta software can get a free copy, which includes the CD, manual, and boot floppies."

An Yggdrasil press release dated 17 May 1994 pointed out another of the company's contributions to the free software world: "Five dollars per copy of Motif purchased from Yggdrasil goes to the development of a free Motif clone." Motif was a programming toolkit that enabled the Unix system to offer some of the features found in the graphical user interfaces employed by Apple and Microsoft for their operating systems. It was doubly notable that Yggdrasil was carrying Motif; it was an expensive ($149.95) piece of software for an operating system that was essentially free. Moreover, it was proprietary: It could not be copied, and came with no source code.

Selling proprietary software for use on a GNU/Linux system was anathema to Richard Stallman; it represented the subversion of all his work to create GNU in the first place, because its aim was to allow users to avoid using proprietary software altogether. In many other ways, though, it was an important landmark in the commercialization of Linux. Making Motif available for GNU/Linux users effectively opened for them the entire world of Motif-based software. Although this software was mostly proprietary and expensive, the point was that it removed another barrier to the use of GNU/Linux systems in traditional business environments. GNU/Linux could be judged purely on its rapidly improving technical merits alongside other, commercial Unixes.

At almost the same time that Yggdrasil was taking this major step, another company was about to marry free and proprietary software, but in a different way. In 1994, Mark Bolzern was trying to sell a Unix database product called Flagship, produced by the German company Multisoft. "One of the problems we had was it was costing too much to set up a Unix system to try it," he explains. Then Bolzern came across GNU/Linux. It seemed to offer the perfect solution: He could use it to demonstrate Flagship for almost no cost. "So I convinced Multisoft to do a port of Flagship to Linux, and that was the first commercial product released on Linux," Bolzern asserts.

Using the free operating system brought its own problems, however. "People were always having trouble installing Linux," Bolzern recalls, "and then Flagship wouldn't run right because something had changed about the CD." The issue was the constantly shifting nature of GNU/Linux: Every distribution was different. "I decided that what was needed was a professional distribution that would pick the best and then hold it stable for a period of a year or so before releasing again," Bolzern explains. In this way he could be sure that Flagship would install easily.

"So at that point I garnered the name Linux Pro," he says, "and picked a specific distribution of Slackware and did some various testing to make sure that I had what I thought was a good solid stable CD, and then punched Flagship onto the CD, too. And the next thing I knew we were selling more Linux than we were selling Flagship, not just in terms of numbers, but in terms of dollars. We're talking hundreds [of copies] per month" of GNU/Linux sold in late 1994. Bolzern suddenly found himself in the GNU/Linux distribution business.

The GNU GPL meant not only that Bolzern could take Slackware as the basis of his distribution but that he could drop it without difficulty. For example, Bolzern says, "When the Red Hat distribution came out, I recognized it as the better solution," and so he simply switched to using that as the basis of his Linux Pro.

Red Hat had been set up by Marc Ewing in 1993. "I started Red Hat to produce a development tool I thought the world needed," he said in 1996. "Linux was just becoming available, and I used [it] as my development platform. However, I soon found that I was spending more time managing my Linux box than I was developing my software, and I concluded that what the world really needed was a good Linux distribution; at the time there was only SLS." As for the unusual name, Ewing explained, "In college I used to wear my grandfather's lacrosse hat, which was red and white striped. It was my favorite hat, and I lost it somewhere in Philadelphia in my last year. I named the company to memorialize the hat. Of course, Red and White Hat Software wasn't very catchy, so I took a little liberty."

Ewing had definite ideas about what was lacking in current distributions. "It was clear that Linux needed a lot of help in the areas of installation, configuration, and package management," he explained. "Until Red Hat, there really was no such thing as upgrading to a new Linux distribution; you had to reinstall. That was a huge drawback. It was also difficult to incrementally upgrade your machine. You either got the sources and configured and rebuilt them yourself"—something only real hackers would want to do—"or you took a chance with prebuilt binaries. Package management is what solves these problems."

What is interesting about these remarks is that Ewing was aiming to provide solutions to user problems. From the start, he was concentrating on the new market of less technically able users. As he explained, "Linux is becoming so popular that a lot of people with no Unix experience are using it, and they are generally not trained in the arcane Unix administration skills—nor should they have to be in our opinion."

This was an important development because it showed how commerce was starting to move GNU/Linux into areas that Linus and his kernel hackers, for example, could not address directly. This was not a question of programming, but packaging, which new companies like Red Hat were ideally placed to address.

Unlike some, more opportunistic, companies, Red Hat fully believed in the new way of creating and distributing software. "All the software we write is GPL'ed," Ewing said in 1996. That is, whenever the company added new features to its GNU/Linux system it made them freely available under the GNU GPL, even to competitors. This was something new in business, and an early indication of the broader implications the free software movement would have on the entire computer world.

"Our relationships with free software developers around the world are absolutely vital," Ewing said, recognizing that his company depended on them for the continuing progress of the product they sold. "We help developers out by contributing hardware and money to organizations like the Free Software Foundation, the Linux Documentation Project, the XFree86 Project, and others. We are absolutely committed to the free software community."

In addition to demonstrating its commitment to the developer community, Red Hat had to win the confidence of users, particularly those in the business world, which was just starting to explore GNU/Linux as an option; a lack of direct support from the developers was one of the corporates' main concerns.

A strength of the GNU/Linux development model was that practically every software author could be contacted directly by e-mail, or indirectly using Usenet newsgroups. Stories abound of people's posting queries about bugs in software and receiving fixes within hours from the original author. But for companies, this novel and slightly ad hoc approach was not enough; they needed someone they could turn to who would be reliable. As a result of this demand, Red Hat and other GNU/Linux distributions started to offer free and paid-for support with their products. "We offer free installation support with Red Hat Linux, and we offer support contracts for those that need long-term security," Ewing said in 1996.

Apparently a minor point, the provision of support for GNU/Linux system would prove a key development. On the one hand, it provided security for companies that were contemplating using free software in a business context; on the other, and just as important, it provided a vital new source of income for companies that were, after all, selling software that was also generally freely available.

Despite GNU/Linux's growing success, in 1996 Ewing was still unsure how Red Hat would ultimately fare in the corporate world. "As a solution to drop on a secretary's desk Linux is pretty lacking at the moment," he admitted. "Our Applixware products"—proprietary software from Applix, and one of the earliest business applications for GNU/Linux— "does bring a high-quality office suite to Linux, but there are not a lot of other end-user applications available. How this pans out in the years to come remains to be seen."

In summary, he described the issue of how important GNU/Linux would become in a business context as "the $1,000,000 question." Ewing was out by a factor of over 1,000: Just three years later, Red Hat's value was several billion dollars. And yet in 1996, the company that nearly everybody expected to become the top supplier of GNU/Linux to business was not Red Hat, but Caldera.

Even Linus, in 1996, said that "Caldera is kind of a step beyond" Red Hat in the way it addressed the corporate market. He continued, "I think what's interesting about Caldera is they based their stuff mostly on Red Hat and then they add the dimension of a commercial kind of approach."

Caldera began as a project within Novell, at that time the leader in corporate networking products, and also the owner of Unix. The man behind this work, originally code-named "Exposé," and later renamed "Corsair," was Bryan Sparks. "We were doing a research project at Novell the last year I was there, using Linux as a way to come out with technologies using nontraditional development means," he recalled in 1996, by which time he had become CEO of Caldera.

"Unfortunately there was a kind of management change at Novell and Ray Noorda [the founder of Novell] left, and a new president came in." Priorities changed: "Any rate, the project was kind of cancelled," Sparks said. But by then he had caught the bug. "[I] personally was kind of enamoured with the idea that we could produce something really interesting here. So I approached Ray, who was now not a part of Novell, and asked if he would fund this idea outside and I'm grateful he agreed."

Sparks's description of the aims of the Noorda-funded start-up are significant: "Our goal is to move Linux along as best we can," he said, "participate in the Linux community but also perhaps more importantly for us to provide commercial products that surround it and create a product that has more commercial appeal." Caldera, as it came to be known, was specifically founded to "surround" Linux with commercial products to increase its appeal to businesses.

Caldera was set up in October 1994, and released betas of its first product, the Caldera Network Desktop (CND) in 1995. The final version came out in February 1996, and offered a novel graphical desktop rather like Windows 95. This "Looking Glass" desktop, as it was called, was proprietary, as were several other applications that Caldera bundled with the package. Because it was not easy to separate these out, it was hard to make legal copies of the Caldera distribution, a dangerous precedent for the new world of commercial GNU/Linux.

Nor did Caldera make any friends when it decided to rename its product OpenLinux, the suggestion being that somehow all the other GNU/Linux distributions were not open. Some people compared this move to Stallman's attempt to rename Linux "LiGNUx." There were three versions of OpenLinux. "We create a very low-end product for the

Linux community, for the hackers on the Net," Sparks explained. "We then do two other products targeted towards resellers and the commercial environment, with many more commercial components, features, management capabilities and so forth."

The commercial components came on a separate Solutions CD, and were ports of applications from major software vendors such as the German company Software AG, which produced the heavyweight Adabas D database. As Sparks recognized, "One of the dilemmas we or anyone has when introducing a new operating system or system-level product is you have got to have the application base. An operating system in and of itself only solves a certain set of solutions, a pretty tight niche, but if you can bundle it with third-party products the range of solutions it can offer is quite large."

The ports of commercial software often arose in a peculiar manner. Sparks explained, "The Software AG partnership has kind of stemmed from the fact that many people inside of Software AG, particularly the engineers, had started to port without management's knowledge—that isn't uncommon, we find. We just called a company not long ago and said we would like to talk to you about your Linux port, and they insisted they didn't have one when we knew that they did. And we said, well, you may want to go check with your engineers because you really do have a port done."

The arrival of these proprietary commercial packages enabled GNU/Linux systems to be offered as solutions in a wide range of applications. But Caldera tended to concentrate on one area where GNU/Linux was now particularly strong. As Sparks said, "Many people perceive Linux as a kind of a hacker's Unix, and we come in and say, well, yes, it's that, but do you know what it really is? Linux is a connectivity product; you want to connect to a remote office, you want to connect to the Internet, you want to connect to this or that peripheral device, Linux can do that."

This was a shrewd move on Caldera's part in several ways. The business use of the Internet was growing rapidly at this time, and many IT departments had to meet two apparently contradictory requirements: to get their company online fast with reliable software, and to do it without any extra budget. GNU/Linux systems offered the perfect solution. They were now robust and yet extremely low-cost. As a result, many companies were using GNU/Linux without even knowing it.

Sparks described a typical situation. "We had a company call up," he said, "an MIS [Management Information Systems] guy at a large company here in the U.S., who said, 'We're using Linux for gateways and other things to attach all our Internet sites. My MIS director just found out that I'm running our company on Linux.' And he said, 'My MIS director said we're not going to run our company on no free software.' So he said, 'Can you help me,' and I said, 'Well, you bet I can.' We set up a meeting, I went out and said, 'Yes, Linux is free, but we're a real vendor. If you have problems we'll stand up and take the bullet. We'll fix it for you and we'll give you more value-added than you expect.' And that is very typical, we've done that kind of presentation now dozens of times here in the U.S."

This provides interesting evidence that GNU/Linux was already being widely used in business, but that few companies would own up to using it. Mark Bolzern confirmed this. Around the same time, in 1996, he said, "Nearly every one of the Fortune 5000 have bought our product and use it in various ways. In most cases, management does not yet know and denies it." He added, "Even Microsoft uses our Linux extensively and has bought hundreds of copies."

Alongside this burgeoning if hidden commercial activity based directly on GNU/Linux software, ancillary sectors began to emerge. For example, companies sprang up that offered ready-built systems optimized for running GNU/Linux. One of the earliest of these was VA Research, a company that would grow to become one of the main players in the GNU/Linux world.

Its founder was Larry Augustin, born in Dayton, Ohio, in 1962. "I was a graduate student at Stanford in electrical engineering," he says. "Most of the work we did at the time was on Sun workstations. I thought, gee, if I had a Unix workstation at home I'd be a lot more efficient and I'd graduate sooner. Now, I couldn't afford a Sun SparcStation"—which cost around $7,000 at the time—but "I'd seen this thing called Linux." He decided to build his own system, and run GNU/Linux on it. "I was able to put together a machine for about $2,000 that was one and a half to two times faster than that $7,000 Sun machine.

"Other people saw what I'd put together, and they said, 'Gee, can you do one of those for me?'" Augustin recalls. "So people started paying me to put these systems together for them." To begin with, Augustin sold the systems through a pre-existing company called Fintronic. Although this business soon prospered—"About a year later I had three people full-time just putting systems together," Augustin says—his life had almost taken a different course.

While he was at university, he got to know two fellow students, Dave Filo and Jerry Yang. "Dave and Jerry had started doing this directory of Internet sites," Augustin says, "that they were running out of their rooms at Stanford." Augustin was also into the Internet by this time. "I had put up this Web page in November '93, which was something very new. In fact, at the time Intel had just barely started a Web site. Intel had five companies listed on their home page that sold systems [using Intel processors] over the Internet. We were one of them."

As a result of their common interest, Augustin recalls, "Dave Filo, Jerry, and I said, 'Gee, there's something going on around this Internet thing, we should figure out a way to create a business.' I was doing a pretty good e-commerce business over the Internet, and they had this directory, and we started writing a business plan about how to build companies around the Internet."

Despite this, "the end-result was they decided to go off and try and do something with this Internet directory they were building," Augustin explains. "And I looked and said, 'Gee, that's just marketing.' I want actually to make computers, right? So I went off and kept doing systems, based around Linux." What he describes as "just marketing" would soon be the pre-eminent Internet company Yahoo, and worth tens of billions of dollars.

But Augustin has no regrets, not least because his own company would also do well. VA Research was spun out of Fintronic in February 1995. "VA" stood for Vera and Augustin: "James Vera originally founded the company with me when we were at Stanford," Augustin explains. VA Research's IPO in 1999 would show the largest opening gain ever, though few would have believed this when looking at the muddy black-and-white advertisement for what was called "VA research" in the July 1995 issue of *Linux Journal*. The top system on offer there was a 90 MHz Intel Pentium with 16 Mbytes of RAM and a 1 Gigabyte hard disk, for $3,755, including a 17-inch monitor.

Augustin says, "We were one of four advertisers in the first issue of *Linux Journal*," which bore a cover date of May 1994. The man behind the first hard-copy publication devoted to the GNU/Linux world was Phil Hughes. "In 1993, I started talking with a few friends about the idea of starting a Free Software magazine," he recalls. "We quickly figured out that we couldn't afford to start something like this because, to be nonbiased, it would need to have no advertising. I suggested, initially as a joke, that we start a magazine on just Linux."

After various problems, *Linux Journal* was eventually launched with help from the Canadian-born entrepreneur Bob Young. At that time, Young was publishing a local newsletter called *New York Unix*, and running the ACC Bookstore, which sold many GNU/Linux distributions and books. Young later merged his company with Red Hat, adding his valuable sales and marketing experience to Ewing's own technical expertise.

Hughes says:

> We started up with four people: Bob as publisher, myself as editor, a layout person and a part-time ad sales rep. We had two offices: publisher and layout in a spare room in Bob's house, editor and ad sales in my basement. We printed 20,000 copies of the first two issues. By the time the second issue was about to ship to the printer, both Bob and I realized this setup wasn't going to work. I decided that *Linux Journal* could be rolled into SSC [a publishing company he had founded in 1983] so Bob and I split the losses at that time and I went on to hire an editor, Michael Johnson [an early Linux hacker] and took over the duties of publisher. At that time, we had 926 subscribers.

As well as a magazine, books about GNU/Linux were starting to appear, too. One of the pioneers in this area was O'Reilly & Associates, then best known for its Unix books. Titles such as *Running Linux* and *Linux Network Administrator's Guide* not only provided invaluable reference material for GNU/Linux users but also allowed the respective authors, Matt Welsh and Olaf Kirch, to receive some remuneration for their many years' service in documenting GNU/Linux.

Linux Journal, ACC Bookstore, O'Reilly & Associates, and other companies like them helped spread the GNU/Linux message through their various activities and associated advertising. Further marketing came from a body that had been set up with more noncommercial promotion in mind. Linux International had been created by Patrick D'Cruze, then a student in Australia. As he wrote in a posting to the Linux-Activists mailing list on 2 March 1994, it was "a new not-for-profit organization," which had as its principal aim "international marketing and support of Linux. It is envisioned that a suitable marketing campaign will be mounted and the 'Linux solution' be expounded upon in the general media and to potential customers."

Despite its emphasis on marketing, it was mainly top hackers such as Alan Cox and Ted Ts'o who initially helped out with Linux International. But as the nascent Linux industry grew, so more of its players became involved. Bob Young was one, and he happened to speak to Mark Bolzern about Linux International at Fall Comdex 1994. Bolzern recalls, "I said, 'Oh, if an organization like that exists, let's make it into what it needs to be rather than starting a new one'" for the purposes of raising the profile of GNU/Linux.

After being invited to joined Linux International, Bolzern says, "I then kind of by default became the marketing force behind Linux International." As Linux International became more active in promoting GNU/Linux, Bolzern in turn became the semiofficial marketing force behind the entire movement.

Bolzern explains his aim at the time: "I figured the best way to reach Linux International's goals as a benevolent entity that would help Linux to develop and help promote it commercially, etc., etc., would be to get vendors involved," an important change from Linux International's initial approach, and one that reflected the shifting power within the GNU/Linux world. Bolzern's reason was simple: "Vendors are the ones who had reason to spend money to promote Linux," he says. Bolzern decided that the best way of getting vendors involved, and hence co-operating rather than competing, was to raise the profile of GNU/Linux at major shows so companies would want to be associated with it through Linux International.

He put his plans into action at the next major show, UniForum, which was held in Dallas, Texas, in March 1995. "I decided that the way to get Linux International launched was to create pavilions, or areas within larger shows" Bolzern says, "where we had a number of small Linux vendors together able to get much more attention than the sum of what any of us could get separately."

Bolzern also organized Birds of a Feather sessions—informal talks— about GNU/Linux at the show. "We ended up having overflow crowds at the Birds of a Feather sessions, which was noticed by Softbank Comdex," the organizers of the show. This was just what Bolzern wanted, because "as a result," he recalls, "they went ahead and committed with us for [Comdex] Fall 95 to put together a pavilion of six booths where they contributed the Linux International booth."

This work in the area of increasing awareness about GNU/Linux was crowned later in 1995 when Bolzern's own distribution Linux Pro was a nominee for Best of Comdex, a major boost given that GNU/Linux was still almost unknown in the wider world of computing at this point, and Comdex was the leading show in the computing calendar. As Bolzern recalls: "When that award happened, [the GNU/Linux vendors] all of a sudden got the picture of hey, wow, if we get together, we can get more attention than we can separately"—his original aim.

Bolzern calls this a turning point in Linux International; perhaps it was for the young vendor community too, as they realized that they were all essentially on the same side in their common fight to make

GNU/Linux an acceptable alternative within business, and that more united than divided them.

The evolution of Linux International into a vendor-based organization with money to spend on promoting GNU/Linux reflected the emergence not only of a new force in the free software world but also of its symbiotic relationship with hackers and users. In this respect, it mirrors Linus's own position in the Linux community, where, as he had explained to Tanenbaum in 1992, his leadership is predicated on his serving that constituency and earning their respect.

But the interesting knock-on effect of all this was that as business entered the GNU/Linux arena and started to change it dramatically, what had begun as a pure hacker movement, born from the creation of a new way of writing and distributing free software, was in its turn starting to change the very basis of how those businesses needed to operate. Increasing commercialization meant that the world of GNU/Linux would never be the same again, but neither would commerce.

7

Linus 2.0

IF LINUX WAS CHANGING, SO WAS LINUS.

True, he remained as aloof as ever from what he called "user space": anything not directly concerned with the kernel, from end-user applications through to distributions. "I really don't keep up at all, almost," he said in 1996. "I'm so kernel-centered, I really don't even care technically about any packaging"—the slightly disparaging way hackers typically regard distributions. The main things that interested him about the growing commercialization of his kernel were the possible technical benefits it might bring.

"I don't care about the market per se," Linus said, "but I find it very interesting to see Linux used in different places. Because I think that's how Linux should be used. Not necessarily should [it] be used in commercial places, but Linux should be able to be used in those places, too. I think getting more and different markets shows you the weaknesses better of a system, so I expect to get some feedback related to these issues." Despite this unwavering concentration on milking every opportunity to improve his code, he, too, gradually began to wage his own marketing campaign. He started speaking at shows and conferences as people's curiosity grew about GNU/Linux—and Linus.

Speaking in public was not easy for him: "I really had to force myself to do it the first time. I was so nervous, I was so shy, I really hated the whole idea, but I knew that I had to do it because I started to get lots of invitations." But Linus turned down the first one. "I said 'no' to an invitation to Madrid," he says; this was "some Unix conference" in spring 1993. "Linux wasn't really well known," he explains, "but it was starting to be something that some people talked about." And yet, "I really wanted to go," he says, "I'd never been in Spain, but I was so nervous about giving a talk there.

"I started to feel so bad about it later that I decided that the next conference I had to do it. So I gave my first talk in Holland to five hundred people." It required considerable effort on his part. "I'd never given a talk anywhere before," he explains. "This was in a foreign language"—English. "I felt really badly, I couldn't sleep the night before, people noticed I was very nervous. But it was a kind of shock treatment, and it certainly got a lot easier in that sense."

One of the first places he spoke was at a meeting of DECUS, the Digital Equipment Corporation User's Society, held in New Orleans in the spring of 1994. He had been invited by Jon "maddog" Hall, senior marketing manager for the Unix Software Group at Digital—the DEC in DECUS. Hall had never heard of GNU/Linux until then, but a colleague, Kurt Reisler, had convinced him to fund Linus's trip. As Hall wrote in an article that appeared in the October 1995 issue of *Linux Journal*, "I had my doubts about this funding as Kurt struggled to get Linux installed on that first PC, but after some able assistance from Linus, he did get it working. I had my first look at the operating system running, and in less than ten minutes I had convinced myself that 'this was Unix enough for me.'"

The result of this conviction was that Hall persuaded Digital to lend Linus a powerful personal computer based on its Alpha microprocessor chip. The idea was that Linus would port Linux to this architecture, which was completely different from that of the Intel chips in ordinary PCs.

Unix had become the portable operating system par excellence, one reason Richard Stallman had chosen it as the model for his GNU project. Linux, by contrast, had grown out of a series of explorations of the Intel 80386 processor; the first versions of Linux even contained code written in assembler for that chip. For this reason, Linus had emphasized in his first official announcement of the Linux project, on 25 August 1991, that "it is not portable."

Later, Linus explained. "The reason Linux wasn't really portable at first was not because I conceived portability bad, but because I considered portability to be a nonissue. In the sense that I didn't think that there was any interest in it, and because the PC platform is so good price-performance-wise, that making a portable Linux to anything [else] didn't quite seem to make much sense. Especially when most of the other architectures already had perfectly good operating systems. And only in the last few years has that really changed, because Linux got so good that it actually made sense even though there were alternatives."

Despite Linus's insistence otherwise, the attraction of being able to run Linux on other hardware proved too strong for hackers around the world. As a result, many porting projects were begun; Linux would eventually be available on a huge range of architectures, from those used by micros such as the Amiga and the Atari (both based on Motorola's 68000 processor family), the PowerPC platform (used by Apple and IBM), and industrial-strength workstations machines employing the MIPS R4000 processors.

Without doubt, though, one of the most significant porting projects was for Sun's Sparc processor. As well as making GNU/Linux available on one of the most powerful hardware systems, widely used in business, the Sparc port is of great historical importance because it was initiated and led by Dave Miller, who was to become one of the most senior Linux lieutenants.

Miller was born in New Jersey, in 1974. The five years' difference between him and other top hackers such as Linus, Alan Cox, Ted Ts'o, and Stephen Tweedie, amounted almost to a generation in hacker terms. Miller's father was "always doing something with computers," Miller says, and his mother ran various retail businesses. As boy, Miller played with a range of Atari micros, but these did not become an all-consuming passion for him. After using computers for a while, "I then went off to other things until I went to university," he says. "I skateboarded, played guitar for three years, and then spent about two years being a socialite towards the end of high school."

In 1991, he went to Penn State, where he first encountered GNU/Linux. "I think the first time I ran Linux was on one of the PC login terminals at the Penn State computing lab," he recalls. "I booted it up in single-user mode from a floppy and just played around at the shell prompt. There wasn't much, but to me at the time it was new and fun. I believe I got evicted from the lab that day for doing what I did. I just came back the next day and continued playing." Unlike his fellow top hackers, Miller had had little previous experience with the Unix culture. "I think I had used Unix twice before I downloaded Linux," he says. Moreover, when he started looking at the source code, "I had no idea what I was looking at actually," Miller explains. "I didn't even know C at all."

Despite his lack of Unix experience, Miller was soon hacking the kernel code and sending the results to Linus. "At this point, I knew C for two days," he notes, "and I had no idea what I was doing. I think the response was something like 'I think a better idea would be to try and'. . . So picture this, I'm clueless, I have no idea what I'm doing, and yet he sends suggestions back as if I did have a clue." As Miller emphasizes, "It's probably this part of Linus's attitude which placed us where we are today. When you got treated like this, you just wanted to work on such a project."

Miller stayed at Penn State for only a semester. After realizing that he "didn't belong there," he went to Rutgers. It was here that his GNU/Linux hacking took off, but not his academic career. Even though he was studying computer science, "I also considered chemistry for a while," but decided that "I'd rather play with Linux than listen to what some nitwit wants me to regurgitate onto a test." As a result, "I failed out of school after two semesters," he says. "My final semester was pure perfection; I failed every class."

Luckily, alongside his studies Miller had picked up a job as student systems administrator at the Center for Advanced Information Processing (CAIP) on the university campus. "My job at the CAIP research center was the key, actually," he says. "It gave me access to huge numbers of nice computers, of all types. There were lots of Sun machines, old and new. Several HP workstations, a few PC systems, SGI servers and workstations, you name it. I was in geek heaven.

"I had noticed some older Sparc systems were gathering dust," he continues. "I had played a lot with Linux on Intel machines, so I wondered what kind of work would be needed to make it work on this Sun box. I programmed before; how difficult could this be, right?" This is a classic young hacker thought, born in part of arrogance and in part of naïveté; and it has driven much of the finest free coding.

"I started to actually toy with the work [of porting Linux to the Sun Sparc] about two or three months after beginning to work at CAIP" in 1993, Miller recalls. "I think three weeks later, I got a very simple minikernel to run; all it did was say 'Hello.' The amount of effort it took to get something so simple made me realize what I had gotten myself into."

As for his motivation, Miller suggests it was "probably boredom. I mean, after I'd run the backups, put paper in the printers, and finished the other sysadmin work that I need to do, there was some time left." He adds in a more serious tone, "I suppose also, now that I had gotten involved with Linux to a certain extent, I must have had some desire to do something significant, mostly to see if I could do it. I had these old Sparcs sitting around; Linux didn't run on Sparcs. Hey, let's give it a go, who knows what will happen and I might even learn something."

Miller did more than "learn something." He brought into being a major project that resulted in the port of GNU/Linux to perhaps the leading high-end commercial hardware platform; this was apparently worlds apart from the Intel 80386 processor that Linux had appeared on first, and which had been perceived by many as little more than a toy. The release of the first complete working version of GNU/Linux running on the Sparc in November 1995 was a major milestone, and marked an important shift of emphasis towards the corporate environment.

The other key advance in porting was made by Linus. Perhaps spurred on by Miller's work and the increasing activity on other platforms, Linus had decided to carry out the first official port of GNU/Linux to a new chip architecture (Miller's Sparc port would only become part of the official Linux kernel later on). There was another, more personal reason, too.

He explains that there "was a stage in Linux that I felt, OK, I've done this. There's never been a stage where I have nothing to do, but there's been a few stages when I've wondered is there something fundamentally interesting left. So when [Digital] offered an Alpha, I thought, hey, this might be it." Once more, Linus's search for the next hacking challenge emerges as one of the key motivators in his decisions.

There were some compelling reasons for making Alpha the first official port. "The Alpha had a few good points," he says, "mainly 64-bits and very radically different architecture from Intel chips. And so in one sense the offer was the perfect porting object because it was so different that if I had an Intel port and an Alpha port, then OK, I proved it, it can be ported to just about anything." This was a totally different situation from the "unportable" code he had first produced.

His choosing the Alpha chip, which processed data in 64-bit chunks rather than the 32 bits employed by the Intel 80386, would turn out to be yet another inspired move on Linus's part. In particular, it would give his kernel a huge head start over Microsoft's Windows NT when, a few years later, the enterprise computing world began moving to 64-bit chips.

Linus's extraordinary knack for turning solutions to specific challenges into larger, long-term benefits manifested itself here as elsewhere. Rather than porting the code in the simplest way possible, he took the opportunity to review his original work, and to rewrite and reorganize everything.

"What happened was that I really had to clean up a lot of code," he explains, "especially in the memory management, because it was very specific to one architecture and I had to really take a completely different approach. I never wanted to have two separate versions; I wanted to have one Linux that worked on both Intel and Alpha and anything else. So I had to abstract away all the hardware dependencies, create a special subdirectory for hardware specific stuff. So it resulted in quite a lot of organizational changes in the kernel."

The changes were drastic. "When I did the portability stuff on the networking code, for something like three weeks I didn't have a kernel that worked, on either Alpha or Intel," Linus explains. "Because I was restructuring everything, and I was doing it one part at a time, and at first the problem was that it doesn't work until everything is perfect. So you actually have to get everything correct before you can even test it.

"I spent one year doing mainly porting [from 1994 to 1995]. Although my main work was spent on e-mail, keeping up with Linux, when I coded I mainly coded for the Alpha." The main thread of kernel development proceeded at what had now become a typically steady rhythm. But along the way there were some novelties. For example, less than a month after Linux 1.0 was released, in March 1994, Linus put out what he called 1.1. But this was not just a simple point upgrade; it represented the beginning of an important addition to the Linux development methodology.

One of the key elements of the methodology was the frequent release cycle of a new kernel version—sometimes every few days. This drove the rate of development at a furious pace, but proved something of a problem for the proliferating nonhacker users. New kernels were sometimes just fixing bugs, and sometimes adding major new features—that were often just beta code. This left users in something of a quandary: Should they attempt to keep up-to-date with each new version, or stick with an older, perhaps more stable one, but miss out on important new features? The tension was exacerbated by the flowering of the commercial GNU/Linux sector. Because it was not possible to revise an entire distribution every time that new kernel was released, GNU/Linux companies were forced to create snapshots of the development process. Inevitably, different vendors created different snapshots, which resulted in an increasingly fragmented market.

Linus's solution was brilliant: to serve both the hacker and the user by creating two strands of kernel development. Those with even point numbers—for example, 1.0, 1.2—were the stable releases. Updates to them would fix outstanding bugs, not add new features. Odd-numbered point releases—1.1, 1.3—were experimental versions, often with novel elements, designed for the hacker community to try out and debug.

At a certain point, the code for the development version would be frozen: No new features would be added, and subsequent work would be limited to debugging this code. Once debugged, it would then become the next release for the stable strand. For example, 1.1.x was frozen, debugged, and then became 1.2.0, etc., and a new 1.3.0 strand allowed more features to be added. In this way, users and vendors could make slower, larger jumps between stable versions, and hackers could track almost daily the constant additions to the kernel.

Linux 1.2 came out in March 1995, almost a year after 1.0. At this time, the computing world was obsessed with the imminent arrival of Windows 95, which was still going through its own beta-testing process, which was very different from that employed by the GNU/Linux world.

This provoked Linus to produce some extremely detailed release notes for version 1.2:

> Ok, the final release of Linux'95, also known among those in the know as "v1.2.0" is now out. After the extensive beta-release-period, Linux'95 is reality.
>
> Before you get Linux'95, I'd like to outline the Licensing stuff, and remind you that copyright infringement is a crime.

After this surprising beginning, Linus went on to detail various licensing arrangements, of decreasing plausibility, culminating in

> * The "I've got too much money" License
> Contact us for details on this exclusive licensing deal, we'll work something out. Please contact "ivemoney@linux.Helsinki.FI" directly.

Linus was less flippant in his announcement of Linux 2.0, which he posted on 9 June 1996. He signaled three key novelties, two of which he thought so important that he jumped straight from 1.2 to 2.0 in the numbering of the kernel, rather than to 1.4.

But the first of them was rather different:

> Linux now has a logo thanks to the artistic talents of Larry Ewing, and one version (the "pretty" version) is included with the kernel. Some people have told me they don't think a fat penguin really embodies the grace of Linux, which just tells me they have never seen an angry penguin charging at them in excess of 100 mph. They'd be a lot more careful about what they say if they had.

What Linus didn't mention here was that he chose the penguin for Linux's logo partly as the result of an encounter on one of his trips abroad, this time to Australia, at the end of 1993. His host for the Canberra leg of the trip was fellow hacker Andrew Tridgell.

"We went to the national aquarium here in Canberra," Tridgell explains. "It's an aquarium plus a little animal park, and one of the things there is a little pen of fairy penguins. Fairy penguins are quite small, they're sort of like ten inches tall, they're very cute little things. And there's a little sign up saying don't put your hand in the pen. And of course Linus ignored that, and put his hand in, and one of the fairy penguins gave him a very friendly little nip—just a little inquisitive 'I wonder what that tastes like?'-type nip."

"And I thought nothing of it," Tridgell says. Later, when Linus was looking for a mascot for Linux, "he decided to make it a penguin," Tridgell explains, "he'd already liked penguins, apparently." But Tridgell says that Linus also explained his choice with a "story about this penguin in Canberra that mauled him—it was a six-foot penguin by this stage. He wrote his story to the Linux kernel mailing list, and I wrote back to the list saying that it was slightly exaggerated. So he wrote to me and said that I have no sense of the dramatic."

The penguin has proved a remarkably shrewd choice. Its uncorporate nature accords well with the spirit that imbues the entire Linux movement. It seems somehow appropriate that software created by someone from the Swedish Duck Pond in Finland should have a bird for its mascot.

In his announcement for version 2.0., Linus continued with the two main additions since 1.2:

multiarchitecture support. The standard Linux-2.0 kernel directly supports both Intel x86 (and clones) and Digital Alpha machines. Quite a few other architectures are also very close to being "official."

multiprocessor support. Yes, you can buy one of those dual Pentium (or Pentium Pro) motherboards, and Linux will actually take advantage of multiple CPUs.

These were dramatic developments. The new multiarchitecture support turned GNU/Linux from being tied to the Intel platform into a widely portable solution, and broadened its reach horizontally, so to speak. Similarly, the addition of the ability to use more than one processor would potentially allow GNU/Linux systems to address bigger problems and extend its reach vertically, into minicomputer-, mainframe-, and even supercomputer-class performance.

The second feature would address one of the biggest limitations of the Linux kernel: that it did not "scale" in power as more chips were added. The provision of multiprocessor support, however rudimentary, was a crucial development for the future, and was tantamount to a declaration that henceforth GNU/Linux should no longer be regarded as simply a PC system, but a complete Unix clone. One, moreover, that potentially could be the equal of commercial systems costing thousands of dollars and hence, implicitly, a match for its most formidable rival in the enterprise, Microsoft's Windows NT.

This key step was carried out by the person who had emerged as the perhaps most versatile kernel hacker, and who was now de facto number two in the Linux movement, Alan Cox. After he had sorted out the TCP/IP code, he looked for a new challenge. The complex task of adding multiprocessor—strictly speaking Symmetric Multi-Processor (SMP)—capabilities was a perfect opportunity for him to try something new.

The equipment was supplied by Caldera as part of its efforts to add more commercial features to Linux. "They sent me the motherboard, two CPUs, and 8 Megs of RAM for it," Cox recalls. "In fact they sent me more memory, but I specifically wanted only 8 Megs for it because you don't find a lot of the bugs unless your machine is actually being hammered hard." In addition, he says, "I used to load it down with everything I could throw at it" in terms of strange peripherals.

Once again, what might be called the Linux method is evident: Rather than trying to develop software on the best possible environment—a fast processor, lots of memory, no strange peripherals—you use an underpowered machine with lots of extras to winkle out unusual bugs. This was the reason Cox had become involved with Linux's TCP/IP in the first place, where the extreme demands his network set-up made on the code allowed him to find and fix bugs no one else had suspected existed.

Meanwhile, Linus had a more immediate project to complete: the thesis for his master's degree.

After his early years as a simple student, Linus had become a teaching assistant at the university. In 1996, he explained how his career at the university had progressed. "I started out as a teaching assistant and did some very limited teaching that way—no course of my own—pretty early on. That's kind of normal for any good student because they always need people to go through test papers and handle these small groups of people going through the weekly exercises." It was in one of these small groups that Linus had bluffed his way to a solution so effectively a few years before.

"The 'real' teaching I did was in '93 and '94," he explained, "when I was in charge of the 'Introduction to Computing' class in Swedish. Not rocket science, and the classes were pretty small, but hey, I can use it on my résumé if I want to. The last two years [1995 and 1996] the powers that be have avoided having me do much teaching so that I could concentrate on research—Linux in my case."

Linus chose to write his master's thesis about Linux portability—fruit of his experience with Digital's Alpha PC. "It's very much the issues, what the problems were, what the solutions were. Porting Linux not just to the Alpha, but the Alpha is certainly one of the examples," Linus explained in 1996, when he was still working on the document—a task he admitted he was not enjoying.

Linus's thesis was in English. "I wouldn't say it's normal, but it's not totally unusual either. For me, it's much easier because I know all the terms in English," he said. His English is first-rate, with only a very slight sing-song accent that is characteristic of Swedish speakers of that language. English was also convenient for the two supervisors of his thesis who would have to read and approve it. As Linus pointed out in 1996: "My mother language is Swedish and they would actually have had more problems finding Swedish-speaking people to comment on the language than it is for them to comment on the English."

Linus also uses English in another situation. "When I program I tend to think in English," he said. The way he codes is similar to Richard Stallman's method: "I never use paper," Linus explained. "If I have something that's tricky and I have to think out exact details, I occasionally write down small figures, stuff like that. But in general, what happens is that I do it straight on the machine; if it's something major, before I start coding I just think of all the issues for a few weeks, and try to come up with the right way to do it—that's completely no paperwork.

"When I have something I'm working on, I don't care what happens around me. I'll think about it on the bus, I'll think about it in bed when I'm trying to sleep. I don't rush out of bed, I just take paper and pen and write it down and go back to bed and hope it makes sense in the morning. But that's pretty rare," he acknowledged. Not only does Linus generally never write things down first, "I never print out parts of the code to find stuff," he said, "and I don't use any other electronic help to index it for me. I keep a mental index of the kernel at all times."

The thesis may have been a less than pleasant experience for him, but at least he knew what was needed. Less clear was the answer to the perennial student question that posed itself afterwards: What would he do after he had finished his university studies?

Matters were complicated by major changes that had occurred in his life. He had left home in the east of Helsinki, where he had been living with his mother and sister, and moved to a small, one-bedroom flat in a nineteenth-century building on the western side of the city. Linus shared the house with not one but two cats, and with someone he described in 1996 as his "common-law wife," Tove Monni, a former karate champion of Finland.

Linus dubbed Tove his "manager" in a mock press release that he posted to the comp.os.linux.announce newsgroup on December 8, 1996:

> Helsinki, Dec 5th, 6:22 A.M. For immediate release.
>
> In order to allay fears about the continuity of the Linux project, Linus Torvalds together with his manager Tove Monni have released "Linus v2.0", affectionately known as "Kernel Hacker—The Next Generation."

Linus 2.0 was Patricia Miranda Torvalds, born at 6.22 AM, 5 December 1996, the time-stamp of the press release. One of her godfathers was Jon "maddog" Hall. Because Linus has always been a private person, the announcement that he not only had a wife but a daughter came as something of a shock to many in the Linux community. It also tended to undercut stereotypes about the kind of person a computer hacker was. But if the surprise over Linus 2.0 was great, that caused by another posting Linus made a couple of months earlier was even greater, because it had implied an imminent event that could not be greeted with such unequivocal joy.

Appropriately enough, perhaps, because the subject had been at the center of Linus's hacking for the last two years, it turned up on a mailing list about Linux for the Alpha processor. Replying to a "2.1.4 exception question," on the morning of October 16 1996, after reams of fairly heavy technical matters, Linus ended his posting with the following throwaway line:

> I'll be leaving for a week in the U.S. this Sunday (house hunting), and quite frankly I'd like to get the five "critical" points above fixed first.

Needless to say, the parenthetical "house hunting" did not escape people's attention. A few hours later, someone asked whether this meant that Linus was moving to the United States and that he now had a job. Linus replied the same day with a characteristic posting that began:

> Ok, folks, DON'T PANIC.

[inline: Linus running around in circles and tearing his hair out]

Now, it had to be told some day. I have a life. There. I did it. I came out of the closet. It's sad, it's shocking, but it's true. I even have a girlfriend [collective GASP], and it all adds up to the fact that it had to happen sooner or later. I'm getting a RealJob(tm).

And concluded:

P.S. Company called Transmeta. Don't bother looking them up, they aren't advertising. They are in the business of getting the best minds in the industry and doing cool things that I won't tell you about. Not selling Linux, so it's not unfair competition in that field.

As usual, hidden among the wit are some serious points. The first is that Linus was well aware of the effect his decision would have. The development process that had evolved over the previous five years was centered on him so absolutely that even his smallest decisions were felt throughout the entire movement; this made his choice of company to work for critical, as his closing remark indicates. He explained at the end of 1996, "I wanted to do something that wasn't directly related to Linux. I was actually offered work from Linux distributors, but I didn't want to go work for them because I didn't want to give my implicit stamp of approval of any one specific distribution, just because I worked there. So I wanted to have something neutral."

His solution was typically resourceful. On the one hand, even though Transmeta was "not selling Linux," he said in 1996, "it's actually in my contract that I'm doing Linux part-time there. It hasn't been formalized. I don't want to be in the position where I actually count the number of hours I spend doing Linux. I think sometimes I will do almost only Linux, and at other times what this Transmeta company is doing."

But Transmeta also offered something else very important. "I just wanted it to be something interesting, something new," Linus said. "Exactly the reason I decided to move was that I'd been at the university something like seven years. Part of that I've been both working and studying there. It seemed to be a good time to try to see the other side of the world"—the world of commerce—"not just the academic side."

Throughout his life, Linus had always looked for the next challenge. As a teenager, he had felt compelled to replace his Vic-20 microcomputer because he had grown to know it too well. He had later taken on the Alpha port because he thought, "Hey, this might be it," when he was beginning to wonder whether there was "something fundamentally interesting left."

And similarly, in 1996, at around the time he accepted the Transmeta job, he said: "I wouldn't say that the technical issues [of Linux] have been done, because there's always going to be a lot of details, always going to be new device drivers, new hardware, new ports, new ways of doing stuff. But even when they interest me they tend to be incremental, which means that while I will enjoy doing them and while I will continue to support Linux, I want to make sure that I have something else to do on the side."

The company that was giving him this "something else to do on the side," Transmeta, was based in Santa Clara, in the heart of Silicon Valley. This was attractive not so much because it would take him from the periphery to the center of computing but for quite a different reason. "The location was interesting more due to other concerns like weather," he said shortly before moving there.

About Transmeta, Linus would say nothing except that the company designed advanced computer chips. "They aren't advertising" was an understatement. Even the Web site consisted of the single line "This web page is not here yet!"; those seeking secret messages in the underlying code found:

> <!—There are no secret messages in the source code to this web page.— >

> <!—There are no tyops in this web page.— >

The Linux world was left a mystery that would not be revealed for more than three years. But it was also left with an astonishing achievement.

The Linux kernel had grown by a factor of nearly 100, from version 0.01, an 80K student exercise in C and 386 assembler, to version 2.0, almost 5 Mbytes of compressed code. It had progressed from something that could barely even run on a PC to an almost complete Unix kernel clone; it supported X Window, TCP/IP networking, several completely different architectures, and multiprocessor machines, although in a fairly rudimentary manner.

A high-speed development methodology had evolved that was unprecedented in the way it drew on thousands of users around the world, connected via the Internet, supplying bug reports and often fixes to senior Linux coders—the "lieutenants"—who fed them through to Linus. He, in turn, chose the most suitable of these fixes to produce the next experimental release of the kernel—while he tended a more slowly moving stable release aimed at users—in a unique twin-development approach.

As a result, the Linux community had expanded by an even larger factor than the kernel. At the end of 1991, Linus guessed that there were tens of users; in early 1992, there were hundreds. Thereafter it becomes harder to ascertain the number as a consequence of the unusual distribution system and licensing terms of Linux. People could download the software freely from online sites, and anyone could copy CD-ROMs containing the GNU/Linux operating system as many times as they liked. This made conventional measures like sales figures almost meaningless.

But the new GNU/Linux companies that were springing up in the mid-1990s needed to have at least estimates of the user-base if they were to make forecasts for their businesses. This led them to investigate just how big the Linux market was. For example, Caldera's Bryan Sparks said in 1996, "we have done some preliminary research, both ourselves and through third parties, and it's a million-plus—some people say it's reached 2 million at this point, I'm more comfortable saying I think we're in a million-plus users." Marc Ewing from Red Hat was more bullish: "Our guess is that there are somewhere between 3 and 5 million Linux users worldwide," he said at this time. Whatever the exact figure, it was extraordinary that there were millions of GNU/Linux users at this point, just five years after Linus started his kernel. It was testimony, above all, to the results of the GNU/Linux development process: code whose "quality is often second to none," as Ewing put it in 1996.

Caldera's Bryan Sparks had no doubts about why the Linux process has been so successful in producing software of such high quality. "Linus has been the perfect individual to act as the benevolent dictator, so to speak, of the Linux community," he said. "If he were any more abrasive or a different personality, I don't think Linux would be nearly as popular." Ewing concurred wholeheartedly: "Linus is quite brilliant, and is definitely the perfect person for the job."

And now that "perfect person" was moving on. Even Linus seemed unsure at the time of his move what exactly would happen. "I definitely want a continuity," he said in 1996. "There's obviously going to be changes, and I don't even know what they are yet. I think more due to the family addition than to the move, but certainly due to the move, too."

A new daughter, a new job, a new country: a new Linus. The question everyone in the free software community was asking was: Did the end of this first, Finnish phase also signal the end of the Golden Age of Linux development?

8

Learning from Berkeley

THE YEAR 1969 WAS IMPORTANT because it saw the birth of Unix —
and of Linus. It was also then that the first steps were taken in the creation of a network that would eventually become the Internet.

Originally called ARPAnet, it was funded by the Defense Advanced Research Projects Agency (DARPA), part of the U.S. Department of Defense. In some ways, ARPAnet was close to the Internet; for example, it
employed what is called packet-switching whereby data is broken into
small packets that are routed over the network separately, and then re-
assembled on their arrival. Packet-switching contrasts with circuit-
switching, employed for ordinary telephone links, for example, where a
single circuit exists between origin and destination for the duration of
the connection.

The key step from ARPAnet to Internet was the move to open architecture networking. As a history of the Internet put together by its creators
and held on the Internet Society's Web site, explains, "In this approach,
the choice of any individual network technology was not dictated by a
particular network architecture but rather could be selected freely by a
provider and made to inter work with the other networks."

From the beginning, then, openness lay at the Internet's heart, and its
subsequent development has been intimately bound up with core specifications implemented through free software. One of the key players in
that story is Eric Allman, who helped make the Internet what it is today;

he is one of the fathers of the free software movement that draws so much of its power from the availability of a global network.

Allman was born in 1955, in California, and started using computers when he was twelve. He says that it was "just one of these after-school programs." But he soon got bored with this, and a couple of years later, he had already moved on to something more challenging. "I developed an interest in operating systems," he says, "so I was actually hacking the operating system."

Studying computer science at the University of California at Berkeley would prove the key step in his career, but almost didn't happen. "Ironically enough, I didn't think I was smart enough to go to Berkeley," Allman says. "I didn't even apply." But luckily, "I had a teacher who insisted that I apply," he explains, "and I did get accepted." Berkeley would later become synonymous with a certain kind of Unix—often cited as one of the fonts of today's free software—but when Allman arrived, Unix had not yet made its appearance. "When I got there, there was this big CDC 6400—a supercomputer for the time, made by Control Data Corporation. You submitted card decks and you got your line printer output. You never ever touched the machine," he recalls.

Something that struck Allman about Unix when it turned up was its documentation: "One of the great things about the Unix documentation at the time was they said, 'We're going to document the bugs as well as the features.'" Allman notes that this "was most emphatically a novelty" and says of this new openness, "I think actually the concept of share and expose, which is really fundamental to what later turned into this open source concept, came from those days. Back in the old days when you didn't have access to things and you had to kind of guess what a program was doing, to suddenly go into this environment where you could see everything, that was an amazing—I am tempted to use this psychobabble term and say 'empowering'—thing."

In this new "empowering" environment Allman wrote his first important program, Delivermail. At the time, he was working as the systems administrator for the Ingres database project at Berkeley. Allman recalls, "What happened was, Ingres got an ARPAnet link. And everyone in the department wanted access to that machine, whether they had anything to do with the Ingres project or not, so that they could have ARPAnet mail. Which is interesting," he notes, "because even back then it was all driven by e-mail.

"I didn't want to have to deal with managing all of those accounts, for various reasons. But we did already have a local network around Berkeley. And I realized that I could just write a program that would forward mail from one network to the other network, and then they wouldn't need an account," Allman says, and adds with characteristic modesty, "you know, there's this saying that all innovation is done by lazy people; and I'm fundamentally a lazy person. So if I was less lazy, I wouldn't have objected to managing all of the user accounts."

But he did object, and created Delivermail to handle the forwarding between the Berkeley network and ARPAnet automatically through what would now be called a gateway. "I wrote that program, and the configuration for it was all compiled in," he explains; that is, setting up the program for each machine on the network required some small fiddling with the source code. This was acceptable, Allman says, because "there were like five or six [computers] on the Berkeley network then, so recompiling it on five or six machines wasn't a problem.

"Delivermail was an interesting thing because I wasn't actually trying to produce anything that anyone else would use. I just had this problem that I wanted to handle as easily as possible." Nonetheless, other people did start to use Delivermail once the program was included in Berkeley's distribution of Unix, BSD, starting with the 4.1BSD version, which came out in 1981.

And when Allman had other users, he also received feedback. "I did get some, although it didn't really start to explode until the Internet came along. We actually got a fair amount from Berkeley, though. Berkeley was always very good about taking input from the outside world, their user base, if you will, and folding it back in," he says.

Allman notes that "we had this ethos of picking up information from folks in the outside world, and turning it back in, which I think is an important part of the open source model." Therefore, "instead of having the information from the users filtered through five or six layers before it gets to the implementers," as happens with conventional software development in companies, "the implementers talked to the users and could find out exactly what it is they need." Allman emphasizes that, as far as free software is concerned, "it's much, much more than just a legal license, it's a way of doing developing; it's a process of involving the users in the development at a very early stage," and he sees this as firmly rooted in the Berkeley tradition.

Soon, however, Delivermail wasn't enough. "Berkeley got bigger fast and [the network grew] to twenty or so machines, and so recompiling for each individual machine got to be painful," he recalls. The increased work required was bad enough, but there was another, more difficult problem. "The other issue was that the network configuration got more complicated," Allman says. "We got other network links."

Sending the university e-mail to the right place was no longer a simple matter, and the system employed by Delivermail couldn't cope with the various kinds of networks that were being hooked into Berkeley. Allman decided that he needed to rewrite Delivermail so that machines could be configured without fiddling with the software itself, and to build more intelligence into the program so that it could decipher from the e-mail addresses where messages should be sent.

He called the result Sendmail. Its success was driven in part by the new flexibility it offered. "If you had a new network, you could integrate that into Sendmail more quickly than you could into the others," Allman explains. "This was long before everyone was doing Internet, and so new networks would show up, mushrooms in the night."

Another factor was more fortuitous. "DARPA had decide to standardize on BSD [Unix] as their research operating system of choice," Allman says. "And BSD came with Sendmail. So to a certain extent there was at least a piece of my being in the right place at the right time." By now the Internet had come into existence, and operated on a completely different scale from the earlier ARPAnet.

"There was a lot of excitement going on," Allman recalls, "it was really clear that there were going to be a lot more people available on the Internet. The ARPAnet only had capacity for 256 hosts, and the Internet [people] realized that this was too small; so they took a 32-bit field [for addresses], so there were 4 billion possible hosts. And a lot of people suddenly realized that they were going to be able to have Internet access. So it exploded pretty quickly. Now, this is still in the research area, but it meant that it was going to be able to get into more computer science departments, more research labs, etc. And those people were very avid users" of the Internet and of Sendmail.

If Sendmail fed off the huge growth of the Internet at this time, it might also be said to have helped create the global network as we know it today. For as Allman explains, central to Sendmail was "the concept that you could send email between different kinds of networks, even when they weren't designed to work together." This was pretty revolutionary at the time: "Other people tell me that Sendmail invented it; I don't know if it did. There may have been prior art. That was definitely one of my goals, and I think I did a very good job of that."

In effect, Sendmail created a kind of virtual Internet out of the heterogeneous networks of the time. In doing so, it may well have been at least partly instrumental in convincing people of the virtues of a homogeneous global network that would allow many different services, not just e-mail, to circulate freely. This is the situation today; the Internet has become a collection of smaller networks all employing the same standard, whereas Sendmail allowed collections of disparate networks to function together, but only for e-mail.

Unifying today's Internet is the underlying TCP/IP (Transport Control Protocol/Internet Protocol), the fundamental rules that establish how communications take place. As with Sendmail, the software that implemented these protocols, in what is generally called a stack, derives mainly from work done at Berkeley. The key figure here was Bill Joy. As Allman says, "no story of Berkeley is complete without discussing Bill. He was both an incredibly brilliant person, very prolific, but what was probably more important about Bill, he inspired people around him to do good work. He just sucked up information like a sponge, and a lot of that information came from the users" in true Berkeley fashion.

Joy's TCP/IP implementation was also included with the Berkeley Unix distribution. The liberal Berkeley license under which it and other components such as Sendmail were released, which essentially allowed any use to be made of the software provided the copyright of the regents of the University of California was recognized, meant that many commercial TCP/IP stacks were derived from this work. Linux possesses one of the few TCP/IP implementations not based on Berkeley, because at the time Linux's stack was written, AT&T's lawsuit against Berkeley's Unix was underway and the Linux community decided to avoid legal problems by writing the TCP/IP code from scratch.

Part of the TCP/IP suite of protocols describes how the individual packets of data are routed from origin to destination using Internet addresses, which take the form of 123.45.67.89; but it is doubtful whether the Internet would ever have taken off as a mass medium if users had been required to enter 204.71.200.66 instead of www.yahoo.com.

The use of these easy-to-remember names is possible thanks to the Domain Name System (DNS) that converts between the two forms. It was devised by Paul Mockapetris, who explains, "The DNS system specs were first published in 1983, and the first implementations were Jeeves, on a TOPS-20 system [a Digital mainframe], a version on Unix from Stanford, and a version for Unix from Berkeley."

Mockapetris's Jeeves software (the name was inspired by P. G. Wodehouse's butler) "was rock-solid, if not feature-rich," he says. It ran all the top-level DNS directories at the beginning, and "let people come to depend on the DNS," as they still do. Because it was tied to the TOPS-20, however, when that hardware was phased out, so was Jeeves.

Berkeley's software was called the Berkeley Internet Name Domain, or BIND. Like Sendmail, it soon became the de facto standard, in part because it, too, was included with Berkeley's Unix distribution as standard and was released under the Berkeley license. "Of the two Unix versions," Mockapetris says, "the Stanford version was superior, but the Berkeley folks had the distribution channel. So they won out." As with Sendmail, BIND was free Unix software that developed through the suggestions and bug reports of its growing band of users around the world. For most of its existence, it was maintained through the selfless efforts of one person, Paul Vixie.

Just as few people today are aware that their e-mail is sent and arrives so efficiently thanks largely to free software programs like Sendmail and BIND, it is often forgotten that the other great Net success, the World Wide Web, was made freely available from the beginning. Indeed, as the Web's creator, Tim Berners-Lee, relates in his book, *Weaving the Web*, he even switched from an initial idea of using Richard Stallman's GNU GPL to putting all the Web technology in the public domain in 1993 to ensure that it had the widest possible deployment.

One of the first to take up Berners-Lee's new technology was the National Center for Supercomputing Applications (NCSA), part of the University of Illinois at Urbana-Champaign, where Rob McCool wrote a Web server called HTTPd. This stood for HyperText Transport Protocol daemon: HTTP was the protocol or set of rules devised by Berners-Lee for transporting Web pages across networks, and a daemon was the name given to a certain kind of software process running in the background under Unix. NCSA's HTTPd server, which was free, soon dominated the sector.

NCSA's ascendancy as the leading Web player was only halted when, in a striking parallel to the move by Symbolics to employ the top coders at the MIT AI Lab, a start-up hired away most of the university's software developers in this area. The new company later came to be known as Netscape Communications. Because Netscape's Web servers cost thousands of dollars, many people preferred to continue using the free NCSA HTTPd server software.

One person doing so was Brian Behlendorf. Born, like Allman, in California, but nearly two decades later, in 1973, Behlendorf also went to Berkeley, where he became involved with the Internet. "When I got to Berkeley, everyone there was using e-mail," he says, "so I signed up with various music discussion forums, and stuff like that, started sending e-mail around to various people. And realizing that, hey, this was kind of fun." Investigating further, Behlendorf soon found out about the then-new World Wide Web.

In mid-1993, he happened to talk to a friend who worked at *Wired* magazine about this new technology. "They had an e-mail robot," Behlendorf recalls. "You could request articles from it, and they would send those articles out. I came in and upgraded that to a Gopher server that also happened coincidentally to do this thing called HTTP, which no one really knew much about at that point." Gophers, a series of nested menus as opposed to the Web's hypertext links, were an alternative way to navigate through information on the Internet. In his book, Berners-Lee suggests that one reason that the Gopher system failed to take off as the Web did was because the University of Minnesota, where Gopher had been developed, decided to ask for a license fee from some users instead of releasing it freely as he had.

This "thing called HTTP" was a Web server. Behlendorf recalls, "That started getting a lot of traffic, and eventually grew to the point where it didn't make sense to have the Gopher site around any more. We were getting 3 to 5 thousand hits a day." This was at the end of 1993.

"So around middle of 1994 it was clear that this could be something interesting," Behlendorf continues. "We started creating HTML [Hyper-Text Markup Language] at that point"—new Web pages—"adding in extra content that wasn't in the magazine. It kind of became clear that this could be a platform for a unique brand or a unique publication. That was the genesis of HotWired," one of the first online magazines. Even though ultimately it failed to establish itself as an independent, profitable concern, HotWired was soon recognized as a showcase for Web technologies.

Behlendorf became chief engineer at HotWired, and chose the NCSA HTTPd server to run the site. "I'd started using it pretty heavily," he says, "and then there was a security hole that needed to be closed. Somebody published a patch to close it, and then there were other various patches floating around. There were a couple of performance-related ones, and a couple of 'this is just dumb, needs to be fixed' kind of patches." These were posted to a mailing list called WWW-Talk, which was hosted by CERN, the European subnuclear research establishment in Geneva, Switzerland, that had been the birthplace of the Web. In the past, these patches had been picked up by the development team at NCSA and used to improve the code. Then things changed.

Behlendorf recalls that "there was somebody who posted to WWW-Talk: Is NCSA ever going to respond to the patches that we send them? No one had heard anything back from NCSA so there wasn't any explicit 'no thank you,' it was a nonresponse." He believes the explanation is simple: "They weren't responding partly because they had lost Rob Mc-Cool and a bunch of other people to Netscape. They were probably simply overwhelmed by the number of people who were writing in, asking for help, offering things and stuff. They probably didn't know how to answer them."

In the face of this lack of response, people on the WWW-Talk mailing list came up with a simple solution. Behlendorf recalls, "Someone else proposed, 'Why don't we combine forces?'"—to fill the gap left by NCSA's team—"and then I volunteered resources to be able to do that." Those resources were fairly rudimentary. "It was a pretty simple box," Behlendorf notes, "it was like 16 Mbytes, 486, nothing to speak of. But it was more than enough power to run a mailing list or two and a Web site, an FTP site, and things like that. It was on a private machine that I'd had sitting on the network at HotWired, so I was independent from any company." As well as his machine, Behlendorf brought something else to the project: a name.

The name he offered was one that he had already used for another project. "I had some friends at a company called EIT—Enterprise Integration Technologies," Behlendorf explains. "I had had discussions there about what, if someone were to write a commercial Web server, should be in it. So I wrote up a page on a bunch of different features, and just put a name on it—Apache. Because I thought it was an interesting name, something that wasn't Web this or Spider that, or Arachnid, or any of the kind of metaphors being used [then]. It was something that was abstract and not related to anything specifically, but just connoted a kind of powerful server."

Nothing ever came of the commercial Web server Apache, and so Behlendorf decided to recycle this "interesting name." He recalls, "When I finally got together with a few other people and started passing patches [for HTTPd] and saying, 'Shall we do our own distribution?' I volunteered the name 'Apache' and that seemed to go over pretty well. That's kind of the genesis of the name, but when I volunteered it, people said that's a very funny pun" because the new Apache server was indeed "a patchy server," created as it was out of patches to the NCSA code.

The Apache mailing list caught on quickly. "I think in the first day there was probably something around 30 to 40 subscribers," Behlendorf remembers, "and subsequently I think that built up to about 150 within the next three or four months. It was fairly popular." Everything was done by volunteers. "It was kind of haphazard and very gradual, it wasn't somebody declaring at the beginning, 'This is how we'll do it.' It was really everyone kind of pitching in and making it happen," he recalls. "People started posting those patches to the list, somebody stepped up and said, 'I'll volunteer to do the integration into a standard kind of set that we can roll out.' People would volunteer at different points in time. We would do a release. I registered Apache.org and started pointing it to this machine."

Because the Apache group was based entirely around volunteers spread across the world, most of whom had full-time jobs running Web sites, for example, it was decided to employ an unusual model for running the list and software development. Behlendorf describes how they arrived at this. "We bootstrapped by choosing around nine or ten people who we felt had contributed most," he explains, "and said, 'Let's establish this as the core group, and we can always expand this core group.'" This core group then ran things according to a fairly complicated series of voting rules. Outside the core group were people submitting bug reports and patches just as with Linux or other free software projects.

Behlendorf sums up the philosophy of this approach as "share the responsibility for the code very widely amongst people that you trust, and we'll do more than any one person can do." It was inspired by the way the Internet was run and progresses. "I think it was something that had shared a lot of similarities to the IETF process," Behlendorf says; "you use rough consensus and running code." The IETF is the Internet Engineering Task Force, whose specialist working groups, open to all, publish what are known as RFCs, Requests For Comments. These documents lay out suggested technical standards. Although there is no body to enforce them, the "rough consensus" amongst those in the working groups, together with the hard-won authority of the IETF, means that the most important RFCs are usually adopted by the Internet community in due course.

Behlendorf says this method is successful partly because, in the world of software, "things either work or they don't work. When it comes down to which algorithm [mathematical technique] is the better way to solve this problem or which is the better security model etc., it tends to be pretty clear." The IETF's approach of "rough consensus and running code" might stand equally as the motto for Apache, Linux, and all the major free software projects.

Apache took NCSA's HTTPd 1.3 as its starting point, and then added patches to produce its first official release, Apache 0.6.2, in April 1995. "We decided to adopt a license that looked and felt a lot like the BSD license," Behlendorf says, because of its simplicity and the close ties between the Apache and Berkeley Unix development communities. Work continued, but soon it was decided that a complete redesign was needed. "We benefited from a rewrite that was done by [Robert Thau], one of the developers, who separated out a lot of the functionality in the server, between the core of the server and a set of modules," Behlendorf explains. This approach of making the code modular was similar to that adopted by Linus for the Linux kernel; it lent itself well to the distributed development model employed by most free software efforts.

Apache 1.0, using the new architecture, was released in December 1995. A couple of months later, a year after the Apache group had been formed, Apache became the most widely used Web server on the Internet, according to the survey produced by Netcraft. Since then, its market share has risen almost every month, and as of the year 2000 it outpaces Web servers from Netscape and Microsoft by a huge margin.

Behlendorf attributes this extraordinary success in part to timing because Netscape and Microsoft had failed to deliver the advanced Web server users wanted at the time Apache appeared. Apache also received a boost from the new Web hosting services being offered by Internet Service Providers (ISPs). Alongside the Net connectivity that ISPs had always offered, they now ran Web servers on which companies could set up corporate sites more cheaply than by creating them in-house.

Apache was popular for Web hosting, Behlendorf believes, because these ISPs had "needs that couldn't easily be captured by a single company," for example, "the ability to host on one box 10,000 different [Web] domains," he says. Because Apache's code was available, ISPs could adapt it to meet these needs without having to wait for commercial companies such as Netscape or Microsoft to get around to adopting various features.

Although the Apache team has no animus against either Netscape or Microsoft, being able to present Apache as a serious alternative to commercial servers was an important consideration. Behlendorf explains why: "Had Apache not existed," he says, "I definitely think we would start seeing people having to build Microsoft-specific Web sites, hosted on Microsoft servers, to talk to Microsoft clients, and then Netscape servers to talk to Netscape clients, and have to maintain two different sets of Web sites essentially to talk to these two different clients."

Without Apache, then, it is highly likely that the browser wars that erupted in 1996 would have spilled over into the world of server software. This, in turn, would have led to a serious schism in the World Wide Web, with companies forced to align with either Microsoft or Netscape—and so missing out on huge swathes of potential customers— or needing to create two Web sites to serve the whole market. In this sense, Apache has played a key role in ensuring that the Web's unitary standards have been preserved. And this, in its turn, has allowed e-commerce to flourish. Paradoxical as it may seem, the dot-com world with its volatile IPOs and outlandish valuations owes much to this piece of free software.

Apache has had another crucial effect. From the very first release of Apache, Behlendorf explains, "it was being used on sites like HotWired, and by MIT—Yahoo's been using it for three or four years, I think. So it very quickly was something people considered a tier-one product right on the same level as Microsoft Internet Information Server, or Netscape's Web server." As a result, he says, "the most important thing we've proved, and probably proved more successfully than the others, is that you can use open source in a mission-critical situation."

Free software such as Sendmail and BIND had been used in a similar mission-critical context for far longer, but had the misfortune to be almost invisible, not least because they worked so well. With the visible and measurable success of Apache, shown in the monthly Netcraft reports detailing how many public Web servers were using which program, people were increasingly aware not only that free software was widely used by companies but that it was running the single most important new development in computing for decades: the World Wide Web.

As such, Apache played a crucial role in preparing the ground for the later and continuing success of GNU/Linux, and for the dramatic uptake of open source programs and methods in the late 1990s. In one respect, Apache still leads the field among free software projects. Although the debate still rages fiercely about whether open source software such as GNU/Linux can ever hope to best Microsoft, Apache has already done it.

And yet even this achievement has been surpassed by Perl, a freely available programming language universally used for system administration tasks and to power complex e-commerce sites. Apache may beat Microsoft and Netscape by a wide margin, but Perl has no serious rivals at all from the commercial sector. Its creator, now routinely referred to as the "Perl god," is Larry Wall, one of best-known and most influential figures in the free software community, alongside Richard Stallman and Linus.

Wall was born in California, in 1954. His father was a minister, and Wall's religious upbringing has strongly marked his life and work. Unlike many other top hackers, computers never loomed large early on "The first computer I ever actually saw was the programmable calculator that we got at our high school in our senior year," Wall says, "so I didn't have much exposure to computers before that. But as soon as it showed up I was quite interested." He first used "real computers" at university.

Wall studied at Seattle Pacific University, where his choice of subjects was unusual—and characteristic. "I started off majoring in chemistry and music," he says. "I played the violin from about fifth grade, you know, pretty good at it, and I've always been interested in anything scientific, so it seemed like sort of a natural thing. My problem is I'm interested in too many things"—a trait that would bear fruit decades later when he came to create the extraordinarily rich and protean world of Perl, one of whose mottoes asserts that "there's more than one way to do it."

Initially, though, this tendency made life difficult. "The problem with both music and chemistry is that they sort of expect you to only do that," he explains, "and so that was not for me." Wall tried a different tack. "For a while I called myself a pre-med major, but that was just an excuse to take a smattering of sciences," he admits. Wall graduated eight years after entering college, although he spent three of those working as chief programmer at the university's computer center.

He graduated with another idiosyncratic combination of subjects: natural and artificial languages. In part, Wall was being purely pragmatic. "It looked like I was going to have enough linguistics and computer courses" to make a degree, he says, "if I sort of combined them." As far as the natural languages were concerned, he says, "it had more to do with learning about how languages work in the sense of taking a data set from an arbitrary language and looking for patterns." Finding patterns was to prove a recurrent theme of Wall's programming career.

The linguistics side did have a practical point, although an unusual one. "One of the reasons for doing the linguistics part of the degree was that my wife and I were thinking about being missionaries," Wall says, "and joining a group called the Wycliffe Bible Translators." The idea was to go out to some relatively uncharted part of the world, learn a hitherto unstudied local language, and then translate the Bible into it for missionary purposes. Once again, this would have allowed Wall to combine several of his many interests. "We thought it would be something that would be fun and be useful simultaneously—definitely the theme of my life," Wall acknowledges. "Unfortunately," he explains, "I came down with food allergies while I was in the middle of grad school, so that sort of put the kibosh on doing any missionary work." He was a graduate student at Berkeley in 1980–1981 and yet never formed part of the flourishing hacker group there.

Wall did not have the luxury of time to spend thinking about what to do next. "Well, we were expecting," he explains. "My wife wanted to be near her mom when we had this baby, so we transferred down to UCLA [University of California Los Angeles] before we actually made this decision to drop out entirely. So that summer I needed a job, and my father-in-law worked for a company called Systems Development Corporation (SDC). He got me hired on there, with hopefully not too much nepotism."

Wall's work at SDC was classified, but alongside this he found time to do some programming on his own account. "We had a Usenet feed," he says. "And there was a newsreader that came with it, but it was really badly designed. I thought I could do a little better than that." Wall created rn—named in memory of the original readnews program he had been so unimpressed with. "I think I was developing in '83 and sent it out in '84," he says. "And what I discovered was people liked it."

When he released his free software to the general computing community, he also discovered something else. "People would find bugs and I'd patch them and make enhancements," he says, "and I would send out these patches, and people would not apply them. Or, worse, they would apply them helter-skelter, and not in any kind of sequence, and that just made for a maintenance nightmare, trying to do this distributed stuff on the Net." In effect, Wall was grappling with a new set of problems raised by the novel distribution medium of the Internet, which had only come into being shortly before, in 1982.

As a result, Wall says, "basically in self-defense I wrote the Patch program." This is a fairly small program whose job is to make sure that the program corrections, the patches, are applied in exactly the right way. Wall points out that his little Patch program, trivial as it sounds, "in some ways actually changed the culture of computing more than Perl did" later on. Wall's Patch can be considered the small but significant leap forward that made the distributed development model possible, and which led, as a result, to a blossoming of free software that continues to this day.

For a couple of years, Wall concentrated on developing his two main projects, rn and Patch; but then practical needs in his daily life as system administrator inspired him to tackle the new challenge that led to the creation of Perl. His employer, SDC, had a problem: "Half of our classified project was in Santa Monica [California], and half of it was in Paoli, Pennsylvania," Wall explains. "We had to exchange configuration control information, but it was all classified. So we had an encrypted link between Santa Monica and Paoli that ran at like 1200 baud, something like that.

"In terms of networking, we could not predict when the thing would be up or down," Wall continues, "so we needed a way of pushing stuff across when the thing went up, automatically, without actually having to intervene and say, 'Start the process.' Well, this is what the Usenet news system does all the time," he notes. "I said, let's just take the Usenet news and make a few tweaks to it. And then it will automatically send [the control information] across when the link goes up.

"That's what I did," Wall says, "and it worked great. But then all our information was out in lots of little article files." These could be read using the rn newsreader, but Wall's management didn't want its information in a heap of "little article files": "They wanted reports," he says. Wall needed an easy way to take all the small files that came across the link and automatically combine them into a report suitable for management. "So I looked around at the tools that I had available," Wall recalls, "and started trying to cobble something together, and realized it just wasn't going to work real good. That's when I began to realize where the problem with the Unix toolbox philosophy was."

This philosophy said that every tool should do one thing well, and had led to the many small, powerful tools that made up Unix; it represented a big break with previous operating systems, and had made the entire GNU project possible. Wall discovered, however, that its strength could also be a weakness. "Since each tool is a separate process," he says, "they tend to be sort of complicated, and have a lot of options. But they're limited, and if you try to push them beyond their capabilities, you can't do it."

For example, one popular tool is the Unix shell. Wall comments, "Shells were very good at whipping things up—so there was the whipping-things-up dimension—and rapid prototyping." However, the "C [language] was good for manipulating things at a very low level, but that's different dimension. And they were both good at that thing and not at the other. So there was this big gap where there was nothing that was good at both of those things. There's a big ecological niche out there that ought to be filled," he says, and adds, "so right from the start, I was planning in a sense to take over the world."

His planned take-over was purely benevolent, and was rooted in a long-standing desire to create tools that would be as useful as possible. With his new tool, Wall wanted to create something that was so useful it would be taken up by many people. Drawing on his previous experiences with rn and Patch, already widely used, he had a pretty good idea about how to go about this.

"From the very beginning I understood that I would probably be distributing it," he says, "and that people would probably like to use it. People are surprised when I say that, because most people will tell you they didn't expect what happened to their tool, but you have to understand that I'd already written languages that other people had used. And I'd already distributed programs like rn and Patch, so I had a sneaking suspicion that anything that I'd like, other people might like too."

As he set about designing his new language, he took his favorite features from pre-existing languages. "I know what I like about various languages, and what I don't like—mostly what I don't like," he says. "The things that bother me about some languages is when they take some point and drive it into the ground." Another source of inspiration, however, was just as important. "I also wanted to borrow ideas from natural languages," he explains. This was a fairly radical thing to do, and was born in part from his own personal interests and training. "It had been talked about before," he says, "but it had never actually been done as far as I've researched. [The business programming language] Cobol was claimed to be self-documenting because it was English, but all that meant was you'd take pseudo-English phrases and plug things in instead of words. So it's actually English-like at a very shallow level. I wanted something that worked at a much deeper level," he says.

Above all, he wanted to add a key feature to his new computing language. "I wanted expressiveness," he says. "I didn't want a language that dictated how you were supposed to solve a problem. Because so many languages have this idea that they should be minimalistic—it's partly because of the math background of most of the people who did computer science." Wall points out that with natural languages, people "want to use expressive words; they don't want to talk in basic English." He thought that they should be able to do the same with programming languages.

"My overarching theme of my life is actually trying to help people," he explains. "So it's sort of natural that I would open up a language in a way that I would think would be most useful to people." Opening up the language means that he should "try to make it easy for the other people to do what they want to do, not what you think they ought to do," he says.

An interesting parallel arises between Wall's approach with his new language and with open source software in general. Where the latter gives users the freedom to do things their way—by changing the source code if need be—so Wall's creation lets them employ the language in ways that represent a closer fit to their way of thinking and working. What came to be known as Perl offers the same freedom as open source, but this time explicitly built in to the structure of the language, not implicitly as a consequence of the availability of source code.

Wall's choice of a name, and the way he went looking for it, was characteristic. "This is another indication that I was already thinking that it would have wide use [because] I wanted a name with a positive connotation," he says. This goes back to his linguistic training: "A word in a natural language fuzzes off in many different directions; it can be used in many different ways. It has many different shades of meaning and you can't help but think negative thoughts about something that has negative connotations, even if you're using it in a positive context," he notes.

He explains how this led to the name "Perl." "What I did was," he says, "I looked through the online dictionary, and looked at every three- and four-letter word, to see if any of them were suitable names for a language, and I actually rejected all three- and four-letter words—'Perl' not being in the dictionary. I thought of several other things, and eventually settled on 'Pearl' because I thought it has positive connotations." He justified his choice retrospectively by coming up with the explanation Practical Extraction And Report Language. "You can tell it still had the 'a' in there because of the 'and,'" he notes.

The explanatory name is apt. Throughout his programming career, Wall has been concerned with making things that were practical so that they might be used by as many people as possible. Extraction had also formed a continuing theme: His newsreader rn was partly about extracting threads of information from the undifferentiated stream of Usenet postings, and Patch was built around the idea of extracting only the changes that needed to be applied to source code. Above all, as a text-processing tool par excellence, Perl is another manifestation of Wall's fascination with manipulating and analyzing the streams of words and characters that make up natural and artificial languages.

Apt as it was, the name "Pearl" had to be modified, rather as "Monix," Tanenbaum's original name for Minix, had to be tweaked. "I heard rumors of another language called 'Pearl,' an obscure graphics language," Wall says. "So I decided I need to change the spelling of it, and I might as well shorten it, because I'm a lazy typist. I wanted a name that had positive connotations, [but] I also wanted one that was short, because I thought people would be typing it all the time." "Pearl" became "Perl."

In 1986, Wall started working on what became Perl, and finished the first version after around six months' work. The official Perl 1.0 was released in October 1987. He says that he often programmed for long stretches, and rarely wrote anything down: "The only thing I use paper for is to make notes of to do's—not extensively: a short 'fix this,' 'implement that,'" he explains.

Wall recalls that after he released Perl, "it took off pretty quickly. Of course there's always early adopters," he says, but points out that "there were things that I did explicitly to help it take off faster," another indication of the extraordinarily conscious way in which Wall was hoping to make his free program widely used. For example, he provided users of other programming languages with translation programs that would take their code and convert it automatically to Perl. Wall says he did this "because I thought people needed a migration path from what they had, and that would make it easier for them to start using it and get an idea of what the corresponding Perl would look like."

This was a fairly remarkable thing to do, especially for a noncommercial language that might well have turned out to be of no interest to anyone; it required even more work from Wall over and above creating Perl in the first place. Once more, it flowed naturally from his desire to help users. "It's complexifying my life in order to simplify other people's lives," he says, and then adds with a kind of mock arrogance that is simultaneously self-deflating: "I talk about helping people, but the flip side of that is yeah, I want to take over the world. Maybe I'm a megalomaniac, or something, and I'd like to make my mark on the world."

Aside from the light that this statement throws on Wall's complex character, it is also fascinating to see the same behavior as exhibited by Linus years later when he was creating his kernel. He, too, frequently talks of "world domination" as his aim; like Wall, he means to puncture his own self-importance. Wall, of course, is well aware of the parallel, and likes to assert a kind of precedence for his world domination plans: "Well, I predate him," he says, referring to the young upstart Linus.

Wall's promotion of Perl has been equally premeditated. For example, contrary to what others might have done, he did not set up a Usenet newsgroup to muster support for Perl. Once more, his reasoning shows a shrewd understanding of the process through which information about free software is spread.

"Pretty soon after [Perl] was released there were requests for a Perl newsgroup," he recalls, "and I put that off. I didn't want a Perl newsgroup because I didn't want to be ghettoized. The dynamics of how Usenet worked, at least back then, was if you posted something off-topic for the newsgroup then people would say, 'Well, take it to this other newsgroup,'" he explains.

"I didn't want people to be able to say that about Perl, so basically we infested the shell programming newsgroup, and whenever anyone would say, 'How can I do such and so?' we would very politely say, 'Well, here's how you might do it in a shell, but it's easier in Perl, you do it this way,'" he says. It is interesting to see Wall engaging in a kind of missionary work here, living among speakers of strange tongues such as shell languages and converting them by solving their problems with his own linguistic gospel.

Wall eventually created a newsgroup for Perl; this helped foster a sense of community and provided a forum for feedback. But alongside bug reports and bug fixes, one type of feedback was particularly important. "There's one message I send out again and again," Wall says. "Somebody will send me some sort of thank you or whatever, and I'll respond, 'Thanks, I run on encouragement like that.'"

This encouragement proved enough to keep Wall hacking on Perl in his own time for many years. "I did all of the maintenance up through the first four versions," he recalls, "and I realized it was actually getting too big for me to handle. There were getting to be more and more pressures to keep growing the language and I realized it was because there was no extension mechanism. And that was actually stunting its growth."

Wall made a major decision. "The thing that started in 1993 was basically me throwing the prototype away," he says, "and redesigning the whole thing. And I realized it was my first chance and last chance to do it, in a sense. And so I basically went down a list of all the buzz words that I wanted to comply with, and designed with those in mind.

"The last version of Perl 4 came out in the summer of 1993," he recalls. "I was already working on Perl 5 by then, and Perl 5 actually came out in '94, on 18 October. Part of the thing was that I realized I needed to learn to delegate too, and so even while we were developing, going through the alpha versions of Perl 5, I would hand off the sources to various people," he explains. Thus, around the time that Linus was creating his own system of delegation, Wall was tackling the same problem—one eventually faced by all successful free software projects. But as might be expected, Perl developed its own original approach.

Initially, things were informal. "Somebody would say, 'I'd like to work on such and so,'" Wall recalls. "And I'd say, 'OK, you've got the baton,' and they would do a release, and I would take it back. That developed into what we call the pumpkin-holder system. Essentially the pumpkin is the baton. Chip Salzenberg,"—one of the Perl lieutenants—"invented that term," Wall says.

"What it evolved into is that we have essentially a chief integrator who is called the pumpkin holder," he explains. This integration involves taking the approved patches and adding them into the main Perl source code. "We have the mailing list that does most of the discussion, called Perl 5 porters, and then there's me. I retain veto power over what the pumpkin holder does." This leaves Wall with ultimate control but offloads the day-to-day running of Perl to the pumpkin holder.

Thanks in part to these changes, Perl is thriving, particularly in the sphere of Web servers. "That was one that did blindside me," Wall acknowledges,

> I say that I thought that Perl would take off, but I thought it would take off primarily as a system administration language, and as a text-processing language. I did not anticipate the Web, but [Perl] was a natural for it. What I did anticipate was that people wanted a language with two qualities: that it could edit text well, and that it was good at gluing things together. If you think about what a Web server has to do, it has to do text processing [to manipulate Web pages] and it has to have data from somewhere, so a language that can do text processing and can hook up to anything else is exactly what the doctor ordered. I wanted Perl to be a humble language in the sense that it can compete by co-operating."

Thanks to its humility and usefulness, Perl is now probably the most widely used "glue" language in e-commerce, from giants such as Yahoo and Amazon.com (both of which use Perl extensively) downwards. As far as estimating how many Perl users there are, Wall thinks "a million is the right order of magnitude," and adds, "I usually say 'a million, plus or minus a million.'"

Wall's achievement goes much further than simply writing a great language. Perl was one of the key enabling technologies that made possible the first wave of interactive Web sites, and hence e-commerce itself. It established yet another field—that of programming languages—where the Net-based open-development process had produced better results than those traditionally employed within software companies to create their black box products.

It is significant that the success of Perl was not an accident, as had been the case with Sendmail, say, or even with Linux. Even though Perl grew out of Wall's own needs, from the beginning he designed it to be not only generally applicable but widely popular. This unusual strategy worked because Wall was self-aware about what he was trying to do and what the processes for achieving this were—an awareness doubtless born of his natural bent and intensified through his dual linguistic training.

This awareness has been displayed most entertainingly in the verbal pyrotechnics Wall routinely employs in his State of the Onion talks at the annual Perl conferences; these have taken place since 1997 and are run by O'Reilly & Associates, which also publishes numerous books about Perl (including one by Wall). In these talks, Wall has talked about, and around, in the most tangential but illuminating ways, the ideas at the heart of Perl programming. The analytical and theoretical side sets him somewhat apart from the other free software leaders, who tend to be more intuitive and practical in their approach to coding.

Partly as a result of this highly personal intellectual approach that he has adopted in his speeches, Wall has made another important contribution to the free software movement. He offers an example of a top programmer who is highly articulate, witty, and deeply concerned with the broader implications of his work. Soft-spoken and avuncular, Wall's calm presence at conferences and before the press has helped to combat clichéd images of hackers as unstable, antisocial individuals with little sense of morality and no sense of humor. If Richard Stallman is the father of today's free software movement, Larry Wall can be rightly considered its favorite uncle.

9

The Art of Code

LONG BEFORE LARRY WALL WAS THINKING about how to make Perl successful, Richard Stallman had analyzed why the hacker community at the MIT AI Lab had worked so well. He then set about re-creating that community, consciously taking steps that would maximize the chances for its survival. As GNU/Linux and the other free software projects such as Perl, Apache, and the rest grew not only in maturity but in visibility, others, too, began to notice a larger trend, and a few tried to understand it.

One of the first formal attempts to analyze the GNU/Linux phenomenon was written by Larry McVoy. He was born in Concord, Massachusetts, in 1962, and so was a good measure older than the likes of the other top Linux hackers such as Linus, Alan Cox, and Ted Ts'o. McVoy was steeped in the mainstream Unix tradition, having worked first for The Santa Cruz Operation (SCO)—which later bought Unix from Novell—and then for Sun, in both its software and hardware divisions. This work experience gave him a depth of practical knowledge in how the software industry functioned that few others in the GNU/Linux movement could match.

While he was at Sun, McVoy put together what he called his Sourceware Operating System Proposal, written during September and October 1993. In it, he suggested that Sun give away the source code to its SunOS 4 version of Unix so that a united Unix platform could be created that could take on the rapidly rising might of Microsoft. As an alternative proposal, McVoy suggested that the Unix industry adopt GNU/Linux as this common platform—an extraordinarily bold move in 1993, when Linux was barely two years old.

McVoy was concerned about nothing less than the future of Unix. In the early 1990s, he says, "the Unix industry is all excited about what they're doing, and they think they're going to win and blah-blah-blah. But the real answer is, if you look out a few years, as an engineer you could see very, very clearly that they were committing suicide," for reasons his paper would spell out.

There was also a specific impetus to write the paper: Sun's decision to change the version of Unix it would offer with its hardware. Up to that point, its operating system, called SunOS, had drawn on the BSD version of Unix that had been put together largely by hackers at the University of California at Berkeley; SunOS was a strong competitor to AT&T's commercial offering, then called UnixWare.

Even within Sun, that hacker tradition continued. "SunOS was a source base that had engineers putting effort into it more out of love for intellectual correctness and excellence than out of rewards of my salary or my stock options," McVoy explains. "It was seven or eight years of engineers sitting there on weekends polishing that thing."

Despite this, Sun's CEO Scott McNealy announced that the company was throwing away this unique asset and moving to AT&T's "official" version of Unix. "I don't think there was a single engineer or even manager that didn't make the journey to the Mecca of Scott's office and say, 'You're out of your mind, don't do this.'" But in the end, McVoy says, "McNealy did this as a business decision."

As a result, McVoy remembers, "I fumed, I fumed, I fumed—I was very upset." He thought that with the move from SunOS to what would come to be called Solaris, the company was losing not only a great product but a unique environment. "It was the sort of place that as a systems engineer, as an OS [operating system] person, you would do anything you could to get into that organization," he says. "The best minds in the industry were there. If you wanted to be working with the best, and learning the most that you could learn, you went to Sun, there was no question about it."

But the move to Solaris would not only discard the fruit of the labors of all those who made up that unique organization but also destroy its spirit. In effect, then, McVoy was about to be cast out of the Unix paradise that had been present at Sun, just as Stallman was cast out of the hackers' Eden at MIT. Like Stallman, McVoy decided to fight back: "The

[Sourceware] paper was in some ways a backhanded way of trying to make McNealy reverse his decision."

McVoy began his Sourceware white paper by offering an insightful and damning report on the parlous state of the Unix world of that time. It spelled out why Microsoft would be so successful with its then-new Windows NT, and explained, too, why GNU/Linux was later welcomed with alacrity by so many Unix users.

"Unix needs our help because Unix is dying. Unix is no longer even close to competitive," he began his paper, and proceeded to catalogue the woes afflicting the Unix world. He estimated that collectively the Unix vendors were spending around $1 billion on what they called development. He noted that "a great deal of this expenditure is redundant over the set of vendors." That is, every Unix vendor came up with its own solution to the same problem, resulting in a huge duplication of effort. By contrast, he pointed out, "Microsoft spends much less than this and produces a better product. Their product is better in terms of ease of use, installation, and administration."

McVoy believes that Unix programmers were as much to blame as their management for this waste. "It's ridiculous," he says, "you look at that billion dollars, and the real answer was . . . there was this pool of OS engineering talent, and these guys would encourage their managers to do this sort of [duplication]. Because they really didn't want to get out of the OS business, they liked being the kings of the heap, being the kernel jocks. They kind of liked this situation where every OS vendor was doing their own version of Unix and the kernel [engineers] could move from company to company, and continue to be the big studs."

The result was a staggering fragmentation. As McVoy wrote, "The major Unix vendors each provide their own version of Unix, resulting in at least ten major Unix systems all competing for about 3 percent of the computer market." This lack of direct competition led to high costs for the end users: "Licensing ranges from $20 to $100 per seat, with vendor mark up for their costly 'value add' resulting in customer seat costs of $600—$3000. Microsoft sells Windows/NT for about $150."

Customers were receiving little in return for the high costs, the Sourceware paper pointed out. "Unix has become stagnant. Unix has ceased to be the platform of choice for the development and deployment of innovative technology." McVoy then went on to note one reason for this: "A great deal of the early development of Unix was done by researchers because of Unix's ready accessibility." That is, when Unix was open, it was innovative; now it was closed and moribund.

McVoy noted in his paper that "the Unix problems are not being addressed. The vendors think 'standards' are the answers. The programmers think 'free' software is the answer. The customers think NT is the answer." Unfortunately, as McVoy explains, when vendors pushed for "standards," they really meant something else. "It was just so incredibly pathetic," he says. "Each of these Unix vendors said they wanted to do a 'let's unify'—and then the next statement was, 'OK, you dump yours, and we'll use mine.' And it was sort of like, jeez, we're really not getting anywhere." Because McVoy was trying to avoid recourse to the "customer solution" of NT, that left the programmers' solution: free software, or "sourceware," as he termed it.

McVoy wrote: "More and more traditional Unix developers have given up on the proprietary Unix implementations and are focusing their energy on sourceware." Among the "results of their labors," he singled out GNU software (GCC and GNU Emacs), the X Window system, and GNU/Linux, which he described as having "many features found only in mature operating systems," and noted that it was "feature rich but lacks the quality and stability of a commercial product," a fair assessment for the state of Linux in 1993.

McVoy pointed out that "almost every good feature in computer operating systems today, including most features in DOS, Windows, and Windows/NT, came from the mind of one hacker or another. Typically, the work was not commissioned by a company." He commented that "for the business community to dismiss the hackers as 'nuts' is a disaster," and suggested, presciently, that "it is far better to figure out a way to allow the business world and the hacker world to coexist and benefit one another. If businesses want the best technology, then businesses should move towards sourceware."

McVoy's Sourceware proposal to solve the problems of Unix fragmentation, cost, and stagnation, called for the vendor community to rally around a single Unix version whose source code would be freely available. Ideally, this would be his beloved SunOS, but if that were not possible, GNU/Linux would still be "a win on the political front," even if something of "a lose on the maturity front," as he put it.

"I never really published it, it just sort of made the rounds," McVoy says of his paper. "And I asked people to distribute it amongst people that could have some influence. I was hoping to try and build up a groundswell of pressure on McNealy and the other executives. I got in to see most of them, and spent a lot of time talking to them about this stuff." The response was encouraging: "Every body who read it was very gung-ho," he recalls. "I was viewed as a savior of Unix to these guys." Even many senior executives were supportive—in private. Ultimately, though, none of this helped. "Of course, nothing happened," McVoy says, "and it was all very disappointing."

As he looks back, McVoy now understands what was going on. "The role I played at Sun was the idiot that would open his mouth and say that the emperor had no clothes," he explains. "I was this guy who was idealistic enough and passionate to do this, and it completely torpedoed my career over and over. I mean, man, talk about stupid, I had it printed on my forehead."

McVoy's Sourceware proposal was, in retrospect, prophetic. It exposed the weaknesses within the Unix vendor community that would lead to its increasing marginalization, and to the corresponding rise of Windows NT as an enterprise operating system. More important, the proposal recognized GNU/Linux and Sourceware—free software—as an important new force, and the one bright spot in an otherwise dismal outlook.

The role of chief theoretician to the nascent opensource world eventually passed to someone who would also later grow into a key figure there. Like McVoy, Eric Raymond has a gift for sharp analysis and colorful prose, but in most other respects the two could not be more in contrast. Where McVoy's activity as free software apologist was accidental and peripheral to his main concerns, Raymond's assumption of that role was conscious; it was almost inevitable in light of his previous trajectory through the world of computing.

Raymond was born in the same state as McVoy, in Boston, Massachusetts, but even earlier, in 1957. He was the eldest of five children. His father was one of the first computer programmers, beginning in the 1950s, and was an executive with Sperry-Univac, one of the original vendors of mainframe computers. Says Raymond, "I like to describe myself as a second-generation hacker."

His father's work meant that Raymond lived abroad as a child, in Venezuela, Italy and England. As he puts it with a typically Raymondian flourish, "I lived on three continents and forgot two languages before I was thirteen." The family moved back to the United States when he was thirteen, to Pennsylvania, where Raymond still lives.

Aside from residues of these forgotten languages, the travelling seems not to have influenced him. "It was just part of my environment, and I didn't really have a judgement about it," he says. But something else did leave a deep mark. "I've an extremely mild case of spastic palsy," he explains, "impaired motor control of my left leg, basically. It's completely static: It doesn't get any better, it doesn't get any worse. What changes is how well you adapt to it over time." Raymond would later describe himself as an "anxious, angry, frustrated child." He explains, "Other people gave me a hard time. There are certain things that are pretty tough to do if you have impaired physical co-ordination. Kind of threw me back on my mental resources."

He describes how the shift to computers occurred. "I got interested in computers in college mainly as a sideline, and then I burned out on mathematics," his original field of study. "Well, computers were there." Raymond was entirely self-taught: "The books didn't exist then," he points out. "That was only a few years after the first degree in computer science, actually. Most of the learning apparatus we have today didn't yet exist. People who were programmers then basically did what I did; they drifted in from other fields and taught themselves."

Someone else who had taught himself, and was also originally a mathematician, was Richard Stallman. Raymond says he knew Stallman not just seven years before he started the GNU project but before he had acquired his trademark mane and beard. As Raymond explains, "I have occasionally stood beside him, and said to people, yes, I knew Richard before he had long hair and a Jesus complex. To his credit, Richard laughs when I say this."

Through Stallman, Raymond got to know the MIT culture, which he characterizes as "organized around PDP-10, assembler language, and LISP." He already knew about the Unix and C culture, which meant that "I got to see both sides of that [hacker] scene pretty early on," he says.

Even in the early 1980s, then, Raymond was a privileged observer of a wide range of coding activity. He likes to emphasize that much of this was disconnected, or at least connected only from time to time; there was no unified hacker culture as we know it today. "That period was very different from the open-source culture now," he says, "because the technological infrastructure to do software sharing the way we do it today didn't exist. The only way you could pass around software during that stage was on magnetic tapes, and so it was only done sporadically. The cultures that did that were very small and very isolated from each other.

"There's a certain school of historical interpretation that views today's free software as a return to a pre-proprietary golden age. That golden age never existed," Raymond insists. "I was there and I know. From '77 to the early '90s, the free software culture, or the open-source culture as we think of it today, only existed in the sense that there were a bunch of people doing things not grossly dissimilar from what we do today.

"But it had no self-consciousness," he points out. "It had no cultural identity; there was nobody who was thinking 'let's do these things for particular reasons.' It was just a bunch of people doing solutions to problems and scratching itches that happened to know about each other and pass information around. One of Richard's contributions was that he made that culture self-conscious." One of Raymond's core contributions would be to strengthen that self-consciousness and to help mobilize the community it engendered.

He began this work with a new edition of the Jargon File, a major collection of hacker lore arranged as a dictionary of terms and usages. It was first put together in 1975, but had languished somewhat in the 1980s, partly, no doubt, as a result of the destruction of the MIT hacker community, one of the main sources for Jargon File entries.

"I stumbled over a copy of it in 1990," Raymond recalls, "and realized, wow, (a) this is a little out of date, there's a lot of new stuff in the culture that ought to be in here, and (b) I've got the seniority to do something about this now. It just never occurred to me before that the document could be modified. . . . I spent a weekend adding entries and I realized, wow, this is pretty interesting; it deserves to be dusted off and maintained. And when I asked the person who was essentially responsible for it at that time [he said], 'Well, you know, there's been some demand for a second edition of the dictionary, why don't you do it.'"

The second edition was published in 1991 as *The New Hacker's Dictionary*. Raymond's motives for undertaking this major project are significant.

I realized that a book like that could do a number of worthwhile things. One major motive that I had at the time was that, like Richard, but independently of him, I thought that it would be worthwhile to strengthen the self-awareness, the cultural consciousness, if you will, of the people that contributed to the dictionary.

I had partly different motives from Richard. He was already on his moral crusade to abolish proprietary software at that time; had been for five years. I was concerned that ugly things were happening to the public image of the hacker culture—which was already a culture in embryo, then. I was concerned that that might create the political conditions under which the Internet and other new communications media could be severely politically restricted. I wanted hundreds of thousands of people in the mainstream culture to sympathize and laugh with my tribe so that when the politics started getting nasty we had some allies.

Another goal was that I thought that even back then the Internet was growing much faster than it had been in the mid- or late '70s when I first got involved with it, and I was concerned that the growth of the Internet was outstripping our ability to acculturate new people. And I wanted to make it easier to acculturate new people.

One person at least partly "acculturated" in this way was Linus. "When we first met in 1996," Raymond recalls, "*he* wanted *my* autograph."

Finally, *The New Hacker's Dictionary* was, as Raymond puts it, "a way of paying tribute to my roots." Already by the late 1980s he was beginning to think of the global hacker community as not just a distinct, well-defined tribe, united by a culture and a set of beliefs (both of which *The New Hacker's Dictionary* was hoping to record and stimulate), but more specifically as his own tribe: a tribe, moreover, that tended to judge people by their real achievements in hacking and that was indifferent to mundane issues of who you were—or whether you have cerebral palsy.

Aside from these novel motivations, *The New Hacker's Dictionary* was also unusual in the way it was put together. "I consciously approached it as a large-scale collaborative process," Raymond explains, "in which I would be a central nexus, but not assert as much control of the process as a conventional editor does."

The New Hacker's Dictionary was published—appropriately enough— by MIT Press, and became something of a best-seller; as such, it achieved one of Raymond's major aims in evangelizing about his tribe and its lore. The resulting interest also allowed Raymond to develop his skills in handling the media, an extremely rare ability among hackers, and gave him "some street cred among journalists" as he puts it, which he would put to good use later on.

The New Hacker's Dictionary nearly had one other dramatic consequence, as Raymond describes. "In 1991, I was working on the first edition of *The New Hacker's Dictionary*, and I was sent an interesting hunk of code by a guy named Ray Gardner. It was what we would now think of as a hypertext viewer for the Jargon File." That is, you could use links within the text to jump to other entries as with a Web browser.

"Ray had written it for MS-DOS," Raymond continues. "He sent me the first build, and I thought this was a cool idea. I completely rewrote it, and generalized and ported it to Unix, and I turned it into a baby hypertext reader which I called VH, or VolksHypertext." He explains the rather unwieldy name: "At the time I was aware of the Xanadu project, which was this huge complex Cadillac of a hypertext system." Raymond had been invited to join the Xanadu project in 1980. "VH was a very stripped down, simple, lightweight hypertext system, so I thought of it sort of as a Volkswagen to Xanadu's Cadillac. No chrome, no tail fins, but it got the job done. So I called it VolksHypertext."

Xanadu wasn't the only hypertext system that was being developed in this period. "It was late '91, I think, I got mail from Tim Berners-Lee—who nobody had heard of at the time—saying, 'I hear you've been doing some interesting things with hypertext; shall we collaborate?' And so I sent him back some mail, basically saying sure, standards are good. And I didn't hear back from him. I still don't know why." Happily for Raymond, he has many other claims to fame other than almost co-inventing the World Wide Web.

Probably his most important achievement, the essay *The Cathedral and the Bazaar*, which analyzes the success of Linux and open-source software, arose in part because of a CD-ROM that turned up on his doorstep in late 1993. The CD-ROM was from the GNU/Linux distributor Yggdrasil, and as Raymond recalls was "the first available CD-ROM Linux distribution. That landed on my doorstep because I had already written enough free software that some of my stuff was on that disk." As mentioned previously, this was the "token of appreciation" that Yggdrasil had sent to "the many free software developers" who had contributed to its distribution, often unwittingly as in Raymond's case.

He admits that he was skeptical of Linux until he tried it; and he might never have tried it had it meant wiping his current system, as would have been the case with any GNU/Linux distribution other than Yggdrasil. But "Yggdrasil had an interesting feature," Raymond notes. "It was possible to run Linux as a demo without changing any partitions on your hard disc"—in other words, without needing to delete or install anything. "And that's what I did for a few hours, and I was astonished at what I saw. I abandoned the rest of my plans for that day, scrubbed the commercial [AT&T] System V that I had been using off my disk, and installed Linux."

Raymond was more than astonished, he says: "Flabbergasted wouldn't be too strong a way to put it. Because it completely contradicted all my expectations about the quality of a project like that. I still had the classically Brooksian idea that you couldn't do high-quality software with a mob," another reference to Brooks's *The Mythical Man-Month* paper. Raymond set out to study and understand this interesting phenomenon.

"The turning point for me in terms of getting to know the people of the culture deeply was in 1996 when I was on the program committee for the first Freely Redistributable Software Conference." This conference was held in Boston, from 3 February to 6 February 1996. It had been organized by Peter Salus, and was being run under the auspices of the Free Software Foundation.

"I was already pretty sure that [Linux] was my personal place to stand," Raymond says, "and the hacker culture's place to stand in a shifting world. And going to the conference certainly reinforced my sense that there were a lot of people out there with a lot of energy who were beginning to work on this." The conference had a further and unexpected effect on Raymond, who met Linus face-to-face for the first time there.

That conference "was when I first became consciously aware that the leadership role in the culture was passing from RMS and the old MIT AI Lab crowd to the Linux people," he says—and that a new generation of hackers had taken over. It was a subtle thing, Raymond recalls, apparent "in what people were talking about, and who they were looking towards." It was also perceptible in what should have been the highlight of the conference and the crowning glory of Stallman's GNU project.

"One of the day-long tutorials there was the first public outing of the new Hurd design, which of course was the Free Software Foundation's shot at a free kernel," Raymond recalls. In the intervening twelve years after Stallman had initiated the GNU project, the Hurd kernel had attained a kind of mythic status that made its arrival all the more eagerly awaited and, perhaps, its ultimate revelation all the more disappointing.

Raymond describes the moment. "I remember Keith Bostic—again, this was also significant, he being one of the key BSD people—asking what I thought of the presentation. And I remember saying to him, 'It's elegant, it's beautiful, it's elaborate, and it's going to get killed by its performance overhead.' And Keith nodding in glum agreement." The reason for his glumness was that "like all of us," Raymond says, "he wanted it to succeed. But Keith and I and other people there sort of looked at that and went, 'It's beautiful but it will never fly, it's too complicated.'" Subtle and fleeting as that moment of realization was, it represented the end of a hacker era.

And also the beginning of the next. "The tribe as a whole wasn't that conscious about realizing that the Linux kernel was going to be it yet," Raymond says, "but I think we already knew it." Raymond emerged from the conference changed by the experience. He believes "that conference was one of the things that pushed me over the edge" to set down his theory about Linux and its development methodology in what became *The Cathedral and Bazaar*.

Before doing so, Raymond resolved to do something extraordinary: to test that theory first. "I have the mental attitude of a scientist," he says. "If you're a scientist, when you form a theory, you test it by experiment; that's just what you do." His test required a piece of free software to which he could attempt to apply a Linux-like development approach. Raymond wanted to find out whether applying the methodology in itself would be enough to create a community around the software that would see to its constant improvement.

"I was quite consciously on the lookout for something suitable," he says. A piece of software called Popclient presented itself. Raymond began the project in June 1996; in October he released the first beta version of what he had renamed Fetchmail; as its name implies, Fetchmail's main job is to fetch mail from mail servers, unlike Allman's more famous Sendmail, which sends it on. Through his experiences with Fetchmail, Raymond was able to test and refine his ideas about how it might be possible to "do high quality software with a mob," as he put it. The result was his essay *The Cathedral and the Bazaar*, which he wrote in late 1996 and finished in early 1997. As well as being freely available online, the essay has also been published in book form by O'Reilly & Associates, along with Raymond's other essays.

The Cathedral and the Bazaar begins with a challenge to the software world: "Linux is subversive." Raymond then goes on to explain the basic metaphors of his paper: "I believed that the most important software (operating systems and really large tools like Emacs) needed to be built like cathedrals, carefully crafted by individual wizards or small bands of mages working in splendid isolation, with no beta to be released before its time."

As a result, Raymond writes, "Linus Torvalds's style of development— release early and often, delegate everything you can, be open to the point of promiscuity—came as a surprise. . . . the Linux community seemed to resemble a great babbling bazaar of differing agendas and approaches. . . . out of which a coherent and stable system could seemingly emerge only by a succession of miracles."

The rest of the essay consists of a series of aphorisms about the open-source process, together with commentary. The form is indicative of Raymond's literary tastes: the aphorism—a short, pithy saying—provides a perfect showcase for his gifts as a writer. One of the reasons he has been so influential in the world of free software is his ability to encapsulate complex ideas in snappy slogans. As the self-appointed front-man for free software, Raymond is continuing Mark Bolzern's pioneering work as the de facto marketing director for GNU/Linux—with a similarly nonexistent remuneration other than peer esteem.

Raymond's first aphorism: "Every good work of software starts by scratching a developer's personal itch." "Scratching an itch" is a memorable way to describe the act of beginning a free software project, even if it does gloss over the complex reasons that top hackers such as Linus start coding, as the genesis of Linux demonstrates.

His second aphorism, "Good programmers know what to write. Great ones know what to rewrite (and reuse)" is close to a similar phrase that is usually attributed to Pablo Picasso: "Good artists borrow, great artists steal." Raymond says the "parallelism was intentional." The key point, of course, is that traditional, black box closed software does not permit such rewriting and reusing, and so cannot enjoy the benefits they bring.

"Plan to throw one away; you will, anyhow" is not just similar to the words of someone else, but a direct quotation, in this case of Fred Brooks. Brooks hovers as a constant presence over not only Raymond's paper but of the entire free software movement. Although Brooks was writing about the creation of mainframe software decades ago, the essays in which he described and warned against the pitfalls of large-scale development projects also indirectly suggest ways of avoiding them—do things in a radically different manner. Much of *The Cathedral and the Bazaar* is about understanding how to realize that difference in practical terms.

The next three aphorisms form the heart of Raymond's paper. "Treating your users as co-developers is your least-hassle route to rapid code improvement and effective debugging," he writes. "Release early. Release often. And listen to your customers." And last: "given a large enough beta-tester and co-developer base, almost every problem will be characterized quickly and the fix obvious to someone."

Raymond recasts the last of these in the more punchy phrase "Given enough eyeballs, all bugs are shallow," and dubs it Linus's Law; in many ways this stands as the resolution of the conundrum posed by what is known as Brooks's Law: "Adding manpower to a late software project makes it later." Linus's Law, taken with the previous two aphorisms, states that the strength of open source lies in its ability to harness a huge user base, notably via the Internet.

Raymond rightly calls Linus's Law the "core difference" between the cathedral-builder and the bazaar modes. As he writes, "In the cathedral-builder view of programming, bugs and development problems are tricky, insidious, deep phenomena. It takes months of scrutiny by a dedicated few to develop confidence that you've winkled them all out. Thus the long release intervals, and the inevitable disappointment when long-awaited releases are not perfect.

"In the bazaar view, on the other hand," he continues, "you assume that bugs are generally shallow phenomena—or, at least, that they turn shallow pretty quick when exposed to a thousand eager co-developers pounding on every single new release. Accordingly you release often in order to get more corrections, and as a beneficial side effect you have less to lose if an occasional botch gets out the door." In other words, Linus's Law implies the other two aphorisms, and taken together represent the open-source process boiled down to its very essence.

Raymond throws some important light on the formulation of this key section. Linus, he says, "saw the drafts before it was finished, and he did two important things. One was he said that he thought I generally had it right. And the second thing was he modified my statement of Linus's Law in a crucial way. The original version of the law was 'given a sufficiently large number of eyeballs, all bugs will be fixed'; he modified that to 'given a sufficiently large number of eyeballs, all bugs will be characterized,' which is a somewhat different statement. Fortunately, characterization is the hard part. Once you have a bug characterized, it's generally easy to fix it."

Raymond also offers some interesting thoughts on the extent to which *The Cathedral and the Bazaar* was restating something that Linus already knew. "My impression at the time was that he had those conclusions as latent knowledge, but that I was causing that knowledge to become explicit in his mind. So I think that when he read my draft, he essentially consciously discovered what he already knew."

The paper had a similar effect on many other hackers. For example, at the first public reading, to the Philadelphia Linux User Group in early 1997, Raymond says that "reading this paper to a bunch of hackers was like putting a spark to tinder. That was my experience all through '97, that people would get exposed to this paper, and their whole view of the cultural world they inhabited would change instantly."

One of his aims in creating *The New Hacker's Dictionary* was giving his tribe a greater consciousness about what they were doing. "Over and over, I had the experience of watching people getting exposed to that paper," he says, "and suddenly their level of understanding of what they had been doing for years would jump. And their energy level would jump with it."

Although there were more immediate effects of *The Cathedral and the Bazaar*, the ability to energize the hacker community was in itself a major achievement. At a stroke Raymond gave an already impressive movement new impetus, and as a result played a major part in preparing for its later successes.

Raymond has also presented these growing successes in a way that the mainstream media can understand and respond to them positively. "I like to describe myself as Linus's minister of propaganda," he says. A side effect of this has been that many more traditional members of the free software community see Raymond as promoting himself more than the tribe. In part, this is a natural suspicion in the face of that rarest of beasts, the extrovert hacker. But these critics miss the point: Those who are good at this role have to push themselves in the face of the media. To ask them to be successful and retiring is simply a contradiction in terms.

Raymond has been effective in this role not only because of his ability to coin quotable sound-bytes but also because his wide and unusual range of interests make him into what journalists like best: a "colorful" figure.

Raymond possesses a black belt in the martial art Tae Kwon Do and describes himself as a "happy gun nut"; he has even persuaded people as diverse as Linus and Stallman to join some of his shooting parties. A hacker into firearms is striking enough perhaps, but Raymond manages to cap that by calling himself a neo-pagan.

"I'm a third-degree witch" in the Wiccan religion—the highest level, he says. "Wicca is a relaxed, nature-centered polytheism long on direct experience and short on dogma," he explains. "My beliefs don't involve much resembling anything that you would call traditional religious faith," he says, and in any case, he adds, "I don't practice a lot anymore."

But Raymond believes that "the techniques and attitudes that I've learned from Zen and neo-paganism are very much part of what makes me publicly effective." They are also completely consistent with the other beliefs that are central to his life: free software, no gun control—or "an armed and self-reliant citizenry" as Raymond prefers to put it—and libertarianism, which he explains as "the original individualist-, small-government, free-trade, rely-on-the-market-not-on-coercion ideology." More specifically, he describes himself as belonging to a group called "market anarchists" who "would like to abolish government altogether."

It is not hard to divine where this thoroughgoing dislike of centralized powers—be it in the world of software, religion, or politics—has its roots. "I hated feeling powerless as a child," Raymond says. "And it wasn't just the palsy: Even if I had not had the palsy, I would not have liked being a child, because I was in a condition of dependence all the time. Some people can readily live with that; I could not. I guess in some sense I've generalized that; I want everybody to feel empowered."

His latest project in empowering people is called *The Art of Unix Programming*. "This is a book about how to think like a Unix guru," he says. "You can view it as a continuation of a theme that's been present in my work all along, which is the conscious elucidation of unconscious knowledge.

"The specific motivation in this case," he says, "is that there are thousands of eager young Linux programmers who are running around with bits and pieces of this Unix tradition, but they don't have the whole thing; they don't have this synthetic overview, the philosophy, and it will make them more effective if they have that." As with *The New Hacker's Dictionary*, Raymond views this as a collaborative venture. "But the population that I expect to be involved with this is somewhat more restricted," he notes, given the more rarefied nature of its contents.

Unix programming is an art, Raymond believes, because "when you do it at a high enough level, there's a very strong aesthetic satisfaction that you get from writing an elegant program. If you don't get that kind of gratification, you never join the culture. Just as you don't get composers without an ear for music, you don't get hackers without an ability to be aesthetically gratified by writing programs." This element of aesthetic gratification perhaps provides the key to explaining one of the missing pieces of Raymond's otherwise comprehensive explanation of the open-source process.

In a follow-up essay to *The Cathedral and the Bazaar*, called *Homesteading the Noosphere*, Raymond explored an apparent paradox at the heart of open-source software: If everyone is free to take the code and modify it, why do major projects like Linux or Apache rarely split, or 'fork,' as hackers say, just as the old-style commercial Unixes did? He suggests that peer esteem, the key driving force for people working in the world of free software, explains the effect. He demonstrates well that the dynamics of such a "gift economy"—where prestige is measured not by what you have, but by what you give away—tend to reduce the threat of forking.

Certainly this analysis goes a long way to explaining why so many coders around the world willingly devote themselves to these projects with no immediate thought of material reward. In one respect, it is unsatisfactory: It does not explain why top hackers—Linus or Larry Wall—began and then devoted so much effort to their fledgling projects. Raymond's "scratching an itch" does not suffice, either: The itches would have been amply scratched by projects far less ambitious—and far less impressive—than what became Linux or Perl, say.

There are precedents for gifted individuals who conceive and work on huge projects, often with little hope not only of recompense but of recognition. In other spheres, these people are called artists, and much of the history of art is the story of those who create masterworks out of an inner necessity to do so, over and above what they may have been paid to produce.

Striking parallels exist between the stories of top hackers and famous artists. For example, generous funding from aristocratic patrons enabled Ludwig van Beethoven to devote himself to writing works of such originality that they were often incomprehensible to his contemporaries, and also to promote the then-radical ideals of liberty he believed in. In the same way, Richard Stallman has been able to devote himself to his coding and campaigning thanks in part to patronage such as the McArthur Foundation fellowship.

Johann Wolfgang von Goethe was a minister of state at the German court of Weimar, and took his duties there as seriously as his work on such projects as his masterpiece *Faust*, a vast patchwork of poetry that occupied him for fifty years. Alongside these major responsibilities, Goethe managed to juggle a family life (unlike Beethoven), rather as Linus somehow does (unlike Stallman) while holding down a full-time job at Transmeta and pushing forward his own life work that grows through constant accretion.

Perceptive analyst that he is, Raymond is well aware of this aspect. In *Homesteading the Noosphere*, he writes, "In making this 'reputation game' analysis, by the way, I do not mean to devalue or ignore the pure artistic satisfaction of designing beautiful software and making it work. We all experience this kind of satisfaction and thrive on it." But he tends to downplay it and subsume it in the 'reputation model.'

Support for the view that artistic satisfaction is a better explanation, at least for the key initiating figures of the free software movement, is provided by someone to whom Raymond made a nod of respect in his choice of the title *The Art of Unix Programming* for his next book. "It was a conscious reference to Donald Knuth's *The Art of Computer Programming*," he says.

Although not well known outside computing circles, Donald Knuth towers over the discipline of computer science; he is a kind of grandfather of the free software movement and foreshadowed many of its ideas and techniques with his own important and widely used programs, all freely available.

Knuth was born in 1938, in Milwaukee, Wisconsin. During a brilliant early career as a physicist and mathematician at Case Institute of Technology—where he was awarded a master's degree contemporaneously with his B.S.—he became interested in the young world of computer science.

In 1962, he started work on a book that was originally intended to be about the design of compilers—the programs that convert source code into binaries. The project blossomed and became the multivolume work

The Art of Computer Programming. The first volume appeared in 1968, the second in 1969, and the third in 1973. Although these three books already contain over 2,000 pages, Knuth plans several more volumes. This huge opus is not about how to program in a particular language; it is about the theoretical underpinnings of all such programs. Knuth is the acknowledged expert on algorithms, the ways of carrying out basic computer operations such as ordering, searching, etc.

He explained why he chose the word "art" for this work in a speech given in 1974 when he received the A. M. Turing Award of the Association for Computing Machinery, the world's oldest computer society. Knuth's speech was later published in the book titled *Literate Programming*. "When I speak about computer programming as an art," he said, "I am thinking primarily of it as an art *form*, in an aesthetic sense. The chief goal of my work as educator and author is to help people learn how to write *beautiful programs*." He later explained, "My feeling is that when we prepare a program, the experience can be just like composing poetry or music."

Knuth went further. Programming was not just an artistic activity but an art-form that could be enjoyed by others. "When we read other people's programs, we can recognize some of them as genuine works of art." This assumes that the source is available, as is the case for open-source software. The resulting aesthetic experience is not minor or incidental: "My claim is that it is possible to write *grand* programs, *noble* programs, truly *magnificent* ones!" (The emphases in this and the previous paragraph are Knuth's.).

Knuth summarizes his views this way: "Computer programming is an art, because it applies accumulated knowledge to the world, because it requires skill and ingenuity, and especially because it produces objects of beauty. Programmers who subconsciously view themselves as artists will enjoy what they do and will do it better."

Knuth's own pursuit of beauty was not restricted to programming. As he said in a later lecture given on the receipt of another award—the 1996 Kyoto Prize for Advanced Technology—"I was excited to see these volumes [of *The Art of Computer Programming*] not only because I was pleased with the information they contained but also because of the beautiful typography and layout."

They are classics of mathematical writing and gentle wit, too, notably through the many quotations from texts selected from Knuth's wide reading. At the head of the preface to Volume 2 of *The Art of Computer Programming*, which deals with "Seminumerical Algorithms," Knuth quotes Shakespeare's Hamlet: "O dear Ophelia! I am ill at these numbers: I have not art to reckon my groans."

When later editions deteriorated in typography and layout because of the lower quality of the photo-optical typesetting technology introduced in the 1970s, Knuth did what any true hacker would do: He sat down and wrote some code to solve the problem.

The result was T_EX, "a new typesetting program for the creation of beautiful books" as Knuth describes it in the Preface to *The $T_EX$book*, his own handbook to the program, and written to provide users with absolute control over the appearance of characters on the page. T_EX allowed him to re-create the effects of hot-lead typesetting that had been used for the first editions of his book but which had now all but disappeared.

The name T_EX is derived from the Greek word τεχνη (tekhne), which means "art," and is also the root of the words "technology" and "technique." As well as coming with its own idiosyncratic form, T_EX also has a particular pronunciation: The "X" in T_EX is like the "ch" in the name of German author Bertolt Brecht.

Although Knuth wrote T_EX for his own needs—"I first intended it to be for myself and my secretary," he says—it soon spread more widely as others recognized its power and usefulness. Knuth had started coding it in March 1978, but as he was later to write in a 1989 piece called *The Errors of T_EX*, "other people had begun to use T_EX in August of 1978, and I was surprised to see how fast the system was propagating." As with other free software projects, the more users T_EX had, the more bugs they found. Well before Eric Raymond had formulated the idea, Knuth had discovered that "new users find new bugs," as he later put it.

"The previous software that I had written for wide consumption had been compilers primarily, so I didn't have as wide a family of users," Knuth explains. "So [the insight about users and bugs] was something that came to me after just from the experience that I had after, because T_EX [had] a much larger, more diverse set of users." This growing community caused Knuth to spend more time on the project than he had intended. The existence of these users was not an unmixed blessing: "It was a stimulus," Knuth says, "and it was a terror."

On the one hand, he recalls, "it was encouraging in the sense [that] I could see how this could really be useful." He rejoiced that what had started out as a private project had turned out to be so generally applicable—just as Linux would. Today, Knuth estimates, there are around 1 million T_EX users, and "95 percent of all publications in physics and mathematics" use it, he says.

On the other, though, "I didn't want it to take over my whole life. I had only one life to live," he explains, "and that had already been decided:

The Art of Computer Programming. I was supposed to finish [T$_E$X] in one year." Instead, he was faced with the prospect of spending decades of his life making "the best typesetting systems for the world." As a compromise between these conflicting demands, he asked himself, "What's the minimum I can do and get back to writing *The Art of Computer Programming* without being totally irresponsible?"

He decided that "instead of patching what I have, let me go to what I wish I had done originally. I'm going to give it my absolute best shot, and then I'm going to finish it. It's going to be good enough to cover 98 percent of everything that people need and then I'm going to freeze it."

Having written T$_E$X78, Knuth started over with a new version that he called T$_E$X82. As well as building on what he had learned about writing the program itself, Knuth was also able to exploit more efficiently what later became known as the Linux method. As he wrote in *The Errors of T$_E$X*: "from the beginning there were hundreds of users. . . . But now there was a new dimension: Several dozen people were also reading the code and making well-informed comments on how to improve it." He was adopting a classic open-source strategy; Knuth even had his own T$_E$X lieutenants. "I had regular meetings with volunteer helpers who represented many different points of view," he wrote. "So I had a golden opportunity to hone the ideas to a new state of perfection," just as Linus would do with his inner circle of advisors.

Knuth's quest for beauty and perfection has been more single-minded than that of Linus or other open-source captains. For example, he not only has kept a log of all the errors that have been found in T$_E$X but has written the article referred to above detailing the entire saga. To further encourage the debugging process, Knuth has taken the unprecedented step of offering financial rewards to anyone who finds errors in his books or software.

The difference in attitude between Knuth and vendors of proprietary software is noteworthy; the latter not only don't pay when users find bugs in their products but charge customers for the privilege of reporting them, because typically the only way to do so is to take out often expensive support contracts. Fortunately for Knuth, few of his bounty checks have been cashed because their owners value them more for having been awarded by him than for their nominal value.

In part because of this dedication to perfection—and because the program is effectively frozen now—T$_E$X may well be the first and only completely debugged piece of complex software ever written.

Currently, Knuth is busy working on the remaining volumes of *The Art of Computer Programming.* He is releasing these in 128-page fascicles, in-

spired in part by the example of Charles Dickens, whose novels were se-
rialized in a similar way. The main advantage in serialization is that
Knuth will receive feedback from his readers as he goes along; thus the
debugging process will move faster.

Knuth's masterwork would not have been possible had he not had access to the work of his fellow computer scientists and the academic tradition they formed part of. The ready availability of their results meant
that he could draw ideas from many sources. "You put together two ideas
that are in two different journals," he says; "maybe the authors never
knew each other. I'm the first person that really knew that these two people were working on the same subject, which happens an awful lot."
Putting them together in this way often enabled Knuth to come up with
important and original results, but far more quickly and efficiently than
if he had performed all the preliminary work, too. In this sense, *The Art
of Computer Programming* is one of the greatest monuments to the openness and sharing that lies at the heart not only of open-source software
but of the entire scientific tradition.

Conscious of the magnitude of the task still before him, Knuth has not
used e-mail since 1990. This apparently extreme decision to cut himself
off from the outside world to minimize distractions during the creative
process is not without precedents. In the early years of the twentieth
century, Marcel Proust was similarly engaged in a work that would dominate his life: his vast, autobiographical novel *A la recherche du temps
perdu* (In search of lost time). To aid his concentration, Proust had the
room where he worked in his Paris home lined with cork to muffle the
sounds from the outside world. It is hard to think of a better physical
correlate for Knuth's act of online disconnection.

The link between Proust and Knuth goes deeper. The opening page of
The Art of Computer Programming reads, "This series of books is affec-
tionately dedicated to the Type 650 computer once installed at Case Institute of Technology, in remembrance of many pleasant evenings"—a
conscious reference, Knuth acknowledges, to the title of Charles Scott-
Moncrieff's standard English translation of Proust's masterwork: *Remembrance of Things Past*.

It seems appropriate that somebody who began his career working
with the then-new IBM 650 computer system now finds himself an hon-
orary and highly honored member of today's computer vanguard: open
source. Given his personal track record of openness and free distribution
of software, it is not surprising that he should be such a staunch sup-
porter of source code availability. "I'm more than sympathetic to that; I
consider that absolutely indispensable for progress," he says.

Knuth uses GNU/Linux for his own computing, and one of the main programs he runs is Emacs: "That's my favorite piece of open-source software," he says. Knuth has even sent Stallman suggestions for Emacs. "He hasn't put them in yet," he notes, but acknowledges that "I didn't send them by e-mail," because he never uses it, and that this omission may have had an influence. Nonetheless, Stallman remains something of a personal hero for him. "He's on the right side of the crusade," Knuth says.

As well as being a distinguished academic, a prolific author of key books and papers in his field, and what can only be described as one of the most senior proto-hackers, Knuth is also a keen musician: He even contemplated studying music at university instead of physics. More recently, he had a fine two-manual baroque organ built in a specially designed room of his house.

Knuth shares a love of music with many of his fellow programmers of free software: Larry Wall trained as a musician, Richard Stallman takes music and instruments with him wherever he goes, Ted Ts'o and Stephen Tweedie sing in choirs (and Tweedie conducts them, too), Dave Miller has variously played guitar, drums, and piano, and Eric Raymond has been a session flutist on two albums. The Victorian art historian and theorist Walter Pater wrote in his 1877 essay "The School of Giorgione" that "all art constantly aspires towards the condition of music"; perhaps this applies to the art of code, too.

But whatever the close links between coding and artistic creation, it would be a mistake to regard hacking as an ivory tower activity, of interest only to some inner circle of adepts. Knuth himself wrote in his essay *Computer Programming as an Art*: "The ideal situation occurs when the things we regard as beautiful are also regarded by other people as useful." He adds, "I especially enjoy writing programs which do the greatest good, in some sense," a clear echo of Stallman's comment about the pride he felt early on in his programs that were useful to people.

Just as the best source code always implies the existence of a usable binary, so there seems to be a sense among hackers that the best software— the most beautiful as Knuth and others would say—implies that it serves its users as much as possible. Time and again, the top hackers refer to the sense of community their work creates, a community defined by the users of the binaries generated from their code.

This sense of creating and serving a community, perhaps as much as any aesthetic sense, is the commonest motivation for the greatest hackers. The community was the goal, not just a result, of Stallman's creation of the GNU project. Sendmail's creator Eric Allman says that for him free software is "about society," and adds, "I suppose that sounds fairly out there, but that really does it for me." Similarly, speaking for the core members of the Apache Group, Brian Behlendorf puts it this way: "To us the primary benefit of using Apache was using it as part of the community at large, rather than just using it for the 1s and 0s it represented."

Perhaps the most articulate exponent of the centrality of the community to open source is Larry Wall. He has spoken of wanting to serve people through Perl, and realized that this "needed the culture around the language," as he says—and cultures are generated by a community of users.

"That starts off small with the feedback loop," he says, "but I also realized that there's not only the first-order feedback loop going on there, there's the interactions among people, and that it's probably more valuable what the other people exchange among themselves in terms of Perl scripts than what I'm exchanging with them. Because the second-order effects are many-to-many, whereas the relationship with the center is one-to-many."

In a sense, Wall wrote Perl and distributed it freely to give members of the community that grew around it the possibility of a similar generosity in their interactions with each other—but one on an even larger scale, thanks to the network effect. "By and large I think I've got my wish on that," Wall says. "People really do help people for the sake of helping people."

For Wall, a committed Christian, this hoped-for effect is nothing less than "theological." Wall draws explicit parallels between his creation of Perl, artistic creation in general, and the primordial Creation. "The metaphor of messianic overtones is certainly there," he admits, and adds with a characteristic ambiguity, "I simultaneously try to take them seriously and not seriously."

Surely it is no accident that Knuth, too, is a deeply religious man, as are other leading hackers such as Ted Ts'o, and that even those who are not religious, such as Richard Stallman and Linus, have a strong underlying ethical component to their characters. This pervasive aspect means that, unlike commercial software vendors, which at most can promise material rewards, the free software projects can offer something much more valuable on a human level, if more intangible. Tapping into the best that is in people, it calls forth the best in all sorts of ways, not least in code quality.

After 1996, even the most cynical and jaded observers of the technology scene were beginning to notice this. Free software, the Internet's best-kept secret, was about to enter the mainstream.

10

Low-Down in the Valley

IT WOULD BE MORE THAN THREE YEARS after he left Finland before the world discovered exactly what Linus was doing at Transmeta, down in Silicon Valley. All was finally revealed on 19 January 2000, at one of the most eagerly awaited and intensively reported launches in recent computing history.

Transmeta's founder and CEO Dave Ditzel announced the Crusoe family of processor chips designed for mobile computers. In their design, Ditzel asserted, Transmeta had "rethought the microprocessor," and with some justice. Observing that the current generation of chips such as the Intel Pentium family were too complicated to design and debug, too expensive to build, and much too hot to use in the kind of lightweight mobile devices users increasingly wanted, Ditzel offered a chip design that aimed to be none of these.

Taking advantage of latest advances in technology, Transmeta had come up with a family of fast, low-power processors that handled data in 128-bit chunks—compared to the 32-bits of the Intel Pentium. But there was a problem: Such chips would not run the thousands of PC programs written for the family of Intel processors that ranged from the 80386 (whose appearance finally reconciled Linus to the Intel range) to the Pentium generically known as the x86 processors.

Transmeta's solution was simple but innovative: to use software to provide the x86 compatibility. That is, when an ordinary PC program ran on a Transmeta chip, special software would convert the programs written for the x86 chip family into a version designed for the 128-bit Crusoe chip. The chips were so fast, Transmeta proclaimed, that the translation process did not materially slow down the performance.

This, then was Transmeta's great secret: It was taking on the most powerful hardware company in the PC business—Intel—just as GNU/Linux was challenging the top PC software vendor, Microsoft. As a result, Linus, one of the least aggressive individuals imaginable, found himself at the center of not one but two frontal attacks on the central bastion of the late twentieth-century computer industry: the Wintel (Windows-Intel) duopoly.

Transmeta does not market computers based on its chips directly; instead, it sells chips and software to what are called OEMs (Original Equipment Manufacturers). Nonetheless, to demonstrate its claims, Transmeta did have some mobile computers using its chips at the launch. One of these was based on the TM5400 chip and was a lightweight notebook running Microsoft Windows. There was also a smaller mobile Internet appliance based on another member of the Crusoe family, the TM3120. It ran something called Mobile Linux.

According to Ditzel, "the TM3120 is fully compatible with all x86 PC applications and operating systems, though we have found the greatest customer interest is for mobile Internet appliances running a version of the Linux operating system." This explanation confirms what Linus had said in 1996. He had insisted that his work at Transmeta was not directly related to Linux, and that Transmeta was not in any way a Linux company. The appearance of Mobile Linux represents a more recent element of the company's strategy, one born from the growing presence of and demand for GNU/Linux in the mobile user community.

After the main presentations, Linus took part in a question-and-answer session with the press. The pale and thin young man from Finland had filled out noticeably since moving to the United States: mentioning his incipient paunch soon became a tick-box item for journalists when they wrote about him. Linus gave some background on the development of Transmeta's GNU/Linux distribution. "Mobile Linux really is fairly standard Linux," he said. "What we've done partly to show off the technology is that in-house we made kind of a small distribution to give to OEMs so that they could have something to run."

As for the effect his work on Mobile Linux might have on the main Linux kernel, he pointed out, "My interests have always affected kernel development, so that's not about to change. And I actually believe strongly in mobility. I find myself using my laptop more than I find myself using my eight-way Pentium Xeon"—a super-PC sporting no less than eight Intel Xeon processors—themselves supercharged versions of the Pentium chip. "I love the eight-way, but it takes forever to boot, and I can't carry it around."

Linus then went on to make an important point. The Transmeta platform is "also a very cool vehicle for doing debugging," he said, because "when you control the whole chip, there are lots of interesting things that can be done." That is, because the x86 processor was created by Transmeta's new Code Morphing Software—which he helped to write—Linus was able to get inside the processor and examine and even hack around with the way the Intel family worked; this was a powerful and unprecedented mechanism for software designers.

Even Ditzel had underplayed this aspect, limiting himself to an interesting anecdote. It concerned a Transmeta customer in Japan who needed a bug fixed in the processor itself (chips are in some ways just software that has been turned into silicon and need to be debugged like programs). "Normally," Ditzel explained, "to get a new CPU [processor chip] would take weeks of fabrication time, testing, and shipping it to them." The design of the chip would have to be modified, and then new realizations in silicon produced, tested, and sent out to Japan by air.

"What Transmeta did was to send them a new CPU over the Internet. In fact, we simply e-mailed it to them," Ditzel explained. This was possible because bugs in the silicon could be worked around by modifying the Code Morphing Software. Sending updates to the Code Morphing Software was as simple as sending a patch to any piece of software. "Crusoe is the only CPU that is software-upgradeable over the Internet," he went on.

This was the real innovation of Transmeta: The company had managed to turn the closed, black-box chip of Intel into a hackable piece of technology. It was half way to producing a chip that could be changed at will; it would need only to release the source-code to the Code Morphing Software and anyone could reprogram the chip—in just the same way that anyone could reprogram the Linux kernel to suit a particular need.

Not that Transmeta was contemplating such a step. One of the ironies of Linus's move to Silicon Valley was that it saw him working for a hypersecretive company that produced closed-source products. The point was that it had come up with a radically new approach that included what might be called the open-source chip as a possibility.

Linus's enthusiasm for his new job doubtless accounts in part for a slightly more leisurely pace of kernel development. In 1996, before he joined Transmeta, there had been over one hundred versions of the kernel released, including no less than sixteen in April alone. In 1997, at the beginning of which Linus moved with his wife, Tove, and daughter to Silicon Valley, there were under sixty—still an astonishing number, of course, were it not Linux.

As a result, 1997 might have seemed a relatively quiet year for GNU/Linux. But beneath the surface, much was happening, particularly as far as increasing people's awareness was concerned. An important catalyst for these changes was the appearance of Eric Raymond's essay *The Cathedral and the Bazaar*, which he had finished in January 1997. "One of the first people I bounced the paper off was Erik Troan," Raymond explains. "He was a key developer at Red Hat, and a good friend of mine.

"And he said, 'Wow, you've really got something interesting here, and you should give it at the next conference. And I happen to know that the people at Linux Kongress are looking for good material.' So I sent it to them," Raymond explains, "and they said, 'Wow, yeah, we want you to come to Bavaria and give this paper.'"

The Linux Kongress was one of the most venerable annual meetings in the Linux calendar, and was already in its fourth year when Raymond went in May 1997. It was held in Würzburg, Germany, and other speakers included top hackers such as Dave Miller, Ted Ts'o, and Stephen Tweedie, as well as the publisher Tim O'Reilly.

"When I heard Eric's talk," O'Reilly explains, "I said, this is fantastic, and that was when I invited him to be the keynote speaker for our upcoming Perl conference that summer. I had decided that one of the things that I needed to do was to raise the visibility of some of these programs [like Perl]," he says. "There was just some part of me that was just really irritated by the fact that the computer industry was ignoring these incredibly important people and programs." O'Reilly had been alerted to the rise of free software by a surge in sales of the Perl titles he published. "Eric's thinking certainly shaped mine at that point," O'Reilly says. "We bounced off each other a lot, and so I used some of his ideas in setting up the conference. Really in a lot of ways that first Perl conference was themed around some of Eric's ideas."

The conference took place in San Jose, California, on 20 August 1997. Larry Wall made his first idiosyncratic keynote, which bore the punning and yet descriptive title of 'Perl Culture,' and Raymond read *The Cathedral and the Bazaar*. This time, Raymond notes, there was a subtle difference to the response he received from that of the audience in Germany. "In the intervening couple of months," he explains, "the paper had spread through the culture so rapidly that at the Perl conference there was already a sense of celebration that hadn't been present in Bavaria," where it had nonetheless been received with "wild enthusiasm," as he recalls.

O'Reilly also noticed something at that conference. "At that first Perl conference we had six or seven hundred people and it was kind of the first time that many of these people had ever seen each other," even though "so many of these people had worked together for years over the Net. It was a very, very powerful experience," he recalls.

O'Reilly decided to organize another meeting. "Late in the fall [of 1997] I started organizing a meeting for the spring, which was really this summit, which we called the Freeware Summit. Where I thought, gosh, let me just see if I can get the heads of these various well-known projects . . . together and meet." Those heads included Linus, Larry Wall, Brian Behlendorf, Eric Allman, Paul Vixie and Eric Raymond. Originally planned as a meeting for hackers who were based on the West Coast of the United States, it was later broadened to be more inclusive. Although not the only gap in the line-up—there was no representative from the free BSD variants, for example—the key name conspicuous by its absence was that of Richard Stallman.

"RMS was not invited," Raymond explains. "I argued that he should be, and lost the argument. Tim O'Reilly and the other co-organizers thought he would disrupt the effort to achieve a consensus from which we could go forward." The exclusion turned out to be symbolic. As well as allowing the others to meet and swap experiences, the Freeware Summit signaled a key shift within that world and made explicit a tension that is still unresolved.

It all centered on the word "free" in "free software." For Stallman, freedom is absolutely central to everything he does, and so there could be no question of choosing anything else. But even his admirers have trouble with the word, if not the idea. For example, Bruce Perens has described the GNU GPL as "one of the revolutionary documents of our century." But he acknowledges, "The word 'free' is somewhat intimidating to business in that they think they can't make money if it's free. English has this problem that most of the time when we say 'free' we mean without cost, and the way that Richard Stallman applies 'free' to 'free software' it means 'with liberty.' So he was talking about rights not price; that didn't really come over."

A couple of months before the Freeware Summit, Raymond began looking for a new name that would be less ambiguous than the existing "free software." The trigger for this search was Netscape's announcement in January 1998 that it was releasing the source code for its Communicator browser suite (discussed in Chapter 11). In the wake of this move,

Raymond saw that the free software community had a unique opportunity to exploit the media interest it had generated.

After visiting Netscape at its headquarters in Mountain View, California, Raymond convened a meeting at the offices of the GNU/Linux hardware company VA Research, at that time also located in Mountain View, on 3 February 1998. "I put forward the proposition that we needed a new label that was less threatening to the mainstream," he remembers, "and we brainstormed it and we came up with 'open source.'"

Those taking part included Raymond; Larry Augustin, the CEO of VA Research; John "maddog" Hall, who was there by telephone for part of the meeting; Sam Ockman, from the Silicon Valley Linux User Group; and Christine Peterson, president of Foresight Institute. Raymond explains, "The Foresight Institute [is] a bunch of thinkers who are concerned about nanotechnology," building machines on a molecular scale, "trying to bring it into existence, and trying to control it so that we use it properly." It was Peterson, he says, "who actually came up with the term 'open source.'"

One of the main items of business for the Freeware Summit organized by O'Reilly, which took place on 7 April 1998, in Palo Alto, was to find an alternative to the name "free software" that all the leaders present were happy to rally behind. Suggestions included not only the newly coined "open source," but also "freeware," "sourceware," and "freed software." After some discussion, a vote was held, and "open source" won.

In addition to the name, Raymond had also come up with the idea of an Open Source Definition. He wanted something that allowed licenses other than that of the GNU GPL, but that still promoted the key ideas behind free software. The same issue had been confronted by the Debian group a year earlier. As Perens, who was Debian leader at the time, explains, "We wanted Debian to be 100 percent free software, and at the time we sort of knew what free software was from the philosophy of Richard Stallman and the Free Software Foundation. But we wanted to be able to accept more licenses than just the GNU one, and we had already put together a system that we thought was all free software, but we hadn't really formalized what free software was."

"So I sat down and wrote the first draft of the entire Debian Social Contract," Perens says. "I submitted the first [draft] in early June [1997]. We discussed on the private mailing list for an entire month, and then we voted it into project policy." An important part of the Social Contract was the Debian Free Software Guidelines, which, Perens adds, essentially outlined "what we would give back to that [free software] community in return for all of the great programs we were getting from them."

Perens explains how the Open Source Definition came about. "Eric Raymond called me up," he says, "the day after the meeting at which the term 'open source' had been coined. Raymond explained the thinking behind the new name, and said he was looking for definition to go with it. When Eric called me, I said, 'OK, that sounds like a good idea, let's trademark "open source" and let's bind it to [the] Debian Free Software Guidelines; we'll call that the Open Source Definition.'" Little needed to be changed: "I did not make any substantive changes to the document," Perens says. "I only changed it from Debian to make it general."

The Open Source Definition lays down nine criteria that the distribution license of software must meet to be called "open source." The first three—the ability to distribute the software freely, the availability of the source code, and the right to create derived works through modifications—enshrine the basic characteristics that lie at the heart of the new software methodology. The other criteria spell out ancillary requirements; for example, they ensure that the license does not discriminate against persons or groups or fields of endeavor (such as business), and they close loopholes that might otherwise be exploited.

In a press release issued before the Freeware Summit, the software projects it embraced were called "freeware"; after the summit, another press release called them "open source" ("sourceware" was also mentioned). The reason given for the shift is significant: "While this type of software has often been called 'freeware' or 'free software' in the past, the developers agreed that commercial development of the software is part of the picture, and that the terms 'open source' or 'sourceware' best describe the development method they support."

That is, the meeting represented a conscious attempt to make comprehensible and acceptable to software companies what had hitherto been something of a fragmented and fringe activity. This was an important repositioning. The leaders present at the Freeware Summit had agreed that to drive the uptake of their software further they needed to adopt a more business-friendly approach—including an easily remembered and understood name. In other words, a brand.

Richard Stallman has always viewed this shift with alarm. "The open source movement is Eric Raymond's attempt to redirect the free software movement away from a focus on freedom," he says. "He does not agree that freedom to share software is an ethical/social issue. So he decided to try to replace the term 'free software' with another term, one that would in no way call to mind that way of framing the issue.

"In the GNU Project," Stallman emphasizes, "we want to talk about freedom, so we continue to describe our software as 'free software'; we do not use the term 'open source.' Raymond hopes that using the term 'open source' will convince existing software companies to release useful programs as free software. This is useful when you can do it, but what our community needs most is to be full of users who value their freedom and will not easily let it go."

There was little that Stallman could do to prevent the others from carrying out what amounted to a rebranding exercise. The marketing aspect of the summit had been one of the key considerations even while it was being planned. "As we thought about it," O'Reilly recalls, "we said, gosh, this is also a great PR opportunity—we're a company that has learned to work the PR angles on things. So part of the agenda for the summit was hey, just to meet and find out what we had in common. And the second agenda was really to make a statement of some kind about this was a movement, that all these different programs had something in common."

At the end of the summit, a press conference was held. Nothing could symbolize better the new approach than this phalanx of top hackers facing the press for all the world like the board of some conventional corporation. O'Reilly recalls that "the basic message was, you guys [in the press] are talking about 'are you going to beat Microsoft?'—and I said, look at these [open source] guys. Every one of them has dominant market share, with no money, nothing but the power of their ideas, and this new model. And I went down the list and said look, here's Apache, here's Sendmail, all these programs that are the market leader. I said, so tell me this isn't a winning model."

The Freeware Summit was a key moment in the history of free software. And as Eric Raymond points out, "One of the things that was interesting about it was [that it was] the first intentional act of community." All the key players—except for Stallman—had not only agreed to operate collectively but had also sketched out the strategy for growing this new community.

The summit and these decisions would have important long-term effects, but even in the short term they produced a heightened awareness among the media. That awareness was furthered at another meeting, which would also have direct and significant consequences, held in Silicon Valley three months later.

Called the "Future of Linux," it was organized on 14 July 1998 by the Silicon Valley Linux User Group (SVLUG) at the Santa Clara Convention Center, with support from Taos, a company offering interim staffing in the Unix and Windows NT fields, and VA Research. As the report on the user group's Web site explained afterwards, it took the form of a panel discussion that offered "some frank talk about things Linux needs to be able to do and barriers Linux needs to break through." Among those on the panel was Linus, who was obviously able to attend such meetings more easily now that he was a resident of Santa Clara.

Also present was VA Research's Larry Augustin. "It was an incredible event," he recalls. "The room held 800 people or so," Augustin says. "We had standing room only, around 1,000 people packed in. To me, that really stands out as the point where we were able to convince a lot of people that this was for real, that there were a lot of real users out there. It was that event that was the catalyst for a lot of things happening."

In addition to plenty of hackers, there was a large press turnout. In August, the *San Francisco Gate* ran a report on the July 14 SVLUG meeting together with an interview with Linus conducted the following week. August 1998 also saw at least three major features: in two computer titles, *Computerworld* and *Sun World,* and in no less a business magazine than *Forbes*.

The article, which was called "For the Love of Hacking," was the most important coverage for the movement yet, and even featured Linus on the front cover. It dealt not only with Linux but also with Apache, Sendmail, Perl, Richard Stallman, and Eric Raymond. *Time* added its own contribution to the high-profile and heavyweight coverage in October 1998 with a feature called "The Mighty Finn." Compared even to six months earlier, this level of press coverage represented a considerable shift; but it turned out that a heavy price would be paid for Linus's new-found celebrity.

When Linus moved to Silicon Valley, there was concern that he would have difficulty maintaining the febrile pace of development that the Linux community had come to expect. After all, he was moving to a new country to take a job at a start-up company, and he had recently become a father. Surely, many feared, it would be impossible for him to devote as much time to Linux as before.

It is true that the pace of development had slowed somewhat, but there was no evidence that Linus was having difficulty coping. As well as being a great coder and an even greater leader, Linus was also a virtuoso at sustaining a remarkably challenging and multifaceted life style.

Now, though, came additional demands on his already thinly stretched energy and time. As he became something of a media celebrity, so he devoted more of his time to giving full-scale interviews or answering journalists' questions as they struggled to understand this (to them) strange and alien Linux phenomenon. As if all that weren't enough, in spring 1998 a second child, Daniela, was born to Linus and Tove. As many parents with several children will confirm, the second child often comes as a shock in a way that the first does not.

In the face of this steadily mounting pressure, it would have been miraculous had Linus carried on as smoothly as before. As it turned out, he was stretched to breaking point, and 1998 saw the Linux community facing an even more serious crisis than the Net wars of 1993; indeed, this crisis threatened to split and perhaps destroy the pivotal co-operative spirit that had pushed Linux so far and so fast. In September 1998, there loomed the terrible threat of a fork.

Large-scale forking is generally regarded as a kind of fratricidal civil war, the worst thing that can happen to a hacker community and to be avoided at all costs. Forking is quite different from the ideological differences that exist between the supporters of, say, the original free software movement and the newer open source; it is not only possible but common for people from both sides to work together on a single project. In effect, there may be a rainbow of ideologies involved in a given project. A fork, however, is an either/or matter, and unless the two opposing camps manage to effect a coming together, a process called "healing the fork," the divergence between them is likely to grow and the gulf become ever more unbridgeable.

One of the most famous forks in the free software world took place in 1993, not in Linux but in Emacs, when a group of hackers decided to start their own Emacs development line, separate from the work led by Richard Stallman. Among the leaders of this group was Jamie Zawinski, who had been involved in free software for many years and was one of the senior figures at the Freeware Summit in April 1998.

Speaking from that bitter experience, he says, "Forks are really bad." It was a decision that he and the other hackers took only with extreme reluctance. "We felt that we had exhausted all our other options," he explains. Unfortunately, Zawinski sees little chance that the Emacs fork will heal: "They've diverged too far, and the cultural and technical differences still exist."

The "cultural and technical differences" were compounded by the slow development of GNU Emacs 19, which frustrated some Emacs users. Various people tried to speed the process by contributing to the development, but as Zawinski explains on his Web site, "our attempts to help the FSF complete their Emacs 19 project were pretty much a disaster, and we reached the point where we just couldn't wait any longer. So we bundled up our work on GNU Emacs 19, called it Lucid Emacs, and released it to the world." Richard Stallman has a different view of the episode. "Zawinski and others wrote major changes in [Emacs] without even telling us. When I found out and phoned Zawinski, he told me that their plans were already half implemented and it was too late to accept any input from us; he said he expected us to use all their changes precisely as supplied and refused to adapt them in any way to make them do what we wanted. If their aim was to help, they ought to have started by talking with us about how to proceed."

The events that brought Linux perilously close to a fork show interesting parallels to the Emacs situation. The events of autumn 1998 were triggered when Linus was unable to keep up with the flow of patches that were being sent to him; as with the XEmacs split, "cultural and technical" differences arose between the two main factions.

Things began in the most innocent way imaginable. On 28 September 1998, Michael Harnois, a kernel hacker, posted a simple technical question to the Linux-kernel mailing list, long the key debating chamber of the inner core of top hackers. Harnois asked:

Am I the only one for whom "2.1.123 fbcon.c" doesn't compile?

That is, he wanted to know why a small piece of code didn't work in version 123 of the 2.1 development kernel. As is usual, somebody soon came along with an explanation for the problem, and attached a patch that would sort things out.

But then another hacker, Geert Uytterhoeven, stepped in and said

Please don't waste your time on creating these patches. These things are functional in the "vger" tree.

"Vger" has entered into Linux mythology, and refers to a computer located at Rutgers University that ran the Linux-kernel mailing list, among others. It was set up by Dave Miller when he was studying and working there. Miller explains how this came about. "The [mailing] lists which existed when I showed up were run in Finland," he recalls, "and were starting to reach a state of being unmaintained. People began to complain, the lists worked only every other day, you couldn't get responses to help unsubscribe when one had problems, etc.

"So I asked my co-workers [at Rutgers], 'Can I run a few small mailing lists here on this old machine that doesn't get used much?' The response was something like, 'Test one, and if no problems show up you can add the others.' I think they all were moved over to Rutgers within the next two weeks or so," Miller continues. "The machine's name at Rutgers has always been vger. Vger sounds like a funny name, doesn't it? Remember Star Trek, where the spaceship named 'Voyager' flies past the screen, and some of its letters had been scuffed off? The remaining letters spelled out VGER. Hey, I'm not a Trekkie and I hadn't named this machine, but it's an interesting Linux history tidbit, I suppose."

Vger was also used for running a program called Concurrent Version System (CVS). This is special software that is used to manage software development; essentially, it allows people to keep track of the current state of a project, for example, which patches have been applied. It is widely used, and is a boon for keeping on top of a complex and fast-moving project such as Linux. Uytterhoeven's message that things were "functional in the vger tree" meant simply that the patches had been applied to the code in the CVS system on the vger machine. There was only one problem: Linus did not use CVS on vger.

As a result, when replying to the previous message about not wasting time creating new patches, Linus wrote:

> He's not wasting time.
>   I have stopped synching up to vger a _long_ time ago. Anybody who still thinks vger has _any_ relevance to the standard kernel is very much misguided.

Linus no longer bothered to look at whether the snapshot of the Linux kernel held on vger matched up with the one he was working on.

One of the people running the vger site, Cort Dougan, wrote:

> We're painfully aware of this. We do sync up with you though, so the vger tree does have what he needs along with your changes.

To which Linus replied:

> Note that saying "it's in vger, so you're wasting your time" is still completely and utterly stupid. The fact that it is in vger has absolutely no bearing, especially as there's a _lot_ of stuff in vger that will probably never make it into 2.2.

That is, patches had been entered into the vger CVS system that Linus was not going to take; therefore, the snapshot of the kernel was still out of sync with his, despite Dougan's efforts and those of others. This meant the kernel held there had elements that would not be used in the official release of the upcoming 2.2 version of Linux.

After Linus's comments about not syncing with vger, the specter of a fork was raised by Kurt Garloff:

And you think it's a good idea to have the linux community divide into to parts: The Linus party and the VGER party? One of the problems of free software is to have one version accepted as the standard one and to have people fix this one and not their highly customized one. Don't do that!

This time, Linus responded to the question at some length, beginning:

No. I've tried to tell the vger people that.
   The problem is that some people think that once they are in vger, they're golden and no longer have to worry. Those kinds of people I don't care about, I don't want to hear about, and I refuse to discuss with.

A few hours later, Martin Mares brought up the issue of having patches ignored:

Some time ago, you promised you'll accept a single large video patch before 2.2 and I did send it to you, but I got ignored.

Dave Miller then pointed out to Linus that it was this large video patch that was at the root of vger's difference from Linus's code:

everyone who maintains the video driver layer is telling you "look at Martins patch," nothing more. If you continually ignore him, you are the roadblock, plain and simple. So instead of being a roadblock, please express your grievances about Martin's attempt to merge things with you.

Miller then went on to describe what he saw as the central problem:

Stop pointing fingers towards "vger," people are sending you patches, continually, and are being ignored and not being told why _even_ after you had told them you would accept such a patch for the video subsystem.

Garloff voiced a growing fear to Linus about where all this might lead:

I see, it's not your fault.
   I still think that you and DaveM and some others should really take care to prevent a split. I think it's worth some effort.

We all know that there are and will be splits. But the problem is that vger is sort of important, because some really strong people use it (DaveM . . .)

Seems it's hard for some of the vger people to accept that you are still the Maintainer of the official release.

But please spend some time to have this cleared. And please tell us, what the outcome of this is and whether one should care about vger, if we want to fix things . . .

But his comment, "I see, it's not your fault" provoked Miller's wrath:

Bullshit, nobody has told him "Linus, go look at vger and take that code," this is utter crap and want this claim to cease immediately.

He reiterated his view that the basic problem was Linus's dropping patches:

People have been trying over and over to send him a patch which fixes bugs and gets the drivers/video directory sync'd up driver wise for other architectures, which he said he would put in, and over and over this person is being flat out ignored by Linus.

Responding first to Martin Mares, Linus wrote:

The reason I'm disappointed is that vger in particular has been acting as a "buffer" between me and bug-fixes, so that now we're in the situation that there are obviously bugs, and there are obviously bug-fixes, but I don't see it as such, I only see this humongous patch.

and concluded:

I'm going to ask David once again to just shut vger down, because these problems keep on happening.

At this point, Ted Ts'o, perhaps the most senior Linux lieutenant in length of service, and therefore a figure of considerable authority within the movement, entered the debate with comments and wise words addressed to Linus on the subject of what Ts'o termed "bandwidth constraints," which referred to Linus's inability to keep up with the flood of patches.

To be fair to the vger people, one of the problems which the vger CVS tree is trying to fix is that sometimes you don't take patches very quickly. There's been at least one set of . . . patches which I had to send you two or three times before you finally accepted it—and they were short patches (1-3 line changes in 4 files), and with a full explanation of what it did. Heck, in the most recent case you and Alan [Cox] and I discussed different approaches for solving this problem before I even started coding the patch.

So we have a problem, and perhaps vger isn't the best solution. . . . But before you go slamming the vger folks because this patch batching effect which you don't like, it might be nice for you to acknowledge that some of your bandwidth constraints may have contributed to the problem, and they were simply trying to find a way around it.

What had begun as a simple question about an obscure bug some forty hours earlier had turned into an increasingly heated argument raging across two continents and ten time zones. Suddenly, Linus has had enough.

First, he fires off a shot directed specifically at Dave Miller:

Quite frankly, I just got very fed up with a lot of people. David, when I come back, I expect a public apology from you.

And then adds one for everybody else:

Others, look yourself in the mirror, and ask yourself whether you feel confident that you could do a better job maintaining this. If you can, get back to me, and maybe we can work something out.

In one last message a couple of hours later, he first explains why he dropped Ted Ts'o's patches (and so, by implication, of everyone else's, too), and then issues one dangerously exasperated statement of annoyance:

Note that if some person cannot be bothered to re-submit, I don't WANT the patch. Anybody who is not willing to take that much care of his patches that he can't maintain it while I haven't accepted it, I don't want to accept patches from anyway.

   The basic point is that I get a _lot_ of patches, and I have to prioritize my work. That means that I require people who send me patches to keep at it until they make it into the kernel.

Quite frankly, this particular discussion (and others before it) has just made me irritable, and is ADDING pressure. Instead, I'd suggest that if you have a complaint about how I handle patches, you think about what I end up having to deal with for five minutes.

Go away, people. Or at least don't Cc me any more. I'm not interested, I'm taking a vacation, and I don't want to hear about it any more. In short, get the hell out of my mailbox.

From these exchanges, nobody could mistake the dire state of relationships between the key hackers on the kernel mailing list.

A few hours after Linus's final posting, Eric Raymond added his comments on the situation.

People, these are the early-warning signs of potential burnout. Heed them and take warning. Linus's stamina has been astonishing, but it's not limitless. All of us (and yes, that means you too, Linus) need to cooperate to *reduce* the pressure on the critical man in the middle, rather than increasing it.

He points out one central fact for the Linux development process:

Linus is god until *he* says otherwise. Period. Flaming him doesn't help, and isn't fair—and you need to have been the key man in development of a must-never-fail piece of software before you even have standing to *think* about doing it.

But Raymond is also unsparing in his analysis of the broader effects of what has been happening:

Patches get lost. Patches get dropped. Patches get missed. This is bad and wasteful in itself, but it has a secondary effect that is worse—it degrades the feedback loop that makes the whole process work. . . . The effect of rising uncertainty as to whether good work will make it in at all is certainly worse than that. Anybody who starts to believe they're throwing good work down a rat hole will be *gone*. If that happens too many times, we're history.

In other words, Linus's dropping patches too often was not just inconvenient but undermined the very mechanism that powered the open source development model.

Raymond concludes with a warning couched in characteristically graphic and appropriate terms:

These risks are bound to get worse over time because both system complexity and the developer pool are increasing. And the critical man in the middle—the "Jesus nut" in our helicopter—has a stress limit. We're going to hit that limit someday. Maybe we're pushing it now.

He concludes:

I've been worrying about this problem for months. (I'm our anthropologist, remember? It's part of my *job* to notice how the social machinery works and where the failure modes are.) I was reluctant to say anything while it was still theoretical, but I take the above as a neon-lit warning that it's damn well not any more.

Raymond was not the only person observing these developments with disquiet. "There are some of us, myself among them, that have been worried about this for a while and are working on a solution," commented Larry McVoy—author of the original Sourceware document and now one of one of the most committed Linux hackers—the day after Linus announced his "vacation."

Like Raymond, McVoy had a memorable way of describing the situation: "The problem is that Linus doesn't scale," he wrote in his posting to the Linux-kernel list. This is a sly reference to one of the common accusations against Linux: that it does not scale up to handle enterprise-level tasks. McVoy then went on: "We can't expect to see the rate of change to the kernel, which gets more complex and larger daily, continue to increase and expect Linus to keep up. But we also don't want to have Linus lose control and final say over the kernel, he's demonstrated over and over that he is good at that."

As well as an analysis, McVoy thought he had a solution, or at least the blueprint for one. His idea was to create a new piece of software that addressed the growing problems of kernel development.

He explains why he was willing to go to such efforts to resolve the problem back then in the autumn of 1998. "If you look back at my view of how the Unix vendors splintered," he says, as explained in his Sourceware proposal, "and how that was universally a bad thing for the source base itself, and the product itself, my point of view was the worst thing that you could do to a project is split the source stream. There's nothing worse. Two leaders, doesn't work."

McVoy provides a little more background on what nearly led to this happening for Linux. "Linus has an overload mechanism," he says, "and his overload mechanism is you send him mail or patches or whatever, and he just drops it on the floor. He just deletes it with no acknowledgement—no negative acknowledgement, no positive acknowledgement, it just gets deleted out of his mailbox: I don't have time to deal with this right now.

"The result of this was that people would get frustrated with [Linus] because their patches were getting dropped"—even to the point of threatening to fork. This time, however, it was much worse. Alan Cox and Dave Miller, the two most senior lieutenants, were seriously contemplating taking this drastic action as a result of their growing frustration. Something had to be done.

"It started to become obvious to me," McVoy says, "that one way to solve the scaling problem was to put tools in place that would essentially make the development process kind of a star [shape], with Linus in the center, surrounded by a ring of lieutenants, and these lieutenants surrounded by a ring of flunkies, maybe the flunkies surrounded by a ring of flunkies' flunkies, but the flow of the information is through this star, and there are filters. So that you end up with Linus getting stuff that most of the time he doesn't have to work on very hard, because somebody he trusts has already filtered it."

This is roughly what has been happening for some years; but McVoy emphasizes, "It was very informal and it was with the lieutenants doing all the work. Linus had to still sort of browse over the work and there was no mechanism put in place." McVoy thought he could do better by using the formal source management software he was proposing, which he called BitKeeper; but first he had to sell the idea to the key people involved.

"So I had this vision," McVoy explains, "that gee, source management would solve all the world's problems, let's get these guys together. And so it took a lot of arm-twisting, but all of them ended up coming up for dinner one day—they were spread out, but all of us were in the Bay area." Because Linus now lived in Silicon Valley, such a meeting was possible, if still exceptional.

"Miller was extremely influential in making this meeting happen," McVoy recalls. "Because it's hard to get Linus to take time out to really focus on something unless he considers it very important. He was frustrated and a little burned out, and Miller basically said come to this meeting or we're splitting the tree. I don't know if he said exactly those words, but he certainly applied the pressure and I wouldn't be a bit surprised if he did say exactly those words."

Adds Miller, "I got very frustrated and emotional about the whole ordeal; I'd lost my mind and my common sense. Things were working in slow motion; we'd been in a development series kernel for nearly two years with no end in sight. Linus was overextended and he was probably just as frustrated as the rest of us about how backed up and busy he was with other things. Linux is his baby, so I'm rather confident about that statement. I'm pretty sure that he just didn't have the time to allocate what was needed during this period, he had so many other things happening in his life."

Miller then goes on to make an interesting point: "Really, when [Linus] has the time to put towards it, nobody can keep up with him. So in the end, the issue really wasn't so much a 'Linus doesn't scale' thing as it was a 'Linus has too much other crap happening in his life right now' thing"—involving a complex mix of his work at Transmeta, his growing family, and those increasingly demanding journalists.

"It was an evening session," McVoy says of this critical meeting. "They showed up by probably somewhere between 5 and 7 in the evening. Linus was pretty frustrated and burned out. It was a very tough time for him. And legitimately so, right? Everybody viewed him as a superhuman guy, and everybody wanted him to drop what he was doing and pay attention to their patch, and nobody had really realized yet that wait, this guy is human, there are limits to what he can do. Because so far there had been no limits.

"I think we talked technical stuff before we hit dinner for a number of hours," McVoy adds, "and then talked a number of hours after dinner." Miller recalls: "Initially, the discussions were procedural, about what things we were doing as developers that made more work for Linus, and how we could alleviate some of that.

"Then I started describing how I thought this [BitKeeper] stuff could work," McVoy continues. "And it took several go-arounds; I think it took a couple of hours. I described the architecture, and I described how information would flow through it, and how this would solve problems." Miller was supportive: "Dave was pushing anything that would help the process," McVoy says. "[BitKeeper] has a lot of the kinds of things we need," Miller explains. "And I'll say one thing, Larry really listened to Linus about what he'd like if he ever used BitKeeper for managing the Linux kernel sources."

As to whether Linus will use the system for day-to-day work on the kernel, McVoy says, "I get the impression that Linus will use it—he's stated what he will do." But on one important condition: "He will use it if it's the best," McVoy notes. "The best in his mind is not better than anybody else's; the best is the best, as good as it could possibly be. The question is, where's his bar? His bar's pretty high. How close am I to reaching that bar? Well, I don't think I'm there yet, but I'm damned close."

In September 1998, BitKeeper 1.0 lay far in the future. Meanwhile, other measures were put in place to relieve at least some of the pressure on Linus. Alan Cox says, "Once we figured out the right way to get patch submissions flowing smoothly, it all worked out fine." During 1999, Linus gradually began to reduce his time with the press, until by the fall of that year he had more or less ceased to give interviews. Eric Raymond says, "One reason I took on the 'minister of propaganda' role was so Linus himself would be able to do less of it."

Against this background, what is remarkable about the "Linus does not scale" episode is that nobody outside the Linux world noticed. Even though the equivalent of a major boardroom power struggle took place—one that might have been seen as exposing a potentially fatal weakness in the Linux phenomenon—the mainstream press completely missed out on this hot story.

The press probably overlooked the story because it played out through the Linux-kernel mailing list. Although publicly accessible, this list is hardly the sort of forum that journalists just discovering open source would be monitoring closely, even though in some senses it represented the interior dialogue within the "brain" of the Linux organism. As a result, the Linux-kernel mailing list functioned rather like the Swedish community's Ankdammen, or Duck Pond, where everybody knew everybody, but where the group as a whole tended to keep to themselves.

The other significant reason the national and general technical press missed the gripping drama being played out in this obscure if important arena was that 1998 also saw an accelerating uptake of GNU/Linux and open source by the giants of the commercial computer world. Reporters were too busy trying to keep up with and understand the enormous cultural shift this represented to be worrying about a few dropped patches.

11

Free the Lizard

WHEN NETSCAPE ANNOUNCED ON 22 JANUARY 1998 that it was making the source code for the next generation of its Web browser software freely available, this not only marked a watershed in the history of commercial software but also represented the final and symbolic coming together of two great currents in the field of computing: the Internet and open source.

As described previously, the main Internet services are run almost entirely by free software on the server side: BIND for the Domain Name System, Sendmail for e-mail, and Apache and Perl for the Web. The rise of the World Wide Web occasioned a battle between open and closed software in the increasingly important area of the client—the browser software that ran on what soon amounted to millions of desktops as the Web was quickly taken up by business and end-users.

The silent struggle begins in October 1991, around the time Linus posted version 0.02 of Linux. At the end of that month, Tim Berners-Lee had inaugurated a mailing list called WWW-Talk for all those interested in the new World Wide Web, which he had only recently released to the public. The following day, Berners-Lee told the members of the list that somebody called Dan Connolly was working on an X11 browser; that is, software to access the Web that made use of the X Window system, also known as X11.

Berners-Lee had written a line browser capable of displaying lines of text along with any hypertext links they contained. This approach was acceptable in the early days because there were no graphics in Web pages. His program ran on the NeXT computer—the machine that Steve Jobs had created after he had been ousted from Apple—which had a small following and employed idiosyncratic software. Berners-Lee was therefore keen to develop a version that ran using the X11 system; this was widely used throughout the Unix community and such a browser would broaden the constituency of the Web considerably.

But there was a problem with Connolly's X11 browser: because Connolly worked for the software company Convex, the code was not freely available. Berners-Lee was trying to persuade Convex to release the source code to its browser, just as Netscape would do six years later.

On the 8 November 1991, Berners-Lee made an eloquent plea for open standards: "The concept of the web is of universal readership. If you publish a document on the web, it is important that anyone who has access to it can read it and link to it."

To make universal readership possible, Berners-Lee called for open standards and "free implementations" of them. He then went on to list some of the advantages that Convex would gain if it made Connolly's X11 browser available to the Web community, and concluded: "I don't know whether your company has a mechanism for allowing code to be released into the public domain (or General Public License). If it is politically impossible, then that's a pity."

Apparently it did prove "politically impossible," as he reported to the mailing list a month later:

> Dan Conolly (Convex Inc) has put together a W3 browser for X but could not release the code. A group of students in Finland were also going to do this for a project—I don't know the status of that work. Anyone who makes a good X11 W3 browser will be very popular.

The "group of students" was not just in Finland, but working under Ari Lemmke, the person who cajoled Linus into giving his kernel the name "Linux" rather than "Freax." There were at least two other X11 browser projects—ViolaWWW and MidasWWW—alongside the Finnish software, which was called Erwise. But it was another that was to prove, as Berners-Lee had put it, "very popular": Mosaic.

Mosaic had been written at the National Center for Supercomputing Applications (NCSA), part of the University of Indiana at Urbana-Champaign. The Mosaic project was led by a young man named Marc Andreessen, who not only became one of the founders of Netscape but played a key role in defining the Web as we know it.

Andreessen's first appearance on the WWW-Talk list is unassuming enough. On 16 November 1992 he asked:

> Anyone written code to construct HTML files in Emacs? I'm hacking something up; let me know if you're interested.

This message is remarkably close in spirit to Linus's early request for information about the Posix standards.

Although none other than Dan Connolly answered Andreessen's question and sent some code that would help, Andreessen had already come up with his own solution. Just a day after posting his first message, he wrote:

> OK, here's a first pass at an html-mode for Emacs. Comments, bug reports, and enhancements are welcome.

The html-mode for Emacs was a way of turning Richard Stallman's infinitely adaptable tool into what would be called an HTML editor today. In fact, Andreessen was one of the top Emacs hackers at NCSA. As an extension to Emacs, his html-mode was naturally released under the GPL, just as Berners-Lee had hoped Connolly's X11 browser might have been.

After this fairly low-key start, Andreessen was soon posting regularly. He quickly became the third most frequent name on the WWW-Talk list, after Connolly and Berners-Lee. On 1 December there appeared what would turn out to be a prescient posting from Berners-Lee, who was sounding a note of mild alarm:

> I am . . . a little worried about the proliferation of implementations. (I know, I'm rather pleased about it too! :-)

He went on to warn against what had already started to happen:

> If you are thinking of a smart extra to EITHER HTTP or HTML then please define it and discuss it here on www-talk. Don't try just to get it out before the next guy. He is probably doing it too, a different way, and these are all exciting ideas which benefit from being hacked around on the net.

As he had emphasized the previous year, "It is important that anyone who has access to [a Web document] can read it and link to it." If standards fragmented, however, this might become impossible; instead of a unified sea, islands of compatibility might result.

Although no one could have guessed it at the time, the seeds of that fragmentation were contained in a posting Andreessen made on 14 January 1993, when Andreessen wrote to the WWW-Talk list:

> People interesting in alpha- and beta-testing a new Motif-based WWW browser at various stages in its development, contact me . . . initially it's hypertext only, but will soon have multimedia capabilities also.

Motif provided a proprietary set of libraries that created a neat graphical interface for Unix. But Andreessen's last comment was the important one. One of the most vexed issues in the Web community at the time was how images should be added to pages written in HTML. Berners-Lee was arguing for a careful exploration of the possible ways of using images and of the implications of the technology employed. As his posting of 14 January had indicated, Andreessen and the NCSA team had already served notice of their intent to proceed—alone if necessary.

Version 0.5 of Mosaic, released on 23 January 1993, was text only, but it was not long before Andreessen indicated the approach the NCSA would be taking to display graphics within the browser. On 25 February, he wrote:

> I'd like to propose a new, optional HTML tag: IMG.

Although this is precisely how images are handled today, at the time it was controversial because it added a new HTML tag, and Berners-Lee was then in the process of formally defining HTML. The last thing he wanted were new tags popping up when he was trying to nail the old ones down. It also raised the spectre of others coming up with their own solutions, and a fragmentation of Web standards.

But as Andreessen pointed out:

> My purpose in suggesting IMG is that things are reaching the point where some browsers are going to be implementing this feature somehow, even if it's not standard, just because it's the logical next step, and it would be great to have consistency from the beginning.

In other words, given that somebody was about to implement his or her own approach, Andreessen wanted to get in early with his own solution and pre-empt the work of others. "It would be great to have consistency from the beginning" was a beautifully judged way of saying "we want everyone to adopt our standard."

On 12 March, Andreessen staked his team's claims more strongly when he announced the imminent arrival of the new browser:

Back to the inlined image thread again—I'm getting close to releasing Mosaic v0.10, which will support inlined GIF and XBM images/bitmaps, as mentioned previously.

Version 1.0 of Mosaic for X followed fairly shortly afterwards, on 21 April 1993, and rapidly established itself as the leading browser for that platform. Versions for Microsoft Windows and the Apple Macintosh were added later that year; and the more widely used Mosaic became, the harder it was for Berners-Lee to resist the new IMG tag for HTML.

It is significant that in the usual academic tradition, the full source code for the X Window version of Mosaic was available for "individual personal use, for use at an academic institution, or for internal business use," yet for the personal computer platforms it was available only for "academic institutions and United States government agencies for internal use."

Commercial use of the Mosaic code was later handled on behalf of the NSCA by a company called Spyglass, which was also based in Illinois, and had been set up by University of Illinois alumni. The agreement between the University and Spyglass was signed 19 May 1994, doubtless prompted by the creation shortly before of a new company that rather cheekily bore the name "Mosaic Communications."

Formed to sell Web technology to the business world, Mosaic Communications was based in Mountain View, California, and had been set up in April 1994 by Jim Clark, the founder of the workstation company Silicon Graphics, Inc. (SGI), and Marc Andreessen. The company not only borrowed the name from the pioneering NSCA browser; it also hired away most of the programmers who had worked on it and the corresponding Web server.

On 13 October 1994, Marc Andreessen made the historic announcement that the first public beta version of Mosaic Communications' product was available: "Mosaic Communications Corporation is making a public version of Mosaic Netscape 0.9 Beta available for anonymous FTP. Mosaic Netscape is a built-from-scratch Internet navigator featuring performance optimized for 14.4 modems, native JPEG support, and more."

Versions were available for X Window, Microsoft Windows, and the Apple Macintosh from the beginning, an indication of the extent to which the personal computer platforms had reached parity with the original Mosaic X11 browser. Similarly, the performance optimization (for 14,400 baud modems) was a signal that Mosaic Netscape was aimed at users outside universities, since those who were in universities would typically have faster links than this to the Internet and would not be using modems.

The most revolutionary aspect of this announcement is probably not even evident today. That a company was not only making a program freely available—there was no charge for downloading Netscape version 0.9, and the program was "free to individuals for personal use"—but throwing open the entire beta-testing process to the general public was without precedent for a launch product.

The announcement reflected Netscape's origins in the university and free software world where this kind of public debugging was standard and, as much as anything else, heralded Mosaic Communications as the first of a new breed of what would soon be called Net companies. Along with a beta-testing program on a scale that was unprecedented, the decision to allow anyone to download copies of Netscape free had another key effect: It introduced the idea of capturing market share by giving away software, and then generating profits in other ways from the resulting installed base. In other words, the Mosaic Netscape release signaled the first instance of the new Internet economics that have since come to dominate the software world and beyond.

At the time, none of this was apparent. One thing that was obvious to the University of Illinois, though, was that it was losing its browser's name and its dominant position in the browser sector. With most of its programmers gone, there was little the university could do to stem the rising tide of Netscape's success, but it could and did take exception to "Mosaic Communications." As a result, the company became Netscape Communications on 14 November 1994: "To further establish its unique identity in the industry and to accommodate concerns expressed by the University of Illinois," as the press release put it.

A month later, Netscape Communications shipped version 1.0 of its flagship Navigator browser and set the single license price for commercial use at $39. It also released two Web servers from its Netsite Web server line. The Netsite Communications Server cost $1,495, and Netsite Commerce Server, which offered secure transactions through new technology invented by Netscape, cost $5,000.

Partly because the company had shrewdly placed details of its secure transaction technology on the Internet so that others could adopt it— and establish it as the de facto standard—Netscape proudly referred to its new products as "open software," by which it meant that it followed open rather than proprietary standards, not that it was open source.

Netscape took the browser market by storm because Microsoft had missed the Internet revolution at first. As late as 1995, when it was preparing for the launch of its ill-fated proprietary Microsoft Network (MSN), it was still dismissing the Internet as too difficult to use and of interest only to academics.

The early beta versions of Windows 95 had no browser element whatsoever, further evidence of how Microsoft had to scramble in this sector. Microsoft managed to produce a browser in time for the launch of Windows 95 on 25 August 25 1995 only by licensing the NCSA code through Spyglass and placing the browser on the Windows Plus! CD-ROM, which was sold separately. To this day, the About Internet Explorer information box begins: "Based on NCSA Mosaic."

Internet Explorer 1 was weak, and despite Microsoft's later and shameless assertions at the time of the first U.S. Department of Justice lawsuit that it was "integrated" into Windows 95, it was just a last-minute addition. If the history of Microsoft shows anything, it is a dogged determination to improve its often inadequate first attempts at writing software, and Internet Explorer is no exception.

Moreover, Microsoft had by now woken up to the full implications of the Internet revolution—it would have been difficult to overlook the stunning IPO of Netscape on 9 August 1995. After opening at $28, Netscape's shares soared to close at $58.25 on the first day, valuing Netscape at nearly $3 billion after barely eighteen months' existence. It was the most successful IPO in history, and probably marked the zenith of Netscape's power and reputation as the leading Net company.

Microsoft's new strategy, however, would soon seriously challenge that power and reputation. In the famous Pearl Harbor Day speech of 7 December 1995, Bill Gates signaled that the Internet would inform everything that Microsoft did henceforth. This speech implicitly placed Internet Explorer at the very heart of Microsoft's entire strategy, and lent a new urgency to its improvement.

The speech also marked the beginning of what were called the "browser wars," when Microsoft and Netscape tried to outdo each other with successive releases of their Web software for end-users. The first casualty in this struggle was not so much truth as standards—continuing a sad tradition that had begun with the first release of Mosaic. Berners-Lee's dream of a unified, universally accessible Web looked more distant than ever.

Internet Explorer 2, released on 27 November 1995, was not much better than the first version, but version 3, released on 12 August 1996, was close to achieving parity with Netscape Navigator. Because Internet Explorer was free of charge, whereas Navigator had to be paid for by corporations, Internet Explorer's market share started to rise, and with it the credibility of Microsoft as a Net company.

By late 1996, it was clear to people within Netscape that the company was in trouble. One of those thinking deeply about this and related issues was Eric Hahn. Hahn had arrived at the company only recently, in November 1995, after Netscape had bought his start-up, Collabra. "I spent the first four months pretty close to full-time on integrating Collabra into Netscape," Hahn recalls, but after that, "I began to work with Jim [Barksdale]"—the president and CEO of Netscape who had taken over from Jim Clark in January 1995—"on special projects since I had some extra time and I didn't really have any other job," Hahn relates.

This collaboration led to a series of white papers that analyzed the growing malaise at Netscape and proposed radical solutions. "Each document took this relatively narrow topic and presented a completely different view on the issue than was prevailing," Hahn says, "and that was why they were called Heresy Documents"—his own name for them, chosen, he says, as a way of defusing what were otherwise "pretty serious challenges to the thinking" within the company.

Given their controversial nature, the Heresy Documents were circulated confidentially, at only the very highest levels. "It was very inner core," Hahn explains. "They were written very, very freely and openly—no punches were pulled." That inner core consisted of Netscape's executive committee: Jim Barksdale, Marc Andreessen, Mike Homer, who was executive vice president of sales and marketing, the chief administrative officer, Peter Currie, and Hahn.

The first Heresy Document dealt with Netscape's Java strategy. Sun's Java allowed a program to be written once and then run on many kinds of hardware without modification, which made it perfect for Internet use—and also undercut the dominance of Microsoft's Windows platform. Originally, Netscape started writing all its own Java software, but Hahn proposed dropping Sun's own implementations straight into the Netscape browser.

"That was a very controversial document," Hahn recalls, "and it basically received a lot of negative commentary," because many people within Netscape had rallied around the platform-independent Java as a weapon against Microsoft. As late as 26 August 1997, Netscape had issued a press release announcing its intention to create a "100% Pure Java" version of Navigator "by 1998"—a version of its browser written entirely in Java. Later dubbed "Javagator," it never saw the light of day. The idea of throwing all that work away was not popular. "But six months later we did exactly that," Hahn notes, "and that gave me the impetus to write number two" in the Heresy Document series, and several others that followed.

Some of the most important of these, and certainly the ones that had the most dramatic effect on Netscape and the outside world, addressed the issue of Netscape's declining share of the browser market, and proposed not only giving away Netscape's flagship product Communicator (an extended version of the original Navigator browser) to match Microsoft's zero price tag but also releasing the source code.

"I don't know that there was an epiphany or an event" that triggered this idea, Hahn says. Rather, "every week we would wake up and watch our browser market share erode, so it was clearly a front and centre issue for almost every employee."

Instead, the idea had gradually evolved in Hahn's mind. "I had become quite enamoured with what was going on with Linux, and I'd begun to take interest in those things," he recalls. "Eric Raymond's paper [*The Cathedral and the Bazaar*] was clearly influential," he notes, but it was just one more factor for Hahn.

As with his Java Heresy Document, these ideas initially met with much resistance.

"The [Heresy Document] that talked about the browser wars said anybody that thinks . . . we can afford to not win the browser war is wrong. And that obviously was an indictment of some very important people," Hahn notes—Marc Andreessen, for example. In 1997, Hahn explains, "Marc was very vocal that the browser war didn't matter, Netscape wasn't interested in fighting the browser war." For about six months, Hahn says, "there was [an] . . . incorrect and short-lived belief that we could be browser-agnostic and that what really mattered were our servers. And I was running that [server] division for some of that time and I knew darn well that, without the browser on the desktop, the servers didn't have any great place in a customer's mind. It was a very hard sell, compared to everybody else selling servers. It really was the browser plus server link up that was the strategic advantage."

It took considerable courage for Hahn to re-affirm the pivotal importance of the browser to Netscape's strategy because his own relationship with Andreessen was anything but adversarial. "Marc and I had a very,

very great relationship," Hahn emphasizes, "all throughout this period, a lot of mutual respect and support."

"And I had told Marc," Hahn says, "that under no circumstances would my role as CTO"—chief technical officer, a post Hahn was appointed to 10 October 1997, replacing Andreessen, who took on the nebulous role of executive vice president of products—"or publishing these documents ever be positioned as undermining his judgement. If there was controversy, I thought it was more important for the company to follow one clear message from Marc than it was for there to be any division in the executive ranks. So even when he and I disagreed, as we did for a while regarding Linux, and open source and a couple of others, these documents had to be carefully controlled because they would point to a pretty big difference of opinion."

In this situation, few executives would have persisted with their brutally frank analyses of the situation. Fortunately for Netscape, Hahn found himself in a unique position. "I had nothing to lose," he says. "I was completely vested for my shares"—following the purchase of Collabra. "I'd always felt a little bit the outsider there, because I came in through an acquisition, so I didn't have any organizational agenda, or advancement agenda. I really was in a great spot to be cavalier."

And just as Hahn's decision to contradict his fellow board member by emphasizing the critical importance of the browser was unavoidable, if personally difficult, so was the action that needed to be taken: releasing the source code for Netscape's browser.

"If you worked the logic of it," Hahn says, "it is an unassailable conclusion, I think." The conclusion may have been "unassailable," but it was still a huge step for the company to take. Fortunately, it turned out that Hahn was not alone in pushing this radical solution. "If I were to summarize it, I would say that it wasn't any one individual or one document or one meeting in which it was, quote, decided. There were, I think, three strands to the rope cord.

"Jamie Zawinski and all of the folks who'd been working in the trenches had been thinking about this for some time and obviously were intrigued by it for a variety of reasons," Hahn continues. There was also "a gentleman named Frank Hecker [who] had the great advantage of being outside the kind of headquarters influence: He was out in the field, with real customers, and sales people, and I think had been with the company a very long time, and had a lot of credibility."

Before he joined Netscape as employee number 20, Jamie Zawinski had long been involved with free software. "I guess you could say I've

been doing free software since I've been doing software," he explains. Zawinski had been one of the leaders in making the painful decision to fork
the Emacs code in 1993.

Zawinski joined Netscape in June 1994. He says, "That was like a
month or two after the company was founded; there was basically no
code written yet." His task was to create the X Window version of what
would become Netscape—and to do it just a few months. On his personal Web site, Zawinski has placed excerpts from his diary at the time
in a piece called "netscape dorm." As he writes there: "This is the time
period that is traditionally referred to as 'the good old days,' but time always softens the pain and makes things look like more fun than they really were. But who said everything has to be fun? Pain builds character.
(Sometimes it builds products, too.)"

"Netscape dorm" provides a vivid picture of what those heady early
days at Netscape were like: "I slept at work again last night; two and a
half hours curled up in a quilt underneath my desk, from 11 A.M. to 1:30
P.M. or so." And, "I just got home; the last time I was asleep was, let's see,
39 hours ago."

It was around this time that alongside his feverish coding Zawinski
made another important contribution to the company. "We were sitting
around a conference table—this was probably July 1994—trying to come
up with product names," he recalls, "and someone said, 'we need to
crush NCSA like a bug,' since back then, taking away NCSA Mosaic's
market share was our primary goal. I thought of Godzilla. Netscape
Communications Corp was at the time still called Mosaic Communications Corp. Thus, 'Mosaic Godzilla' [became] 'Mozilla.'"

Although the more corporate "Netscape" was chosen for the final
product name, "Mozilla" lived on within the company, notably as the
name of Netscape's dinosaur-like mascot, and would finally achieve a
glorious resurrection in the open source browser project.

Zawinksi's practical experience of open source meant that he played an
important if unsung role in evangelizing this development process
within Netscape's engineering department. The third key player in the efforts to get Communicator released became interested through Zawinksi's explanations in the private newsgroups that circulated around
the Netscape intranet of why opening up software development brought
considerable advantages.

Frank Hecker had worked for the computer manufacturers Prime and
Tandem before joining Netscape in February 1995. His Unix background
meant that not only was he familiar with the GNU project but had even
carried out ports of parts of it himself. He became technical manager for

the government sales group at Netscape and worked out of an office located in Bethesda, Maryland. In the autumn of 1997, at around the time Netscape was seriously considering producing Javagator—the "Pure Java" version of Communicator—Hecker was reading the internal newsgroups where engineers discussed various issues of the day.

"One of the things that was brought up in the newsgroups," Hecker remembers, "was, well, if you're using Java as a development language, then we're going to have to find some way to obscure the byte-codes because otherwise people could just disassemble the Java and recover the original source code." The byte-codes were the special kind of binaries that Java produced. The point was that it was easy to go from byte-codes to the original Java language source code, something that is difficult to do with compiled versions of programs written in C, for example.

As Hecker explains, "The implication being there that if we're going to release some stuff as Java-based systems . . . we'd figure out some way to essentially obscure the source code or otherwise keep it confidential" because the prevailing wisdom was that commercial software houses never allowed others to see the source code. "To which some other people, including Jamie Zawinski, replied: Why are you bothering with this? Why don't we just release the source code for this stuff and that way we'll get the benefit of letting other people work with it and help us fix it, improve it and so on," Hecker continues.

"And that struck me as a sort of interesting argument," he says. He knew that people such as Zawinski had been advocating this idea for some time. "Jamie and many other people inside Netscape had proposed it at various times over the past few years, from 1994/95 on." But for all their practical experience in the area, the suggestion had never been taken up. Hecker believes he knows why. "One of the problems I saw there was [that] traditionally releasing source code had been proposed by developers," he notes. "It was obvious to them why it was important. It wasn't really clear from a senior management level why releasing source code could be of use because nobody ever made the business case."

This was what Hecker set out to do in a comprehensive document, which he called "Netscape Source Code as Netscape Product," begun in August 1997. This "somewhat obscure title," Hecker says, "[reflected] my opinion that Netscape should consider treating source code as a product delivered to Netscape customers in the same sense that binary versions were considered products. I felt that proprietary software vendors treated source code as this magical mystic thing—'the crown jewels,' 'the secret sauce'—and as a consequence had a negative reaction when the subject of releasing source code came up.

"If the business benefits of releasing source code outweighed the benefits of keeping it private then companies should seriously consider whether, when, and how to release source." Although logical, this viewpoint was nonetheless radical for the time.

The document also spelled out in detail the various ways in which money could be made from open source software. This emphasis on the commercial rather than technical advantages of releasing proprietary code freely was doubtless the reason it proved such a powerful auxiliary for Hahn when he was making his case to the Netscape board.

The combined efforts of Hahn, Hecker, and Zawinski culminated in a meeting at Barksdale's home in the fall of 1997. Present were the executive committee and Roberta Katz, Netscape's corporate counsel. It was something of a marathon session, and open source was by no means the only item on the agenda.

Although no formal decision was taken at that point, it was nonetheless a key moment. "I think what happened," Hahn says, "was between Jamie and his group's work, Frank Hecker's work and that meeting, we had things sort of supersaturated. There were people at that meeting who really hadn't internalized what open source really meant, and so to go from not really understanding it or not really knowing about that whole model to saying 'yes, let's do it' in one meeting was unrealistic. But I do think it primed everything so that in the weeks that followed we sort of were marched down that path."

Barksdale's approach to what might have seemed a life-or-death decision for the company he ran is striking. "Jim never took an active role in strategy," Hahn recalls, "in product strategy or even business strategy. He really left it to his executive staff to kind of mull it over, and for a winning view to emerge. Then he would get behind that and really help the company execute on it. I don't know that he ever had superstrong opinions on any of these topics. If he did, he never voiced them."

Barksdale was not the only one who got behind the decision, once taken. "It was very hard to get over the hump of flipping some switch," Hahn explains, "but once it was flipped, there was no resistance. The company was on a jihad to get it open sourced, and Marc, and Jim, and Mike Homer, and everybody else—even people who maybe were not so excited by it early on—they were supportive and encouraging."

Although this "jihad" had enormous positive benefits on a company increasingly depressed in the face of the Microsoft's mounting successes, Hahn did not allow himself to be swept along too much by the surrounding excitement. He knew only too well what the company was really doing. To explain his position to others, he would tell a story:

"Two guys go camping, and they're barefoot, and they run into a bear. And one guy stops and puts on his sneakers. And the other guy looks at him and goes: What are you doing? You can't possibly outrun a bear. And the first person says: I don't have to outrun the bear, I just to have to outrun you."

Hahn explains, "I think that's the view that I had about the open source strategy and Netscape. I'm not sure everybody got the message that open source was some sort of wonderful magnificent new thinking, but it became uncontroversial because it was way better than what we doing prior to that [on the browser side]." He notes, though, that Netscape "never got there on the server," where products remained resolutely closed source.

Hahn also says, "We may not have really gotten it, but, boy, we were encouraged to keep going by the Internet and that was a very, very powerful force." The positive response from the Net community had been one of Hahn's subsidiary aims in proposing that Netscape take Communicator open source. "One of the motivations in the Heresy Document for open sourcing it," he explains, "was the observation that Netscape historically was much more successful in the market when it was perceived as the underdog against the Evil Empire.

"We had clearly lost our underdog status; we had been arrogant, obnoxious, and downright insensitive to the technical backbone of the Internet that had really thought the browser was cool in the first place. So this move was in part designed to reposition the company as humble and needing people's help, and wanting to be a team player so that we could all fight the good fight against Microsoft. And that worked very well. The day we announced, there was a deluge of positive enforcement from the market."

The announcement was made 22 January 1998. It began: "Netscape Communications Corporation today announced bold plans to make the source code for the next generation of its highly popular Netscape Communicator client software available for free licensing on the Internet. The company plans to post the source code beginning with the first Netscape Communicator 5.0 developer release, expected by the end of the first quarter of 1998. This aggressive move will enable Netscape to harness the creative power of thousands of programmers on the Internet by incorporating their best enhancements into future versions of Netscape's software."

The announcement introduces an idea hitherto viewed with great skepticism by computer businesses—that of the distributed, global development process that lies at the heart of GNU/Linux and other major open source projects—as if it were the most obvious and natural thing in the world. For a high-profile company such as Netscape to give its stamp of approval in this way was extraordinary.

It was entirely appropriate that Netscape, of all companies, took this step. Netscape had already changed the rules once with its first product, Netscape 0.9. By effectively offering a free download it already drew on the online world to speed up the debugging process and spread the word further in one of the first examples of viral marketing. Making Communicator 5.0 open was the next logical step: a product that was truly free and would, or so it was hoped, be developed in partnership with the entire Net community.

In taking the code open source, Netscape was at last giving Tim Berners-Lee the browser he had been asking for since 1991, and adding the last piece in the Net's free software jigsaw puzzle.

Netscape's announcement did all these at least in theory. But taking the decision to make the source code of Communicator 5 freely available was one thing, and difficult enough; creating a working program—never mind one capable of taking on Microsoft's increasingly polished Web browser—was quite another.

One of the key areas to be addressed involved the license. The press release announcing the release of the source code had promised that "the company will handle free source distribution with a license which allows source code modification and redistribution and provides for free availability of source code versions, building on the heritage of the GNU General Public License (GPL), familiar to developers on the Net."

Netscape had rightly understood that open source development only worked if the licensing terms were couched in such a way as to encourage others to contribute. Its invocation of the GNU General Public License, by far the best-known of the various licenses in this area, was a further sign of its good intentions. Coming up with a license that met the needs both of Netscape and of the hacker community whose aid it was trying to enlist proved a challenge, however.

The person charged with this was Mitchell Baker, who was associate general counsel at the time. "I became involved at the meeting of the Netscape executive staff to make a decision is this something we want to do or not," she recalls. This was in January 1998, just a few days before the public announcement.

The implication was that Netscape was prepared to take this momentous step without knowing which form one of the key pieces—the license under which the code was released—would have. Baker confirms this: "Netscape was self-selected for people who could live comfortably in that setting."

To help draw up the license, the company involved many open source luminaries, including Linus, Richard Stallman, Eric Raymond, and Bruce Perens. Raymond describes the meeting with Netscape at this time as a "tremendously impressive experience" because it was clear that they really "got it." He says the people he met were "intelligent" and "hip" to the issues, and that, most impressive of all, there was no "primate posturing" of the kind he had feared when entering such a corporate environment.

The GNU GPL was not a practical option. Had Netscape simply released Mozilla under this license, software used in conjunction with even part of it would automatically have become GPL'd because of the way the GNU GPL worked. Neither Netscape nor the third parties were able to accept this.

In the end, two new licenses were drawn up, the Netscape Public License (NPL) and the Mozilla Public License (MPL). Mozilla had now been chosen as the official name of the new project, as a further press release dated 23 February 1998 explained: "Netscape Communications Corporation today announced the creation of mozilla.org, a dedicated team within Netscape with an associated Web site that will promote, foster and guide open dialog and development of Netscape's client source code."

Jamie Zawinski recalls, "My first reaction, a few hours after I heard the announcement [to make Communicator 5 open source], was to go register the domain mozilla.org." The creation of a separate identity for the project was an important step in reassuring potential developers that this was not mere window dressing, and that Mozilla really would be independent. It was also highly appropriate that for what amounted to a return to Netscape's roots, it should adopt the coders' original name for its browser.

Despite the complication they represented, two licenses were necessary to resolve an intractable legal problem. Some of the code in Communicator was used elsewhere by Netscape, and some had also been licensed to third parties. The Netscape Public License was used for Netscape's programming and was GPL-like in many respects, but it gave the company special rights to allow the code to be supplied to third parties without passing on its GPL-like properties. It also enabled Netscape to include the initial Communicator source code in other products that would not be subject to open source requirements for two years.

Through newly created newsgroups that were thrown open to all for discussion of licensing and other matters, another unprecedented step for a software company to take, Netscape tried to convince potential contributors why it needed special rights. "We had a discussion through the newsgroups," Baker recalls, "and explained OK, this is why in the NPL stuff those rights are important and why we think we need them.

"And many people came to the point of saying, well, OK, I can sort of understand that for the code that you're releasing," she recalls. "And if I fix bugs, or make some minor contribution to that code, OK, maybe it's OK you get special rights to some piece of my work; I don't like it, but I can sort of understand that. But if I ever do anything significant that's new to me that I want to contribute to your project there is no way that I will do that under the Netscape Public License.

"And so that made sense," Baker continues, "so we went back and said, OK, we feel we need the Netscape Public License for the stuff we're releasing, but we will create the Mozilla Public License, which is exactly the same except that it has no special rights. And if you want to contribute code to our project—we hope you will—here's a license that doesn't give Netscape anything special. And that seemed for most people to resolve the issue."

Netscape came up with the MPL, which is close to the GPL, because "ultimately we decided we should have a license that promoted community," Baker explains. As well as throwing light on the extent to which Netscape understood the process it was attempting to harness, this emphasizes once more the centrality of a community to open source, and how profoundly insightful was Stallman's early insistence on this element.

Even with these licenses, Netscape was unable to keep all the code that it had licensed from third parties. Unless the owner was happy for it to be released as open source, this code had to be removed from Mozilla, and it left some serious gaps. As the Netscape Frequently Asked Questions (FAQ) on the Mozilla source code explained: "This release does not include the source code for the 5.0 version of Communicator's Messenger, Collabra, or Calendar components. It also does not include source code from third parties that were not willing to have their source code distributed under the terms of the Netscape Public License (for example, Java). In addition, the source code does not include elements that are illegal to export under U.S. law (such as cryptography source)."

These were major elements that had been excised. Messenger provided all the e-mail capabilities, and Collabra was used for reading newsgroups. As a result, the initial release of Mozilla code on 31 March 1998 had gaping holes where core functions had been ripped out.

This did not dampen spirits the following day at what was called the mozilla dot party, whose motto was "free the lizard." The party had been thought up and organized by Zawinski, who acted on his own initiative and picked up many of the costs; entrance was free. It took place at the Sound Factory, one of San Francisco's largest nightclubs. Among the DJs that night was Brian Behlendorf, who was a major figure in the Rave music scene as well as a key player in the Apache group. Another open source icon, Eric Raymond, was there too, and even joined in with his flute during the second set of the Kofy Brown Band, who were playing at the event.

Like the Freeware Summit, which took place less than a week later, on 7 April 1998, the mozilla dot party was another highly symbolic coming together of the diverse open source tribes. But where the Freeware Summit was a meeting of the clan chiefs, the mozilla dot party embraced the rank and file, too. "Open Source, Open Party," as Zawinski had put it in his mozilla dot party dot faq. As did the Freeware Summit, the party generated useful press coverage for what was increasingly perceived as a movement.

On 16 April 1998, Netscape issued a press release in which Tom Paquin, Netscape fellow managing mozilla.org, is quoted as saying, "Since Netscape made its Communicator 5.0 source code available through mozilla.org two weeks ago, we have received an overwhelmingly positive and welcoming response from developers around the world." It gave some statistics: "To date, there have been more than 100,000 downloads of the source code from mozilla.org alone, and an estimated 100,000 downloads from more than a hundred mirror sites located around the world. In addition, twenty-four hours after the source code was released on March 31, the first change was checked in to mozilla.org by a developer."

The press release also recorded the donation of a piece of software that was of critical importance in handling eXtensible Markup Language (XML), a kind of generalized version of the Web's HTML and fast emerging as the most important Internet technology since the advent of Web. James Clark, the technical lead of the main XML working group, had made his Expat program available to the Mozilla project—a considerable boost to its advanced capabilities, and something of a publicity coup.

Another was provided just hours after the source code was released. A group in Australia and the U.K. called Cryptozilla had put back the cryptography elements that Netscape had been forced to rip out because of U.S. export laws. It seemed a vindication of everything the open source community had been saying about how the serried ranks of coders around the world would just step forward and fill in the holes. Hecker's assessment is more measured. Cryptozilla's feat "was not really a surprise," he says. "It was obvious that even with the code removed it would not be all that difficult to put the code back." Moreover, "once they'd done that, they didn't really keep up with the code base, and so that code is no longer useful."

On 15 May 1998, Brendan Eich, who is responsible for the architectural and technical direction of Mozilla, outlined what he called the Mozilla Stabilization Schedule—a road map for Mozilla. He identified 1 September 1998 as the date when "features stop going in and aggressive stabilization begins" so that the code would be in a fit state for release as a product. On 26 October 1998, however, Eich posted a new development road map that announced a radical shift. Instead of taking a key browser component called the layout engine—the code that processes the HTML and displays it on the user's screen—from the current Netscape development, they would throw it away and start again with what he called NGLayout (Next Generation Layout), later dubbed "Gecko." As Eich explained, he had arrived at this decision because of his own views as "mozilla.org technical bigshot," taking into account "the judgment of the module owners"—Mozilla's lieutenants—and, most tellingly, "the fervent wishes of Web content authors," as Eich put it.

Above all, the Web content authors wanted adherence to the standards that the World Wide Web Consortium (W3C)—the independent body led by Tim Berners-Lee—had come up with over the last few years. They included such things as Cascading StyleSheets, which allowed complex Web page designs to be constructed in a clean and conceptually simple way; and the Document Object Model (DOM), which was essentially a method to allow such items on a Web page as headings, tables, etc. to be accessed and manipulated as if they were separate elements.

All these standards were well defined, and their benefits well accepted. But Netscape and Microsoft offered only partial support for the W3C standards, and to different degrees, an unfortunate consequence of the browser wars. This meant that a Web page following standards would look different, sometimes wildly so, according to whether it was viewed with Microsoft's or Netscape's browser; this was a nightmare for Web designers, and ran counter to everything Berners-Lee had striven for in his stewardship of the Web.

Users of the Web had made pleas for compliance with standards before, but this time something was different. By opening up Mozilla development, Netscape had also opened up the decisionmaking process. "That's the way it's supposed to work," as Hecker explains. "If you're going to be inviting other people to be involved in your development process, then you're going to have to expect that they may have opinions of their own which may not in all cases agree with your opinions." In the case of Mozilla, Hecker says, "a lot of people involved in it were of the opinion that it was not the right thing to ship a product." Instead, he continues, they thought that "it was a better goal to ship a product that was based on new code that could be fully standards-compliant."

One person who was not surprised by the decision to write new code was Eric Hahn. "I'm a programmer," he says. "Part of my decision process when I was writing the Heresy Documents is I put on my machine the entire source [for Communicator] and compiled it, played with it, looked at it. I don't write code for a living anymore, but I sure can read it. And I looked at it and I said, this is going to be a tough pill to swallow."

He also explains why it was not possible simply to adapt the old layout engine to make it fully standards-compliant. "Netscape made a lot of technical and coding decisions that were very short-sighted," he says, "and those were cumulative. It wasn't that the engineers weren't smart or anything, or that they were bad programmers," it was something much more fundamental. "It was that the culture was to ship so many things out in such a raw state, and never have the time to go back and fix them."

The decision to rewrite huge chunks of the code over six months after it had been released was a huge blow to many in the Mozilla community. As well as throwing away over six months' work, it also meant, inevitably, that they would not be shipping a product for many months to come. For some, this was unacceptable. The most high profile among these was Jamie Zawinski.

Zawinski had already worried about Netscape's takeover by the online giant AOL, announced on 24 November 1998; he saw it as a further move towards the kind of soulless corporation he had no wish to be a part of. He had written another of his highly articulate and strongly worded think pieces called "fear and loathing on the merger trail," which was published on the mozilla.org site. This had one positive benefit: It called forth an e-mail from Steve Case, the founder and CEO of AOL, in which he stressed, "We're very supportive of mozilla.org."

Despite Case's attempts at mollification, Zawinski's disquiet grew hand-in-hand with the receding launch date for a Mozilla-based product. In the end, the symbolism of the date 31 March 1999, the first anniversary of the Mozilla code release, proved too powerful, and he posted on his personal Web site an essay titled "resignation and post mortem," which contained some of his finest and most passionate writing.

It begins: "April 1st, 1999 will be my last day as an employee of the Netscape Communications division of America Online, and my last day working for mozilla.org." He points out the biggest failure of mozilla.org: "The project was not adopted by the outside. . . . The truth is that, by virtue of the fact that the contributors to the Mozilla project included about a hundred full-time Netscape developers, and about thirty part-time outsiders, the project still belonged wholly to Netscape—because only those who write the code truly control the project."

Zawinksi also singles out what is indubitably Mozilla's greatest achievement. "Merely by being who we are and doing what we did, we played a big part in bringing the whole open source development model to the attention of the world at large. We didn't start the mainstream media interest in open source (Linux did that, mostly), but I think we did legitimize it in the eyes of a lot of people, and we did tell the story very well. Lending the Netscape name to this software development strategy brought it to the attention of people who might otherwise have dismissed it."

But this was not enough for Zawinski. "For me, shipping is the thing," he wrote in his resignation paper. "Perhaps my goals were unreasonable; perhaps it should have been obvious to me when we set out on this project that it would take much longer than a year to reach these goals, if we ever did. But, it wasn't obvious to me then, or now."

Because these things were obvious to both Hahn and Hecker, it is interesting to ask why, despite the manifest holes left by the huge chunks of missing software, and the "intractable" nature, as Hahn puts it, of much of the code that did remain, Zawinski seems to have held on to his "unreasonable" goals. The answer suggests an interesting cultural difference between coding as practiced in the commercial and open source worlds.

Zawinski's diary during the prelaunch days of Netscape, when he was working mad, thirty- and forty-hour shifts, is permeated with a sense of the electric if surreal atmosphere that reigned there, and speaks volumes about the buzz he felt at being part of the entire insane endeavor. Zawinski has memorably described his attitude to GNU/Linux as being a "love/hate relationship without the love," and it might be fair to describe similarly his feelings about the commercial development cycles as a "love/hate relationship without the hate."

Mozilla, and by implication the other major open source projects, did not work like this. The distributed development model means that great progress can happen in a short time, but generally as a collection of short bursts. There is no real sense of deadline as there always is with commercial software development, no sustained day-in, day-out pressure to deliver on time, and the often extended periods between major releases of Linux illustrate this: It took more than two and a half years to move from version 2.0 to 2.2.

By realistic criteria, Mozilla did not fail. It simply failed to provide Zawinski with one of the key elements that made him such a good programmer: the rush born from coding against the clock. In a way, perhaps, he looked for his multi-day programming exploits to be as wild and exciting as the mozilla dot party he had organized. As he looks back, Zawinski admits as much: "I was used to doing things fast: Netscape always did things fast. Mozilla.org didn't. I burned out. I felt ineffectual," he says.

Zawinski's great Web lament exposes something of a paradox at the heart of the open source process, which is rightly perceived as an activity that engenders a tremendous sense of excitement among its participants. And yet the thrill seems to be of quite a different quality from the manic "meet the deadlines at all cost" that pervades the world of proprietary software with its intense competitive pressures. Instead, perhaps, open source offers a creative excitement that is more sustained, if less extreme.

Netscape's rise and ultimate fall is, in part, a monument to the failure of the commercial coding model—and a pointer to fundamental weaknesses in other companies that employ it. As Hahn says, "In Internet time"—which Netscape largely defined—"we never had time to go back" to do things again or properly. Similarly, it was commercial, not engineering, considerations that led to the following of standards in a highly selective manner, if at all. It is therefore deeply appropriate that Mozilla, the spiritual heir both of the open Mosaic and closed Netscape browsers, and guided increasingly by the Net community from which they sprang, should be the first browser to support completely the key Web standards.

Zawinski closes his resignation essay with the following: "My biggest fear, and part of the reason I stuck it out as long as I have, is that people will look at the failures of mozilla.org as emblematic of open source in general. Let me assure you that whatever problems the Mozilla project is having are not because open source doesn't work. Open source does work, but it is most definitely not a panacea. If there's a cautionary tale here, it is that you can't take a dying project, sprinkle it with the magic pixie dust of 'open source', and have everything magically work out. Software is hard. The issues aren't that simple."

His insight that open source is no "pixie dust" has certainly proved true, but his fear about the possible knock-on effects of the perceived failure of Mozilla proved unfounded. The unassailable logic that had persuaded three kinds of employee at Netscape—Zawinski in engineering, Hecker in sales, and Hahn in management—to work towards what became Mozilla was already sweeping through other front-rank computer companies by 1998. The announcement of their support would make the rise of open source not only undeniably visible but seemingly unstoppable.

12

A Foothold

NETSCAPE'S ANNOUNCEMENT IN JANUARY 1998 that it was taking its flagship product, Communicator, open source would not, on its own, have been enough to make the free software programs credible for business. For one thing, the move was so daring that to many observers it smacked of desperation. In this view, Mozilla did not validate the open source approach but revealed it as the last chance for companies with nothing better to try.

Netscape's dramatic experiment may have alerted the commercial world to open source, but it would take the backing of a more established and conservative computer company to turn it into a credible option. That backing was provided, and in the most unequivocal manner, by the bluest of blue chip companies: IBM announced on 22 June 1998 that it would ship the Apache Web server with the IBM WebSphere Application Server, a key component of its WebSphere product family, and offer "commercial, enterprise-level support" for the free software.

Eric Hahn, then CTO of Netscape, was depressed by this bold move; it was, he says, "a very dark day for me at Netscape." A couple of months before, in the final of his Heresy Documents—called, appropriately enough, the Uberheresy—was the almost shocking proposal "that we should phase out the Netscape Enterprise [Web] server and switch to an Apache core, and whatever things we thought were secret sauce, build them on top of Apache.

"When IBM announced that they were doing it," he continues, "it made me realize that IBM, which is a big, historically slow-moving company, got it more than Netscape did." It highlighted his own failure to help refashion Netscape to the point of the company's "getting it" as much as IBM did, the Mozilla experiment notwithstanding.

IBM's decision was probably the single most important boost the proponents of free software could have wished for. At a stroke, it elevated an open source program to the level of commercial software and gave it a key official foothold in the enterprise. It helped turn Netscape's earlier move from the singleton act of a maverick company into a prescient foreshadowing of trends to come—and therefore provided an implicit justification for any software house that wanted to back GNU/Linux or other open source software to do so.

One of the key players in this story was James Barry. Barry was not a long-standing employee of IBM; before joining, he had sold his previous company, the startup ResNova, to Microsoft. The ResNova team had written most of Microsoft's main Web server product for Windows NT, Internet Information Server (IIS), and the Personal Web Server for Windows 95. Coming from outside IBM in this way may well have given him freedom to propose bold new ideas.

"I was being brought in to take a look at IBM's lineup in Web server space," Barry explains. The problem there was that "IBM had almost over forty or fifty products at the time," he says. "You've got a commerce suite, you've got payment suites, you've got store catalogues, and you've got things that interpret [Web server] logs and tell you where your visitors came from, things that hook up to mainframes. And these were all separate software pieces that are on the server side.

"So I came back with a report, and basically said you've got some projects out there that make no sense. You've got a lot of them that do almost the same thing, but they've got a different brand." Barry's first report, which came out in December 1997, contained the proposal that everything be rebranded as part of what he called the WebSphere product line.

During his analysis, he had realized something else. "What's the first thing people do when they come into the Web site? You serve up a Web page," he notes. For that, you need a Web server, and IBM had one. "When I first started working, Internet Connection Server, ICS, was what we called it," Barry recalls. "And then it was branded to Domino Go."

IBM's go-it-alone approach to Web servers had a big problem: "We had like .2 of one percent" market share, Barry says. "Basically 90 percent of the market was concentrated in three Web servers"—from Microsoft, Netscape, and Apache. A negligible market share meant that it was difficult—and expensive—to find staff who were trained to use IBM's solutions; this, in turn, meant that IBM's broader Web offering, which became the WebSphere product line, would be difficult to sell against competitive solutions based on more popular Web servers.

Barry drew the obvious conclusion. "The report came back and basically said, hey, we need to tap into a Web server" offered by one of the three market leaders. "So we looked at those three choices," he says. "You look at Netscape, and actually IBM had a talk with them about acquisition, but that for a lot of reasons didn't work out. Microsoft—a little bit expensive to buy. And so that left Apache." The same ineluctable logic that had led Hahn and others to the conclusion that Netscape should take Communicator open source also pushed Barry to recommend something equally revolutionary: that IBM drop development of its own Web server and adopt Apache.

Many in IBM could not conceive of doing such a thing; this was a problem because, as Barry explains, when it comes to adopting a new policy, IBM is "very much consensus driven—if you have one person who's affected by it down the food chain and they say no, you can't go forward until you get their buy-in." Barry was stuck; he had to try twice to get his idea accepted before he succeeded. He prevailed on the third occasion in part only because he teamed up with someone else in IBM who had independently become convinced that Apache was the way forward—and who was just as tenacious as Barry.

His name was Yen-Ping Shan. Speaking about the qualities needed to make breakthroughs within IBM, he says: "You need to have very thick skin, especially on your backside. You just take the hit, and move on. Focus on the issue and focus on what's the benefit to the company, and to the broader community. And forget about those shots."

Shan explains how he came to be involved with the Apache project. "In early '98," he says, "I was working on IBM e-business strategy, and later on I picked up the chief architect responsibility for e-business tools. Looking at the overall situation, I realized that we really, really need a broad-based Web server share for the entire stack to be successful"—just as Barry had. Shan notes, "Of course, this is not a unique revelation. Many people have come to that conclusion before me, and they even tried a couple of times trying to push Apache, but none of them succeeded."

Says Barry, "Shan was the person who made it successful within the process of IBM." Shan concurs, but modestly underlines the role of others. "I believe I was the one who figured out how, with a lot of help from many friends, to move this IBM bureaucracy. IBM is like a big elephant," he says. "Very, very difficult to move an inch, but if you point the elephant toward the right direction and get it moving, it's also very difficult to stop it. So we kind of joke [in IBM that] figuring what's the right thing to do is less than 10 percent of the effort; 90 percent of the effort is to figure out how to leverage the bureaucracy."

Shan explains his approach. "First . . . I went around and asked people what [they did] and how they failed" in previous attempts to get Apache adopted. Apparently there had been others trying even before Barry's own unsuccessful pitches. "And it turns out that it has to do with timing; it also has to do with the parties that you have to get agreement on. You need to have marketing, legal, and development all in agreement; without any one of them you're not going to go anywhere," because of IBM's rigorous consensus-driven approach.

"So in February that year, I started looking into the situation and I determined that, yes, if we do it right there is a chance for us to push it through," he says. Confidentiality was paramount. "Just imagine that . . . you have a team of sixty, seventy developers working in a lab on a product," Shan says, "and you're investigating ways to ditch the product and embrace open source. If the news get out, you're going to have a lot of resignations. You can imagine how difficult it would be to convince the developers that it is the right thing to do." Not only that, "You want to have developers buy in; you want them to embrace open source and see that as a positive thing and [you want them] . . . to contribute to the open source movement," Shan explains—otherwise the entire exercise will be futile.

Shan remembers thinking that "if you have to convince developers, you have to convince their leaders. So I got two of them, and asked them to join me to analyze Apache."

"I asked them to compare and contrast," Shan recalls. "And when they really dug into it they were surprised by the elegance of the architecture. Of course, it took them a little time to get in there and start having an open mind and look at things from a bigger picture perspective. But they did. So with that, I was able to convince myself that technology-wise this was a go, and at the same time we were pushing marketing and legal."

Marketing and legal was being handled largely by Barry; he and Shan had worked together before. "I met him in various meetings," Shan says, "and I've always thought that he's the kind of guy who knows a lot, and wouldn't mind speaking his mind, and stand firm on what he believes. And he also had a lot of respect for my developers."

He and Barry would spend a lot of time together on the Apache project as they traveled around the various IBM divisions trying to win acceptance for the idea. The point was, as Barry explained tirelessly to everyone they pitched to at IBM, "We can't go in half-heartedly. We can't go in and say, yep, we're going to adopt Apache but we're going to keep our Web server. So what we said is, it's going to be on all the systems.

"IBM has probably more VPs than many other companies [have] employees, so it was a sales job," Barry notes. He was well suited to the task. "I've been at executive levels for a while at different companies, so I know how to talk to the VP level," he says. It went much higher than VP level—to Steve Mills, for example, who was a general manager in the software group. Mills reported to John M. Thompson, who was a senior vice president. It may even have gone higher; Barry believes that Thompson took it to Lou Gerstner, the chairman and CEO of IBM. But the key person was Mills: "Once we had Steve Mills and his people aligned with the fact that we needed to do the Apache move," Barry says, "basically that gave me a heavyweight hammer." At this point, mid-March 1998, Barry and Shan were authorized to make contact with the Apache group.

They got in touch with Brian Behlendorf. He had left his job at HotWired, where his official title had been "Unix sherpa," and was working full-time at Organic, a Web-design company he had helped found. Previously, he had worked there in his free time for no salary, but he had taken up the role of chief technical officer in January 1995, when Organic was able to pay him.

Before Behlendorf could meet up with Barry and Shan, a preliminary had to be dealt with. "We gave Brian a call over at Organic," Barry recalls, "and said, 'We need you to sign an NDA [Non-Disclosure Agreement]. We'd like to talk to you.' He had no idea what we [were] doing. So he signed the NDA, and we flew out to meet him, Shan and I." Shan recalls, "The meeting was March 20, at 6 o'clock in the evening, in a little Italian restaurant right across the street" from Organic, which was based in San Francisco.

Shan and Barry dropped the bombshell at the restaurant. Barry recalls saying to Behlendorf, "'We'd like to adopt Apache as our official Web server.' And he kind of looked at us, like, huh? And he goes, 'Well what does that mean?' [I said:] 'Well, we want to participate in the process, we're going to drop our proprietary Web server and adopt it for all platforms. And we really want to see how we can work with you.'"

Behlendorf recalls, "My first thoughts were amazement and, to a certain degree, yeah they finally get it, right. But I wouldn't say it was a surprise. We'd always thought that companies would start very quietly just by assigning a few engineers to watch [Apache] and maybe contributing here and there, and that it would never be a big marketing kind of thing for them. It would just be a kind of quiet yeah, they happen to use it internally kind of thing. But clearly [IBM] wanted to make a bigger statement with it, and that meshed very well with our own plans."

While some internal legal issues were being resolved within IBM, Shan recalls, "the next step is for Brian to visit the Raleigh labs [where IBM's current Web server was developed]. That was on April 9, just a few days after the first meeting, and we signed confidentiality agreements, so essentially it's open kimono." This meeting would be the acid test of whether IBM's Web server developers—the people who would be working with the Apache community—were willing to replace their work with the vastly more successful open source rival.

"I got my architects on all the Web servers," Shan recalls, "and Brian was there. And they talked technology, and how can we work together. Brian came out of it and said, 'Wow, boy, it would be nice to get you guys involved,'" Shan says. Just as important, Shan recalls, "my lead architect came out and said, 'Boy, this guy knows his stuff, he's great.'" Behlendorf has similarly warm memories of the meeting. "I spent . . . a whole day partly with their engineers, partly with their marketing people, and partly with their business people; [I] explained how Apache worked, and what our objectives were as a group, and how we were organized and things like that. I expected them to be maybe 20 or 30 percent clueful, and it [was] more like 90 to 95 percent clueful because they'd spent quite a bit of time watching us, because everything we do is out in the open"—another benefit of the public development process.

Barry and Shan remain astonished at their own achievement. "I thought it was pretty amazing," Barry recalls. And Shan says, "IBM had not done anything like that before. When I started looking at this, most people would give it [a] one percent chance of getting there. It is a small miracle."

As with the Netscape announcement five months earlier, that "small miracle" attracted a lot of press attention. Barry recalls, "We had almost a thousand articles, and if there's any nay-sayers, they pretty well shut up watching that cascade of good press." Just as Hahn had seen the Mozilla move as repositioning Netscape to a "humble" company, in need of support from the Net community, so IBM's espousal of open source suddenly made them one of the good guys—a company that "got it." The lesson would not be lost on many other software companies that watched first with incredulity and then with growing interest IBM's high-profile PR victory.

As with Mozilla, after the elation came the mundane issue of implementation. "In IBM, the executives got it," Barry explains, "and the programmers got it. But it's this huge mid-level of management that didn't get it. They're being judged by profit and loss. They're being judged by a set of metrics that did not include we're going to give away products."

As a result, he says, "Apache took off and then kind of died within IBM." The problem was that "we couldn't market it separately," Barry explains. "We had to bundle it with stuff that we charged for. From a marketing standpoint, we could have taken a huge advantage, but we didn't. Everything got vetoed because we had to make money on it. We had to bundle it with WebSphere. Everything had to mention WebSphere first, Apache as a 'by the way, we run on Apache.' And as a result, it didn't take off as fast as I had actually hoped."

But there were, nonetheless, concrete achievements even in this disappointing first phase. As Shan explains, "We realized that for Apache to be seen as a serious Web server, there's got to be serious support behind it. So we have to get people mobilized to build an IBM 7x24 support team to make it real."

The issue was absolutely crucial—as its mention in the IBM press release in June 1998 attests. Shan's creation of a "7x24 support team"—one that was on call every hour of every day—removed concerns about Apache (at least for IBM customers) and provided an exemplar for other companies.

IBM's decision to replace its own Web server with the open source Apache was a watershed, but by no means the end of the story. Although the company would release all its contributions to the Apache project as open source (as it had to if it wanted to be part of the process), it was not taking the bold step of converting its own proprietary products into open source as Netscape had done. But that move followed soon after the Apache move, and partly as a result of it.

The person who made this happen was David Shields. He had joined IBM's research division in 1987, after working at New York University for twenty years. "For PhDs in research" at IBM, he explains, "there are basically three job titles: research staff member, IBM Fellow, and Nobel Prize winner."

In early 1996, Shields started collaborating with Philippe Charles on a major project called Jikes. This was a Java compiler that took programs written in the Java programming language and produced special code that could run on any system that supported Java—the basis of Java's much-vaunted platform independence. As a research project, Jikes was made freely available on IBM's alphaWorks Web site, but only as binaries for certain operating systems, not as source code. Initially, GNU/Linux was not among the platforms supported.

"We got the first request for a Linux binary version in May of '97," Shields says, "but for various reasons I didn't pursue it. In June of '98 we got increasing requests for a Linux binary version, and I decided to make another go at it." By July, Jikes was available for GNU/Linux, but still only as a binary.

"That met with a very enthusiastic reception," he recalls, "much more than we'd expected, and as part of that we got requests from users for the source, though I wasn't quite sure what to do about it" because it was unprecedented for IBM to give away the source code of its programs. "I said, 'Well, I'll make an effort at it.'" But he acknowledges that "at that time, I didn't think it would happen."

A Jikes user suggested Shields should talk to Brian Behlendorf, who put him in touch with James Barry. "Looking back," Shields says, "I realize the key step was probably that IBM had gotten involved with Apache in June [1998]." This paved the way for Shields's own efforts, and also provided him with somebody to whom he could turn for practical advice.

"I wrote the proposal in August, and the proposal was accepted by early September," he says. As with Netscape's decision to take Mozilla open source, or IBM's move to adopt Apache, things were made easier because little or no revenue would be lost: "It's nothing IBM would ever even think of selling anyway, so it's not as though we're talking about lost income," Shields explains. He argued, "Why not go for good will and show we're committed to Java, open standards, and all that?

"Most of the time was not convincing management, it was just getting an acceptable open source license. That was very much a process of consensus, because it involved the research attorneys, the attorneys at the software division who dealt with Java, the trademark attorneys, patent attorneys, contract attorneys." One reason for caution was that "all the lawyers involved were well aware they were writing IBM's first open source license," he says. Getting it right now would mean that releasing other software as open source would be easier in the future. The initial Jikes open source license of December 1998 was later generalized into the IBM Public License in June 1999.

IBM's increasing backing for open source, and later GNU/Linux, was undoubtedly one of the major catalysts for the later uptake of both. Its adoption of Apache in June 1998 and its release of Jikes as open source, however, did nothing to alleviate perhaps the most serious shortcoming of GNU/Linux at the time: a lack of enterprise-level software. As well as the headline-making moves of Netscape and IBM, 1998 also saw nearly all the major back-end applications ported to GNU/Linux.

The earliest outing of a first-tier corporate software package running under GNU/Linux predated IBM's Apache announcement by some months. Computer Associates (CA), one of the world's largest software companies, demonstrated a beta version of its Ingres II database at CA World in April 1998.

It was highly appropriate that Ingres II led the charge to GNU/Linux. Ingres II was based on the original Ingres project undertaken at Berkeley—the one that Sendmail creator Eric Allman had been a part of. And as early as 1992, there was a port of that first Ingres. On 24 November 1992, *Linux News* reported that "Zeyd M. Ben-Halim announced a new version of his port to GNU/Linux of Ingres, the relational database manager"; this was barely a year after Linux had first been released. The original Ingres project has since turned into the open source PostgreSQL, which is still being developed.

Computer Associates did not release their public beta until October 1998, and the final supported commercial version did not see the light of day until February 2000, by which time there had been over 3,500 downloads of the beta version, and another 4,000 distributed on CDs.

In the meantime, the other top database vendors announced their support for GNU/Linux in an embarrassing about-turn. A news item in *Infoworld*, dated 6 July 1998, and headed "Linux Not Yet Critical Mass, Database Vendors Say," quoted a representative of Oracle, the leading database company, as follows: "Right now, we're not seeing a big demand from our customers that we support it." The story went on to add that IBM, Sybase, and Informix also had "no intentions of releasing versions of their databases on Linux."

And yet two weeks later, on 21 July 1998, Oracle announced that it would be porting its Oracle8 database to GNU/Linux. A day after Oracle's flip, Informix went even further and released a GNU/Linux version of its Informix-SE database, along with free development licenses. As Oracle had done, Informix proclaimed this was "in response to user demand." The actions of IBM and Sybase were more consistent with their July pronouncements. IBM released a beta of its DB2 database in December 1998, and Sybase remained the most skeptical about GNU/Linux, waiting until February 1999 before announcing the port of its SQL Anywhere database.

Without doubt, Oracle's announcement represented the key move, and the one that began to put GNU/Linux on the map as far as serious business use was concerned. Oracle's policy reversal also came as a relief to many hackers. Eric Raymond says he had been "nervously expecting a massive anti-open-source PR offensive from Microsoft" ever since Netscape's Mozilla announcement. He explains, "I and a few others were successfully gaining public attention for the 'open source' brand, but as long as Netscape stood alone, I knew that a few million dollars backing the right spin could make us look like kooks. The Oracle port announcement changed all that; it made the open-source concept unkillable by mere PR."

The person responsible for overseeing the launch of the GNU/Linux version of Oracle8 was Allen Miner. He notes, "My official title was at the outset 'Vice President of Microsoft Alliance.' So I used to hand out my card and say, 'This is my title, but my real job is how do we beat Microsoft.'"

When "it just became obvious that engaging with the open source community was going to be much more interesting for Oracle and for me than trying to figure out how to get Larry [Ellison, Oracle's CEO] and Bill [Gates] to have a pleasant conversation," his title became the more diplomatic "Vice President of Strategic Alliances."

Oracle had been thinking about a GNU/Linux port well before the announcement in July 1998. "As much as a year and a half or two years prior to that," Miner says, "I had seen from time to time on the internal mailing lists various people, most notably Magnus Lonnroth, advocating that we ought to take a look at this thing." Lonnroth is modest about his role. "I was an early user/supporter of Linux, and I argued that Oracle should release Linux ports as early as 1995," he says, "but I think it would be a mistake to name me as the internal evangelist."

Partly as a result of this advocacy, "we had a skunk-works project creating ports to both Linux and FreeBSD," Miner says, "and Oracle was actually running on the platform as early as a year prior to the announcement." Technically, then, there was no problem in releasing a version for GNU/Linux. "When Magnus and others were saying there [are] customers expressing interest and we think there's a lot of potential here," Miner says, "the reason we didn't support it right away is because it was not clear that we could make a large enough business to sustain an ongoing maintenance team and to build out the technical support capabilities and all that goes into supporting Oracle on a platform. Once we release a port on a platform, we basically commit to support that in perpetuity."

These knock-on consequences meant that the announcement of Oracle's forthcoming port effectively amounted to a ringing endorsement of GNU/Linux's viability in the business world by a company that knew it better than most. Given the magnitude of the commitment implied, it is no wonder that Oracle was initially wary of taking such a step. "A couple of big things that happened in early 1998 directly changed that environment," Miner recalls.

"First of all, something as simple as the community coming up with the label 'open source,'" he says, "and all of the marketing savvy that came into the community about how to position it as an attractive alternative to traditional operating systems and as a new way of creating software as opposed to the more radical freeware movement. The engagement between the open source community and Netscape to persuade Netscape to launch the Mozilla project was a huge breakthrough," he adds, "as was IBM's [decision] to license Apache and to collaborate with the Apache group and integrate that into their WebSphere.

"All of those things gave [GNU/Linux] a huge breakthrough in credibility," Miner recalls. "And with all of those activities it began to become clear to many people in Oracle that in fact this was more than just another freeware platform, that there was a reasonable probability that this could become the next big thing. Then the question just became, I think, more a matter of what is the right time for us to make this announcement, as opposed to whether or not we would. So I think by May there was a group of people within Oracle who, though we were publicly saying we don't have any plans yet, had recognized that it was just a matter of time before we did this."

Miner emphasizes that "there were many factors in the decision" when it was finally made in July. But Larry Augustin, the head of VA Research, believes he knows what tipped the balance. He says the "Future of Linux" meeting in Santa Clara on 14 July 1998 "was the catalyst for Oracle's deciding to announce their intention to port to Linux." He remembers that "the people from Oracle were completely overwhelmed" when they saw the size and enthusiasm of the crowd at that meeting. "Everyone just looked at us and went, 'You know, there's something going on here,'" he says. Miner concedes, "The timing of that meeting is not purely coincidental."

Even at this point, Oracle's CEO, Larry Ellison, was "skeptical of whether this would really be a serious commercial platform," Miner believes. "But he'd been aware that we had products working on Linux and FreeBSD for some time, and to his credit in the end he was supportive of the decision to commercialize it and make the commitment to go ahead and support it not as just as a free give-away unsupported product, which is the approach that one or two of Oracle's competitors took, but as a commercial product with a price and full support."

Miner then adds, "We even took a serious look for some time at [Oracle's] providing support for the Linux operating system itself, because that appeared to be one of the factors slowing adoption in corporate environments. We felt that was perhaps a thing we could do to help accelerate both our business on Linux and that of Linux itself." Oracle eventually decided that the growing support from other companies would meet this need.

Fortunately for Miner and the other advocates of the port, the reaction to Oracle's announcement was unprecedented. "I was amazed at the response to the prerelease of the production CD we put out in October," he says. Although the release was low-key—the company "issued one press release, threw up a page on the Web site," he says—"there were several thousand CDs ordered before the CDs were cut. And no one in marketing could recall ever having had that quick a take-up of a new Oracle platform." Miner says this "certainly gave us confidence that as a movement and a potential marketplace there was a lot more possibility than we had imagined prior to that." It also "was a very good validation that in fact the Linux movement was quite large," he says, "and that it wasn't all just hype and PR, that there were real people out there wanting to do real things with it."

This was good news for Oracle, because its commitment to porting Oracle8 to GNU/Linux also meant that its other key enterprise products would follow in due course. As Miner explains, the corporate approach was "once you do something, you basically do it completely." When Oracle delivered the final version of its Oracle8 database for GNU/Linux on 7 October 1998, it also launched Oracle Application Server. The following year, the company not only released its WebDB product, a "database-powered Web publishing tool for end users," for GNU/Linux but set up an entire business unit dedicated to "develop, market and support Linux software." A press release explained that Oracle's products had "received a phenomenal response from the Linux market, establishing Oracle as an enterprise software leader on Linux with more than 50,000 developers and 800 customers."

As with the moves from Netscape and IBM, Oracle's high-profile commitment to the platform, together with the porting of all of the other top databases, lent yet more credibility to the GNU/Linux system for server applications. This was bolstered even further when the German company SAP announced in March 1999 that it would be porting its enterprise resource planning (ERP) software R/3. The SAP press release quoted Hasso Plattner, cochairman and CEO of SAP as saying, "We have received a significant number of serious customer requests for R/3 on

Linux over the past year. After extensive testing in-house and discussions with our partners and customers, we are confident that Linux meets our standards."

Although little known to the general public, SAP's R/3 is the nearest thing that exists to a global standard for enterprise software. On top of the basic R/3 platform run software modules that handle generic corporate tasks such as payroll and human resources, as well as the specialized requirements of industry sectors such as aerospace, automotive, banking, chemical, oil and gas, etc. According to the company, "SAP has more than 10 million licensed users, more than 20,000 installations in more than 100 countries and supports 28 different languages. More than half of the world's top 500 companies use SAP software."

Microsoft may power the world's front offices with its Office suite on Windows, but behind this desktop veneer, SAP provides the core functions that keep companies running. The announcement of the port of SAP R/3 to GNU/Linux was in some ways the culmination of the growing support for open source that had begun barely a year before with Netscape's dramatic move. The first shipment of R/3 to customers was made on 24 August 1999.

SAP's belief in open source was made abundantly clear through some forthright statements in a FAQ document about SAP on Linux that it put up on its Web site. As part of its answer to "What is Linux or Open Source?" it states, "Open Source is a development method that has good chances of revolutionizing the complete software industry." As to "Why does SAP do this?" the answer is unequivocal: "We expect Open Source to be the software model of the future and Linux to be successful in low- and high-end installations." Lest people accuse the company of not practicing what it preaches, it poses and addresses the inevitable question, "If it's so good, why doesn't SAP go Open Source? In fact, we are currently thinking about publishing selected R/3 kernel components as Open Source to start with."

Alongside these remarkably positive statements in the FAQ, one is more ominous, though apparently innocuous enough. In reply to the question, "Where can I get Linux for R/3?" the document explains that although the Linux kernel is standard, the distributions built around it are not. As a result, "Breaking completely new ground with Linux, we decided to concentrate on one distribution to start with, which is Red Hat. We hope that in the future we will be able to support more than one distribution."

Although not the first occasion that Red Hat had been singled out for preferential treatment in this way, it was certainly one of the most significant, given SAP's central role in companies. Just as SAP's announcement that it would be porting R/3 represented the crowning glory for the GNU/Linux movement as a whole, a sign that it had at last and inarguably arrived in the enterprise, so SAP's choice of Red Hat was near enough an official endorsement of it as the preferred distribution for corporate use.

The roots of this development go back to the end of 1998. Among the crescendo of support software vendors were offering to GNU/Linux in general, a quiet announcement came from Intel that it would be investing in Red Hat. The company may not have made much fuss about it, but the media certainly did. Quite rightly, they saw this as a significant strike against Microsoft, Intel's "partner" in the Wintel duopoly that had effectively ruled the computing world for so many years.

Microsoft had enjoyed the upper hand in the relationship, skillfully forming alliances with Intel's competitors when it needed to cow the chip maker. There had been little that Intel could do to retaliate—until GNU/Linux came along; its stake in Red Hat was the first sign that the pattern of power in the industry was shifting, and that maybe Microsoft would no longer have things all its own way.

Intel's investment in Red Hat, and later ones in other GNU/Linux companies such as VA Research, TurboLinux, and SuSE, may have been a mere moving of pawns in the larger chess game with Microsoft, but it had the important knock-on effect of validating Red Hat, just as Netscape and IBM had done for open source earlier that year, and the database companies had validated GNU/Linux. Where Intel led, others were sure to follow, even if it was simply to add their bets to an outsider that had been more or less unknown to the majority of them until Intel had plucked it from obscurity.

One company that got in on the act early was Netscape, which invested in Red Hat at the same time as Intel. This must have looked like a smart move in the light of what happened, but Netscape had let an even bigger opportunity slip through its fingers. As early as the spring of 1998, in the wake of the company's highly successful announcement that it was taking the next generation of its Communicator browser suite open source, Eric Hahn proposed following the logic of this move even further. He says that his Uberheresy document, written at that time, "was mostly about Linux and open source," and that "it made a bunch of assertions."

"One" he recalls, "is that we should immediately stop all work on Windows NT, because there was no scenario in which our products on NT would prevail over Microsoft. It said we should focus those efforts on Linux." And finally—in what forms one of computer history's more interesting what-ifs—it said, "We should buy this little company in North Carolina called Red Hat."

Instead, along with Intel and the two venture capital companies Greylock and Benchmark Partners, Netscape bought just a little of Red Hat. It proved a good investment: Less than a year later, on the day of Red Hat's IPO, "this little company in North Carolina" was worth over $3 billion.

It was cold comfort to Netscape, though, which had been swallowed up by AOL back in November 1998. Nonetheless, the stunning success of the first open source IPO confirmed the shrewdness of all those bets on Red Hat and its position as the leading GNU/Linux company.

13

Alliances and IPOs

ONE STRIKING FEATURE ABOUT THE 1998 GNU/LINUX announcements was that they all came from software companies; these on their own, however, were not enough to make GNU/Linux fully acceptable to corporations. The backing of hardware vendors was indispensable, not so much because it meant that companies could buy machines with the free operating system already installed, but because such systems would be fully supported. The lack of formal support from recognized companies was perhaps the last serious barrier to widespread adoption of the GNU/Linux platform.

The company to break through that barrier, and to kick off another exhilarating year for the GNU/Linux community, this time with announcements of backing from all the leading hardware vendors, was Hewlett-Packard (HP). The press release dated 27 January 1999, stated, "HP will now provide customers with Internet solutions and services based on Linux," and announced that "an alliance with Red Hat to support Official Red Hat Linux 5.2 on the Intel-based HP NetServer family."

The man behind HP's GNU/Linux moves was Wayne Caccamo, who was a strategic planning manager at the time. He explains how HP's moves came about. "It was summer of '98," he says, "and I got involved not because I was assigned to look at Linux as much as I was generally viewed as someone looking out on the horizon." He describes GNU/Linux at that time as "on the list of nuisance issues that kept popping up on our radar screen, and something that seemed like an opportunity."

Such an opportunity was important to his company. "HP at that time had missed some major technology revolutions like the Internet, and Web on the first wave," Caccamo recalls. "If we were going to recapture the old HP image of an innovative, visionary company, we [would] have to demonstrate that we are on top of some key trends and are proactively rather than reactively responding to them." This meant not just taking chances on things such as open source, but doing it before anyone else.

Caccamo started by reviewing the situation at HP. "I did some investigation around the company on the various activities that were happening that were Linux-related or directly involving Linux. It was pretty clear to me that we had actually a lot of stuff going on. So what I recommended was that we form the Open Source Solutions Operation," he says. Its job would be "to surface a lot of the activity that's going on internal to the company, and knit it together into a cohesive story that we could take outbound to our customer base."

The Open Source Solutions Operation (OSSO) was formally launched on 1 March 1999, by which time HP had already started to "surface" some of its GNU/Linux activity. As well as the alliance with Red Hat, announced in January, HP had also ported its Web JetAdmin peripheral management software. On 17 March, it issued a release that it had "optimized its . . . Kayak PC Workstations for the Linux operating system."

Much more significant than these was the announcement on 20 April 1999 that HP would "provide customers with around-the-clock, worldwide support of Linux and HP Linux applications. HP's new support services include a maximum two-hour response-time commitment, and immediate response for critical calls, on multivendor Intel-based platforms." These platforms were spelt out later as Red Hat, Caldera, Pacific HiTech, and SuSE, perhaps the first official recognition of their status as the top four GNU/Linux distributions, running on servers from HP and "other vendors"—Compaq, Dell, and IBM.

Despite the enormous symbolism of this step—with one of the world's leading support organizations offering what amounted to a safety net for the use of GNU/Linux within companies—Caccamo says, "I don't remember there being a lot of consternation about it" among senior management. Nor, surprisingly, was Microsoft's possible reaction to what amounted to the recognition of GNU/Linux as an enterprise-ready operating system and implicitly as a worthy rival to Windows NT a real issue.

In part Microsoft's muted response was attributable to the scrutiny the company was under as a result of the U.S. Department of Justice's antitrust lawsuit. "I think that maybe the whole situation Microsoft was in [meant] they just weren't in a position to make the phone call," Caccamo suggests. "They've done it in the past, saying, 'HP, we'd appreciate it if you would not do this product introduction'—incredibly ballsy—just amazing that they even have the gall to do that. But they did."

Caccamo believes HP's move "was pretty important," but part of a broader "snowball effect." Before the big announcements of 1998 and early 1999, he says, "Linux was very grassroots within corporations," with support coming mainly from the engineers. "What the IBMs and HPs and SAPs and everybody else did is connect that grassroots movement with more of a top-down management interest" by getting the message across at a corporate level. "And when those two ends started to touch, sparks went off."

Sparks started to fly in 1999 as nearly all the main hardware vendors announced their backing. Almost all of them chose to partner with Red Hat, at least initially, rather than with other distributions, or with GNU/Linux in general.

For example, shortly after HP announced its first alliance with Red Hat, Dell dipped its toe in the GNU/Linux waters. On 4 February, Red Hat recorded that it had "designated selected server and workstation configurations from Dell . . . as certified and compatible with Red Hat Linux." Hardware compatibility had always been something of a thorny issue for GNU/Linux, principally because many peripheral vendors had refused to publish details of their hardware to allow software drivers to be written. The press release also contained the interesting information from Dell that "we have been offering Red Hat Linux preinstalled to customer specification for some time," although it had not made this widely known.

A couple of weeks later, IBM joined the hardware club. A press release announced that "a development lab will be established to maximize performance, reliability, and security for Red Hat Linux on IBM server and client systems." IBM followed this up shortly afterwards with the announcement of much broader support for GNU/Linux. A press release dated 2 March trumpeted, "IBM launches biggest Linux line-up ever." Key points were that IBM would "support major versions of Linux globally" and that it would "work with four commercial distributors of Linux"—the same quartet of Caldera, Pacific HiTech, Red Hat, and SuSE that HP would back even more comprehensively a month later—"to pave the way for comarketing, development, training, and support initiatives that will help customers deploy Linux."

IBM also announced some major ports to Linux. These included Web-Sphere products (the family whose creation James Barry had recommended at the time he was working on the Apache announcement), Lotus Domino, the top messaging and collaboration server, and also a port of GNU/Linux to run on some of IBM's RS/6000 machines.

On the same day, Compaq got in on the act, too; it announced the availability of some of its ProLiant servers preloaded with GNU/Linux. Although it did not specify which distribution it was using, its preference was made clear a week later when Compaq, IBM, Novell, and Oracle invested in Red Hat, adding considerably to the boost given by the first round of investment by Intel and Netscape in September 1998. Separately, on 30 March 1999, SAP also made an equity investment in Red Hat.

HP, IBM, Dell, and Compaq formed the principal group of hardware vendors that made high-profile statements of support for GNU/Linux in 1999, and created strategic partnerships with Red Hat. Two other companies joined the party later; these were SGI, which announced an agreement to provide Red Hat on its Intel-based products on 2 August, and Gateway, which entered Red Hat's authorized reseller program on 7 September.

The reason the top hardware companies—Intel, IBM, HP, Dell, Compaq, SGI, and Gateway—had chosen to work with and often invest in Red Hat rather than in Caldera, say, can be found, perhaps, in Allen Miner's experience when he coordinated GNU/Linux at Oracle. "Red Hat was without a doubt the most active at building the Linux industry," he recalls, "in terms of marketing, in terms of [their] proactively approaching potential partners and working to see that they're involved in all aspects of rolling Linux and other open source out into the marketplace."

Red Hat's CEO, Bob Young, a Canadian, although a permanent resident in the United States, was, more than anyone else, responsible for formulating this strategy. His proactive approach to business partners grew out of an equally direct relationship with the customer that was evident even before he teamed up with the founder of Red Hat, Marc Ewing, at the end of 1994.

In 1990, Young was working for a computer rental company. "Our goal at that time was to get into the Unix workstation rental and leasing business," he explains. But then, as now, Young had some formidable rivals. "I was up against some billion-dollar competitors," he says, "so I would cozy up to the technical users, the Unix user groups in Boston and New

York City and Washington, [D.C.], with the idea that the sys[tem] admins and the programmers would be aware of when they needed equipment even before their purchasing department was. And this way I'd get the inside scoop on their equipment requirements."

Getting close to the users had an unforeseen side effect. "I spent a lot of time with these user groups," Young explains. "I was helping them by publishing a little East Coast Unix newsletter to try and attract more members, because of course it was in my interest to have these user groups be as successful as they could be. So I would ask them what articles should I write in this *New York Unix* newsletter that they didn't get in the big national magazines because I needed a niche. And the story that these guys kept talking about was what they termed—this was back in 1992—free software."

Despite his later enthusiasm, Young was initially skeptical about this new world of free software. "I was somewhat astounded by it because I was a capitalist. You would ask these guys, OK, if all this free software is really better than the proprietary stuff, where does it all come from? And they'd give you answers like it's from engineers according to their ability, to engineers according to their need. And I'm going, yeah, right. I was a skeptic, saying Linux is going to make Unix fragmentation look like choirboy stuff." And yet, he says, "every time I looked around, there were more people using these Linux-based OSes, who were more enthusiastic about it."

By this time, Young had left the rental business. Building on his experience in the Unix market, he entered the mail-order world in March 1993. "I was running a small Unix software distribution business called the ACC Bookstore to pay my bills," he explains. "ACC stood for whatever it did for a living; for example, A Connecticut Computer Company when we were in Connecticut. But it was really designed to get us to the top of any alphabetical listing of suppliers.

"My catalogue was called the ACC PC Unix and Linux Catalog," he says. "The theory was that I would use some of this enthusiasm for this Linux and free software stuff to build a mailing list of customers [whom] I could sell, quote unquote, real technology to. The problem was, my sales of real technology, SCO Unix and this sort of thing, never really took off. But meanwhile my sales of Linux-based products—and they were mostly pretty small sort of low-end primitive technologies, like the Slackware CDs from Walnut Creek, and Linux Professional from a little outfit called Morse Communications—the sales from those products just kept growing exponentially.

"So I started doing some research into it, saying I must have this wrong. There's something going on here that even the people I've been asking the advice of haven't been doing a good job explaining to me." Characteristically, Young's research consisted of going back to his customers. "At this point, I was trying to figure out who were the primary users of Linux," he explains.

His travels around the Linux user groups left him more perplexed than ever. The more users he met, the more diverse his target market seemed to be. "I'm going, OK, let's see, my target market is rocket scientists at NASA or it's blue-haired art students in Toronto," he says, mentioning two of the more memorable users he had encountered. "I'm having problems with this, until later that night I was stewing on this conundrum in my room, and finally the penny dropped."

Young had finally realized "that the one unique benefit that was creating this enthusiasm was not that this stuff was better or faster or cheaper, although many will argue that it is all three of those things. The one unique benefit that the customer gets for the first time is control over the technology he's being asked to invest in." Put another way, open source software provides freedom—just as Richard Stallman had planned from the start. Young's starting-point and overall philosophy may have been poles apart from Stallman's, but the end result has been an almost equally fanatical devotion to freedom for the user.

Young also realized that the real business model for GNU/Linux and open source was selling services, not the product. He knew that he needed something around which to base these services. "I was looking for products to brand," he says. Young found one thanks, once more, to his habit of keeping close to the customer. "I would grill my repeat customers on a regular basis: What other products should I add to my catalogue, what other things do you know about out there that I should be paying attention to?" he says. "And a couple of these guys said, 'Yeah, you should take a look at what this Red Hat guy is doing.'"

Young wanted to move beyond just selling Red Hat as one of many distributions. "I was looking for a product that I could add to my catalogue on some sort of exclusive basis," he explains. Fortunately for Young, Marc Ewing "desperately needed some help selling this thing, because he was starving to death in his bedroom of his small apartment near Duke University in Durham," North Carolina.

"So I call up Mark, and say, 'If my customers are right, yours really is a better Linux than Slackware. I'm selling a thousand copies of Linux a month at this point, mostly Slackware, but a certain amount of Yggdrasil.

You know, I should be able to switch-sell 10 percent of my customers, so send me three hundred copies.' I get dead silence at the end of the phone. Turns out he was only thinking of manufacturing three hundred copies a month.

"After this conversation, we recognized we had a perfect fit," Young notes. "He needed some help selling the product, and I needed a product to brand. So about sixty days after that, we formally merged our two little businesses. My little company called ACC Corp bought all the rights to Red Hat from Marc, in return for a bunch of shares, and subsequently changed its name to Red Hat Software" in May 1995. Young had the brand he was looking for.

Combining Young's business acumen and Ewing's technical skills, the new Red Hat began to win a following among the hacker cognoscenti. It started winning awards, too; for example, *Infoworld's* Product of the Year award for 1996. Young says that nobody was more surprised than he and his colleagues.

"We tied with Windows NT 4.0," Young recalls, "and we're going, hold on, there's twenty-three of us down here in the tobacco fields of North Carolina, and the best Microsoft can do with a three-year head start, with a thousand of the world's smartest operating system engineers, and with a billion-dollar budget is to tie us for this award? What's wrong with this picture?" The secret, of course, was the distributed development system built around thousands of hackers who worked to make the components of Red Hat's GNU/Linux distribution so good.

Young and the others at Red Hat may have been surprised by the award, but they were also delighted, because they hoped that it would propel them to the next level: corporate acceptance and sales. And yet this did not happen. "When we won [the *Infoworld* award] for the '97 year," Young explains, "we actually realized we had a problem.

Because here for two years in a row—and the second year we won it outright up against Microsoft—the industry was recognizing that we were building better technology, but everyone was choosing Microsoft nonetheless.

The problem was that at that point there were thirty-five of us, down in the tobacco fields of North Carolina. And push come to shove, if you're going to make a decision for which infrastructure you are going to use to build your Oracle application stacks for your corporation, you're not going to do it on thirty-five guys in North Carolina when you have the choice of the world's most profitable, most successful technology company offering you what they claim to be a much better alternative.

It didn't matter how big we got, we could become twice as big, we could become ten times as big, and we would not overcome that problem. So what we realized is we had to partner ourselves; we couldn't become big enough, but we sure could partner ourselves with the industry who was beginning to take notice [thanks to the Netscape Mozilla project, IBM's Apache announcement, and the rest]. Customers no longer thought of this as Red Hat Linux from your little Red Hat. They would think of it as Red Hat Linux from Dell, running Oracle databases, supported by IBM's global support team. And suddenly the customer goes, 'Oh, OK, that makes sense to me.'

And so that's very directly what led us into the conversations with Intel and Netscape. On my whiteboard at work for the whole of 1998 was a list of the top ten technology companies on the planet in order of size and influence. In that initial round for September '98, we targeted Intel on the hardware side, because they were the guys who had the influence; all the hardware was being built against Intel chips. On the software side, it was much more difficult because it was sort of earlier stages for the software companies. We ended up picking Netscape simply because they had, at that time, the most influence. And they had also opened the source code to the Netscape [browser] technology and clearly were making a commitment in our direction.

The Intel connection brought Red Hat more than money, or even corporate credibility, Young recalls.

Intel, back in March of '98, were the guys who really stressed a particular concept. Their line was, the success of technology platforms has relatively little to do with the guys selling the operating system, and a great deal to do with the success in building out an ecosystem around that operating system.

In other words, Microsoft might be the most profitable supplier in the Windows market place, but they earn a small share of the total revenue of that industry when you start adding up all the support organizations that exist, all the application vendors from Oracle to Corel, Computer Associates, Symantec, all these guys. And then you add all the hardware guys in there in that sort of ecosystem, you recognize the reason you can get almost anything done with a Windows-based computer is because there's some vendor out there who can help you do it.

And what Intel reinforced, but we recognized—in part because of winning this *Infoworld* product of the year award for the second time—was that we had to build out this ecosystem. And that's where we spend a lot of time these days, with the largest technology vendors [as Miner had noted appreciatively] because all the smaller technology vendors tend to follow the lead of the Oracles, and the Computer Associates, and the IBMs.

Young still spends most of his time with vendors and companies, evangelizing the benefits of this ecosystem, of open source. In many ways, it's the perfect job for someone who talks endlessly and entertainingly about a subject dear to his heart. Promotion of his company is surprisingly restrained, although Young is always happy to don his trademark red hat for photo shoots: "I have a business card that reads Red Hat Spokesmodel," he says in gentle self-mockery. But his apparently selfless devotion to the broader cause of open source has some hard-headed business logic behind it.

"The moment we get across this point that Red Hat's brand stands for this commitment of delivering open source technology to the marketplace, then we create massive opportunities for Red Hat's sales team," he says. "If I can't do that, it doesn't matter how much our sales team brag about their products being better, faster, and cheaper, the customer is going to say, 'I can buy it from little Red Hat or I can buy it from big, safe Sun, or Microsoft' and we're going to end up losing the bid."

"Little Red Hat" is not so little now, at least based on market capitalization, which accounts for much of Young's successful approach. On 11 August 1999, the day of its IPO, Red Hat's shares shot from $14 to $52 at the close of business; those people "down in the tobacco fields of North Carolina" now had a market value of $3.5 billion.

This was a notable success, and not only for Red Hat. Just as the investment of Intel and Netscape had provided the first, high-profile validation of Red Hat and therefore of GNU/Linux, so the wild ride of the Red Hat stock was also implicitly a vote of confidence by investors in GNU/Linux and open source. The victories and achievements of Red Hat have been gains for the entire commercial GNU/Linux world.

This halo effect, where the success of one open source company benefits the others too, is nothing new; it made Caldera's pioneering efforts to move GNU/Linux into the corporate environment in 1994 so important. Caldera can claim much of the credit for paving the way for the string of successes during 1998 through its careful nurturing of software retailers and vendors, and its sponsoring of ports to GNU/Linux. Ironically, Caldera's trailblazing meant that it gained least from Netscape's announcement in 1998 that it was taking its browser open source, and its later moves to embrace GNU/Linux as a server platform.

Caldera had worked with Netscape throughout 1997 to offer various products on GNU/Linux. On 7 February 1997, it announced that it would port Netscape's FastTrack Server, the company's entry-level Web server, and Navigator Gold (which would later become Communicator), and these were released on 18 August of that year. Then on 15 December 1997, just a month before Netscape made the Mozilla announcement, Caldera issued a press release in which it described its "exclusive agreement to provide Netscape core server and client software to the Linux community." It also noted that as part of the agreement, "Caldera has the rights to license Netscape software on [its distribution] OpenLinux to other Linux providers."

Ransom Love, who took over from Bryan Sparks as CEO of Caldera in August 1998, and who like Sparks was a former Novell employee, explains the situation. "The only reason we got an exclusive license was because Netscape wanted us to pay them millions of dollars because they did not see any future in Linux at the time. And consequently, we said, 'Well, if we're going to pay you millions of dollars, we have to have a way of recouping this.' And then they turned around and published the client for free" Love points out, "literally weeks after they signed the agreement," when Netscape announced its plans to release the Communicator source code. Netscape's move made it impossible for Caldera to sell client licenses to other GNU/Linux distributions.

This was not the first time Caldera had paid the price for being too early with its innovative ideas. When it launched its first product, it had added to the then plain GNU/Linux a smart graphical user interface. "The Caldera Network Desktop was a Visix desktop product," Love explains. "That's another one of the things that we brought to Linux to try to create more of a validation in the business space." Visix's code, however, was proprietary. "Many of these technologies that we were using to try to create solutions were owned by the companies at the time," he says. "We were trying to kind of leapfrog the process of having to develop everything from scratch. We knew that Linux even then was stable enough for business, but you needed to create a total product"—a running theme in Caldera's strategy, just as the ecosystem is for Red Hat.

Many hackers took exception to what they saw as the pollution of free with proprietary software. Love emphasizes that "business didn't care," they just wanted a solution. "But we did get a lot of criticism, and people were concerned then that Caldera was trying to take Linux proprietary. And they couldn't be more wrong. Because we never had an intention. Never have, never will."

Bob Young regards this willingness to compromise over proprietary software for the sake of creating a "total product" as a fatal mistake for Caldera, the reason that Red Hat, with its unwavering commitment to open source, eventually became market leader. "Bryan Sparks and Ransom Love are friends of mine; they're just princes of human beings," Young stresses, "but as businessmen, as entrepreneurs, [they] spent too many years of their lives at Novell." As a result, Young believes, they still had something of the mindset of conventional software companies.

"Caldera put themselves into a niche," he says, "because they kept saying, 'OK, we understand how open source builds better technology. And we can build a better operating system using this open source and aligning ourselves with all these engineers, but the only way we can make money is to surround this thing with proprietary, added-value components of our own'"—such as the Visix desktop, for example. Love disagrees with this analysis, and also disputes that Red Hat is ahead in market share in the corporate sector—Caldera's main focus. "If you look at business market share, I think the numbers would be quite reversed," he asserts.

Whatever the truth of the matter, Love is surely right about one thing: "We're just getting into true business development and deployment of Linux on a mass scale. So we're right at the tip of the growth curve when it comes to business. The real businesses are kind of all at the point of OK, what do I do with it, how do I deploy it?" he says, "and they need a solution. They need applications, they need support, they need education, they need all these components that make it more viable."

Many seem happy with the strategy. On 10 January 2000, Caldera announced that together with other investors, Sun and Novell were putting money into the company. In March, Caldera made its IPO. Although the shares did not show the same heady gains as Red Hat's—opening at $14 they closed at $29, valuing Caldera at around $1,100 million—the market conditions were quite different. Red Hat's shares, too, were well down from their peak in December 1999.

Love's holding in Caldera should be some consolation to him for the rocky ride he has had with the company so far. It turns out that Caldera's unhappy knack for spotting the key trends ahead of everyone and never being able to capitalize on them goes back a long way—to that original Corsair project at Novell.

Love fills in some details of what he and Bryan Sparks were doing with GNU/Linux back in 1994. "This was back in days of Mosaic Communications; Netscape hadn't even got their name yet," Love points out. "We had created a graphical browser interface that was a virtual world. Using color maps, we could actually point and click and navigate the network. You could go from department to department, within the corporation, or an intranet, by clicking on a map. And you could grab the information you needed without having to understand the complexities of the network itself."

Sparks and Ransom Love had come up with a tool for browsing through information whose navigation model—a virtual world—has not been matched by today's products, never mind those of 1994. "It was funny because we had the Mosaic folks come out," Love says, "and they couldn't get their jaws off the table."

Novell's management had no inkling of what was running down in their labs. "They would have owned the Internet space," Love says simply. But Novell shut down the project; because of its stubborn refusal to fully embrace TCP/IP's open networking standards, the company became increasingly marginalized by the Net instead of owning it. In this sense, Caldera (the word means a volcanic crater, particularly one whose breadth is far greater than the current vents of lava) is a sadly apt name for a company that represents a kind of noble relict of the even more powerful ideas its founders had dabbled in at the beginning.

Novell was also the impetus behind the creation of an outfit that would eventually become the third major distribution in the GNU/Linux Gang of Four, Pacific HiTech.

Pacific HiTech's founder, Cliff Miller, had led a pretty adventurous life up to that point. Born in San Francisco, he had lived in Australia for a year as a child, and then went to Japan for two years, where he stayed with a Japanese family and attended a public school. After he moved back to the United States, Miller attended college, and spent a year in Macedonia, then a part of Yugoslavia, to further his studies of the Macedonian language. "I finished my BA when I was nineteen," he explains, "and then a year later got my MA in linguistics as well," and adds with what amounts to something of an understatement, "I tend to be pretty intense, and just get through things as fast as I can."

Miller's life then took a different turn. "I went to work in a salt factory, and then in the Wyoming oil fields for a little over half a year, driving a big truck." But Miller succumbed to the lure of Asia, one of the fixed points of his world, and returned to Japan to teach English there. He then moved to China, where he taught English at a science university and met and married his wife, Iris, a native of Beijing who speaks fluent English and Japanese.

When the couple returned to the United States, Miller says, he "worked at Xerox for a while, in their multilingual software group. At the time I didn't know much at all about computers and programming, but was really interested. I applied to a number of schools and got accepted into graduate school in computer science, with scholarships at the University of Utah."

In 1992, when he had started a PhD at Utah, Novell had made Miller's wife redundant after it acquired the company where she was working. Rather than look around for another job, Miller and Iris started a new company, Pacific HiTech, in their basement. "Our initial aim was to sell U.S. or Western software into the Japanese market," Miller explains—a business they were well qualified to take on given their shared linguistic and computing skills. "And very quickly we became a CD-ROM publisher, taking free software and shareware from the Internet, publishing it on CD-ROM." Miller notes, "We were one of the first companies to be profitable by basing our business mainly on the Internet."

During their investigation of free software that was available on the Internet, they came across GNU/Linux. "It was another thing that we could take and turn into a product," Miller recalls, and adds: "but it was much more than that as well. We actually used Linux very early on, as a development tool, internally."

This development work paid off a few years later. After selling free software and other people's GNU/Linux distributions, Miller and his wife decided to come out with their own—but with a difference. "We figured well, gee, we're already testing and doing some development on Linux, and Japan was kind of a wide open market for Linux because nobody was doing a real Japanese commercial version of Linux, so we decided to do it there." This was in late 1997.

As with Caldera's first product, Pacific HiTech's distribution included some proprietary software, and largely for the same reasons. A GNU/Linux distribution for Japan largely needed to support the Japanese language fully; GNU/Linux was capable of doing this, but required the addition of Japanese fonts, for example, as well as other specialized elements. Pacific HiTech's product offered these in the form of commercial software. "There were things out there in the free software world," Miller explains, "but they weren't of the same quality, so we have a few different versions" of the distribution, including "a completely free version that doesn't have the commercial stuff. The basic distribution is all GPL."

Pacific HiTech's distribution has done well in Japan, and also in China following the launch of a localized version there in the spring of 1999. Miller says that "nobody really knows" exactly how big their market share is in these markets because distributions can be downloaded and copied freely, "but we figure it's over 50 percent in Asia." Given this success, it was natural that Miller should think about entering the U.S. market. "We've always sold just a trickle of products. We really beefed up our selling efforts last quarter of '99." By this time, the company had changed its name to TurboLinux, reflecting in part that it was no longer concentrating on the Asian market. It was an appropriate choice for a company run by the quietly spoken but intellectually turbocharged Miller.

"In the fourth quarter of [1999] we started selling to retail stores in the United States, and that was mainly our workstation product," Miller says. "Through some pretty aggressive promotions we were able to get a pretty good start in the retail market. But the real emphasis of our strategy is to serve the enterprise market with the server product that we are developing. We concentrate our development on our server product line and on clustering."

Clustering involves taking several machines and running them in a coordinated fashion. "We have what's called a daemon," Miller explains, software "that runs in the background and provides for the high availability. So if one [computer] node in your cluster goes down, then the daemon that's running on all of the nodes will notice that and route around that bad computer." The ability to cope with the failure of individual machines without disturbing the overall running of the system is the main attraction of such high-availability clusters, as they are called, especially in hot areas such as e-commerce.

TurboLinux adopts an unusual licensing approach for this daemon. "It's closed [source] for a period of six months, and then we open it up after that," Miller explains. "So it's kind of a compromise in order to protect our investment on the development." This kind of innovative approach—one that had been pioneered by a program called Ghostscript—is possible because technology is moving so fast that even this six-month window provides purchasers with enough incentive to buy software that will later become free. Miller explains, "For a large company to get clustering software at one or two thousand dollars is really quite a bargain"

Miller seems to have no difficulty convincing investors that his approach is viable. At the end of 1999, Intel invested in TurboLinux, along with a couple of venture capital companies. This round of financing was followed by another, in January 2000, from what Miller calls "a whole slew of companies; Dell was the lead investor, and then there were Compaq, Seagate, Novell, NEC, Fujitsu, NTT, and Legend in China—there are about twenty-five or so corporate investors."The amount of money was pretty substantial," Miller adds, "we got $57 million. But even more important than that was the relationships that we were able to enhance by doing that." Nonetheless, the money will be useful in financing Miller's ambitious expansion plans in Europe. Red Hat and Caldera have been present there for some time, but the dominant distribution in this region comes from the German-based SuSE (pronounced roughly like the American composer "Sousa").

SuSE's original German name was Software- und System-Entwicklung, or Software and System Development. Like Pacific HiTech, the company was created while its founders were still at university. One of them was Roland Dyroff, who today is SuSE's CEO. "The plan for setting up the company was Unix-focused consulting and software development," he says. "But before this plan could really be executed, Linux came in and the focus went to Linux."

The company was formed in 1992. Its first offering to customers was in March 1993, and consisted of Peter MacDonald's pioneering SLS distribution. Later, SuSE used Slackware as the basis of a localized version. Where Japan was attractive to Pacific HiTech because of its lack of GNU/Linux activity, Germany was a good place to sell GNU/Linux distributions for exactly the opposite reason. Then, as now, Germany had some of the most advanced users in terms of awareness and deployment of GNU/Linux. In 1996, SuSE decided to come out with its own distribution. "The reason being the time lag," Dyroff explains, "Slackware released and then we had to apply our patches" to make it suitable for German users. Since then, SuSE has gone on to add many original elements.

When SuSE had established itself as the leading European distribution, it decided in 1997 to open an office in Oakland, California. Dyroff himself describes this as a "ridiculous decision." As he explains, "the reason is, the company was very small at this time. We had a '96 revenue of like 3 million Euros [about $3 million], and we had not much financial liquidity to invest in the United States. And we didn't have much experience. We just did it." When it entered the U.S. market, SuSE used retail as a strategy to promote its brand, as had TurboLinux. "We focused on selling the SuSE box product," Dyroff says. But now it is branching out into professional services, an extension of something SuSE began in Germany back in early 1999.

Although services are "the fastest growing sector of our business by far," as Dyroff says, SuSE's main traditional strength has been in retail sales. "One hundred percent of our customers are private customers, because the individuals we are selling to in the companies are nearly [all technicians]," Dyroff says. "The area of potential customers now expands beyond those where a technician makes a purchase decision or recommends Linux. But this is a very new process," he stresses, and as a percentage of all sales "is not relevant" yet. This echoes Love's comments about how it is still early days in the business GNU/Linux sector and far too soon to declare a victor.

SuSE, like its name, is an enigma. Despite his solid technical background, Dyroff radiates an unbridled enthusiasm, and frequently breaks out into boyish giggles. Perhaps it is this, along with moves such as its "ridiculous decision" to enter the U.S. market, that make SuSE something of a joker in the GNU/Linux distribution pack. Nonetheless, as one of the largest and most profitable players in the sector, SuSE is to be taken seriously. In November 1999, investments worth 12 million Euros (about $12 million) from Intel and Apax Partners bolstered its war-chest further.

The four leading distributions were not the only established players in the GNU/Linux world who benefited from the powerful backing of mainstream computer giants and the financial markets during 1998 and 1999. Another was the GNU/Linux hardware company VA Research, which changed its name to VA Linux in April 1999.

Like Red Hat, VA Linux was plucked from its relative obscurity by an investment, announced on 12 November 1998, this time from Sequoia Capital, which had helped propel companies such as Yahoo to the next level. Intel then added its blessing to VA Linux with an investment on 19 February 1999. VA Linux's IPO took place on 9 December 1999. The shares opened at $30 and closed at $239.25, an increase of nearly 700 percent—a new record for the largest first-day gain of an initial public offering.

True to their countercultural origins, and recognizing the open source community's critical role in their success, Red Hat, Caldera and VA Linux arranged for hackers who had contributed to GNU/Linux to be allocated shares at their opening price, in what were called directed-share schemes. Unfortunately, glitches and practical problems partially stymied these laudable attempts to reward the real creators of the operating system.

Many were concerned that the not inconsiderable sums descending on the hacker community as a result of these IPOs would corrupt the hitherto unspoiled world of open source. Eric Raymond, himself the recipient of no less than 150,000 VA Linux shares in return for his services on the board of that company as what he calls "VA's official corporate conscience," was not one of them.

In one of his most characteristic pieces, called "Surprised by wealth," a by-now familiar commingling of personal history and astute industry analysis, he described how he had found out about VA Linux's stunning entrance on the stock exchange. It begins with a classic Raymondism: "A few hours ago, I learned that I am now (at least in theory) absurdly rich." After a few details, he explains, with studied nonchalance, "I had become worth approximately 41 million dollars while I wasn't looking.

"You may wonder why I am talking about this in public," he teases, and then explains as he turns adroitly from the particular to the general:

> Fairness to the hackers who made me bankable demands that I publicly acknowledge this result—and publicly face the question of how it's going to affect my life and what I'll do with the money. This is a question that a lot of us will be facing as open source sweeps the technology landscape. Money follows where value leads, and the mainstream business and finance world is seeing increasing value in our tribe of scruffy hackers. Red Hat and VA have created a precedent now, with their directed-shares programs designed to reward as many individual contributors as they can identify; future players aiming for community backing and a seat at the high table will have to follow suit.
>
> So while there aren't likely to be a lot more multimillion-dollar bonanzas like mine, lots of hackers are going to have to evolve answers to this question for smaller amounts that will nevertheless make a big difference to individuals; tens or hundreds of thousands of dollars, enough to change your life—or wreck it.

He goes on to point out the irony: "Gee. Remember when the big question was 'How do we make money at this?'" Then, more seriously, he addresses the central question this new-found wealth poses:

"Reporters often ask me these days if I think the open-source community will be corrupted by the influx of big money. I tell them what I believe, which is this: commercial demand for programmers has been so intense for so long that anyone who can be seriously distracted by money is already gone. Our community has been self-selected for caring about other things—accomplishment, pride, artistic passion, and each other."

Raymond emphasizes that, despite the spectacular irruption of money into the open source world, and the transformation of the GNU/Linux distributions into financial powerhouses, the true hacker knows that there is a world of difference between shares—however stratospheric their valuation—and the sharing that lies at the heart of free software.

14

Open for Business

The challenge faced by companies whose business was based around a GNU/Linux distribution—how to make money from software that was also freely available—was by no means a new one, even if it was only in 1999 that such high flyers as Red Hat and VA Linux brought the model to the attention of a bemused general public.

One of the first people to make money from free software was Richard Stallman, who sold tapes of his GNU Emacs for $150 in 1985. He also provided consultancy based around Emacs and, later, his GCC compiler, which turns C programs into the binaries that processor chips can run. Well before Linux was even begun, a company called Cygnus Solutions had pioneered many of the techniques later applied by the GNU/Linux distributions that grew around it, and had shown that building a business based on free software not only was possible but could be highly profitable.

As had happened so often during the history of free software, GCC set things in motion. When Michael Tiemann, one of the founders of Cygnus, came across GCC in 1987, he was so impressed that he went off and read Stallman's manifesto on free software to find out more about the GNU project. Tiemann not only saw the power of Stallman's logic but also discerned in it a latent business plan. "It comes down to my relatively simple belief that free markets are really the right way to run economies," Tiemann explains, "and that if you've got a better way, it should be possible to make that profitable and successful."

GCC was manifestly so much better than any commercial product that Tiemann thought he could create a flourishing business around it. Because it was not possible to make much money from selling something that was freely available, he decided that the secret lay in services—support and consultancy, for example.

He talked to Stallman about his plans. "I did want to get his blessing, as it were," Tiemann recalls. Despite the views about commercial software that are often erroneously ascribed to him, Stallman was delighted. "He said, 'Absolutely,'" Tiemann recalls, "'as long as you adhere to the GNU Public License.'" After all, if Tiemann's venture was successful, it would prove that Stallman's ideals were not incompatible with commerce, and that building a business around free software was possible.

Stallman likes to say that "Cygnus was intended to stand for 'Cygnus, Your GNU Support'"—making it yet another recursive acronym. Tiemann comments, "That's like saying Emacs stands for 'Eight Megabytes And Constantly Swapping.'" (This rather unkind remark referred to the early days, when Emacs required more memory than most machines possessed. It had been necessary therefore to resort to such tricks as swapping parts of the program to and from the hard disc—an approach that slowed things down enormously.)

"The reality of the situation," Tiemann continues, "was that we couldn't find any names that were not previously registered. When I lamented this fact to a couple of my Net friends, one of them searched the dictionary for words that contained 'GNU.' And 'Cygnus' seemed the one that was least obscene. But people very quickly attributed what 'Cygnus' might actually stand for. I'm happy for Richard to own one of those definitions."

"I was completely convinced [Cygnus] would work," Tiemann says. But he realized that he had a problem. "I thought to myself, you know, Richard is probably one of the brightest guys I've ever met when it comes to software," he says. And yet despite this brilliance, even Stallman found it difficult to get companies to accept his ideas about free software. As a result, Tiemann explains, "I sort of felt if I was just another voice in the wilderness I wouldn't be able to get any more critical mass than he got.

"So I explicitly wanted to recruit some cofounders," he says, "to try to create a level of critical mass that would catalyze the business. And I talked with many people about this idea, and the only ones that took me seriously were the other two cofounders," John Gilmore and David Henkel-Wallace.

"John Gilmore's e-mail handle is 'gnu,'" Tiemann explains, "and some claim that he had nicknamed the GNU project." Moreover, "John was employee number 5 at Sun, renowned programmer and civil libertarian, and also independently wealthy because of his Sun stock." The other partner, David Henkel-Wallace, was somebody Tiemann had met while doing his research on compilers, and who "also seemed reasonably bright," he says. "So the three of us pooled our resources. Actually, I was the short end of the stick, I only had $2,000 of liquid money to invest at the time. I told John and also Gumby—David Henkel-Wallace's nickname—that I wasn't tapping them for their money. And so we each put in $2,000, and started the company." This was in November 1989.

The new Cygnus Solutions offered services based around Stallman's GNU software. "Basically, I would go and sell a contract and then John and Gumby would figure out how to deliver it," Tiemann explains. "Initially this worked quite well. However, it got more complicated as I burdened them down. And we needed to build a scalable model. The challenge was we knew that we wanted to be support services for the software, [but] we didn't have [our own] product at the time." In fact, "it took about three years before we really had a credible support offering," he says, and adds, "we probably lost money on every support deal we did before 1992."

While they were casting around for a product, one of them came up with what, in retrospect, was an interesting idea. "John Gilmore proposed that we write a free kernel for the 386," Tiemann recalls. This was in 1990, fully one year before Linus would sit down and do exactly that. "I always considered myself to be an unprejudiced individual," Tiemann explains, "but the thought of taking something like Unix and running it on an Intel 386 just boggled my mind. I didn't feel it was a real processor. And I didn't feel that users who bought PCs were real users." This statement echoes the sentiments of those who had questioned the sense of porting a real operating system to such a footling processor when Linux was first released.

This was not the last time that opportunity in the form of GNU/Linux came knocking. "Adam Richter, who was the purveyor of the first Linux on CD, Yggdrasil, came to me and asked for some business advice," Tiemann recalls. "And I poured out my heart and I told him what mistakes we did and didn't make." Unfortunately, "he was definitely uninterested in joining forces with Cygnus."

Even later, Cygnus once more narrowly missed its chance. "In 1995, Larry McVoy"—author of the Sourceware document—"came to me," Tiemann explains, "and said, 'There's this company in North Carolina that's doing Linux, and they're really making a lot of money for the number of people they've got. You ought to check it out.' And I tried to convince my partners at that time that we attempt to acquire Red Hat, and they would have none of it. In 1990-91, I said no to John Gilmore, and in 1995 he said no to me. So there was a long window of opportunity that we simply ignored."

The problem was hardly lack of vision. After all, in 1992, Tiemann had made a speech to the Sun Users Group conference in which he not only assessed correctly the strengths of the free software movement, but predicted it would become the dominant force in the following years. Nor was the problem caused by a lack of ambition; partly because Cygnus had become so successful—"by 1995 we were doing north of 10 million dollars a year in our core business," Tiemann says—they decided to stick with what they knew. "It's awfully difficult to say we're going to duck out of this race right now," he says, "and we're going to go back to zero."

The product that was driving these impressive revenues was GNUPro, which offered a more comprehensive and integrated development environment based around free software such as GCC. "We subscribed to the theory that we needed to have a focused product that people could identify," Tiemann explains.

One consequence of Cygnus's success was that, in addition to being built around GCC, the company became the guardian of GCC's development. "Stallman wrote the original version" of GCC, Tiemann explains. "GCC 2 actually came out shortly after Cygnus was founded, and a large part of that was already set in motion by work I had done before Cygnus," he says. "But from about 1991 onwards, we had more full-time people working on GCC than any other single entity, and today we've got more by an order of magnitude at least."

Once again, Cygnus here prefigured the approach later taken by other companies based around free software. For example, Red Hat has taken on many of the top kernel hackers. The list is impressive, and includes the lieutenants Alan Cox, Dave Miller, and Stephen Tweedie, and other hacker stars such as the Hungarian, Ingo Molnar. The other company that has built up an impressive portfolio of big names in the open source world is VA Linux. Top figures associated with the company include Ted Ts'o, Eric Raymond, and Jon "maddog" Hall.

Given the parallels between Cygnus and the GNU/Linux distribution companies that have come after it, and the wealth of talent Cygnus possessed in the field of open source tools, it is perhaps no surprise that Red Hat acquired Cygnus, on 15 November 1999. Even before this, Cygnus had put out feelers—and had been turned down. "We talked with Red Hat and were rebuffed early [1999]," Tiemann explains, "because the advice they got from one of their board members was nothing good comes from joining two small companies"—at that time Red Hat had forty people, he recalls.

However, things changed. "After their successful IPO," Tiemann says, "they could go look for strategic partners. It turns out that the fit is actually quite good. Cygnus has a lot of the technical depth that Red Hat needed, especially related to development tools." Cygnus also helped realize Red Hat's vision of deriving more of its revenue from services. At the time of the acquisition, 60 to 70 percent of Cygnus's turnover came from services, and for Red Hat, "their box product was probably more than 80 percent," Tiemann says. Although the philosophies of the two companies—and of Tiemann and Red Hat's Bob Young—are close, in one area Red Hat caused Cygnus to modify its approach slightly.

Unlike Bob Young, who believes that the open source nature of the products he sells is central to the value they deliver to customers, Tiemann has been more pragmatic about including proprietary elements. "At the end of the day," he believes, "in a capitalist society, you're judged against the competition."

But Tiemann has come to recognize that one of the key features of the brand that Red Hat has built is what he calls "the 'always open' promise"—everything the company does will always be open source. "And it turns out that brand trumps almost everything." As a result, he says, "being religiously pro open source for the sake of being religiously pro open source doesn't carry much water with me. But being religiously pro open source as a component of a brand strategy that is effective carries a lot of water."

The question of how or even whether to add proprietary elements to commercial products based around free software remains one of the touchstones for companies working in this area. It was an issue that Eric Allman had to face when he decided to create Sendmail, Inc. Unlike Tiemann, the perennially unassuming Allman was not driven by some belief that his free software was so good that it should be possible to profit from it. "I did not start Sendmail Inc. to make money, although that's a nice thing," he says. "But I did it to make Sendmail sustainable; I did it so we could do great innovation. I did it to make the world smaller"—emphasizing once more his central belief in the community aspect of free software.

In the early days, the Sendmail program was supported by Allman alone—"nights and weekends," as he puts it. He says,

> I love the open source process, but Sendmail was becoming a victim of its own success. We were going through a period when the Internet standards were starting to go through dramatic expansion in the e-mail area. I found I was unable to supply those resources, and so Sendmail was going to become unable to step up to the demand.
>
> When I first started working on what became Sendmail version 8, I set up a mostly open mailing list for people doing testing," [in early 1993.] "It became clear that there were a few people that were exceptionally good [on that list]. They were not only asking good questions and pointing out bugs and so forth, but they were contributing fixes. And so I set up another list which was intended as a support list. It was invitation only, but I would publish that address so that outside folks when they had questions could send to that list and there wouldn't just be me answering. And a lot of the people that started on that list are still there. They're a very hardcore group.

The second list was created around the beginning of 1996, he says.

"As Sendmail evolved," Allman explains, "a lot of the support moved on to those other folks, and I was able to continue to do development. And some of those people, one or two in particular, were helping increasingly with development. But it started to become clear that this was not sustainable. The Internet was exploding, it was growing 100 percent a year or whatever it was, and the user base was growing a lot faster than I could." As a result, he started looking at other solutions.

"My first attempt was to try and create something where I got a small amount of funding," Allman continues. "I had this fantasy if Sun and Digital and IBM and SGI and a few others were each to kick in $50,000, just like maybe the half to a third of the cost of one loaded engineer, I'd be able to do what I wanted. Then they'd get good stuff, and I'd get good stuff, and we'd all be happy. But I couldn't float this." This was in late 1996.

By early 1997, Allman was making a living as a consultant—"primarily on Sendmail," he says. "My fantasy was that I'd charge ridiculous amounts of money, and that would let me work half-time, and the other half-time I could work on Sendmail." Note that Allman's "fantasy" was not to get rich by charging "ridiculous amounts of money," but to support himself so that he could work on Sendmail—and then give away the results. "In the process," he says, "I ran into Greg Olson," an old friend.

"He was doing consulting on market strategy, business development kind of things," Allman continues. Olson asked what he was up to, "and I said, 'Well, I'm trying to find a sustainable model for Sendmail.' And he said, 'Tell you what, you're an old friend, I do this professionally, but I'll take a look at it for you.' So he went off, he did some market research, he talked to customers and he came back and said, 'You know, you've got just the basis of dynamite business here.'"

The reasons were simple. "Fabulous market, incredible market penetration. We usually say 75 percent of the mail servers on the Internet are Sendmail, or Sendmail variants," Allman explains. "The market was not only a huge one already, but it was growing incredibly quickly. E-mail is the killer app of the Internet, and always has been." Sendmail Inc. would be based on offering full, enterprise-level support for current and new users, as well as commercial versions of the software with new features.

Eventually, Allman and Olson managed to raise 1.25 million dollars from such people as Bill Joy and fellow Sun co-founder Andy Bechtolsheim. "We used a portion of that money to do some PR, which turned out to work out very well because when we rolled out the company in March '98, we made the front page of the *New York Times*." In doing so, Sendmail Inc. fuelled the curiosity that Netscape's open source announcement had provoked just a couple of months earlier, and helped keep free software in the public eye until IBM started the avalanche of commercial support announcements with its adoption of Apache in June 1998.

Allman and Olson did not lose sight of hackers' reactions while seeking investment. "We were very concerned about that," Allman says. "And we spent a lot of time thinking about how we were going to assure them that we were not doing a technology rip-off"—taking Sendmail proprietary.

"Both Greg and I feel very strongly that the contribution of the community is an important part of Sendmail's success," Allman emphasizes. "And if we'd lose that, we'd lost a big chunk of how and why we have succeeded. So we've remained very firmly committed to the open source model." But he adds, "Not to say that everything is open source—we are a hybrid company—but the concept is that the core material, the stuff that you need to push forward innovation, to push standards, to essentially move the Internet forward, is open source."

This statement is balanced by what Allman sees as "a moral commitment to our investors to make money for them. And so we can't give everything away. We would undoubtedly make more money right now if we were to say the next release of Sendmail is going to be available for fee only," Allman says. "But in a year, that would be a very bad decision. So from a point of view of a pure capitalist model, we're better off leaving it open source, assuming we believe that we're a long-term play."

This is an important point: Companies that attempt to take free software proprietary—as is possible under some licenses—are effectively cutting themselves off from the very power they seek to tap. For their product to thrive, they need a flourishing free community. As Allman and Olson recognized, the health of their company is intimately linked to the vigor of the community that surrounds it.

Allman's view that Sendmail would have failed to grow had not he or someone else created an open source company to support and nurture it is one shared by a fellow free software pioneer, John Ousterhout (pronounced "oh-ster-howt"). As Allman and many others have, Ousterhout has strong ties with the University of California at Berkeley, where he was a professor of computer science. Ousterhout is best-known for his language Tcl, pronounced "tickle," which began as a "tool command language" for creating design tools for integrated circuits, and Tk, a toolkit for producing graphical interfaces.

Ousterhout originally wrote this for himself and his students, beginning in 1988. Tcl percolated to the outside world in "late '89," he says. "I'd given away a few copies then, and I started getting comments back from people. It was in '90 and '91 when things really picked up." As it had been for Stallman and Wall, this feedback was crucial in spurring him on to develop his software further. "For me, the biggest thrill in building software is knowing that there were lots of people out there using it," he says. Ousterhout points out that this drives a key strength of the open source process.

"It's sort of the opposite of design by committee," he explains. "You get all the benefits of this huge pool of ideas, but it's not a democratic system. There's typically one person who is the god or the tsar who has final authority over everything that goes into the package. One of the great benefits is that you can get a degree of architectural simplicity and uniformity that you can't get if you have design by committee or a zillion people all with total authority to make changes to the core of the system."

Ousterhout acknowledges that he failed to follow up on one idea that came from his users. "We started hearing stories about this crazy physicist who had this weird idea for something called the World Wide Web," he recalls. "Somebody did this package called TkWWW, which was a graphical way of displaying this Web stuff that had been invented by this guy in Switzerland." This was in 1992, barely a year after "this guy in Switzerland"—Tim Berners-Lee—had released the Web publicly, and well before the NCSA's Mosaic browser project at the University of Illinois had begun. To compound his embarrassment, Ousterhout says ruefully, "I never actually started [TkWWW] up. I thought this World Wide Web thing seemed pretty hokey. One of those things you sort of look back and kick yourself for.

"I'd been at Berkeley a dozen years or so by then," he continues, "and I had always wanted to spend a good chunk of my career in industry, as well as in academia." The final push was the realization that as Tcl was becoming more popular, it would need more support than the open source structure could offer. Echoing Eric Allman, Ousterhout says, "I think there's a set of things you can do very well in a purely open source project, and a set of things that tend not to get done in that project. All of the additional kinds of services and value-adds that you need if the company is going to be using this for mission-critical applications—development tools, higher-level kinds of facilities—those tend not to get developed in a project that's purely open source."

As a result, he decided to leave Berkeley and work on Tcl at Sun, which he joined in the early summer of 1994. The move had its critics, notably Richard Stallman, who issued a typically direct call to arms headed "Why You Should Not Use Tcl." Ousterhout explains the reason. "When I went to Sun, that was acknowledging that I felt that it was OK to build a commercial business model around open source software," he says. "That really bugged Stallman, and so he tried to get people to boycott Tcl as a way of showing protest against that." What provoked Stallman's ire was that the commercial model would involve proprietary software.

"The belief was that Sun was going to somehow take Tcl proprietary," Ousterhout says. "And what really was the deal with Sun was we planned to continue developing the open source Tcl and distributing it freely, and that was in my contract with Sun. But we would also build some commercial things. We'd prototyped some commercial products that would be built around Tcl, and if all went well, Sun would sell those products while still giving away the source of Tcl freely.

"We actually had gone so far as to begin to create a new business unit at Sun," Ousterhout recalls. "It was going to be called SunScript. But a few months into the effort, the person who was our angel among the Sun senior staff, Eric Schmidt, he went off to become CEO at Novell. Shortly after he left, it became clear to me that we just didn't have the kind of support and enthusiasm in the top-level management at Sun that we would need in order to make this a success over the long term."

Recognizing that Sun was not likely to be so committed to Tcl, not least because it was around this time that the company began promoting heavily its own Java programming language, Ousterhout asked that the project be cancelled. "But as part of the cancellation," he says, "we agreed that we would take all of the software that we thought we were going to commercialize, and release it all freely on the Internet"—generously sacrificing his own interests for the sake of the Tcl community.

Ousterhout was faced with a critical decision: whether to move on from Tcl entirely, or to set up his own company to support it. "Early summer of '97 we cancelled SunScript," he recalls, "and then over the summer and fall I sort of tested the waters to see if I'd be able to raise enough money to start a company. Things looked good, so in January of '98 I spun out from Sun to start Scriptics." Ousterhout was fortunate that as part of the preparations for creating SunScript, "we'd done a bunch of marketing studies at Sun trying to figure out what kinds of products to build and where there was demand," he says. So "we did have some evidence that at least the community was there, and of the interest in the development tools."

Scriptics's first product, TclPro, offered an extended development environment, as had Cygnus's GNUPro. Ousterhout recalls that, for the most part, Tcl users accepted these new proprietary elements alongside the open source Tcl. That community was already large: Ousterhout estimates that there were around half a million Tcl users when Scriptics was launched, and that there are more like a million now.

"We did our development tools in '98," he explains. "But we were thinking about what might be interesting areas where people need integration applications that we could apply Tcl to. And it converged pretty quickly around B2B [Business-to-Business e-commerce]." The resulting product, Connect, was an ambitious piece of enterprise-level software that allowed companies to link together their respective computer systems by using XML (eXtensible Markup Language) as a platform-independent format for exchanging information across networks such as the Internet, and Tcl to provide the integration.

The subsequent proliferation of global B2B exchanges has shown the shrewdness of Ousterhout's bet on this area. Reflecting the company's new focus, in May 2000, Scriptics was renamed Ajuba Solutions, and Connect became Ajuba2. Not surprisingly, perhaps, Ousterhout says, "We do a lot of services right now. One of the general lessons I've learned over the last couple of years is that if you're doing a business that's purely based around the open source stuff, the biggest opportunity is in the services area."

One person who couldn't agree more is Dave Sifry, co-founder and CTO of Linuxcare, a company set up to provide nothing but services to the business GNU/Linux market. It was born in rather odd surroundings. Sifry and co-founders Arthur Tyde and Dave Le Duke had been pitching an earlier business plan to yet another venture capitalist. "We had this moment of truth in September of 1998," Sifry recalls. "We had just very, very nicely gotten our hats handed to us, one more time. And so we sit around in the parking lot, depressed," he continues. "And we thought, well, what is it that we really do know best? What is it that we're twelve to eighteen months ahead of everybody else in experience and in knowledge? And where is there a real need that we can fill?

"So we're all kind of pondering this," Sifry says, "and then one of us just sort of said, 'Well, there's no 800 number for Linux'"—no one to call for support. "And that was really the seed of the idea that became Linuxcare." The rightness of their new idea was shown by the ease with which they now lined up investors, including such big names as Kleiner Perkins—which had provided the main backing for Netscape—Michael Dell, and Hasso Plattner, CEO of SAP.

Linuxcare offers a range of services, including support, consulting, and education. The software embraces the Linux kernel plus "any additional open source application that came with a Linux distribution," Sifry says. From the beginning, he and his co-founders recognized a fundamental problem with this kind of model. "The single largest problem with service businesses is that they don't scale well, traditionally. Because if you end up being a body shop, the administrative costs per employee start to increase the more people that you have." This was the problem that Cygnus had faced in its early years. Sifry says they decided the solution was to "build a knowledge base that's Web-based [where] we feed everything that we do in the business into that. Because the last thing you ever want to do is you want to answer the same question twice."

As with other companies founded on open source programs, Linuxcare had to address the question of proprietary software. "We are not so religious that we insist that everything be GPL'd," Sifry explains. "We look at it as an educational process. It really comes down to working with the customer and saying, you know what, here's where open source is going to benefit you. Here's where it's going to benefit you in a year. But here's where it's not going to benefit you right now."

Despite this pragmatism—"Customers do come first, no doubt," says Sifry—Linuxcare remains committed to open source rather than to proprietary software. "But we don't force our people to do that. We say, look, we encourage you to work on open source projects while you're here at work." Sifry sees this encouragement as a vital part of the Linuxcare culture—and the recipe for success. "Aside from the purely moral feeling that, hey, this is part of doing the right thing for the world," he says, "there are a number of very significant strategic business reasons why we do this.

"Number one, it encourages us to get the best developers in the world. When you actually are telling people, hey, I want you to work on open source software while you're at work, that is pretty unique. And then once you get some [of the best coders], you end up getting more. Because everybody wants to work with the best people. Number two is, the more good open source software that's out there, the more people who are using open source software. And guess what, that means the more people who are going to need the services of a company like Linuxcare. Number three, when you encourage people to work on open source software while they're here at work, you end up getting leaders and teams of open source engineers who now work for your company. And then lastly, and by no means least," Sifry points out, "it's great PR."

This analysis implies, of course, that the key asset for any open source company, even more perhaps than for conventional companies, is the people it employs. Because the "product" is open source, and freely available, businesses must necessarily be based around a different kind of scarcity: the skills of the people who write and service that software. This also explains in part why Red Hat and VA Linux have been prepared to offer such flexible contracts to the top hackers, many of whom work from home, often outside the United States.

Just as Linuxcare saw that it could abstract the services side from the products still offered by companies selling GNU/Linux distributions, so another innovative venture aims to move one stage further by creating a marketplace in those increasingly valuable programming skills.

The original idea came from Hewlett-Packard, and it was the open source coordinator there, Wayne Caccamo, who helped realize it. "When I was gathering my network of people at HP," he says, "I came across a guy who was very much an expert on Linux. He was doing some project that happened to involve Linux development and he was very frustrated by the process of bringing in [outside software] contractors. The process at HP, like any large company, is very cumbersome.

"He came up with this concept that we could create an intermediary," Caccamo recalls. The idea was that the intermediary would handle the details of finding and hiring open source contractors. At the suggestion of the originator of the idea, Caccamo decided to work with O'Reilly & Associates. He had noted how "they played a positive role bringing people together in the Linux community," he says, "and they also employed people within the open source world that were viewed and known as celebrities and that were all respected from that standpoint." Among these celebrities, few were more respected than Brian Behlendorf, who had recently joined O'Reilly.

The job at O'Reilly came up, Behlendorf says, "when I was fishing around for something new. I sat down with Tim O'Reilly and started talking about what could be done in open source. I really felt it was worth spending the time to see if there was yet another business model that open source could facilitate that wasn't just sell support. He said, 'Well, why don't you incubate those ideas here at O'Reilly?'" Behlendorf recalls. "And so I joined there with the intent of coming up with a set of ideas and testing the commercial viability of them." This was at the beginning of 1999, just when Caccamo was considering O'Reilly for the intermediary he was looking for.

The result was SourceXchange, a site where companies can post proposals for programming work and solicit bids from open source coders. It is intended to form the first of a series of projects exploring new business models based on open source, and which collectively make up Collab.Net. A list of those involved reads like a roll call of the leading players in the open source industry. Employees include Frank Hecker, who played a major role in convincing Netscape to take its browser open source, and James Barry, who helped convert IBM to Apache. Alongside Behlendorf, Tim O'Reilly and Marc Andreessen are board members, and investors in a $35 million round of funding closed in June 2000 included Dell, HP, Intel, Novell, Oracle, Sun, and TurboLinux.

"The SourceXchange model is designed for projects that are substantial in size," Behlendorf explains, "that aren't the 'I need someone to fix this bug, here's $100, or beer money,' which a couple of other sites are based on. But it really is focused on the $5,000 to $25,000 projects, the ones that involve two man-weeks' to four man-months' worth of work." Not surprisingly, given Behlendorf's own history, all the code produced is released as open source, but which particular open source license is adopted is "part of the negotiation," he says.

Behlendorf points out that not only companies can benefit from SourceXchange. "Every open source project out there has a list of unfinished items," he says, "things that no one really wants to tackle because they are complex, because they require specialized knowledge, or for one reason or another they're just not the kind of things that people attack in their spare time. SourceXchange is a way to get past that. That's why it wasn't designed for small little bug fixes; it was designed for the bigger problems, the ones that are keeping bigger projects from getting to the next level."

VA Linux is another company that hopes to provide employment for hackers, promote free software, and make money in the process. Although initially formed to put together hardware optimized for running GNU/Linux, its scope has broadened considerably. "We have our systems business, which is geared towards providing the best hardware and systems to run Linux, particularly for those people building Internet sites," says Larry Augustin, CEO of VA Linux. As well as selling the basic hardware and software, VA Linux is also in the business of providing custom solutions, and in a novel way. "The idea is that the Internet is a great R and D resource. There's a tremendous repository of source code out there on the Internet, and that's what we view as our toolbox.

"A customer comes along and they have a particular feature set they need," Augustin explains. "We can look at this archive of source code that comes from these Internet sites, and say, 'Well, here's an open source piece that's 80 percent of what you want.' We go to the customer and say, 'We can charge the amount of money it will take us to get from 80 percent to 100 percent and it will be all open source.' Our goal is to work with the developers on the Internet sites to actually get that piece of software from 80 percent to 100 percent for that customer."

Augustin's commitment to supporting existing open source projects led him to create one of the community's key resources. "There's a site on the Internet called Freshmeat, where open source software projects are announced," he explains. VA Linux acquired Freshmeat when it bought the parent company, Andover.net, in February 2000. At that time, there were around fifty new free software projects announced on it every day. Even though Freshmeat is a great notice board—"everyone monitors it," Augustin says—it is less useful for finding the code in question; links are often broken, or only one version of the program is available.

Augustin decided "we need a place where every time something is announced on Freshmeat, that piece of software is put into storage somewhere, permanently archived, never deleted—all versions forever. So I came up with this idea of a site that I called ColdStorage; this was meant to go with Freshmeat."

VA Linux started building ColdStorage in 1998, at the same time it was working on another idea, called OpenProjects. The idea behind Open-Projects was to provide hackers with space on an Internet site where they could co-ordinate open source software development. Because this meant setting up Web pages, an FTP area, and mailing lists for each project, "we found ourselves spending a tremendous amount of time just with system administration," Augustin says.

"So we looked at these things, and we said, 'Gee, let's take the ideas of ColdStorage and OpenProjects and pull them together.'" The result was named SourceForge, launched on 4 January 2000 as a free service to open source developers. Just a few months later, SourceForge already had around 5,000 projects, including many of the most important, and over 1 Terabyte—a million Mbytes—of free software.

Though born in part of the business model of VA Linux, the appearance of SourceForge represents a large boost for the open source community. It provides both a historical repository of code—allowing people to track how programs develop; for example, to find out when a certain bug appeared or disappeared—and a high-quality, zero-cost infrastructure for expanding current projects. Perhaps even more important, it makes starting new projects easier. As a result, it may well offer the necessary catalyst for the creation of programs in an area where open source has so far had little impact: that of end-user applications.

15

Trolls Versus Gnomes

GIVEN GNU/LINUX'S ROOTS IN UNIX, and its rise as the ultimate hacker's system, it is perhaps not surprising that the end-user applications initially available were mostly for software developers—editors, compilers, etc.—or were small tools that addressed a single task. Nonetheless, the almost complete absence of complex applications was perturbing because it inevitably raised the question of whether the open source development methodology would ever work for this class of software. Against this background, the appearance of a free program called the GIMP, which originally stood for General Image Manipulation Program, and later became GNU Image Manipulation Program, was viewed with considerable relief.

It had been created by two students at Berkeley, Spencer Kimball and Peter Mattis, although this time the university played no part. Kimball and Mattis represent a wave of free software coders who are younger than the pioneers—Mattis was born in 1975, in Silicon Valley. Mattis explains how, in early 1995, the project came about.

"I was in my second semester of my sophomore year," he says, "studying computer science. We were thinking about [doing] some project. I was just getting into doing stuff with the World Wide Web, and I wanted to make Web pages. I had been a Mac fanatic in high school, and I had Photoshop on a Mac." Adobe's Photoshop program is the de facto standard for image manipulation, and is widely used by Web designers for creating graphic elements for their sites. It dominates this category as much as Excel does that of spreadsheets. "I'd gone to college," Mattis continues, "I switched over to Unix, and I couldn't do cool graphics under Unix at the time. So I said, I just want to be able to do the things that Photoshop did. It didn't seem that complicated at the time. It was very ambitious, but we were pretty naive about that."

The classic young hacker's cry of "It can't be that difficult" aside, it is interesting that Mattis was coming to Unix from the Apple Macintosh, and therefore with a set of expectations concerning application availability and user interface that GNU/Linux at the time was unable to meet. In a sense, Mattis is representative of a new generation of hackers that took rock-solid stability and basic operating system functions for granted, and were now demanding more.

Although he and others would be pushing GNU/Linux much further than its command-line or X Window origins, Mattis started using programs running in these environments for his project, and they affected him profoundly. "We both had Linux installed," he recalls. "I didn't consider Linux as a big free software thing at the time, even though it was. I was mostly thrilled with having a free compiler"—Stallman's GCC—"like wow, we just want to do something and kind of contribute it back to that community." Once again, the existence of high-quality free software acted as a spur to others to create and give back more of it.

Given its enormous popularity and the important role it would later play in the history of open source desktop applications, it is sobering to learn that a trivial occurrence almost caused the GIMP project to be cancelled. "I used to read newsgroups all the time back then," Mattis explains. In one of them, people were asking whether there was a Photoshop-like program for Unix. "And this guy came out responding, 'I have this program I'm going to release in about a month or two.' He listed out this whole feature list and I looked at it, and it's like, Jesus, that does everything we're doing with our program and more.

"For a moment we were like, ah, well, maybe we should just quit," Mattis remembers, "and then we came back and said, 'No, this is a learning experience, let's get ours finished and released out there.' And we did that, and I never heard from this other guy again." As Mattis comments, "It's kind of weird, though, that somebody like that could have really just killed the GIMP before it was even released, and he doesn't even realize it."

As well as the problem of pre-announced rival projects that never materialized, open source applications had to contend with a greater difficulty. One reason it was easier to write server-side programs than those for the desktop was that the former did not require fancy graphical front-ends, and this was where Unix was weak.

Although X Window provided a basic windowing technology, it did not offer programmers what are generally called widgets—the basic building blocks of graphical programs. These include such things as on-screen buttons, selection boxes, and all the familiar components that go to make up a Mac-like or Windows-like desktop. For these, it is necessary to turn to one of the toolkits, which contain sets of widgets that can be used to construct a graphical application.

The main graphics toolkit for Unix was Motif. But, as Mattis says, "we found Motif painful. We didn't have a firm grasp about how it worked internally." He points out one reason for their difficulties: "There were no good examples of how to do stuff in Motif. If I wanted to do something new and interesting, it was very difficult to figure out how to do that." Another reason this was difficult was that Motif was not open source or even zero-cost software. As a result, it was usually employed with proprietary programs, for which the source code was unavailable, making it even harder to learn how to program.

Nonetheless, Kimball and Mattis struggled on with Motif and produced version 0.54 of the GIMP, which came out in February 1996: "It was kind of stable, it did basic stuff," Mattis says. "It wasn't very advanced at all." At this point, he recalls, "Spencer was off playing with the way image manipulation worked." Meanwhile, Mattis was thinking, "You know, this Motif stuff is really frustrating. Let me see, how would I design a better toolkit? I started playing around saying, like, how would I do buttons?"—one of the most basic widgets. "And it kind of just evolved into something like, wow, I have almost all the things you need in a real toolkit." This was how Linux came into being, with the same realization on Linus's part that the result of his "playing around" was almost a Unix-like kernel.

Mattis called his toolkit Gtk: the GIMP Tool Kit. When he showed it to Kimball, "It's like, OK, we'll move over to using Gtk." Doing so brought some major advantages. "[Kimball] was frustrated by not being able to use certain things in Motif," Mattis says, "not because Motif didn't allow it, but because he didn't know how to do it in Motif. But if he wanted to do something in Gtk, I knew instantly how to do that. Or I could add it in for him." Gtk was much better than Motif for their purpose, but still not quite right. "We really found that there were incompletenesses," Mattis says. "There were things that were made difficult by the way Gtk was originally programmed." Mattis rewrote almost all of his toolkit, which he called Gtk+.

The switch to Gtk and then Gtk+ had another, even more important benefit. "When we converted over to using Gtk," Mattis recalls, "there was suddenly a great influx of people starting to look at the internals [of the GIMP], and say, OK, now I can modify this because I have access to the toolkit as well. So it wasn't so much that it made doing things easier, it was more that a lot more people started contributing internally. And that's what really kind of freed Spencer and I eventually to hand over the project to other hands." In other words, the classic open source benefits of bug fixes and new code being sent in began to flow only when users could see all the code, something that was not possible when the proprietary Motif libraries were used. The arrival of Gtk ensured not only the GIMP's further development but also its very survival.

Mattis and Kimball eventually decided that they had contributed enough of their time and energy to their project and the free software world, and wanted to move on. "I guess I was a little bit disgruntled initially to see there weren't people immediately picking up," Mattis acknowledges. "But in hindsight it was hard to expect people to pick it up immediately" because the GIMP is a complex program, and it took time even after the open Gtk libraries were adopted before other hackers felt confident enough to continue development.

The GIMP, for all its deserved fame, was not the only free software graphical application created in early 1995. At the same time, in the German university town of Tübingen, another computer science student, Matthias Ettrich, born in 1972, was starting work on his own ambitious personal project: a document processor for GNU/Linux called LyX (pronounced "lukes").

LyX was a document processor rather than word processor; at its heart it employed Donald Knuth's T_EX typesetting language, which handled many of the design decisions automatically. "[T_EX] does almost everything," Ettrich explains, "things that you don't want to worry about, placement of pictures, how the line or the page breaks were done without having these ugly defects."

Ettrich began LyX for the joy of hacking and as a tool for writing his papers at university. Unlike the GIMP, however, LyX became an official project for a university course. Ettrich optimistically told his professor that he'd have something usable in three weeks. "It was totally wrong," Ettrich notes. "It took me something like three months before I could actually do some typing. I think it was four or five months before I released something, put it on SunSite," one of the big Internet stores where software was placed for download by others.

The move had unforeseen consequences for Ettrich, the same ones Linus had experienced when he uploaded his project to a public server. "The mail started coming," Ettrich recalls, and adds that he had been unprepared for this because "[I] didn't know anything about free software, and how it works. I didn't know the concept of people cooperating or collaborating over the Internet," he says.

"When I released LyX, I said right, people, this is an alpha version, not really stable. The final product I will probably make a shareware thing—because that's what I knew from DOS software." Shareware was a kind of try before you buy: If you continued using a program that you had downloaded, you were required to send a small fee to the author.

"The basic idea was not to become rich with that," Ettrich explains. "My idea was I invested lots of time in that thing, and I don't want it to die, and I need some time to be able to maintain it, because otherwise it's just a big blob of dead code." But now something better than the shareware model presented itself. "I learned with all that feedback I got, during that alpha and beta period, that lots of people wanted to join the project and help me with maintenance, so it was for the project much better to say, OK, we put it under the totally free license, and no money involved whatsoever, please help. And that worked out."

The world of free software may have brought with it unforeseen advantages, but it also revealed equally unsuspected problems. LyX was written using the Motif libraries (as was the first version of the GIMP), "which is not free software," as Ettrich notes. "Then I switched over to the Xforms library, which isn't free software either—I mean, it's perfectly free, you can download it, you can get the source code if you ask the maintainer, but it's not free in the sense of the Free Software Foundation."

That was the problem. What Ettrich calls "hard-core free software zealots" were not happy with this use of nonfree software, and the license under which LyX was released. The criticism came as something of a shock to Ettrich. "The tone of these mails was very aggressive, as if I had committed a crime," he explains. "I said, 'Excuse me, I was sitting half a year there, writing some software. You can use it for free and give me some feedback if you want to, and if you don't want to, don't use it.' So I didn't understand why these people were so aggressive. That was a pretty strange experience," he notes.

Ettrich came across GNU/Linux only at about the time he started work on LyX, but he soon became an enthusiast and an expert. He certainly didn't miss the old DOS system he had used before—"Linux was so much more powerful than DOS," he says—or even Windows, then at version 3.1. "Windows 3.1 was a quite poor graphical interface," he remembers, and he didn't believe his GNU/Linux platform was lacking in any important way.

Two new commercial programs changed Ettrich's views, however. The first was IBM's OS/2 Warp operating system, which, he explains, was much bigger in Germany than elsewhere, thanks to some clever local marketing. The appearance of this smart new GUI (graphical user interface), complete with drag-and-drop capabilities that made working with files and programs much easier for nontechnical users, started raising a few doubts in people's minds about the GNU/Linux desktop. The subsequent arrival of Windows 95, and its enormous success with end-users, added to this growing sense of unease.

It took the experience of a nonhacker using his LyX document processor, not a technical revelation, to shake Ettrich out of his complacency about the superiority of the GNU/Linux way: "I had convinced my girlfriend that she wanted to use [LyX] for writing her masterpieces. I tried my best to strip Linux down and have a nice user interface. I added menus, and a little bit of drag and drop here, and tried to set up something nice, something I always claimed it's possible to do, you just have to want it.

"And I did that, and she was working on the computer, starting the word processor from an icon, but she discovered so many nasty things: This doesn't work, this is inconsistent, and how do I do this? I was going oops, people are actually using these new graphical user interfaces. And I had a closer look and I saw that it was just terrible." It was terrible because the graphical programs that ran under GNU/Linux used half a dozen toolkits, each with its own idiosyncratic appearances and approaches, making it a nightmare for nontechnical users.

Ettrich started exploring the possibilities, trying to find a way to recreate the simplicity of the Warp/Windows 95 approach, whose strengths he now saw. "I browsed the software mirrors"—the major stores of downloadable programs—"to find alternatives," he says. While searching, he came across a new toolkit called Qt. "I downloaded the thing, and played around with it, and had the feeling, wow, it's really easy to program." Moreover, although a commercial program, it was available free to those producing free software on all operating systems that support the X Window system—as GNU/Linux did.

Qt came from a small Norwegian company called Trolltech, based in Oslo. It had been founded in 1994 by Eirik Eng and Haavard Nord, and was originally called Quasar Technologies. "Qt" was the Quasar Toolkit, and is pronounced "cute" by those inside the company. The name Trolltech came about because the company founders thought it "sounded a bit more Norwegian," as Nord explains. "Many Norwegian companies are called Troll this, Troll that." And he adds, "Trolls are big creatures, they live in the forests, or inside mountains. Some of them can be evil and bad, and some of them can be good as well."

These trolls were certainly trying to do good. Alongside the commercial licenses for their Qt toolkit, they also offered a free version for free software programmers. "We did that right from the very first day," Nord notes. The reasons for this were a mixture of the pragmatic and the idealistic. "One of the options" for promoting the new Qt when it appeared in 1996 "was to get venture capital," he says, "and start spending the money doing advertisements, showing the toolkit to professional customers via magazines and so on. The second one was to simply give away a version for free so people could start using it" and learn about its virtues directly. Trolltech chose the latter course, partly because they had another motivation. "Eirik and I had from the start been using Linux, GCC, and Emacs," Nord explains, "and we appreciate very much using free software. So this was also a way we could contribute back to the community."

The more Ettrich looked at Qt, the more he liked it, and the more he was convinced it might provide him with the desktop solution he had been looking for. And so in October 1996 he sent out an announcement about his idea for KDE [K Desktop Environment]: a complete, free desktop for GNU/Linux, using Qt to provide the basic widgets.

Ettrich's announcement of the KDE project is one of the truly historic documents of the open source movement. Although, almost unbelievably, he says "I just started writing it, in maybe two hours or something," its 3,000 words provide a cogent analysis of all that is wrong with the current graphical interfaces available under Unix, as well as an extremely detailed road map of how to create something new to remedy the situation. One of the most telling aspects is that the second section is headed simply "A GUI for endusers"—suggesting a new emphasis that was revolutionary for the hitherto introverted hacker world.

The perspicacity of Ettrich's KDE announcement document is manifest nowhere more clearly than in its closing paragraphs. There, he lists some of the unhelpful replies such proposals invariably provoke, concluding with "Thanks for not sending these as follow-up to this posting :-) I know I'm a dreamer . . ." He was certainly dreaming if he ever imagined that his words could ward off the negative comments that began to flood in immediately. Ettrich says, "We were accused of being too Windows-like, and just, yeah, oh no, you want to destroy my Linux" by moving from the good old text-based command line to what Ettrich believes "many old hackers" saw as "this sissy 'GUI' thing."

But alongside such die-hard traditionalists there was another, more articulate group who had problems with the KDE project. Ettrich had already predicted what they would say in his list of likely responses to his proposal: "Why Qt? I prefer schnurz-purz-widgets with xyz-lisp-shell. GPL! Check it out!" The key element here was the GNU GPL, or rather the lack of it. Although Qt could indeed be used without payment by free software hackers, and its source code was available (later, anyway—initially Qt was shipped only in binary form—"We were a bit scared people could like steal our good ideas," Trolltech's Nord explains), it wasn't free software in the sense that Richard Stallman and the Free Software Foundation understood it.

The new KDE team did not ignore this wave of protests. "Everybody joining looked at alternatives [to Qt]," Ettrich explains, "and we had a long discussion: Shall we do it with Qt? And the result was [we decided] it's the best technical solution if we want to reach the goal that we have." As a result, the KDE project became the focus of one of the most intense and divisive struggles ever seen within the free software world, and one that exposes more clearly than anywhere the two great currents that flow through it.

In one camp are the pragmatists who, like Ettrich, say, "It's the best technical solution if we want to reach the goal that we have." As far as the licenses under which software is released are concerned, "for me it was a matter of personal opinion," he says. "If somebody tells me I will not use your free software because of the library that has a license I don't like, I didn't really care because I had experienced the same thing with LyX. There's basically two kinds of software," Ettrich believes, "good software and bad software."

This belief that licenses come down to "a matter of personal opinion" does not mean that the pragmatists are indifferent to what others think. For Ettrich, one of the key events during the early days of KDE was the February 1997 Linux Kongress at Würzburg in Germany. This was where Eric Raymond first read his paper, *The Cathedral and the Bazaar,* to an international audience. Trolltech's Haavard Nord gave a presentation, and so did Ettrich. Ettrich says that one factor that gave him the confidence to continue basing his KDE project on Qt despite the criticism from some circles was that at Würzburg "nobody was complaining about the license, nobody." As a result, "I said, OK, the problems are not that big."

The problems were big enough for the other camp in the world of free software, that of the purists. They believed with the pragmatists that there were just two kinds of software, but for purists like Stallman and his followers, those two kinds were free and proprietary. Technical issues were secondary or even irrelevant to the principle concern of liberty.

Qt's lack of the full freedom they required troubled the purists. Many of the fundamental rights granted by the GNU GPL—the right to modify the source code and to redistribute those modifications—were absent under the free Qt. This meant that, whatever Qt's other virtues, any desktop built using Qt would rest on nonfree foundations; Qt was therefore to be deprecated, according to the Free Software Foundation adherents. The great danger, as the purists saw it, was that KDE might well succeed, creating a situation where the free GNU/Linux operating system was used mostly to run the nonfree Qt for KDE applications, a terrible prospect for them.

As a result, the purists tried to persuade Trolltech to change the license terms of Qt to those of the GNU GPL when used for free software, with a commercial license for those who wanted to develop products to be sold. This would have made the KDE project true free software, and provided Trolltech with revenue from commercial applications. But Trolltech saw a danger in this approach. "There were many people in the free software community who did not want us to succeed with Qt," Nord explains. "So they were threatening they would put lots of power behind making some alternative version of Qt."

Under the terms of the GNU GPL, it would be permissible for a large team of free software hackers to take the source code for Qt and develop it faster than Trolltech—and in ways the company might not like. Although Trolltech would have the right to incorporate such changes, this alternative development stream would nonetheless serve to split the Qt world—to fork it. "The fork was maybe the thing we were most worried about," Nord says. As a result, Trolltech refused to consider the GNU GPL, and the free software community decided that the only possible approach was to set in motion an entirely new, and unambiguously free desktop project that would ensure that KDE did not end up as the standard by default.

The person who came to lead the project was the young Mexican, Miguel de Icaza Amozurrita, born, as Ettrich was, in 1972. He had first heard about the GNU project from a friend when he was studying mathematics at the National Autonomous University of Mexico, in his birthplace, Mexico City. Gaining practical experience had to wait until he became a system administrator at the university, parallel to his studies. "When I got my Sun machine at the university," he says, "the first thing I did was install this free stuff that was out there. And I read RMS's manifesto, and I was hooked up with the whole idea of creating a full operating system that was completely free."

De Icaza's first contribution to the GNU project was a file manager, a program for viewing and manipulating the contents of directories. "I wanted to have a good file manager, because I was coming from the DOS world in which they had a similar tool which was pretty good." That "good file manager" from the DOS world was Norton Commander, and provided de Icaza's program with a name: Midnight Commander.

His next project involved the Sun machine he was using for his system administration duties. Dave Miller had started work on a port of GNU/Linux to the platform, and de Icaza offered to help. Miller has some interesting comments on de Icaza at the time. "I think early on his programming/engineering more closely matched his adrenaline-pumped personality," Miller notes. De Icaza's extraordinary energy, famous within the free software community, would stand him in good stead as he took on ever more free software projects.

As well as this phenomenal drive, de Icaza is also notable for his dedication to the GNU cause. For example, one of the projects he contributed to was "the Linux RAID [Redundant Array of Inexpensive Discs] code, which is a thing that lets you have faster reliable access to your hard drives in Linux." De Icaza decided to work on this not out of some personal need: "I didn't have the hardware," he notes, "so I was emulating the actual physical devices for implementing that stuff." That is, he created a software model of a RAID system purely so that he could write a driver for others to use.

After the RAID code, de Icaza moved on to another GNU/Linux port, to an SGI machine. Once again, he was building on the work of Dave Miller, who had begun the port during a summer vacation job at SGI while working for Larry McVoy there. It was at this time, at the end of 1996, that Ettrich announced the KDE project. Initially, de Icaza was pleased that someone was working on a desktop for GNU/Linux. "At the beginning, I didn't understand what was happening," he recalls. "So I said, 'Oh, yeah, well, these are nice efforts, it's free, it's under the GPL'"— KDE itself was released under the GPL, even though the Qt libraries were not.

"So I talked to Erik Troan at Red Hat," de Icaza continues. "I said, 'Here, Erik, you should be shipping this, it's wonderful stuff.' And then I talked to Richard [Stallman], and said, 'Richard, this is great stuff going on, we have to support this project.' And he said, 'Well, no, the problem is the following,' and they both said the same thing: The result is not free. And I said, 'Oh, wait, wait, wait a second, let me see that again.' So I went and read the license, and indeed, the problem was that the [Qt] software was proprietary."

After initial attempts to convince Trolltech to use the GNU GPL for the Qt libraries had failed, people started considering the alternatives. "We tried a number of approaches," de Icaza says. But there were only two real options: One was to come up with a free clone of Qt that would have no licensing problems. Although such a project, called Harmony, was later begun, de Icaza had his doubts about this approach because it had been tried elsewhere without success. The other option was ambitious: to create a new desktop that would be based entirely on GPL'd software.

But this left proponents of the idea with a problem: Which toolkit should they use? The main ones, such as Motif (and Qt), were proprietary, and so out of the question. The solution was daring: They would use the Gtk+ toolkit Peter Mattis had created for the GIMP. In retrospect, it is extraordinary that what became the huge edifice of an entire graphical user interface to GNU/Linux was built on foundations thrown down entirely by chance. As Mattis himself says, "At the time, to write our own toolkit, people would have said that's stupid and crazy. I guess in hindsight that was an incredibly lucky decision. It had a huge impact having a pretty good quality toolkit for people to do graphical programs with, and put a big impetus behind the whole open source explosion."

As well as being able to use a preexisting toolkit, the new project could also recycle a name. The new GUI system would be called GNOME ("guh-nome," the initial "g" pronounced, as is usual for GNU software). GNOME stood for GNU Network Object Model Environment—which seemed to have little to do with graphical user interfaces. In fact, this "old" GNOME project drew its inspiration from the most unlikely source: Microsoft.

In 1997, "just before the GNOME project as a desktop replacement" was started, de Icaza says, "I had visited my friends at Microsoft." They showed him a new technology called ActiveX, which was part of Microsoft's ambitious plans to catch up in the Internet sphere. ActiveX consisted of small programs that could be sent over the Internet to a Web browser, where they would add advanced functions. Unfortunately for Microsoft, this approach proved to be a security nightmare, and ActiveX never caught on for Internet use.

But ActiveX formed part of a broader component strategy whereby software could be built up out of these smaller elements. De Icaza was impressed by this aspect, and wanted to create something similar for GNU/Linux. "GNOME was initially developed to create this component system," he says.

Then along came KDE and the decision to create a rival desktop project. It was decided to adapt the original component-based approach. Just as Ettrich had realized that KDE would need to be a meta-project, made up of many smaller stand-alone programs, so de Icaza and his fellow GNOME supporters saw that the component model offered many advantages for free software coding. "It helps," de Icaza explains, "because that means that if a component is buggy, instead of having to understand a huge application, you just have to understand the [smaller] application in which the problem is actually happening." That is, it takes the modular approach adopted in the Linux kernel and applies it to higher-level applications.

GNOME's component model went through several names. "Eventually the component model was not called GNOME," de Icaza says. "It was originally called Baboon, and then we changed it to Bonobo. My girlfriend was deep into primate behavior," he explains "so I got exposed to a lot of monkeys." In addition to being given a new name, the original Baboon component system was substantially revised and improved before becoming the current Bonobo.

When the GNOME project was announced in August 1997, "there was a lot of good response, and we started working right away on the project," de Icaza says. One of the earliest GNOME coders was Alan Cox. "He has contributed a lot of software, a lot of fixes, a lot of patches," de Icaza notes. "He was working on GNOME because we had a very clean license compared to the other one. Many of the people working on GNOME were actually people who were very concerned with the licensing issues."

One company interested in the licensing issues and in having a completely free desktop was Red Hat. As a consequence, "about four months after the creation of the GNOME project," de Icaza says, "they actually put people working on GNOME." This provided an important boost, he says, because "many of the things that other people wouldn't have done in their spare time [Red Hat] did." de Icaza adds, "They even lost market share due to their commitment to GNOME" because competitors Caldera and SuSE were shipping their distribution with the new and highly attractive KDE while Red Hat was waiting for GNOME to catch up.

Despite all this broad-based effort, de Icaza says, even its most fervent supporters wished that GNOME wouldn't need to be finished. "Initially we were hoping that the existence of the project would make [Trolltech] change their minds, but they didn't. So we just kept working and working until we actually had something to use."

Trolltech may not have been willing to accommodate the demands of the GNOME supporters, but they were certainly trying to improve the situation. As Ettrich explained, Haavard Nord had spoken at the Linux Kongress in February 1997, and even at this stage had made an offer. "At the end of Haavard's talk he said, 'We want to do something about the licensing; we want to set up a legal body, some kind of foundation, to ensure that there will always be a free edition.' He said that, without being really pressed or anything," Ettrich says. "Everybody said, 'Yeah, it's good, we can do that in the future,' and nobody really jumped in and said, 'Yeah, we have to do that, it's really important to do that now.'"

Despite its apparent lack of interest, Trolltech later went ahead and formed the KDE Free Qt Foundation. "We knew that the KDE guys were a bit a squeezed," Nord says, "and they were under pressure from other people." The reason, he explains, was the not unreasonable fear that "OK, [Qt is] free software now, but if the Trolls are going to change the license in a couple of years, we are then stuck with all this KDE software and we can't continue developing it because now Trolltech wants money from the licensing." The KDE Free Qt Foundation, set up in April 1998, ensured that a free version of the Qt libraries would always be available, even if the company were sold or ceased trading.

This development allayed the fears of many, but still did not address the central issue of the license that rankled with the purist wing of free software. As Nord explains, "Now many people complained that they could not send patches or make modifications to Qt." To try to resolve the situation, Trolltech decided that it would go even further. But it was a painful process. "Some people [at Trolltech] threatened to quit their jobs if we made an open source version of Qt," Nord explains, "because they feared that that threatened our income."

Eventually, Trolltech decided to draw up a new license for the Qt libraries, the Q Public License (QPL). Ransom Love, "worried by all the arguments about the Qt licensing," Nord believes, because Caldera was using KDE for its distribution, put Trolltech in touch with Bruce Perens and Eric Raymond, who were asked to take a look at the license. "It was quite overwhelming," Nord says, "they helped us a lot." The resulting QPL, released in November 1998, at last seemed to solve the remaining problems with Qt for all but the most demanding free software advocates. "Many of the people who were against Trolltech and Qt thought that now we had come far enough," Nord says. On 4 September 2000, Trolltech went even further and added the GNU GPL as an alternative.

When the QPL first appeared back in November 1998, GNOME had been in existence for more than a year, and had made substantial progress towards its first official release, which eventually came out in March 1999. There was therefore little prospect that GNOME would cease development or merge with KDE. One interesting difference between the two projects is that an office suite was not part of the original KDE project, "mainly because I never used half the packages," Ettrich explains. "I knew what a word processor was, but I never used Microsoft Office." These office applications were soon added by other programmers. For de Icaza, by contrast, office applications were central to the vision. "The goal of the GNOME project is to run a completely free system without using any proprietary applications. So the office suite is obviously part of this effort. If you want to be able to use a completely free operating system, you need to provide the tools [end-users] need for the day-to-day work."

Even though its final vision was more complete, the purist wing was dilatory in creating a desktop for end-users. Given that there were such superb tools as Emacs, fancy GUI word processors may have seemed superfluous. The pragmatist Ettrich saw that, on the contrary, it was vital to move GNU/Linux forward into new areas, and to give nontechnical users a way to enjoy the benefits of this powerful system. It was the pragmatist KDE project that undertook what appeared to be an insanely ambitious plan to create an entire GUI front-end to GNU/Linux that would be the equal of the new and eye-catching Windows 95.

And it was the pragmatists' decision to use the technically best toolkit at the time—Qt—even though it was not completely free, that spurred the purists into putting together their own desktop project to match KDE in its functions and its suitability to the end-user.

Thus it is down to the sometimes fraught dynamic between the pragmatist and purist wings that the free software world has made one of its most important advances. Without the pragmatists, things might have taken years longer—and Windows would have become even more firmly entrenched. And without the purists' refusal to compromise, Qt might never have moved to the open source QPL, and the KDE desktop would have been dangerously compromised.

In an e-mail dated 10 July 1998, Linus offered his thoughts on the matters of licensing, KDE, and GNOME, and gave a clear indication of where he stood on the matter.

Personally, I like KDE better than gnome right now, on the strength of pretty user interface and it working better. I personally use neither, though. I know there has been a lot of silly license flamage, and I don't particularly like it.

My opinion on licenses is that "he who writes the code gets to chose his license, and nobody else gets to complain." Anybody complaining about a copyright license is a whiner.

This, of course, is the classic pragmatist position.

The anti-KDE people are free to write their own code, but they don't have the moral right to complain about other people writing other code. I despise people who do complain, and I won't be sucked into the argument.

Although Linus seemed to prefer KDE at that time, this was probably more a reflection of its being further along than GNOME. He has since distanced himself from the discussion, and promoted the value of having more than one solution. For example, in September 1998 he said, "It's kind of like politics: You don't need to have a one-party approach to be stable, and in fact it tends to be more stable to have multiple parties that try to vie for power than to have a single rule. I think the KDE versus GNOME issue will just make the system better in the end, even if it means some internal struggles for a while."

Today, KDE and.GNOME are growing vigorously and competing in a healthy fashion. Both have hundreds of developers and many hundreds of applications. There are also moves to make the two approaches more compatible. "We're definitely working closer," de Icaza says. "We're agreeing on a number of standards." And, as Ettrich points out, one reason such cooperation functions is "because we have no commercial interests in all these things."

Those who like to point to the continued existence of the KDE and GNOME projects, with their separate collections of software, as evidence of a fundamental split in the GNU/Linux world forget one important point: It is possible to run both KDE and GNOME applications on the same machine, at the same time, no matter which desktop is running. So there is no real fork between the two projects, just differences in approach and on-screen appearance. As free software, KDE and GNOME are both routinely included with commercial distributions. And choice, after all, has always been at the heart of free software.

The paths the two founders have since taken present an interesting contrast. True to his role as the creator of a meta-project, Ettrich has stepped even further back from a "star" position. Appropriately enough, he is devoting himself to questions of technology, specifically Qt technology, as an employee of Trolltech. His move there in August 1998 is in many ways the perfect solution for everybody. "Trolltech gave me the possibility to improve KDE's toolkit and thus improve KDE," he says. "I can choose whether I want to spend time hacking on KDE or Qt, so I have lots of freedom." It is also the perfect solution for Trolltech, which now employs a gifted coder—the company took him on because "he was an amazing developer," Nord says—as well as someone who is uniquely qualified to act as the link to the KDE project.

De Icaza has chosen what might appear a surprising option: to set up a company based around GNOME software. Of course, the purist wing of free software is not against commercial software as such, only proprietary code. And the example of Cygnus has shown that it is possible to create a highly successful company based on GNU GPL software. De Icaza says he spoke to Michael Tiemann, one of the founders of Cygnus, when setting up his company, Helix Code, with fellow hacker Nat Friedman, as well as to Red Hat's Bob Young.

Reflecting its business plan, the company was originally called International GNOME Support. The current name Helix Code "comes from the fact that we couldn't get any other name," de Icaza says, as well as "all this monkey, evolutionary stuff" that permeates GNOME.

Alongside support work—"We're already finding contracts," de Icaza says—Helix Code has brought out its first product, Helix GNOME—"basically, sort of a distribution for GNOME, easy to install," he explains. "It's just the desktop, so it works on top of many other Linux distributions." Other projects include Gnumeric, a spreadsheet project led by de Icaza that is fully compatible with Microsoft's Excel to the point where "we match the printed output, which is extremely important," and the e-mail client Evolution, which is extensible through the use of Bonobo components.

Not surprisingly, Helix Code and the GNOME project are tightly interwoven. "Many of the people hired by the company"—among whom are most of the top GNOME hackers—"are maintainers of existing GNOME packages," de Icaza explains, "and they keep doing their maintenance work on those packages and updating and development. Obviously all the development we do is GPL'd and it becomes integrated with the GNOME project. So I think it benefits everybody."

Helix Code is not alone in establishing a symbiotic relationship with the free software project. A new company called Eazel, set up in August 1999, is also working on GNOME elements—"they are actually redoing the desktop and the file manager," de Icaza says—and making them freely available. "They're working together with us because we both depend on the component technology."

De Icaza believes this joint work will lead to significant advances. "It's not any more about just providing a desktop; we're actually going beyond that," he says. "We're very focused on usability, we're very focused on human-computer interaction. It's no longer a matter of providing a desktop for Unix users, it's about having people who have never touched a computer before feel comfortable with a free software system.

"We're pushing some of the most innovative technologies here," he emphasises. "I would say that this time we're going to have a clearly technical advantage"—an important point for a system which is often taxed by its competitors as being something of a laggard in user-interface technology. "When you see Gnome 2.0 you're going to see something that nobody else has—not Windows, not Mac, not anybody."

The invocation of the most famous Apple computer is particularly piquant because three of the founders of Eazel were key members of the original Macintosh team. Michael Boich, president and CEO of Eazel, created Apple's software evangelism group for the Macintosh; Bud Tribble, vice president of software engineering, managed the original Macintosh software team; and Andy Hertzfeld, whose job title at Eazel is simply "Software Wizard," designed and implemented a large portion of the original Macintosh system software, including the User Interface Toolbox.

Nothing could symbolize more potently how far GNU/Linux has come from its command-line, hacker-oriented origins in just a few years, and the extent to which it is assuming the mantle of challenger to Microsoft even for ordinary users—once Apple's cherished role—than the decision to create Eazel and work on open source software by these ex-Macintosh gurus. But the fight between GNU/Linux and Microsoft on the desktop lies some way off yet, assuming it arrives at all, which some still doubt.

On the server side, however, the battle has been raging for a while now. The official opening of hostilities can be dated to an attack by Microsoft back in April 1999, when what began as a small-scale covert operation went horribly wrong, and escalated into all-out media war.

16

Lies, Damned Lies, and Benchmarks

AS THE EVENTS OF 1998 AND 1999 brought GNU/Linux to more people's attention, and the growing range of heavyweight applications made it increasingly useful as an enterprise-level solution, a natural question posed itself: Which was better for the task—GNU/Linux or Windows NT? In early 1999, a spate of benchmark testing broke out as computer magazines tried to establish for the benefit of their readers how the two operating systems compared in raw performance.

The first of these comparisons appeared on 25 January, in a Ziff-Davis publication called *Sm@rt Reseller*, a title aimed at the value-added reseller sector of the computer market. GNU/Linux was potentially of great interest to these readers because their livelihoods depended on creating and selling complete solutions to customers. If they could swap in a free operating system instead of Windows NT, and without sacrificing performance, their profits might well increase substantially.

The article, written by Steven J. Vaughan-Nichols and Eric Carr, was unequivocal. Its headline read "Linux Up Close: Time to Switch," and its opening paragraphs were equally forthright: "Forget Linux's hype. Forget Microsoft Corp.'s server market share. The bottom line, according to our hands-on analysis, is that commercial Linux releases can do much more with far less than Windows NT Server can." Later on, the writers rubbed it in even more: "According to ZDLabs' results, each of the commercial Linux releases ate NT's lunch."

The tests used two benchmarks Ziff-Davis had created: WebBench and NetBench. The former measured the performance of GNU/Linux with the Apache Web server, as compared to Windows NT running Microsoft's Internet Information Server, which was bundled free with NT. NetBench tested how well the two systems could send out files to Windows PCs. Acting as a central file server to Windows clients was one of Windows NT's principal roles; for GNU/Linux, which was essentially a Unix system, such activity was alien. That it was possible at all was thanks to yet another piece of free software.

Called Samba, the program represents one of the best-kept secrets of the open source world. Its ability to mimic almost exactly a Windows NT machine acting as a file server has led to its being introduced surreptitiously into thousands of companies whose management have never noticed for the simple reason that the combination of Samba and GNU/Linux performs so flawlessly. Samba is probably the reason GNU/Linux systems are first used within companies otherwise committed to proprietary software. As such, it has played a crucial role, along with the Apache Web server, in establishing the corporate credentials of open source software.

The original author of Samba is Andrew Tridgell, who joined Linuxcare in 1999 as the starriest of its star hires. He was born in 1967, in Australia, and had been Linus's host in Canberra—and the indirect cause of the famous penguin incident. Samba was created to meet a personal need, as with so much free software, and almost entirely by accident.

"The whole thing started back in December 1991; I was a PhD student in the Australian National University of Canberra, and essentially I was looking for ways of procrastinating. An opportunity came up to beta-test something called Windex" Tridgell recalls. Windex was an X server for Microsoft Windows (then at version 3.0), and allowed a PC to display programs running on a Unix server. This was possible thanks to the inherently networked nature of the X Window system: Output from a program could be accessed over a network and displayed in a window created by an X server program—like Windex, say.

But Tridgell had a problem. "I was using PC-NFS to connect to a Sun system to share my files," he explains. That is, he was using an alternative way to swap files on his Windows PC with the main departmental server; it was awkward because a key element of the network connectivity on a PC, the TCP/IP stack, was different for the two approaches. To use Windex, he had to load its own stack. "It had to use the Pathworks one, because it was written by Digital and Pathworks was Digital's implementation of TCP/IP for Windows.

"So I installed Pathworks [on the PC]," he says, "and I could no longer access my PC-NFS server" because the stacks were different. At this point, the classic hacker idea ocurred to him: "So I thought, well, it can't be all that hard, the protocol, so maybe I can try and write a server for SunOS that provides the same functionality that is provided by a Pathworks server running on a Digital Unix box." By writing some software for the departmental Sun machine, he hoped to be able to swap files with his PC using just Pathworks instead of always needing to go back to NFS.

"What I didn't know was that the [Pathworks] protocol wasn't a proprietary Digital protocol," he notes. "In fact, the protocol was the same protocol used by Microsoft in their networking. And I didn't realize that the protocol was called SMB [Server Message Block], and I didn't realize that it was a partly documented protocol. So, in blissful ignorance, I went and implemented the protocol from the wire," he continues, referring to another classic hacker technique, "just watching packets." By looking at what messages were sent over the network, Tridgell was able to write some software to do the same, even though he didn't know how those messages worked.

"[I] implemented a basic server, and that took about a week over Christmas December '91," he recalls. "It's fun doing things over a Christmas break." Coincidentally, Linus was also having "fun doing things over a Christmas break," that year; he was adding the Virtual Memory capability to his very young Linux kernel, which he had begun just a few months before.

Once he had written his server, Tridgell decided to see whether anyone else was interested in using it. "So that was sent out to a Pathworks mailing list, and a number of people were interested in it and tried it out. I released version 0.1, then 0.5, within a couple of days of each other," he recalls. But something happened that caused him to drop the project: The department where he was working changed the hardware he was using and he no longer needed his simple Pathworks server program. "So I just stopped working on the project completely," he says. "I put a note on the FTP site saying, 'If anyone else wants to take over, then feel free to do so.'" Even though he had received "quite a bit of feedback," including several patches, nobody stepped forward to carry on development, and it seemed as if the project would go no further.

GNU/Linux revived the project, which was apt because the future Samba would prove one of its most powerful allies. In November 1992, somebody named Dan Shearer sent Tridgell an e-mail about his old Pathworks server. "Dan told me basically that there was some interest in porting this thing to Linux," Tridgell recalls. "So I wrote back and asked him, 'What's Linux?'—I'd never heard of it. So he told me what Linux was, and I went and downloaded a copy and put it on a PC that I'd got by that time, a 386, and I fell in love with Linux immediately."

As well as alerting him to GNU/Linux, this also raised his consciousness about free software in general. Even though Tridgell used free software—for example, he employed Emacs to look at the contents of the packets being sent over the network by Pathworks—"it was just sort of, oh, there it was, [and] I downloaded it. I didn't think about the whole free software movement," he says. But after his encounter with GNU/Linux, this changed. "Once I started reading the mailing lists, very quickly I understood what was happening, and wanted to participate." Fortunately, another chance event a year later suggested a way he might do this. "This was about the same time that I set up a little network at home." By now, Tridgell was using GNU/Linux, but his wife had a Microsoft Windows machine. The problem was how to network the two very different systems.

"And then I remembered an e-mail that I'd got from somebody saying that my server worked with Microsoft Windows as a client," he recalls. That is, Tridgell's Pathworks server could also talk to PCs running Microsoft Windows, not just to those running Digital's Windex product, which he was using initially.

"I'd dismissed the e-mail at the time," he says, "because I assumed the person didn't know what they were talking about." After all, he says, "I'd written a Pathworks server, not a Windows server. And you get a lot of crazy e-mails. But I went and downloaded the code [for the Pathworks server]—I had to actually go and download it because I didn't have a copy—and tried it" on his GNU/Linux box and "with my wife's Windows box at home. And lo and behold, it did indeed work."

Tridgell realized that his quick Christmas hack was actually something much more valuable: a way of allowing Unix and Windows machines to share files.

Spurred on by this discovery, Tridgell announced on 1 December 1993 a project to improve his old file-sharing code. "Lots of people responded to that," he recalls, "lots being of the order of fifty or a hundred people, which at the time, when you announced free software project, that was a big deal." Linux, after all, had initially only elicited responses from a handful of people. "At that stage, I GPL'd the code," Tridgell says. "I think it was largely out of loyalty to Linux; I was doing this on Linux and

I loved what was happening with GCC, and the other GNU projects, and so I wanted to be part of that."

In a short history of Samba that he wrote, Tridgell explains how the name 'Samba' came to be chosen. "The code in Samba was first called just 'server'; it then got renamed 'smbserver' when I discovered that the protocol is called SMB. Then in April 1994, I got an e-mail from Syntax, the makers of 'TotalNet advanced Server,' a commercial SMB server. They told me that they had a trademark on the name SMBserver and I would have to change the name." So Tridgell looked for words that contained the letters S, M, and B and chose Samba as the best (another was "salmonberry").

Samba developed in classic open source style. "People basically started sending in patches," he says, "and I started working frantically to improve the project. It was not long after that that I first read a specification of the SMB protocol, and discovered that there were lots of holes in the spec."

The holes in the specification make SMB an interesting hybrid between an open and proprietary standard. "Microsoft very much takes the attitude that if the specification, such as it exists, and the implementation in Windows NT differ, then NT is correct and the specification's wrong." This has a direct consequence for Tridgell and the Samba team. "In the SMB world," he says, "the whole point of the protocol these days is for interoperability with Microsoft. And so we always do all of our testing directly against the Microsoft implementations. And we try to remain bug-for-bug compatible where it makes sense. There are some cases where it doesn't make sense, and their bugs are just ridiculous, and you shouldn't emulate them. But in most cases, we emulate the bugs so that we interoperate completely with the Microsoft implementation."

Tridgell makes an important point about Microsoft in this context. "They consider themselves the only implementation of this protocol, even though they know they're not. But they control the server and they control the client, so they can just stick the code at the client and the server and it will work, and they don't really think much beforehand about designing it appropriately." This analysis sounds a note of warning of what might happen should Microsoft ever attain a dominant position on the Web, able to use—and abuse—its power on the client and server sides to mask bad coding. It emphasizes once again the importance of independent projects, such as Apache and Mozilla, dedicated to open standards.

Microsoft's attitude to the SMB protocols means that as it has extended the basic standard, Samba has had to track it. Samba's constant shadowing has led to a certain ambivalence on the software company's part. "Our relationship with Microsoft is rather interesting," Tridgell says. "There are some people in Microsoft who are all out to help us, because they see Samba as providing a critical link for them to the Unix world. We've even got Microsoft engineers ringing us up for help when they're installing Samba at a site because it allows them to roll out NT at an existing Unix shop." On the other hand, he adds, "there's other people trying to hinder us. Microsoft is a big company, and there's a multitude of opinions."

Those opinions were doubtless polarizing even more when the benchmarks started appearing in 1999 because they showed Samba and GNU/Linux in an increasingly favorable light. Following the initial comparison in *Sm@rt Reseller* on 25 January, which had noted that GNU/Linux running Samba "kicks NT's butt" as a file server, on 1 February, *PC Week* Labs reviewed the new Linux 2.2 kernel.

The original *Sm@rt Reseller* test had used version 2.0 of the Linux kernel, which was over two years old at this point. Perhaps it was not too surprising that the *PC Week* article began, "Look out, Microsoft: The new Linux 2.2.0 kernel adds enterprise-critical SMP [Symmetric Multi-Processor] capabilities to the operating system's proven reliability, flexibility and irresistible price, giving users weary of Windows 2000 delays and shortcomings strong reasons to seriously investigate the platform."

Then, on 26 March, the same *Sm@rt Reseller* team that had written the piece on 25 January looked at the recently released Samba 2.0. Once again, their comments left no room for doubt. Under the title "Samba 2.0: A license to kill NT?" they began, "Who needs an NT license? Not us!" and concluded with the following: "Even if your customers seem to have dug their heels into the Microsoft camp, Samba's one-two punch of far faster SMB file and print services without Microsoft licensing fees makes it an option that must be considered. For basic Server Message Block file and print serving, Samba can't be beat. No ifs, ands or buts."

The verdict seemed unanimous, and the defeat stunning: the freely available GNU/Linux and Samba combination beat the proprietary Windows NT as a file server from every viewpoint. But not quite unanimous. Miraculously, just when all seemed lost, a benchmark appeared that asserted the contrary and provided Microsoft with the ammunition it so desperately needed.

On 13 April, a company called Mindcraft issued a press release headed "Mindcraft study shows Windows NT server outperforms Linux." The summary read, "Microsoft Windows NT Server is 2.5 times faster than

Linux as a file server and 3.7 times faster as Web server." Once more, Ziff-Davis's NetBench and WebBench were used for the benchmarks, running on a PC with four Intel Xeon processors and 1 Gigabyte of memory (almost identical to the *PC Week* test machine of 1 February).

Mindcraft was set up in 1985 by Bruce Weiner. "Our current business has really been focused on performance testing over the last four or five years," Weiner explains. This comes in two forms. "One is performance testing for vendors to validate that their products perform the way they expected under circumstances they expected to work in," he says, "and that work is generally not published. The other side is performance marketing; it's nearly always for publishing."

Almost immediately after the press release appeared, an item posted to the *Linux Today* Web site by Dave Whitinger pointed out one extremely relevant fact from the benchmark report not mentioned in the press release. Under the heading "Mindcraft Certification," Whitinger noted, was the following phrase: "Mindcraft, Inc. conducted the performance tests described in this report between March 10 and March 13, 1999. Microsoft Corporation sponsored the testing reported herein."

Of this significant omission, Weiner explains, "Initially the contract had a clause that precluded us from discussing the test in any detail. Other details were approved." Weiner was well-aware that it would have been better to admit this from the start. "I suggested that," he says, and explains Microsoft's about-face as follows: "They're a big company, and I think things got communicated incorrectly or misunderstood somewhere along the way as to what happened. When that became clear, they said, 'Well, sure, go ahead and tell them.' I guess maybe somebody high enough up heard the noise, whatever."

That noise was considerable. "I expected a few things: 'They don't know what they're talking about'—that kind of thing," Weiner says. "But the firestorm that occurred was unbelievable; it's like I killed a baby or something. I didn't kill it, I spanked it, and I said, 'No, no, don't do that, learn how to do it right.'" But the open source community felt that even a spanking was a mortal insult, and Microsoft must have been taken aback by the vehemence of the reaction.

Of Microsoft's initial approach, Weiner says, "They contacted us some short time before; it wasn't months and months." This put a certain amount of pressure on Mindcraft, because "typically there's a lot of setup goes on in these tests ahead of time," he says. Mindcraft and Microsoft agreed that the Ziff-Davis WebBench and NetBench programs would be used. "It's an OK thing to run," Weiner explains, because "nobody can say you rigged the test."

Nonetheless, people in the open source community were soon suggesting precisely that, largely because more details began to emerge about the circumstances of the tests. Appropriately perhaps, it was *Sm@rt Reseller*'s Vaughan-Nichols who was among the first to point out some interesting issues surrounding how the two systems were prepared.

As Vaughan-Nichols's article dated 15 April 1998 explained, Mindcraft was able to draw directly on support from Microsoft when tuning the system to get the best performance. When it came to the GNU/Linux system, however, it could obtain no similar help, either from Red Hat, whose distribution was being used for the test, or from the open source community at large. As a result, the Red Hat system used for the test lacked several important tweaks that would have improved its performance.

Further investigation by the open source community dug up interesting details about Mindcraft's attempts to obtain tuning information for GNU/Linux, which consisted of appeals for help in Usenet newsgroups. Weiner explains what happened. "We did it right at the beginning of the tests," he says. "I think we did one [post] ourselves. We got no real response and then there was another party that did one. And at that time there were just like no responses to this thing that we got, nothing at least meaningful."

To say that "nothing meaningful" was obtained is hardly fair, because a reply was posted on the same day, 11 March 1999, with detailed comments and suggestions. But these included changing the way the system was set up and using a different operating system, and so could not be taken up. If Mindcraft had wanted serious help for the benchmarks, its obvious course would have been to explain why it wanted the information. In these circumstances, open source supporters would have done their utmost to help tune the system.

Weiner explains why he felt it was impossible to take this action. "In the open source community," he says, for "a lot of people there, [Microsoft is] the evil villain, and we knew had we mentioned that, the whole firestorm that occurred after the fact would have occurred" then. This is a fair point, but still left open the possibility of mentioning the benchmarks without naming the company sponsoring them. "Boy, things were tight and rolling fast in terms of timing and what was occurring," Weiner says. "In retrospect, certainly, we could have done it much better, no question about it. And we used that retrospect, and I guess the attention that this brought the first time, to do it right the second time. And there's no question, I think, we got the input we needed the second time."

The "second time" referred to Weiner's decision to rerun the benchmarks, this time soliciting help from the top people in the Linux and Samba worlds. Contrary to Weiner's claim that there was "no question" that they got the input they needed, the open source community, though offering what help it could, was still deeply unhappy with the overall setup, and felt that it was not able to give the necessary input.

At the heart of the matter was Mindcraft's continued refusal to allow anyone from the open source world to be present during the second run. Without access to the test-bed, the open source community believed it was at a considerable disadvantage. Jeremy Allison, who became one of the major actors in the Mindcraft benchmark drama, already had a good idea about the real reason this access was being denied.

Born in Sheffield, England, in 1962, Allison is number two in the Samba world after Andrew Tridgell. "I tend to do the stuff that makes a release go into production, so I am the paranoid one," he says. In this respect, Allison plays a role similar to that of Alan Cox in the Linux world. Allison has had a wide-ranging career, including stints as a software engineer at Sun, Cygnus, SGI and, most recently, VA Linux. His open source credentials are impeccable. In the late 1980s, he came up with a patch to GCC, which he sent off to Richard Stallman, who promptly said, "No." "It was great," Allison says. "It was like getting a reject message from God."

Allison even created an SMB server of his own, though he notes, "No one ever saw that code." As soon as he came across Samba, he says, "I just started hacking on it," and he quickly became the key developer alongside Tridgell. As such, and probably because he was located in Silicon Valley and Tridgell was in Australia, Allison was one of the experts to whom Weiner turned. "Bruce Weiner was calling me up and I was giving him Samba tuning advice," Allison recalls. "The Valley's a kind of small place, and people talk a lot. I knew he was up at Microsoft [in Seattle]. And it was really funny, because I was basically trying to get him to admit that, and he wouldn't."

On 4 May, in a *Linux Today* article titled "Setting the Record Straight: Where *Linux Today* got it right and wrong," Weiner offered his rebuttal to an article of 27 April on the same Web site, in which Dave Whittinger and Dwight Johnson asked, "Will Mindcraft II be better?" In it, among other things, Weiner acknowledged that the Mindcraft bench tests had indeed been carried out at Microsoft. Weiner wrote, "Many have tried to imply that something is wrong with Mindcraft's tests because they were done in a Microsoft lab. You should know that Mindcraft verified the clients were set up as we documented in our report and that Mindcraft, not Microsoft, loaded the server software and tuned it as documented in our report. In essence, we took over the lab we were using and verified it was set up fairly."

There is no reason to dispute this; but suspicions and skepticism about the end results are to be expected when the circumstances of the testing are hidden. Moreover, in one important respect, running the tests in Microsoft's labs did give NT an advantage through the presence of Microsoft's technicians. As Weiner says, "They were available on call to us at any time. And we talked with them up front about tunes for their products, and they recommended a certain set of tunes."

Weiner emphasizes, "The information we're getting is the same as that information that's publicly available. So it wasn't as if we got anything special." He concedes, however, that by being at the Microsoft labs, "we did have the convenience," if nothing else. In any case, the presence of these technicians "at any time" stands in painful contrast with the refusal to allow even one member from the open source community to be present for either of the tests. "I think best way to put it is it was too short notice to make that happen well," he says, citing once more the pressure of time as one of the overriding factors in the way benchmarks were conducted.

Weiner recognizes the importance of the issue. "It was unfortunate," he says. "I know that the guys that helped us were feeling shortchanged because of that. Even if only one of their folks could have come in, that would have been good enough for all of them. And I said to myself, look, the best way to do this thing is let's don't publish these [second] results yet." Because they were conducted in largely the same circumstances, the same accusations would be leveled. Weiner realized that something more was needed. He quotes himself as saying, "'Let's do an open benchmark.' And I talked Microsoft into doing it."

The person overseeing the Mindcraft benchmarks at Microsoft at this time was Jim Ewel, one of the company's most experienced marketing experts. He had joined Microsoft in 1989, and worked on what he describes as an "eclectic mix" of jobs before being appointed general manager of marketing in January 1999 for the upcoming Windows 2000, the final name for Windows NT 5. He worked alongside Mike Nash, the general manager of the Windows 2000 launch. Ewel explains that the Mindcraft benchmarks "started out as a project over in Mike Nash's group." The Microsoft team initiated the Mindcraft benchmarks, Ewel says, because "we were hearing a lot of PR about Linux, and a lot of claims in terms of performance and all that stuff. We just thought that the reality was very different from the perception. So we wanted to get some facts out."

Weiner says that once the open benchmarks were suggested, the attitude of the hackers changed. "It was 'OK, guys, let's call your bluff,'" he recalls. And "all of a sudden, the Linux community was backing away," he adds. In one respect, this was hardly surprising; after all, when the first test results were released, there was no mention that Microsoft had paid for them, nor that they were conducted in a Microsoft lab. The tuning was not optimal for the GNU/Linux system, and even with the second round of tests, representatives of the open source world were refused access to the equipment.

In another respect, however, Weiner may have been right about a certain backing away. After the initial shock and outrage had begun to die down, the top hackers got down to some serious analysis of just what was going on. One of the reasons this took some time was the nature of the Ziff-Davis benchmarks.

As Andrew Tridgell explains, "The problem with NetBench is that it's a very closed benchmark, in the sense that anyone can download it, but you'd need a half-million-dollar lab in order to run it seriously. You can't just go and run it at home and expect to get a result that's at all meaningful. There was really only one location available to the open source community to test this sort of configuration," he continues, "and that was inside SGI, where Jeremy [Allison] was working. And so though he could do that, that was an enormous bottleneck, and it meant that people like Alan [Cox], Linus, and David Miller couldn't really do the tests themselves." In this respect, NetBench and WebBench were taking the community into a new realm where the open source techniques based on the input of the many users running software on their personal computers was no longer enough.

But hackers are nothing if not resourceful. Using SGI's facilities, Allison ran NetBench for just one PC client, and all the details of the data's flowing over the network were recorded. Tridgell then replayed that data to simulate hundreds of clients running simultaneously, employing just two fast GNU/Linux machines linked together. In this way, it was possible to run NetBench without having that half-a-million-dollar laboratory—and hence start investigating what was happening in the Mindcraft benchmarks.

Tridgell also carried out another important piece of work. "One of the things you're doing with benchmarking is you're trying to work out which subsystem on the server is the bottleneck," he says. "So what I did was I created three benchmarks," each one of which tested a different part of the GNU/Linux-Samba combination. The problem was revealed when the NetBench simulation was run using these three benchmarks.

The difficulty was not with Samba, as Tridgell was pleased to find; the tests ran slowly even without it. It turned out that it "was a kernel problem," he explains. "Basically, we weren't scalable to a four-way SMP." This was a variant on the old "Linux does not scale problem," in this case deep within the kernel, that was showing up only under the extreme circumstances of the Mindcraft test. Once he knew what the problem was, Tridgell came up with a way of fixing it. "It was a very ugly hack," he says with the typical disdain a top coder has for such rough-and-ready solutions. "That sped us up by about a factor or two. It wasn't of course valid, it wasn't a patch that you could really put into a production kernel."

The good news was that Tridgell's analysis and the rough fix meant that the problem he had located could be fixed after a little serious hacking. The bad news was that a proper patch would not be available for the open benchmark that Weiner was proposing. As Allison says, "I knew we were going to lose, because I'd already done the benchmarks on Linux in SGI's internal lab. I knew what the bottleneck was, and it wasn't a Samba issue. Basically, the idea at that point was just trying to do damage control as much as we could."

In this sense, Weiner is probably right in that the open source community were backing away from the idea of a rematch: They knew what was wrong, and that at this stage "it was all politics," as Tridgell comments. "It was Mindcraft trying to save face." But "saving face" was important to Weiner; the "firestorm" that the benchmarks had provoked had cast aspersions on his company. Whatever flaws the first two benchmarks may have had, Mindcraft needed to establish that it had not cheated. If doubts remained on that score, Mindcraft would have no future customers.

Weiner originally made his open benchmark invitation on 4 May 1998, and revised it on 18 May to address some of the concerns raised. The first phase of the test had as its stated purpose to "reproduce the results of Mindcraft's second test." As Weiner says, "The reason we wanted that one done is that we wanted Mindcraft to be vindicated that we hadn't rigged a damn thing."

The second phase was where "Linux experts use anything available at the time of Mindcraft's second test. This will show how much better Mindcraft could have done at the time." The final phase aimed to "get the best performance using today's software." Weiner says that allowing this third phase "was a pretty brave thing for Microsoft to say at that point," with some justice. Microsoft had little to gain and much to lose by allowing the GNU/Linux platform to be tuned to the limit.

Ewel explains that "it was a joint decision. I talked to Mike Nash and Jim Allchin"—one of the most senior Microsoft executives—"about it. It was taking a chance, we knew that." But "we know we have a good product and we were pretty confident that [the Linux hackers] weren't going to be able to do a benchmark special to beat us." This was because he and his colleagues had "sat down with our best technologists," he says, to weigh the risks and the rewards of taking part in such an open benchmark. The last point is interesting, because it suggests that Microsoft had been examining GNU/Linux and Samba in great detail, to the point that it knew how much work was required to deal with issues the Mindcraft benchmarks had surfaced. Nonetheless, credit should be given to Ewel and his team for having the courage to take this calculated risk.

Not that Microsoft did not exploit the situation to the full in other ways. On 12 May, it posted a document to its Web site called "Update on Windows NT server vs. Linux performance and capabilities." In this, a typically well-researched Microsoft document, it laid out the previous Mindcraft benchmarks, along with other independent tests; for example, tests that had just appeared in *PC Week* on 10 May, and in *PC Magazine* on 11 May, all of which tended to corroborate Mindcraft's results.

As well as allowing representatives of the open source world to be present, the open benchmark tests sought to address other concerns. For example, it turns out that Samba works better with PCs running Windows NT rather than the Windows 95 and 98 used in the first two Mindcraft tests. "I personally wasn't aware of that at all at the time," Weiner says. But the open benchmark would be run using both Windows 95/98 and Windows NT clients. Moreover, the tests would be run using first one processor and then four processors, with corresponding amounts of memory, because GNU/Linux was designed to run better on leaner systems.

Weiner's final concession was to allow these open benchmarks to be run at an independent laboratory. Weiner explains, "*PC Week* and ZD Labs said, 'Why don't you do it here,' because obviously it was a story. And we said, 'Great, we'd love to do it.'" The benchmarks having originated at Ziff-Davis, a certain justice prevailed in this choice for the scene of the final shoot-out. All parties agreed to participate on this basis, and the bench testing began on 14 June. "We wanted it to happen much earlier," Weiner says, "but [the head of ZD Labs] couldn't arrange that because of their lab schedule."

The event proved anticlimactic after the drama of the previous three months. As everybody knew it would, Windows NT beat GNU/Linux running Apache and Samba. Henry Baltazar and Pankaj Chowdhry reported in *PC Week*: "After a tortuous five days of tests, audited by the best and the brightest from Mindcraft, Microsoft and Red Hat Software Inc., and despite significant tuning improvements made on the Linux side, Windows NT 4.0 still beat Linux using the Apache Web server and Samba in every performance category, although the margin of victory was smaller than in Mindcraft's tests. But far more interesting is that, in all the areas in which the Linux community cried foul, its assumptions were wrong." Weiner says he felt "totally vindicated" by the outcome, and for Microsoft, Ewel comments, "We were very pleased with the final published results."

The Mindcraft benchmarks represented a difficult time for the GNU/Linux community—and an important one. Before, its members had almost reveled in their splendid isolation from the rest of the computer world. Like rebellious adolescents, they had taken a great delight in cocking a snook at authority, in doing things their way—secure in the knowledge that their approach was "obviously" better.

The Mindcraft benchmarks changed all that. They showed that for all its real strengths, the Linux kernel had real weaknesses. It still did not scale well. The failure to shine in these benchmarks shattered the complacent attitude of the hacker community that held they were simply the best in everything. As such, it represented a kind of rite of passage—painful, but necessary—to the grown-up world of real computing. In particular, it provided a messy introduction to the sometimes unfair world of business.

The Mindcraft tests, despite the unsatisfactory way in which the relationship with Microsoft was revealed, showed unequivocally that GNU/Linux did not handle this kind of enterprise-level system as well as Windows NT. Open source advocates might point out that the test system and benchmarks were chosen to show their software at its worst; but companies do use such systems, and such benchmarks, however flawed, do play a role in the framing of corporate IT policies. Linus himself had long before recognized the realities of comparative testing when he wrote of "Lies, damned lies, and benchmarks" during an early exchange about the relative performance of GNU/Linux back in February 1993.

If GNU/Linux was to be taken seriously in the enterprise market, it had to improve its showing in these kinds of tests. Andrew Tridgell's work had already pointed the way, and patches were soon forthcoming. First, Dave Miller did some hacking, but "the person that did the really good work was Ingo Molnar from Red Hat," Tridgell says. Tridgell explains that Molnar "ended up tripling our performance, even quadrupling in some cases."

The Mindcraft saga has done more than give rise to a few handy patches. "It gave a real focus," Tridgell believes. "In particular, from a technical point of view, it made us focus on the larger-scale benchmarks as compared to the microbenchmarks. To a reasonable extent, the kernel developers had been using microbenchmarks like lmbench," which was Larry McVoy's software for tuning at a very low level. In this area, Tridgell contends, "Linux was so far ahead of all the other operating systems in that it's just not funny."

But lmbench "didn't stress the operating system under a load of fifty processors running simultaneously," he says. "Getting scalable kernel-level SMP is a much more difficult task, and nobody had really worked on it. So what this [episode] did was it focused a lot of effort on that." In a sense, then, the Mindcraft benchmarks did Linux a great service.

Linus eventually realized this too, but not before even he lost his usual equanimity and coolheadedness. Weiner says, "I got the firestorm from the top ranks" in the open source world, and Allison recalls that "Linus sent [Weiner] this just unbelievably nasty e-mail calling him a fair few names." Similarly, Ewel says that he and Linus "exchanged some fairly heated e-mails." For a moment, Linus had forgotten that bug reports from users in new situations, pushing and stressing the software in new ways, had always helped make Linux better. And the Mindcraft benchmarks had done this by showing what needed to be done if GNU/Linux was to become an enterprise solution. One concrete result of this input was revealed by Red Hat's announcement on 15 August 2000 that Dell servers running GNU/Linux were "the fastest Web solutions of those tested" and more than twice as powerful as Windows 2000 on the same four-processor system.

The fueling of future improvements in Linux was one way the exercise backfired for Microsoft. The bigger blunder, however, was something more profound. By arranging for GNU/Linux, Apache, and Samba to be benchmarked against Windows NT, Microsoft said in the most emphatic manner possible that these were rivals; after all, there is no point benchmarking things that are not in some sense comparable. This was a significant shift from Microsoft's previous stance that GNU/Linux was not up to enterprise-level tasks, and nobody was using it anyway.

The Mindcraft benchmarks gave the lie to this position more effectively than anything the open source community could have done. At a stroke, Microsoft had anointed GNU/Linux as an official rival. Moreover, through its inept initial handling of the resulting furor, it hammered home this message for over three months, just in case anybody missed the first announcement in April.

Whatever its public statements, Microsoft changed its attitude to GNU/Linux internally at this time. Ewel explains that "we had some technical people who were looking at Linux, but we didn't really have any kind of what we call a business and product planning team looking at it." Around the time of the Mindcraft benchmarks, the omission was remedied.

This "Linux competitive" team, as it is called within Microsoft, reports ultimately to Ewel, and is quite small. "On Linux, we only have actually one guy full-time," Ewel explains. This compares to five people on the marketing side for the entire competitive team, which monitors Sun and Novell as well as Linux. Meanwhile, "on the tech side," Ewel says, there is "one guy full-time, and four or five guys who probably spend 10 to 20 percent of their time" looking at Linux."

Perhaps recognizing that the Mindcraft benchmarks had gone badly wrong by generating positive publicity for GNU/Linux, Microsoft returned to the attack in October, when it published what it called "Linux Myths" on its Web site. "With all the recent attention around Linux as an operating system," it began, "it's important to step back from the hype and look at the reality."

The first section, dealing with performance, leads with the Mindcraft bench tests (as carried out by *PC Week*), and then adds other supporting reports and articles. The second section deals with reliability, and says that "Linux lacks a commercial quality Journaling File System." It points out that without such a system, "in the event of a system failure, such as a power outage, data loss or corruption is possible." This had been an important missing component from GNU/Linux for a long time. Since the Linux Myths document appeared, however, several journaling file system projects have begun. Two of them come from commercial vendors: IBM and SGI have offered their respective software to the open source community. Another is being led by Stephen Tweedie, one of the most senior kernel hackers.

Microsoft's comment that "there are no commercially proven clustering technologies to provide High Availability for Linux" was similarly true at the time. Such high-availability clustering allows one machine in a group to fail without an overall break in service. The many noncommercial clustering projects that existed then have now matured considerably, and some, like that of TurboLinux, have been sold and fully supported for some time. That the highly popular Web search engine Google depends on a GNU/Linux cluster consisting of no fewer than 4,000 machines is evidence enough of the "commercially proven" nature of these technologies.

The third myth that Microsoft seeks to demolish is that "Linux is free." It rightly points out that "the cost of the operating system is only a small percentage of the overall total cost of ownership (TCO). In general Windows NT has proven to have a lower cost of ownership than UNIX." But its statement that "there is no reason to believe that Linux is significantly different than other versions of UNIX when it comes to TCO" conveniently forgets that Unix's high costs were largely caused by the fragmented nature of the sector, which in turn led to higher software and training costs.

The next point addresses security. Microsoft asserts that the "Linux security model is weak." But many believe it is the Microsoft security model that is fundamentally flawed. One such person is Bruce Schneier, author of the classic book *Applied Cryptography*, and widely respected as an independent authority on computer security. In the September 1999 issue of his free monthly newsletter *Crypto-Gram*, Schneier examined the relative security of closed and open source software. He wrote, "As a cryptography and computer security expert, I have never understood the current fuss about the open source software movement. In the cryptography world, we consider open source necessary for good security; we have for decades." Schneier concluded, "Comparing the security of Linux with that of Microsoft Windows is not very instructive. Microsoft has done such a terrible job with security that it is not really a fair comparison."

Microsoft's last point in the Linux Myths document states that "Linux as a desktop operating system makes no sense. A user would end up with a system that has fewer applications, is more complex to use and manage, and is less intuitive." The comment about GNU/Linux's being less intuitive has been overtaken to a large extent by enormous progress in the KDE and GNOME projects, which offer most of the benefits of Microsoft Windows. However, GNU/Linux support for PC hardware technologies such as Plug and Play (allowing automatic configuration of devices), PCMCIA (credit-card-sized peripherals commonly used with notebooks) and USB (another easy way of adding hardware) has undoubtedly lagged behind Windows, which does indeed make the system more difficult to use and manage.

There is also much truth in the comment about software availability. Tens of thousands of applications run under Windows 95/8 and NT; GNU/Linux cannot yet come close. But things are changing rapidly, as the growing flood of announcements on sites such as Freshmeat indicates. Moreover, the picture could change almost at a stroke if a long-running open source project called Wine comes to fruition.

Started in June 1993, Wine aims to allow GNU/Linux systems to run unmodified Windows applications directly. According to the current leader of the project, the Swiss-born Alexandre Julliard, "there are two meanings to the name," which, in typical hacker fashion, happen to be contradictory. "The original meaning is WINdows Emulator, and the other meaning is a recursive acronym, Wine Is Not an Emulator," he explains. "The goal is to run just about everything. I don't think we can really reach that goal, but I think we can get good enough compatibility to run things like Microsoft Office," which would be a huge breakthrough.

If successful, the Wine project would be a tremendous boon for users of the GNU/Linux system; it would give them access to the wide range of Windows programs without the need to install Windows itself. An important side-effect is that Wine would also allow companies with Windows software to sell to GNU/Linux users without porting their programs directly.

Note that in this last Linux Myth, which deals with applications, Microsoft switches from the server side, the focus of all the other points, to the desktop. In 1998 and 1999, GNU/Linux made great strides in gaining significant server-side applications support, as Chapter 12 detailed. This has been reflected in a corresponding rise in the deployment of GNU/Linux as a server platform. For example, figures from the market analyst company IDC indicate that of all server operating systems bought worldwide in 1999, paid GNU/Linux licenses represented 24.4 percent; in 1998 it was 15.8 percent.

Several main headings of the Linux Myths mirror closely the original goals of the Windows NT project, presumably because most of these goals remain priorities. In his foreword to *Inside Windows NT*, the official history of the project written by Helen Custer, NT's architect, Dave Cutler, included four areas not touched on in the Linux Myths document: portability, Posix compliance, extensibility, and internationalization. Their omission later is understandable; in all but one of them—internationalization—GNU/Linux is clearly ahead of Windows NT. In the area of portability—the ability to run on different processors—GNU/Linux's lead is so significant as to constitute an increasingly serious problem for Microsoft's operating system.

Initially, Windows NT ran on the Intel x86 family, and the MIPS R4000 family. Support for the Alpha AXP chips from Digital and the Motorola PowerPC was added later, but Microsoft dropped the MIPS and PowerPC chips in 1996. Alpha support survived until August 1999, when Digital's owner, Compaq, announced that it was dropping Windows NT on that platform. This left Microsoft NT on just one processor, Intel's x86 family.

Where NT varieties have dwindled, GNU/Linux ports have multiplied extraordinarily to embrace practically every processor chip capable of running the operating system, even those employed in such unlikely platforms as the Palm handheld. But without doubt, the most important port of all is to an Intel chip that in 1999 was still shrouded in mystery: code-named Merced, later dubbed officially "Itanium," and often referred to as the IA-64. The "64" was significant because it indicated that this was the 64-bit version of the venerable Intel x86 family.

GNU/Linux took an early lead here thanks to the efforts of VA Linux's Larry Augustin. He approached Intel with the idea of porting GNU/Linux to the IA-64 platform because he had noted how traditionally the open source community always saw hardware and documentation long after everyone else. This meant that GNU/Linux ports lagged behind those of other companies that were given documentation confidentially—and early.

"We looked and said, 'Gee, you know, we want to try and change that,'" Augustin recalls. "'We'd like to get ahead of the curve for once.' And we saw Intel's new processor as an opportunity to create a new standard for development. That is, when the hardware is released, open source and Linux support is available on day one. We put together a proposal how we'd do the development, and the plans for releasing it to the open source community. That was a very important piece, that we were going to work with Linus and the development community to make sure that what we produced was not VA software, it was standard, everyone used it. And Intel liked the approach."

Augustin believes there were two important factors in Intel's decision to give its backing to his proposal. "I can tell you that that 'Future of Linux' panel" held in Silicon Valley in July 1998, "had an impact," he says—just as it did on Oracle, when it prompted the database company to announce its port of Oracle8 to GNU/Linux. The other factor was "plain economic," Augustin says. "Intel wanted to be in the server space, and was not doing a good job of it. They saw in Linux an opportunity to do that."

The agreement for VA Linux to lead the port of GNU/Linux to the IA-64 was announced on 2 March 1999. Other companies mentioned in the press release as joining the effort were Hewlett-Packard—which had helped to design the IA-64 chip—SGI, IBM, Compaq and Dell, as well as Caldera, Debian, Red Hat and SuSE.

As a result of this initiative, and the broad support it received from the entire computer industry, GNU/Linux was soon well ahead in the race to port to the new Intel processor. For example, at the beginning of 2000,

Michael Tiemann, who became Red Hat's CTO after it acquired Cygnus, gave a course on the GNU development tools that Cygnus had ported to the IA-64, at a conference for developers on the new platform. "Microsoft was nowhere to be seen at the conference," he recalls. "And I asked, did they actually manage to demo Windows 2000 booting on IA-64? And what people told me was they got up on stage on the first day of the conference, they showed it booting, they shut it down, and their machine went back into cold storage.

"However, there was a third-party solutions booth where NEC and SGI and IBM and Compaq and everybody else [were] demonstrating IA-64. Those machines were running all day long, all throughout the conference, and they were all running Linux."

Microsoft doesn't talk much about GNU/Linux's lead here. Instead, it prefers to characterize open source as "kind of chasing taillights" as Jim Ewel puts it. There is some justice in this because, as Augustin had noted, GNU/Linux developers were denied timely access to proprietary hardware specifications.

Now, though, Intel had not only provided details about the Itanium chip to the GNU/Linux community, it had even placed what were once tightly guarded trade secrets about the IA-64 architecture online for all to see—a stunning conversion to open source ideas. Tiemann says, "IA-64 is the first time where we got an even start instead of being behind by six months or a year." And Augustin points out, "It's the first time that we've seen a major launch of a new processor where Linux was the default operating system. That to me is just a tremendous milestone, it moves Linux from being the number two player to being the number one player."

Not only is it in the new market defined by the Intel Itanium chip that GNU/Linux is reshaping the computing landscape. Parallel to the move to 64-bit enterprise systems, practically every sector of the industry is reinventing itself as a result of GNU/Linux and open source. And this was revealed nowhere more dramatically or visibly than in the extraordinary announcements made by IBM at the beginning of 2000.

17

Tomorrow's Hothouse

AFTER ITS TRAILBLAZING ADOPTION OF APACHE as its Web server in June 1998, IBM's embrace of GNU/Linux and open source was steady but unspectacular. In December 1998, shortly before it released the Jikes Java compiler, IBM also made available a beta version of its DB2 database for GNU/Linux. At the beginning of 1999, it donated Jakarta, which provides advanced capabilities to the Apache Web server project, as well as key XML technologies. Later that year, it gradually added GNU/Linux support to some of its PCs and ThinkPad notebooks. None of this, however, could have prepared for the bombshell that the company dropped at the beginning of the year 2000.

On 10 January, IBM announced that it "intends to make all of its server platforms Linux-friendly, including S/390, AS/400, RS/6000 and Netfinity servers, and the work is already well underway." The release continued, "IBM has released source code modifications that enable Linux to run on S/390 servers. These modifications can be downloaded free of charge from the IBM developerWorks Web site. IBM is not providing services support or maintenance for this source code. However, IBM is currently conducting a joint customer study to gauge customer interest and support requirements for Linux running on S/390 servers." Official IBM support arrived on 17 May 2000, when it was also announced that SuSE and TurboLinux would be offering GNU/Linux for the S/390 as a product.

It would be hard to think of a better symbol of the rise of Linux, which had begun life less than nine years before in the Helsinki bedroom of a twenty-one-year-old hacker, than its appearance on the mightiest and most prestigious of corporate mainframes, the IBM S/390. IBM's move was not purely symbolic, however, even though the phrase "Linux-friendly" was vague. Alongside the ports, IBM was announcing something just as historic and what amounted to a Linux Tsar for the company: Irving Wladawsky-Berger.

Despite his middle-European name, Wladawsky-Berger speaks with a noticeable Spanish accent, a legacy of his Cuban origins. He entered IBM as a researcher, and later created and ran with great success IBM's Internet division. At this time, IBM took the key first step of adopting Apache: "I was very involved with my colleagues in the software group" in taking that decision, Wladawsky-Berger says.

Wladawsky-Berger drew an important lesson from the move. "We all realized that in the areas where it's most important to choose technologies that facilitate interoperability, integration, application portability, let's work with the industry," he says. "Let's work with our competitors, let's work with the open source movement, because that's the layer that we'll facilitate pulling it all together. That still leaves plenty of areas to go add value and compete in the marketplace: how well you support your customers, how well you put it together, what happens when they have a problem."

He also notes an important parallel with the world of the Internet. "We saw this happening with TCP/IP . . . where the industry adopted TCP/IP as the common networking protocol to facilitate connectivity, and life went on. It was possible to both work with the industry on TCP/IP and then compete aggressively on systems that connect via TCP/IP."

Wladawsky-Berger explains how the company awoke to the GNU/Linux revolution. "Since the fall of '98 there started to be more and more activity in IBM around Linux. I think what happened is that around the middle of '99, Linux seemed to have hit a kind of inflection point where it went from being a great research technology to all of a sudden being a great technology with potential commercial value."

Then, in a process that mirrors closely the events that led to Netscape's decision to take its browser open source, various groups started pushing independently for IBM to adopt GNU/Linux. During the summer of 1999, Wladawsky-Berger says, "there were probably three trains of thought that all came together.

"One of them was the fact that Linux was becoming a Unix platform with an increasing amount of market share. Our software group had started to put all of our middleware on Linux: databases, transaction managers"—used for ensuring the integrity of customer operations in e-commerce, for example—"Domino for e-mail and collaboration.

"A second stream," he recalls, "was led primarily by our people in research that were studying Linux and the open source movement. [They] realized that just like TCP/IP helps set standards for networking, Linux and the Linux application interfaces had the potential to set the standard for application development and application deployment.

"And then the third track," he says, "came from the supercomputing community that increasingly saw Linux as basis for building very large supercomputers using clusters of machines." A long-running open source project known as Beowulf had already helped to create several of the world's most powerful supercomputers by using off-the-shelf hardware components and a slightly modified form of GNU/Linux for a fraction of the price such machines would normally have cost.

"So through the fall [of 1999]," Wladawsky-Berger continues, "all of those three forces were leading us to a conclusion that IBM should embrace Linux as part of our Internet and e-business effort and make it run across all of our platforms, make it a major platform for all of our middleware, and develop more and more the business services around Linux. And finally, we made the decision just before Christmas of '99."

The person who took that final step was Sam Palmisano, Wladawsky-Berger's boss. "I think that the ultimate decision was on Sam's shoulders," Wladawsky-Berger says, "because it was part of his overall business responsibility, which is the whole area of operating systems." At the time, Palmisano was general manager of the enterprise systems group, in which Wladawsky-Berger is formally vice president of technology and strategy. On 24 July 2000 Palmisano was named president and chief operating officer of IBM.

The widely held view that Palmisano will take over from Gerstner as head of IBM in due course makes Palmisano's decision to back GNU/Linux and open source particularly significant. It could lead to the interesting situation where a man who has staked his career on the success of open source within IBM will, assuming that approach prospers, find himself in a position to place it at the very heart of the computer giant's strategy.

The overarching logic of the decision notwithstanding, the practical benefits to IBM are clear. Possessing, as it does, the widest range of disparate hardware systems—from portable computers up to supercomputers—the company more than any other has had to live with the consequences of incompatible software. By making GNU/Linux run on all its hardware, it immediately unites all its systems into a single family and offers customers perfect scalability.

When IBM has delivered on its promise to make all its server platforms "Linux friendly," the same piece of software that is created on a desktop PC, tested on an RS/6000 system, and then run on an AS/400 minicomputer can, as the company grows, be moved onto an S/390 without changing a line of the code. "We've been so trapped into the paradigm that says once you develop the application on a platform, you are trapped," Wladawsky-Berger says. "And porting from that platform to some other platform is a custom effort that takes a lot of manpower. All of a sudden, that can start becoming something from the past."

He emphasizes again that, although radical, this approach is not unprecedented.

Before TCP/IP came along, the notion of connecting different systems was considered a major custom job. You'd hire very specialized programmers because you usually had different systems that talked different networking languages and then they had to very carefully handcraft a way for the systems to work together. Once TCP/IP became a de facto standard for any system that wanted to be part of the Internet, then all of a sudden every system supported TCP/IP and it no longer was an issue how do you connect to the network; you just connect.

Now what's happening with Linux is this cultural shift that says that if you can agree on standards for applications then you can develop an application and then separately choose your deployment platform depending on what works best. The whole notion separating application development from the underlying deployment platform has been a Holy Grail of the industry because it would all of the sudden unshackle the application developers from worrying about all that plumbing. I think with Linux we now have the best opportunity to do that. The fact that it's not owned by any one company, and that it's open source, is a huge part of what enables us to do that. If the answer had been, well, IBM has invented a new operating system, let's get everybody in the world to adopt it, you can imagine how far that would go with our competitors.

IBM's plans represent as big a boost to the open source movement as its initial support for Apache. They will also have enormous repercussions, even for companies that might not share Big Blue's sudden enthusiasm for GNU/Linux. For example, one small but important element of IBM's strategy is to add GNU/Linux compatibility interfaces to its variant of Unix, AIX; this will allow users to employ programs written for

GNU/Linux on IBM's powerful hardware systems running AIX. The GNU/Linux platform will become even more attractive to software vendors, who are likely to port more of their programs, making GNU/Linux more appealing to users. The position of GNU/Linux will, in turn, strengthen within the Unix world, and weaken that of other, proprietary variants of Unix—including, ultimately, AIX.

SGI, one of the earliest supporters of this new approach, has already recognized this. Its first move towards the world of open source was with Samba, not GNU/Linux; Samba's number two, Jeremy Allison, largely made that happen. He recalls, "Basically SGI said, 'Well, if you come to work for us, we'll make Samba our official product [for file serving].' So that was too big an opportunity to miss,"—both for himself, and for Samba. SGI announced its support on 8 December 1998, proclaiming itself "the first commercial Unix vendor to support Samba software."

SGI's adoption of Samba was a triumph for the free-software world, and offered hope that others might follow. But Allison was in for a surprise when he arrived at the company. "It was funny," he says, "because I expected to be an open source island in a proprietary company. And Linux was running riot inside SGI already. Everybody was using it, everybody knew about it."

Allison explains why SGI's move to prefer GNU/Linux over its own Unix variant, Irix, was inevitable at this point. "The problem that they saw was that Irix was failing to get application capture." That is, Irix had too small a share of the Unix market to warrant the effort and expense required to port software to it. "If you have to pay ISVs [Independent Software Vendors] to port to your platform, it's not a viable long-term market." By adopting the increasingly popular GNU/Linux operating system, SGI would be able to tap into the large and growing body of applications without having to pay for special ports.

SGI announced its official "Linux debut" on 17 May 1999. Although it became one of the most fervent backers of GNU/Linux, it was by no means isolated in its support before IBM joined the club in January 2000. Hewlett-Packard, for example, announced on 1 March 1999 that it would "provide Linux-compatible APIs on HP-UX." That is, it would make a compatibility layer available so that users of its HP-UX system could run GNU/Linux applications.

Similarly, on 8 June 1999, a press release recorded that "Compaq Computer Corporation and Red Hat Software, Inc. today announced a joint development and marketing agreement which will result in enhanced interoperability and compatibility between Compaq Tru64 UNIX and the Red Hat Linux operating system." This development was bolstered on 17

August 1999 by "a new release of SuSE Linux 6.1 AXP"—SuSE's version of GNU/Linux running on the Alpha AXP chip—"with enhanced inter-operability and compatibility features between Compaq Tru64 UNIX and the SuSE Linux operating system."

Even Sun has felt obliged to respond progressively to the growing phenomenon of GNU/Linux as the de facto Unix standard. Its first approach was to match the price of the open source operating system with its "Free Solaris Program," which started in August 1998, and provided a free Solaris license for noncommercial use on Intel-based PCs.

More dramatic was Sun's announcement on 26 January 2000, when it unveiled version 8 of its Solaris operating system, that starting with that release, "Sun will no longer charge an end-user license fee for the right to use the runtime software on systems with eight or fewer processors." Moreover, "the company is providing free access to Sun's source code to foster innovation and ubiquity." As Mindcraft's Bruce Weiner, long an observer of the Unix scene, comments: "There's no way they would have done that without Linux."

In addition to matching GNU/Linux on price in some sectors of the market, Sun has also been forced to reach an accommodation with its emerging main rival. For example, on 8 December 1998, it announced that "it has teamed with the Linux community to complete a port of the popular freeware Linux operating environment to the UltraSparc architectures."

The upbeat tone of the press release—it proclaimed that "every copy of Linux is another win for Unix and open standards"—contrasts starkly with Sun's attitude to Dave Miller's first port of Linux to its machines, which he started in 1994. Until the 1998 announcement, Miller recalls, Sun gave no help to his efforts. "In fact," he says, "I would get publicly flamed often on Usenet by Sun engineers. I had a bad attitude back then, and I'd go off the wall on how kick-butt my Linux on Sparc was going to be." He acknowledges, "I sort of asked for it."

Perhaps more important than Sun's support for the UltraSparc port was its announcement in December 1998 that "it intends to add Linux compatibility to the Solaris environment so that customers can take advantage of the breadth of new Linux applications within the highly reliable Solaris environment," a subtle dig at GNU/Linux's youth and relatively unproven state. The appearance of this code, called lxrun, once again extended the reach of GNU/Linux; software companies now had another reason to write for the free operating system—and one less to write for proprietary versions of Unix. Other signs that Sun is gradually embracing open source include the release of the StarOffice productivity suite, which it acquired in August 1999, under the GNU GPL in October 2000, and the adoption of GNOME 2.0 as the default desktop for Solaris.

Although Sun's relationship with GNU/Linux and open source may have been bumpy, as a manufacturer of hardware it has been able to find alternative models of revenue generation even while giving away its entry-level Solaris 8 operating system. Other companies are not so fortunate.

A case in point is Berkeley Software Design, Inc. (BSDI), formed in 1991 by many of the key developers of the original Berkeley Unix. On 14 December 1998, BSDI announced that it would be adding Linux application support to its version of Unix, called BSD/OS; but in addition to providing their customers with a means to run GNU/Linux applications, the move also lessens the incentive to port to BSD/OS, its strengths notwithstanding. The announcement on 10 March 2000 that BSDI would merge with Walnut Creek CDROM, the distributor and sponsor of the popular FreeBSD operating system (which also derives from Berkeley Unix) is evidence that BSD/OS is feeling the effect of GNU/Linux. This move allows BSD/OS development to tap into the enthusiasm and creativity of the skilled and dedicated FreeBSD hackers, and provides more formal support for FreeBSD.

The situation for the other major software-only Unix vendor, SCO, was more problematic—and ironic. In the early 1980s, SCO excelled as a company in almost the same space as GNU/Linux would in the early 1990s: that of Unix running on Intel processors. SCO's achievements were crowned in 1995 when it purchased UnixWare from Novell, which had, in turn, bought it from AT&T in 1993. In acquiring the rights to Thompson and Ritchie's original Unix work of 1969, SCO became, in effect, the keeper of the sacred Unix flame. But hackers have no piety and little pity when it comes to technology; for them, SCO's products were old proprietary versions of something that would reach its culmination in GNU/Linux.

SCO tried to fight back. It had been providing "students, educators and Unix system enthusiasts" with free copies of its latest software for some years, but in binary form only. Then, on 12 May 1998, it offered low-cost licenses for an "ancient" release of Unix, including the source code. But despite these moves, GNU/Linux continued its march into the hearts of hackers and onto the desktops of companies. Along with the other vendors of proprietary Unixes, SCO bowed to the inevitable, and on 2 March 1999 "affirmed its long-standing support for the Linux and Open Source movements by adding Linux application support to its award-winning UnixWare 7 platform."

It is amusing to note the heading of the press release: "Linux, Open Source movements shift spotlight back to Unix systems innovation and away from single-vendor lock-in." The Unix vendors' attempts to achieve lock-in over the previous decade had fragmented the Unix world to such an extent that it was powerless when faced by the onslaught of Microsoft's Windows NT.

The final humiliation for the old guard occurred on 2 August 2000, when SCO announced that it was selling two out of its three divisions—including the original Unix—to Caldera. The hackers had triumphed over the establishment.

However halting the moves by the proprietary Unix vendors first to acknowledge and then to work with the open source version, the final result is clear: GNU/Linux will eventually become the de facto standard for Unix. Many would say that it is already. Moreover, IBM's ambitious moves to make GNU/Linux the universal programming standard within the company means that it will also be employed for high-end computing, notably supercomputers; this will serve to block Windows 2000's ascent into such arenas just as GNU/Linux seriously challenges it from below—a pincer movement that will be increasingly dangerous for Microsoft.

Against the background of these major shifts in the world of the Unix computing market, the personal computer company Apple might seem relatively secure. After all, the GNU/Linux platform is immature in the field of end-user software, and it is closely wedded to the Intel family—historically and emotionally, at least. By contrast, Apple is essentially a desktop company built on the PowerPC chip architecture. Ports of GNU/Linux for the PowerPC exist; one of them, called MkLinux, was even actively encouraged by Apple. But it is not so much this direct, if minor, rival that threatens Apple as the entire GNU/Linux phenomenon.

Apple's relationship with GNU/Linux has always been problematic because the original Apple Macintosh was intentionally created as a closed machine, unlike the open IBM PC. It was intended as a kind of appliance about whose internal workings users need know nothing. This was a logical approach to take for the market the machine was aimed at; but it was, of course, anathema to the hacker spirit.

The first port of the Apple Macintosh was undertaken almost out sheer bloody-mindedness. One of the main coders was Alan Cox, who describes the work as having "the supreme virtue of being both completely pointless and challenging." Writing about the experience later, he thanked various people who had helped in this epic endeavor, but concluded with "no thanks" to "Steve Jobs—for refusing to provide any [Macintosh] documentation."

Given this starting point, and its subsequent tepid enthusiasm for efforts to port GNU/Linux to later Macintosh hardware, Apple's announcement on 16 March 1999 that it was releasing what it called Darwin, the foundation of its new Mac OS X Server operating system, as open source was an important step. With elements taken from Berkeley Unix and microkernel technologies of the kind Andrew Tanenbaum (the creator of Minix) favored, Darwin is a close relative to GNU/Linux.

Although Apple's move, and its subsequent release of other code as open source, may well help "Apple and their customers to benefit from the inventive energy and enthusiasm of a huge community of programmers," as the original March press release hoped, it fails to address a more fundamental problem for the company.

This had already been raised in a prescient essay titled "A Modest Proposal," written by Don Yacktman in 1998. He noted, "There is a finite amount of 'serious' development happening at any given time. Of that development, very little happens for non-Windows operating systems. Apple is competing with Linux to obtain third-party support. As Linux overtakes Mac OS, it is likely to absorb the non-Windows development pool. If third party support for Mac OS were to dwindle, then Apple's future could be in serious jeopardy," whether or not the company uses open source development techniques for its operating system. Fewer new applications means fewer users. SGI understood this, which is why it switched emphasis from Irix to GNU/Linux. As Yacktman correctly pointed out, the same could happen to Apple if GNU/Linux becomes viable as a desktop system.

The foundations for this viability have been laid with the creation of the KDE and GNOME environments. One of the first software vendors to take advantage of this was the Canadian company Corel, which ported its well-known Windows programs using an innovative approach based on technology from the open source Wine project. Corel's founder, Michael Cowpland, has described GNU/Linux as "the lever that has finally pried open the single-vendor situation," breaking Microsoft's stranglehold on the desktop. This view makes Microsoft's $135 million investment in Corel, part of a "strategic alliance" announced on 2 October 2000, interesting, to say the least. But that "single-vendor situation" does not obtain in plenty of sectors in the computer market, where the prospects for GNU/Linux look particularly rosy.

For example, GNU/Linux is already flourishing in the server appliance area where the idea is to create a low-cost system with minimal configuration or maintenance requirements. GNU/Linux is ideal in these circumstances. Moreover, it can be put together with other robust and free software—Apache, Sendmail, Samba—to create dedicated boxes designed to perform common tasks such as Web-serving, e-mail, file-sharing, and so forth.

One of the leaders in this area, and certainly one of the longest established, is Cobalt Networks. The company was founded in 1996, and counted Larry McVoy and Dave Miller among its employees at one time. The GNOME hacker Miguel de Icaza almost joined the company, but was unable to obtain the requisite U.S. visa. In October 1999, Cobalt announced an agreement to supply Gateway with server appliance technologies, the computer manufacturer's first dabble in the world of open source. A few months after Gateway unveiled its Micro Server system, arch-rival Dell joined the fray with its PowerApp line. Sun, too, has entered this sector through its purchase in September 2000 of Cobalt Networks for $2 billion worth of Sun shares. The accompanying press release was remarkable for omitting any mention of the fact that Cobalt systems run GNU/Linux—further evidence of Sun's ambivalence toward its operating system rival.

But GNU/Linux offers the perfect solution not only at the top-end of the appliance market. Its qualities of low cost, tight coding, and proven reliability make it ideal for a range of smaller devices, too. These are called a variety of names, depending on their end-function, but one popular designation is the Net appliance.

Many players compete in this sector, but none is more significant than the leading online service, AOL, which had more than 25 million members at the start of 2001. On 5 April 2000, AOL announced its new "family of specialized Internet appliances." These appliances are based on Transmeta's Crusoe chip, and they use that company's Mobile Linux, put together in part by Linus himself. They also employ Netscape's Gecko layout engine to provide the browser capabilities. In a sense, the AOL Internet appliances represent the first post-PC, post-Microsoft architecture: no Intel, no Windows, and no Internet Explorer.

Flexibility is one of the great strengths of GNU/Linux; that it can be applied in the most diverse circumstances is already evident from the range of innovative devices that employ it. For example, TiVo uses GNU/Linux for its digital TV recorder. Kerbango Radio and PenguinRadio, two Internet appliances that allow users to tune into audio streams from around the world, are both based on GNU/Linux, as is a new home communications device from the Swedish company Ericsson. The Screen Phone uses Red Hat Linux, with a graphical interface from Trolltech displayed on a color touch-screen, to offer telephony, e-mail, and Web browsing in a cordless unit. According to Ericsson, the Screen Phone is the first of "a new range of consumer products and services for home communications" that it will be developing jointly with Red Hat.

One characteristic common to these systems is that users are not expected to configure or upgrade them as they routinely do for PCs; whether server appliances, Internet radios, or extended communication devices, they are simply switched on and used. The so-called embedded-devices market embraces everything that is not a computer in the conventional sense but that uses computer chips. Although less apparent, this sector is much larger than the computer market, and many believe that the opportunities for GNU/Linux here are correspondingly greater.

One company subscribing to this view is Lineo. Spun out of Caldera in July 1999, the new company came into being as a result of customers' demands. As Bryan Sparks, the former CEO of Caldera and now head of Lineo, explains, "We did some custom work for a couple of companies" in providing GNU/Linux for embedded systems, "and it was April of [1999] we said, 'Boy, you know what, let's turn this ship, let's just focus on that.'"

One of GNU/Linux's great strengths in this sector is its ability to address the needs of any kind of embedded device; it is also "better, cheaper, faster" than proprietary rivals. Lineo has consciously built on these qualities through the six early acquisitions it made of other companies that were working on GNU/Linux for embedded systems. "We needed to grow quite rapidly," Sparks notes, "just in terms of humans for a company, and in the process we felt that there were some strategic gaps that we needed to fill. So if you're a customer doing anything with embedded Linux, or anything with embedded and are evaluating Linux, we can cover the whole spectrum from very, very small to very high end."

Lineo's business model differs from that of other GNU/Linux companies, many of which see services as the way forward with a product that is essentially free. "We are a product company, primarily," Sparks says. "We do services, but only as it relates to product sales." One company in the embedded market that does believe strongly in basing its business on services rather than products is Red Hat. Through its acquisition of Cygnus in November 1999, it finds itself competing with Lineo as well as with its old rival Caldera.

Cygnus was active in the embedded market before Linux existed. After porting its programming tools to the various embedded chips, the next logical step was to create an operating system for that sector. But instead of using GNU/Linux, as might have been expected, Cygnus came up with its own solution, called eCos, which it released in September 1998 as open source. Although eCos was not based on Linux, Cygnus's next project in the embedded space, EL/IX, was, but with a twist. In September 1999, the company proposed not just another embedded GNU/Linux, of which there were by now many, but a way for competing products to preserve compatibility among themselves. The press release called EL/IX "a major step to pre-empt the fragmentation of embedded Linux."

This sounds fine in principle, but some, like Lineo's Sparks, have their doubts. "We think it's nonsense," he says. "There's no technology there at all; it's just marketing slicks." Despite his disdain for EL/IX, Sparks has plenty of respect for Cygnus/Red Hat in the embedded space. At the very least, he says, "we see them as a competitor in the things that they could do."

The danger of fragmentation within the embedded space is probably less than it is for the server or desktop sectors. By their very nature, embedded devices address certain needs and usually run custom software. As a result, detailed compatibility between the many platforms that exist is less important than for servers, say.

There is another interesting consequence of this inherently balkanized nature of the embedded sector. The Linux kernel has flourished and grown because so many hackers have been able to try out the code, find bugs, and make suggestions. Because embedded systems are specialized, it is unlikely that many hackers will be playing around with code written for them; this means that the classic open source development methodology has little to offer in the embedded space, or in any other domain where few people look at the code, namely, specialized niche markets.

Their differences in philosophy notwithstanding, Bryan Sparks and Michael Tiemann, cofounder of Cygnus and now CTO of Red Hat, agree on one thing: the huge potential of the area. Tiemann says, "I believe that the real name of the game is going to be Internet appliances. The PC form factor is going to go the way of the universal motor." Sparks adds, "We believe that the next wave of Linux is embedded, and we think that the next wave in embedded is Linux."

Some big names agree. In May 2000, Lineo received $37 million from Mitsubishi, Motorola, and Samsung; in September Motorola invested a further $22.5 million, while Samsung and Lineo formed an embedded systems joint development in Korea. Earlier in 2000, Lynx Real-Time Systems, another embedded systems company, received investments from Intel, Motorola, and TurboLinux. Lynx launched its embedded Linux product BlueCat in February 2000, and in May changed its name to LynuxWorks "to reflect its new focus on bringing the benefits of Linux to the embedded market," as the press release put it.

Motorola's strong commitment to GNU/Linux in the embedded sphere was signaled not only by its participation in both these investments but also by the announcement in March 2000 that it was coming out with its own distribution for the telecoms industry, called High Availability Linux. As the press release explained, this is designed for "carrier-grade networking, wireless and Internet applications that require 99.999% availability."

This "5Nines" availability is equivalent to less than five minutes of downtime per year. Perhaps the ultimate testimonial to the exceptional reliability of the open source operating system is that Motorola, whose sales were over $30 billion in 1999, chose GNU/Linux to provide this extreme level of availability; it stands with IBM's announcements in January 2000 as one of the most significant statements of support from a technology company with impeccable credentials.

The embedded sector may well offer a bigger opportunity for GNU/Linux than the server and client markets represent. Many believe, however, that the impact of the open source philosophy will spread far wider—even beyond computing. For example, an obvious application of its development methodology is to content rather than to code. Alongside the GNU General Public License, the GNU Free Documentation License (FDL) aims to promote the sharing of documents just as the GNU GPL does for software. But where the GNU GPL is well established as the leading license in its field, the GNU FDL faces stronger competition; for example, the Open Publication License from the Open Content project, and the IDG Open Content License from the Open Book Project.

Despite the underdeveloped state of content licensing, content collaboration is thriving. The Open Directory, for example, is creating a Yahoo-style classification of Internet content with volunteers instead of with paid researchers. The benefit of this approach, as for open source software development, is that it scales. At the end of 2000, the Open Directory had well over 30,000 contributors selecting and organizing 2 million Web sites in 300,000 categories to form a freely available database. Originally called GnuHoo and then NewHoo, the Open Directory was bought by Netscape in November 1998 and used on its portal. Since then, the Open Directory database has been taken up by several other high-profile sites, including Lycos, Google and HotBot, in some cases displacing proprietary content.

Open source methodology has also been applied with great success in what might be called open journalism; it is best exemplified by the

Slashdot.org Web site, created in September 1997 by Rob "CmdrTaco" Malda, which has as its motto "News for nerds. Stuff that matters." The "stuff that matters" is essentially free software, together with a range of related subjects. The site's most important feature is that it offers not so much news for nerds as news *by* nerds: Most of the material is sent in by readers and the stories that appear each day on the site are chosen from the submissions. Visitors can post their comments and add further information. The analogy with the continued honing of the Linux kernel through the successive application of patches sent in by hackers around the world is clear.

The "Slashdot effect"—the deluge of visitors to a Web site if it is mentioned in a story—is by now famous, but more important is the other Slashdot effect of creating a powerful distributed news gathering and filtering machine that is independent of the ordinary media companies (Slashdot is owned by VA Linux). Slashdot is a highly visible example of where the open source philosophy challenges the traditional structures of information, especially economic and legal, and its dissemination. But some believe that open source software itself may have just as great an impact as open journalism in reshaping the landscape of intellectual property.

One such is Professor Eben Moglen, professor of legal history at Columbia University and general counsel to the Free Software Foundation. His contention is that the current overlapping legal systems of patents, copyright law, and trade secrets are becoming unworkable. Moglen says that the history of law offers precedents to suggest that such unstable situations cannot persist. His more controversial belief is that an important catalyst for the final collapse of these mutually conflicting systems will be free software such as GNU/Linux: "What we are headed for is the great war over free software," he predicts.

Let's think about the Net for a change as a collection of pipes and switches, rather than thinking of it as a thing or a space.

There's lot of data moving through those pipes, and the switches determine who gets which data and how much they have to pay for it downstream. And of course those switches are by and large what we think of as digital computers.

The basic media company theory at the opening of the twenty-first century is to create a leak-proof pipe all the way from production studio to eyeball and eardrum. The switch that most threatens that pipe is the one at the end. If the switch closest to your eyeball and your eardrum is under your complete technical control, the whole rest of the aqueduct can be as leak-proof as they like, and it won't do them any good. And the switch is under your control, of course, if the software is free software.

That these are not simply the interesting but theoretical musings of an academic who has spent too much time playing with GNU software and reading the GNU GPL has been demonstrated by the case of two open source programs that circumvent the Content Scramble System (CSS) used to block unauthorized viewing of DVDs.

Because the GNU/Linux platform was not a supported platform, it was not possible to use that system to watch DVDs. In the usual way, hackers started LiViD, the Linux Video and DVD Project, to craft some code so they could view DVDs on their computers. Even though it has no evidence, the film industry sees the software that has grown out of the project as an attempt to subvert the encryption system for the purpose of piracy; hackers regard it as freedom to watch their DVDs under GNU/Linux.

This case is particularly interesting because DVD software for both GNU/Linux and Windows (called css-auth and DeCSS, respectively) has been released under the GNU GPL. As such it can—and has—been copied all over the world; this puts the film industry in a difficult position. As Moglen notes, "Now they have to go to some court somewhere and say, 'Give us an injunction to make everybody in the whole world stop talking about this.' And that's not going to work, because courts are going . . . to see that this is an impossibility. They're going to recognize that there's no factual way to accomplish it, and that there's something repugnant about being asked to do what's impossible."

Although the U.S. film industry appears to fear this software, its potential impact on the intellectual property landscape pales into insignificance beside two other open source projects. Called Gnutella—a combination of "GNU" and "Nutella," an Italian chocolate and hazelnut spread—and Freenet, these programs create a means for locating files that may be distributed anywhere across a collection of computers linked by the Net and running the Gnutella or Freenet software.

The key feature of both is that no central directory lists where those files are held, unlike the more famous Napster file-sharing system. Instead, requests for an item are passed on from computer to computer; if the item is found, it is then sent to the originator of the request. The lack of a central node means that it is extremely hard to track down the where the file is held on the Gnutella network; Freenet is specifically designed to make this impossible and also preserves the anonymity of the originator of the request.

The way these new programs nullify attempts to police copyright in-fringement is particularly interesting. Both Gnutella and Freenet overlay a kind of virtual network on top of the current Internet; this severs all links between files and their physical locations. Content is just "on" the network; "where" is irrelevant to the user. It seems appropriate that the distributed development methodology known as open source, born of the Internet and largely powering it, should also lead to its reinvention in an even purer, more powerful form.

18

Beyond the Market

AN ARRAY OF BLUE-SKY POSSIBILITIES depend critically on the continuing progress of GNU/Linux and open source. But plenty of skeptics as well as competitors see many reasons for the free-software revolution to stumble and even fall.

According to these naysayers, fragmentation is the greatest specter haunting the open source world. In particular, the commercial distributions of GNU/Linux, they explain, are just like the variants of Unix—and look what happened to them. Moreover, the ability to fork is one of the key features built into the GNU GPL; indeed, the pessimists could say with some justice that forking is not so much a risk as a right.

Critics might point to the XEmacs saga, discussed in Chapter 10, which demonstrates that serious forks not only have occurred in the free-software world but remain unhealed. They fail to note, however, that this fork occurred in the area of applications, and was born out of a desire by some users for an alternative approach. Although it is true that the Emacs/XEmacs split reduces the amount of developer attention each can receive, this damage does not propagate; no other programs depend critically on having one version of Emacs. The forking here promotes user choice without diminishing the power of either branch of the fork.

A fork of GNU/Linux would be a different matter. As well as splitting the development effort, such forks would also cause irreparable harm to the entire GNU/Linux platform because users and applications developers would have to choose which fork to support. Incompatibilities between forks of GNU/Linux would result in an overall reduction in the user base for each fork, less incentive to port to that fork, and weaker, poorer systems for everyone as a result. As a consequence, there are huge pressures against forking at the operating system level. A user choosing to support a minor fork would run the risk of losing many of the benefits of future GNU/Linux applications; this on its own would throttle renegade versions.

It is still conceivable that such forks would thrive by addressing, for instance, an important but hitherto unmet need; in this case, however, it would be possible for the main GNU/Linux stream to take some or all of the innovations added by the fork and fold them back into the main line of development to meet that need. As well as guaranteeing the right to fork, the GNU GPL also provides a built-in mechanism for its healing.

Recognizing, perhaps, that the forking argument has critical weaknesses, others have argued that, on the contrary, the risk for free software is not fragmentation, but concentration. For example, many have descried in Red Hat, the leading open source company, a new Microsoft, which one day may be prepared to sacrifice the interests of users on the altar of profitability.

It is undeniable that the arrival of commerce changes the dynamics of the open source development process. In particular, it brings its own set of priorities that may clash with those of the hackers. However, a previous episode in the history of free software indicates what happens in these circumstances—and who gets to adjudicate.

Cygnus Solutions, introduced in Chapter 14, had built its business around creating new ports of GCC and then handing them to the community as open source. As Cygnus cofounder Michael Tiemann explains, "Basically, our business depended on our ability to help bring new microprocessor vendors into the GNUPro product platform." But in 1997, a problem arose. "More and more of our ports of the compiler and enhancements to the compiler got backed up in the patch reviewing process," Tiemann says. That is, the work of Cygnus was not being folded back into the official GCC distribution fast enough. As a result, he says, "the FSF process became a limiter of our business."

Tiemann makes an important point in this context: "The technical community sometimes has more patience and tolerance" than a business might have. "If one project is stalling," he says, "an enterprising young hacker may decide to go and work on a different project. But if you've got $10 million of revenue per year that you've got to handle, and you've got a 50 percent-plus growth rate that you're trying to maintain, stalls in the patch process become unacceptable."

Here, then, was a critical test of what happens when commerce collides with the community development process. Cygnus's solution was fairly extreme: It decided to fork the GCC code. With its new EGCS (Experimental GNU Compiler System, pronounced "eggs"), it could incorporate all the changes that it needed for its products. But, in effect, it was hijacking the GCC standard. "We tried to do it in a way that could be reconciled, but we were forceful in our leadership," Tiemann says. "What was very gratifying was that basically the entire Net community was behind us."

This last point is crucial. Had Cygnus simply created EGCS to satisfy its own commercial requirements, it would have become a fork divorced from the main GCC user community. This would have been perfectly valid and legal in itself, but it would have meant that Cygnus would have lost all the benefits of the open source development methodology that provided much of its strength. By creating a fork that had large-scale user support, it put pressure on the main branch—controlled ultimately by Stallman—to reach an accommodation (which was why Cygnus tried to "do it in a way that could be reconciled," as Tiemann puts it).

Tiemann explains what happened after the decision to fork. "While EGCS was alive," he says, "Stallman was basically trying to evaluate what would be the consequences of endorsing this Cygnus-sponsored fork. At the end of the day, I think the integrity of the people who are currently working on the GNU compiler [at Cygnus] was so unimpeachable that he was able to make the very risky decision and say, 'Wow, I'm going to put all of the eggs in this basket which is controlled by a commercial company.'"

That is, Stallman healed the fork by using the Cygnus version as the basis for future developments of the official GCC, renamed GNU Compiler Collection (from GNU C Compiler) to reflect the expanded goals of the project. This was obviously a courageous step, but not entirely a leap in the dark. As Tiemann correctly emphasizes, the EGCS fork was not controlled so much by Cygnus as by its engineers. On the basis of their past work—and their "integrity" in the context of GCC development—Stallman was confident that they would continue to develop GCC for the good of the community, while also addressing Cygnus's concerns.

This suggests one way that a company such as Red Hat, say, might assume a more active role in determining the future course of GNU/Linux without hijacking it in any way. Just as Stallman—hardly a man to compromise—was willing to place the development of GCC in the hands of its key developers, and to depend upon their "integrity" to ensure its independence, so Linus might not be too concerned to see Red Hat emerge as the dominant force in the Linux world. Alan Cox and Dave Miller are employed by the company, and nobody would think of calling into question their integrity. In a sense, their presence acts as a guarantee that Red Hat will always be a responsible guardian of the Linux community's interests, just as Cygnus was for GCC.

The power of the users, realized through such top hackers as Cox and Miller, who amount almost to the community's representatives in the commercial distribution world, is one major reason that Red Hat and companies like it will never be able to impose its will on the free-software movements. But there is another; this flows from the unique dynamics of business based around open source software.

To understand why Red Hat will never become another Microsoft, consider what a company has to do to go head-to-head with the Redmond giant. Because the Windows operating system is proprietary and closed, producing a good clone of it is a mammoth undertaking. A perfect clone is probably impossible. As a result, Microsoft will always have the advantage of current compatibility and future innovation.

In the world of GNU/Linux, the situation is different. Because, to its credit, Red Hat releases all its work under the GNU GPL, anybody can take it and use it. This means that where the barriers to entry for competitors to Microsoft Windows are so high they are effectively insurmountable, they are more or less nonexistent for rivals to Red Hat. It is noteworthy that this dynamic allows not only current competitors of Red Hat to catch up with it technically very quickly but new entrants, too. The rise of MandrakeSoft shows that this is no mere theoretical possibility.

In 1995, Gaël Duval, a 22-year-old Frenchman from Caen, Normandy, who was studying computer science, was looking for a Unix to put on his 386 PC—a familiar enough story. "I searched through the Internet and naturally found Linux, [which] I grabbed on fifty diskettes," he recalls. As many before him had been, Duval was impressed with what he saw.

Again, as with countless others before him, Duval tracked Linux's steady improvements, trying out Red Hat and GNU/Debian alongside the Slackware distribution he had downloaded first. He particularly liked Red Hat's distribution format and its installation procedure. Then, when the KDE desktop was announced at the end of 1997, Duval started to follow this project, too. "I'm a graphical operating systems lover," he confesses.

But now he had a problem. Because KDE used Trolltech's Qt libraries (which initially were not open source), Red Hat refused to ship it. But

Duval wanted to use KDE while keeping the Red Hat distribution he had come to know. The solution was obvious for a hacker: He would just create his own distribution that put together Red Hat and KDE.

Following the numbering of the Red Hat version it was based on, Duval called his distribution Linux-Mandrake 5.1. In July 1998, Duval placed this on an FTP server for others to download—as Linus had done with his original Linux code. Just as Linus had been encouraged by the feedback he received to his early kernel, so Duval was spurred on by the response to his home-brew distribution. It was "incredible," he says. "I immediately got hundreds of e-mails [from] people who enjoyed the project and the product. I also got first patches and ideas." He was even more struck by two e-mails from the United States and one from Australia. "The most incredible," he says, "were three companies who announced that they had started to sell GPL CDs of Mandrake."

This opened his eyes to a possibility he had not considered. When he created Linux-Mandrake, he had no thought of selling it. "I just ended my studies at Uni," he says, "I had no money and I was looking for a job as Unix systems administrator or programmer." But now, "because of the demand, I started to sell some Mandrake CDs." Duval teamed up with two other Frenchmen, Jacques Le Marois and Frederic Bastok, and together they founded MandrakeSoft in December 1998, its headquarters in Paris.

Although things began small—"we started with private fundings plus auto financing by selling Mandrake powerpacks"—MandrakeSoft grew rapidly. By the end of its first year it had fifty employees; and soon after, one hundred. One of MandrakeSoft's first coups was to sign a deal with the U.S. publisher Macmillan to provide a retail distribution, launched in June 1999. "Macmillan is present in many retail stores in the U.S.A. and several European countries," Duval says. "Macmillan was looking for an alternative to Red Hat; they thought that Mandrake was the best choice for them." According to a press release dated 27 October 1999, Macmillan's Mandrake-based product "accounted for 52% of total Linux software units sold at retail" in the United States during August 1999, less than a year after Linux-Mandrake was put together.

Macmillan was not alone in singling out this young company and its new distribution. Also in August 1999, Linux-Mandrake 6 won two LinuxWorld Editors' Choice Awards, for Product of the Year and Distribution/Server (and was runner-up in the Distribution/Client category). The same month, the investment fund of AXA, "one of the world's leading insurers and asset managers," with nearly $655 billion of assets under management, took an equity position in MandrakeSoft. Nor was that the end of the investments: The total venture capital obtained in one year was $15 million.

Like its longer-established rivals, MandrakeSoft has started hiring top hackers, and even bought projects so that it can release them as open source software. As a result, MandrakeSoft is emerging as a showcase example of all the strengths of the open source model in commerce. The GNU GPL allowed a more or less penniless computer student to create a new distribution that has taken on the well-financed Red Hat, and to win in many cases. It also means that others can take Mandrake's product as the starting point for yet more new distributions. "That happened several times," Duval says. He welcomes it: "It's good for us because it makes us still more known and spread"—just as Mandrake promotes the Red Hat distribution.

These counterintuitive dynamics act as a brake on the dominance of any one distribution. They also ensure that user needs are soon met. If none of the existing distributions—there are currently more than one hundred—serves a market well enough, it is an easy matter for someone, with only the most basic of resources, to create that distribution and possibly rise to become the next MandrakeSoft, or even Red Hat.

MandrakeSoft chose to begin as a Red Hat clone, and still maintains compatibility with Red Hat. That is, "when a software company releases an application . . . targeted to Red Hat systems, it will install on Mandrake," Duval explains. However, this feature of Linux-Mandrake does reveal a continuing issue for the GNU/Linux world: cross-distribution incompatibilities.

These have to do with how software is selected and packaged, not with forks in the programs themselves. For example, decisions about which version of the kernel will be adopted, how many patches will be applied, and where a library will be placed when it is installed can make all the difference as to whether an application package will run or not on a particular distribution. Many software vendors have created four or more slightly different versions of their products to cope with the tiny divergences between distributions.

Recognizing the inefficiency of this approach, and the danger that such differences might grow, Bruce Perens, author of the original Open Source Definition and the second leader of the Debian project, created the Linux Standard Base (LSB) in 1998. The main aim of the LSB is "to be able to have an application move from one distribution to another without being recompiled," Perens says. Unfortunately, he adds, "it's taking longer than I would have liked."

The main pressure to establish standards is likely to come from the companies most affected by it. Given its embrace of GNU/Linux as a strategic platform unifying all of its hardware solutions, IBM has more to lose from the divergences between the main GNU/Linux distributions than most. It therefore comes as no surprise that IBM's GNU/Linux chief, Irving Wladawsky-Berger, says of the LSB, "It is very important, and I think it's going to be like the IETF [Internet Engineering Task Force, which draws up technical standards] has been to the Internet. I think that the LSB will help us get the Linux standards defined, and think that's where the support of many companies, including IBM and Silicon Graphics and others, helps a lot."

This support of IBM will make LSB a reality. As Wladawsky-Berger says, "We're encouraging everybody to work closely with the LSB." It is not hard to imagine the kind of "encouragement" that IBM might offer a GNU/Linux distribution that, for whatever reasons, fails to support the LSB standard fully. For example, being dropped from IBM's list of approved distributions would probably "encourage" anybody, even the largest open source company, to toe the line.

Even assuming that projects like LSB succeed, and that the open source worlds do not become excessively fragmented or consolidated, open source must still face plenty of other challenges before its full potential is realized. One threat is that commercial software houses may use patents—currently being awarded, in the United States at least, for surprisingly trivial ideas—to prevent hackers from employing certain programming techniques in their free software. Another threat, even more insidious, was outlined in 1998 by the Microsoft engineer Vinod Valloppillil in the first Halloween document.

In a section headed "Blunting OSS [Open Source Software] attacks," he suggests that one approach would be to "de-commoditize protocols & applications." As he explains, one of the reasons open source projects have been able to flourish is the existence of fundamental protocols (sets of rules) that determine how things such as the Web and e-mail work. To "de-commoditize" means to remove standards that open source has proved so efficient at implementing. As Valloppillil puts it: "By extending these protocols and developing new protocols, we can deny OSS projects entry into the market." The sheer cynicism of this approach is astonishing; it suggests fragmenting standards, not for customer benefit, but to place obstacles in the way of open source.

De-commoditization is no mere theory. Microsoft's chosen target for first putting it into practice was an open security protocol called Kerberos, named after the three-headed guard-dog of the gates of hell—the Greek form of the Latin *Cerberus*. Kerberos grew out of MIT's Project Athena, begun in 1983, and which also gave rise to X Window. It has been published as an Internet standard by the IETF, and is freely available for anyone to use.

Microsoft offered Kerberos for the first time with Windows 2000, launched on 17 February 2000. In a classic example of "embrace, extend and extinguish," Microsoft added its own extension to Kerberos; this prevented other implementations from working with it fully. Even though it was building on open protocols, Microsoft refused initially to release details about its extension.

Microsoft placed a document describing those extensions on its Web site at the end of April 2000. It added a typically clever twist, however: Although the specifications could be freely downloaded, they could be viewed only once a license agreement had been accepted. That license forbade attempts to implement the extension in new code—for example, in Samba. Indeed, Samba's Jeremy Allison points out that "if this had been available to [Microsoft] in the early days of SMB, Samba would have been stillborn."

On its own, the Kerberos saga would be a depressing story of how Microsoft felt confident enough blatantly to "de-commoditize" a protocol and use its clout on the desktop to impose a proprietary extension at the moment it was about to be judged in the U.S. antitrust case for its previous monopolistic behavior. But the story took an even more interesting turn when hackers flouted the licensing requirements and posted the full details of Microsoft's extension to the Slashdot.org site at the beginning of May.

On 11 May 2000, Microsoft responded by sending an e-mail to Slashdot regarding what it termed "unauthorized reproductions of Microsoft's copyrighted work" on the site. That is, Microsoft invoked copyright law, specifically the relatively new U.S. Digital Millennium Copyright Act, which grants copyright owners wide-ranging powers to pursue copyright infringement. Slashdot responded by declaring its "hesitation to engage in censorship" through withdrawal of postings made by its readers. The Kerberos saga therefore makes explicit the increasingly tangled relationships between trade secrets, free software, copyright, and freedom—as Eben Moglen, general counsel to the Free Software Foundation, had predicted.

Moglen is able to speak directly from experience regarding another area where free software potentially faces legal challenges. Some have suggested that the GNU GPL, the de facto constitution for the entire free-software movement, may not stand up in court. If this happens, it would cast a huge chill over the world of open source because it depends on the GNU GPL to regulate much of its operation.

So far, enforcement has not proved a problem. "About a dozen times a year," Moglen says, "somebody does something [that] violates the GPL. Most of the time, they're doing so inadvertently, they haven't thought through what the requirements are. And I call them up and I say, 'Look, you're violating the GPL. What you need to do is do this. Would you help us?'" The answer is invariably yes, he says.

"What is true," Moglen admits, "is that no large American software company has engaged in a public controversy with us over the enforceability of the GPL." And although some might conclude "that means . . . there's something about the GPL [that] is not enforceable, I would turn that proposition around," Moglen says. "There have been no such controversies because nobody thinks they're going to win them."

But, he adds, "I think that sometime it's probably going to become necessary, in order to dispel a little FUD [Fear, Uncertainty and Doubt] on these subjects, for us to choose to take the judicial enforcement route with a case [that] we would otherwise feel comfortable working out in our traditional way." This would be to demonstrate, once and for all, the validity of the GNU GPL and hence of the foundation of free software.

In one respect, the open source world is fortunate there are companies with the resources needed to back a long-drawn-out legal tussle with some well-financed violator. As Moglen says, "Our advantage from the great elopement of Wall Street with anarchism" in 1999, when companies such as Red Hat and VA Linux enjoyed highly successful IPOs, is "that . . . some money [is] lying around that can be used for these purposes."

But only "within limits," he adds, and notes that "each one of those enterprises looks the way it does because it has a zero cost of manufacture. Each of their models depends upon the idea that this is a very inexpensive business to be in, because your product is manufactured for you for nothing by other people." Moglen's observation touches on perhaps the most serious question mark hanging over open source: Will the business models based on it work in the long term?

One person who doubts it is Larry McVoy. "I believe that the next problem that the open source community is going to face is how to make a revenue stream appear and stick around," he says. As the author of the Sourceware proposal, which foresaw many of the features of today's operating system landscape, his words carry a particular weight.

"The problem with open source," he explains, "is that the things that meet the Open Source Definition are all focused on rights for the end users, to the detriment of any rights for the vendor." The end result, McVoy believes, is that companies based around open source software can never equal Netscape, Sun, and Microsoft as industry behemoths. McVoy also thinks such companies are laboring under a fundamental misapprehension about the open source development model. "It's easy to do the easy work," he says. "You can have a weekend hack attack, or even a month-long hack attack and do something significant and get a lot of praise from the community." But he points out that after the easy work comes the grind.

McVoy doesn't even allow that unpaid hackers will be useful at finding bugs in code written by paid professionals. If "college students sitting in their dorm room on your stuff that you've spent fifteen man-years working on, spend a week, or a weekend, or a day, or an hour working on it, they can't possibly grasp how it all fits together. There are companies who are betting that part of their development costs will be gone because of the open source model," McVoy says. "And I think they're betting on a failing model."

McVoy's litany of open source woes continues. He believes not only that such companies are doomed but that in the process of failing they will take swathes of the existing software industry with them. As the uptake of GNU/Linux and other open source programs increases, it will inevitably drive out solutions from other vendors—particularly in the Unix arena. McVoy contends, however, that these vendors paid for what we now call open source.

"The preceding [software] ecosystem had a built-in pad," he explains. "It charged more money than what the stuff you were getting was worth. The extra money paid for having engineers sitting around at Sun labs, and HP labs, and the rest of these places. The open source in the world didn't happen [thanks to] volunteers," he insists. "It happened [thanks to] engineers at places like Sun.

"This is a discussion that [Red Hat's] Bob Young and I have all the time," McVoy continues, "where he's worried as hell about this. Because, basically, Red Hat is well on its way to putting [Sun's software division] out of business. Well, that's kind of cool for Red Hat, except for one problem. Red Hat doesn't generate enough revenues to pay for the software that they get—and they actually get some of that software from Sun. This is known in the industry as killing your supplier. It's not a good idea." McVoy's reasoning raises critical questions about the viability of the companies based around free software. If he's right, the new open source companies whose flames have burned so brightly in recent years are destined to gutter into oblivion, and, in the process, starve fires of other companies that depend on Unix.

McVoy's analysis appears to underestimate the significant contribution students make to free software, whether in their spare time (the GIMP and Gtk), or through course projects (the LyX document processor)—and as both, like Linux, which began as an idle bedroom hack and turned into material for a master's thesis. But even if students' contributions are relatively small, and if open source companies really do drive some traditional software vendors out of business before following them into oblivion, it still may not matter.

As the previous chapter described, the open source revolution has moved on from the pioneers. Today, mainstream companies—IBM, HP, Compaq and SGI—have all taken up open source in various ways. They depend critically neither on Unix, as Sun does, nor on open source, as Red Hat and the other distributions do. Instead, they use both as elements of a broader strategy; for example, selling hardware and services.

Against this background, then, whether or not the new open source companies succeed is in some senses a secondary concern, although not for them and their shareholders. Development of GNU/Linux and open source within other companies will almost certainly continue, anyway. McVoy's own analysis explains why. The "built-in pad" he refers to means that traditional computer companies "can afford to have some percentage of their engineers working on stuff that they don't understand and they don't agree with," he notes. The reason this goes on is because "the engineers [are] passionate enough about it that they say, 'Look, I'm going to do this or I quit.' And [the companies] say, 'OK, you can do it.'"

Given that at least some of these companies will thrive as businesses—however great the impact of open source, it is not possible that the entire software business will disappear—those passionate engineers will still be working in their midst. The fruits of their passion will supplement the work of new generations of students in educational establishments, or of enthusiastic hobbyists programming at home, to say nothing of such dedicated hackers as Richard Stallman and the FSF who do not code to live, but live to code. This, ultimately, is the reason free software does not depend on open source companies for its own survival: It exists beyond the market.

The central issue, then, is not whether open source companies can flourish and blossom into multibillion dollar concerns but whether free software can continue to grow and progress as it has for the last decade and a half. Another scaling challenge presents itself: How can the open source methodology take on more and increasingly ambitious projects?

GNU/Linux, Apache, Sendmail, Perl, and the rest are continuing proof that the development approach does allow growth and change—although a little bumpily at times—to embrace ever-larger bodies of code. But projects can be expanded, and more of them undertaken, only if enough hackers devote significant amounts of time, energy, and enthusiasm: The success of free software depends on a constant supply of fresh coding talent. The problem is even worse than it might seem at first sight because open source needs this constant supply of new hackers just to keep its current projects ticking over.

Although high-profile coders—Richard Stallman, Larry Wall and Linus—appear to be fixtures in the hacker firmament, this is by no means true for the vast majority of those in the free-software world. For example, after a couple of years of working more or less on their own, the GIMP's creators Peter Mattis and Spencer Kimball decided it was time to move on, even though the software was not quite finished and no successors were lined up.

Two people more aware than most of the constant turnover of coders are Miguel de Icaza and Matthias Ettrich. To cope, both of them consciously structured their ambitious graphical interface projects as a collection of smaller subprojects. "What you have is that people contribute for a period of time," de Icaza explains, "then they have other obligations, like school, or marriage, or job changes, or family, and they have to stop working on the project." Ettrich is even more specific: "A generation for free-software programming is very short; it's between half a year and maybe two years for those more dedicated."

A central concern for the free-software world is therefore whether there will be enough new hackers, and where they will come from. The scale of this problem is unique to the open source software method; commercial software houses can always offer extra financial incentives to keep programmers who are thinking of leaving. It may well be that, as the open source world grows and enters the mainstream, enough additional professional programmers will start to contribute. Even if they don't, free software possesses unique advantages that will allow it to find those programmers from new sources: regions where computing is still in its early stages.

In the absence of a well-developed local support infrastructure, reliability becomes a key consideration, and GNU/Linux plus free software may be the only feasible option, especially if financial resources are limited. For example, the New York-based Sustainable Development Networking Programme (SDNP), part of the United Nations Development Programme, has routinely been using a GNU/Linux-based approach to provide around forty-five nations with some of their earliest connections to the Internet. Free software has been used for this purpose since 1994, an indication of its early stability and continuing utility.

The small size of the computer market in many of these countries often means that proprietary Western software is simply not available in a localized version. For example, in Ethiopia, "the market wasn't considered important enough for Microsoft-type products," Donald Knuth explains. "But volunteers could take the open source [of the free typesetting program T_EX] and then adapt it themselves." As a result, he says, computer users in Ethiopia "could have good fonts in Amharic [the main national language, with its own alphabet] that were made by somebody in [his] garage."

For certain parts of the world, other factors may favor open source over proprietary software. In China—an area that TurboLinux's Cliff Miller knows better than most—"the government mindset is that they don't want to be locked into something" that comes from the United States, he says. As a result, "they look at a company that sells closed, proprietary software coming from the U.S. [as] being a pretty big threat. Linux is much more in line with their political and economic needs than Microsoft Windows is." Indeed, there have been persistent rumors that the Chinese government might even forbid the use of Microsoft's Windows 2000 and adopt GNU/Linux as an "official" Chinese operating system. "You certainly hear in meetings a great deal of dissatisfaction with Microsoft in China," Miller comments, "but nobody goes on record saying that." However, "there is a lot of excitement around Linux," he says, and whether official of not, GNU/Linux is well on the way to becoming the de facto standard for China. "I'm sure it will," Miller says.

Potentially, then, the impact of millions of Chinese users on open source could be immense. But in the short term, at least, India's contribution promises to be even more dramatic. India has the advantage not only of a widespread use of English—the lingua franca for hacker collaboration over the Net—but also of a huge and highly educated middle class with ready access to computers. In short, India represents perhaps the perfect recruiting ground for free-software coders in the future.

India is already a significant force in the programming world; this came to many Westerners' attention through its work in fixing software issues arising out of the Year 2000 problem. And it is surely no coincidence that IBM has chosen to set up a GNU/Linux center in India as part of its move to embrace open source. "One of the appeals of Linux is that not only is there a hotbed in the U.S.," says IBM's Wladawsky-Berger, "but that there are even bigger hotbeds in Europe, India, and China. You can imagine there are lots and lots of wonderful Indian engineers."

There are likely to be even more such engineers if an Indian open source project called the Simputer—from SIMPle compUTER—succeeds. As a press release of 26 May 2000 explains, the Simputer is a "mobile computing device for the common man . . . based entirely on free software," principally GNU/Linux, Perl, and Tk. It is designed as a "shared computing device for a local community of users" and to "make available the benefits of Information Technology to the rural masses" in India. The unit's low price—around $200—is crucially important if it is to be widely deployed to these users, and that price would be impossible to achieve without open source software.

Other countries, too, are likely to become major contributors to the free-software world—Mexico, for example, thanks to a major distance learning project that is already underway there. Details about it first appeared in October 1998, when Arturo Espinosa Aldama posted to a mailing list for GNOME—a project to which he has close personal links. As Miguel de Icaza explains, "He was my roommate in Mexico," and in August 2000, Espinosa joined de Icaza's company Helix Code.

Espinosa wrote in 1998:

> I work as the project leader of the "Scholar Net," a program that aims to bring computers and the net to every elementary and mid-level school in Mexico. We expect to install from 20 to 35 thousand labs per year to a total of 140,000 centers in the next five years.

At the time, this message led to wild assertions in some quarters that 140,000 Mexican schools would soon be using GNU/Linux.

But Espinosa emphasizes, "Our Linux solution is just an option. It is not something that is being installed by decree. What happens is that every state in the country decides by itself what's going to be its technological solution" for implementing Scholar Net. So far, he says, six out of thirty-two Mexican states have shown an interest in adopting his GNU/Linux approach. "Realistically, I think that in a year we will have something near five states," he says. "So that's around maybe 1,500 schools installed."

Although far fewer than the 140,000 touted by some, this number is significant and would represent an important test-bed for the use of GNU/Linux in schools. Moreover, if even a small percentage of the children involved became free-software hackers, this could have a major impact on GNU/Linux. As de Icaza says, this and similar projects mean that "there are going to be more people who do not depend on proprietary technologies, who know how to use the free software alternatives, and know how to develop the free-software alternatives."

In a sense, though, such schemes to introduce GNU/Linux-based systems into schools are inefficient as a way of fostering new coders to drive free-software development; it places the onus on the individual—the child or young person—to get to know more about the underlying software, to learn programming, and to start hacking. Alongside such worthy undertakings, a more formal approach to teaching programming that would naturally lead people to contribute to open source projects is needed. This is one of the aims of a project called Computer Programming For Everybody (CP4E), the brainchild of another key figure in the world of open source.

Guido van Rossum was born in 1956, in the Netherlands. In the late 1980s, while living in Amsterdam, he worked on a branch of the Amoeba project, the main research interest of Andrew Tanenbaum, the creator of Minix, who is a professor at the Free University in the city. "I remember Tanenbaum asking me once, 'Are you a researcher or a developer?'" van Rossum says. "And I still don't know the answer. I guess I'm a bit of both."

While he was working on the Amoeba operating system, van Rossum came up with the idea for a new language. "One of the things we were trying to do was to make [Amoeba] a sufficiently usable system that we could run it on our workstations and use it for our day-to-day use," he says. "We realized that one of things that made it difficult was that we didn't have a good scripting language"—a method for creating programs quickly and easily. And so van Rossum wrote one, which he called Python after the BBC TV comedy series *Monty Python's Flying Circus*. "It was one of my favorite TV shows at the time," he explains.

As he later wrote in the foreword to *Programming Python*: "In December 1989, I was looking for a 'hobby' programming project that would keep me occupied during the week around Christmas." Note that he called this a "hobby," the term Linus employed to describe his kernel when he announced it to the world; and that van Rossum wrote it over Christmas 1989, just as Linus wrote the Virtual Memory code during Christmas 1991, and for the same reasons: to stave off boredom.

Python was released in February 1991, and it soon enjoyed a devoted following. Python is in many ways a rival to Perl—the leading scripting language—but van Rossum emphasizes that no animosity exists between him and Perl's creator, Larry Wall. "I think Larry is a great guy, and Perl is a very useful language, but I have a different philosophy about language design."

Because of that different philosophy—born in part from ideas borrowed from an earlier, educational programming language called ABC, which he "remembered fondly"—van Rossum says, "it gradually dawned on me that Python was actually a very good language to teach to beginners."

The projects van Rossum was working on for his employer at the time, the Corporation for National Research Initiatives (CNRI), based in Reston, Virginia, were coming to an end, and he was casting around for something new. "I was convinced that I wanted to work on Python full-time," he says. "The educational thing just popped up as one of the ideas that might work."

This project democratizes open source. Currently, hackers either start their own major projects or join someone else's; with van Rossum's approach, far more people would be able to hack up a simple script to meet their own needs. Once they get the taste for this, they might well go on to bigger things.

Van Rossum believes his approach could have a significant effect on open source. "Sometimes I think I'm crazy," he says, "but sometimes I think that it's not unreasonable to assume that lots of people will have some basic programming skills so they can make their computers do what they want them to do. There will be an open source community of people who share small and large things they created for their computers that is different from the existing open source community only in the fact that this is many more millions of people who are probably less sophisticated but nevertheless interested computer users."

The entire CP4E project is intimately bound up with open source. It will it create not only a huge body of potential coders but also a new demand for open source software. "If most software is proprietary, a lot of the ideals of CP4E won't be fully realized," van Rossum says. "Because one of the ideals is that people won't only want to create new software from scratch, because that's a tedious process, but people will want to take existing software and make changes."

Assuming that new pools of coding talent do evolve—in China and India, in the schools of Mexico, and through broad educational projects such as CP4E—one possible point of failure remains for the open source movements: at the top. Even with a constant supply of gifted hackers, without the right kind of leadership and a process that allows power to pass smoothly to successors, energy will dissipate and free-software projects worldwide will dwindle into irrelevant programming pastimes.

Most of the main open source projects have already tackled this issue. Apache's core group allows new members to be added as others drop out. Larry Wall has stepped back from the day-to-day running of Perl so that others can shoulder the burden in turn. Projects such as Sendmail and Tcl have companies with teams of paid engineers that can move the standards forward while preserving their openness. But questions of succession remain unanswered for the two key free-software projects: Linux and GNU.

Because Linux has a high profile and more and more companies are betting their futures on its continued development, the question of what happens after Linus has been the more discussed of the two. Opinions within the open source world differ. Larry McVoy, for example, believes that "Linux is held together by Linus, and he is a unique human being. The way I always put it is, great programmer, great [software] architect, nice guy—pick any two: You can't have all three in one human being"— except in Linus.

Stephen Tweedie is more sanguine. "There are so many other people involved," he says, "who have the ability to take on increasing parts of the workload, that I really can't see there being a long-term problem." Another senior hacker, Ted Ts'o, agrees: "There are a number of people who can do the job. Someone would have to get designated as the successor, or we might decide to use a different model—such as perhaps something like what Apache, or Perl, development communities use— it's not clear what we would do." And Ts'o emphasizes, "A lot of it has to do with enough people in the developer community being mature."

Fortunately, the Linux community seems to have both strength-in-depth and the requisite maturity to cope with any situation that might arise. For example, Alan Cox and Dave Miller are leading candidates to take over should this be necessary. Alan Cox is already running the stable branch of the code, leaving Linus to concentrate on the development version. Although Alan Cox is an obvious choice, he believes that "there are several people who could take over." He adds, "I'm told Linus has directions for the event filed away somewhere. I've never seen the contents and hopefully will never need to."

Dave Miller, too, has been handling an alternative kernel source tree that is held on the vger machine: "That's a huge tranche of development which is now being carried out entirely independently of Linus," as Tweedie points out. Nonetheless, even someone as gifted and ambitious as Miller, who almost took the momentous step of forking the Linux code during the 1998 "Linus does not scale" incident, recognizes that the time is not yet right for him to contemplate taking over. "I don't think I'm personally 100 percent mature enough to do it right at this moment," he says. "If I had to do it, I would. Maybe a year or two from now I could keep a grip on such a large project and make intelligent and well thought-out decisions. But I hope I never have too." And he adds, with knowing understatement, "Linus is pretty good at the task."

The two positions—that Linus is unique and that he is replaceable—are not, ultimately irreconcilable. Linus's greatest achievement is not his software: One day, Linux will be superseded. As Alan Cox says, "There will eventually come a point where someone is trying to do something [that] requires you fundamentally break Linux. So you will end up with something [that] replaces Linux, built just using Linux as kit of useful parts to get you going."

Linus's enduring contribution, rather, lies in his perfecting of the development model that he inherited in slightly different forms from the hacker cultures of Berkeley, the GNU project, and Minix. Linus opened the process to be inclusive: Anyone can download the latest kernel, anyone can send in patches. Linus added the vital element of rapid review—sometimes producing updated kernels on an almost daily basis—that took the open source process to the next level. Linus allowed his lieutenants progressively to take over parts of the kernel, thus ensuring its greater scalability and long-term viability.

Linus is unique because he was able to serve as a focal point for all these advances to come together to create a complete methodology that is now central to the continuing success of the open source movement and that offers the first plausible alternative to the current—and creaking—model of software development. But Linus is also replaceable because of this methodology, which allows programming and architectural decisions to be delegated to specialized circles of experts; and thanks to this methodology, even his leadership style—that of power wielded in subservience to the user base—can be distributed more widely.

This devolution of power has been possible because Linus is a pragmatist and the Linux development process inherently consensus-driven. In the purist wing, however, things are not so easy. Compromise is not an option when it involves fundamental issues of principle, as selecting a future leader of the GNU movement inevitably does. Given that there can be no fuzziness in the GNU project's goals, so leadership by committee—an inherently fuzzy approach—is hardly practical. What is needed is someone able to command unqualified respect within the purist hacker community not just for technical ability but also for an unswerving record of commitment to the ideals that stand at the heart of the GNU GPL and the GNU project.

Stallman says despairingly, "I'm going to keep working on the free-software movement because I don't see who's going to replace me." Nevertheless, a worthy successor who has the rare mix of qualities necessary may already be emerging in the person of Miguel de Icaza. His managerial skills, manifest in the smooth marshalling of hundreds of programmers in the GNOME project, as well as his own programming prowess, revealed through his coding of Midnight Commander and Gnumeric, are beyond question, as is his abiding and deep-seated commitment to the ideals of free software.

His own take on those ideals is striking. "As the years pass and you're working in this framework," he says, "you start to reevaluate in many areas your relationship with your friends and with your family. The same ideas about free software and sharing and caring about other people start to permeate other aspects of your life." De Icaza here makes explicit aspects that have always been implied in Stallman's crusade for free software and the creation of a community that can share it.

Although De Icaza hopes that "somebody with [fewer] responsibilities than I have would be able to take over" from Stallman if the need ever arose, he says that "if Richard asked, I would do it." As a result, he provides the entire free-software movement with the guarantee of a continuity and a future, no matter what happens.

De Icaza's readiness to accept such an onerous task—one that has already required Stallman to forgo much in his life—also hints at the reason free software and open source will continue to thrive and progress. Somewhere, whether in Boston, Helsinki, Mexico City, Beijing, or Delhi, somebody—probably young, and, with increasing likelihood in the future, a woman—will be willing to take on a similar burden when the need arises, despite the personal cost.

In the end, GNU/Linux and the open source projects are not about software code only. As this book has described, they are also about freedom, sharing, and community; they are about creation, beauty, and what hackers call "fun"—though "joy" would be nearer the mark. They are about the code within that is at the root of all that is best in us, that rebels against the worst, and that will exist as long as humanity endures.

INDEX

ACC Bookstore, 102, 103, 224–226
ActiveX, 262
Adabas D database, 100
Ajuba Solutions, 246
Allison, Jeremy, 277, 293
Allman, Eric, 120–123, 241–244
Alpha processor, 110–111, 294
Amazon.com, 138
America Online (AOL), 201–202, 298
Amsterdam Compiler Kit (ACK),
    21–22
Andreessen, Marc, 183–186, 190–191,
    249
Apache (computer program), 127–130,
    182
  and IBM, 205–219, 289–290
  versus Microsoft Internet Information
    Server, 270, 282
Apple computers, 183, 268
  and image manipulation, 252–253
  and GNU/Linux, 296–297
Applied Cryptography, 285
Applix (computer program), 98
ARPAnet, 120–123
Artificial Intelligence (AI) Laboratory,
    15–16, 17–19
Art of Computer Programming, The, 155
Art of Unix Programming, The, 153,
    155–159
AT&T, 66, 73, 124

Augustin, Larry, 101–102, 167, 170,
    250–251, 287–288

Baker, Mitchell, 196–197
Baltazar, Henry, 281–282
Barksdale, Jim, 189, 194
Barry, James, 206–211, 249
Bash (Bourne Again Shell) program,
    24–25
Bastok, Frederic, 309
Bechtolsheim, Andy, 243
Behlendorf, Brian, 125–130, 161, 199,
    209–210, 249
Ben-Halim, Zeyd M., 213
Berkeley Internet Name Domain (BIND),
    125, 182
Berkeley Software Design, Inc. (BSDI),
    295
Berkeley Systems Distribution (BSD),
    65–67, 73, 84–85, 122–125
  and GNU/Linux, 295
  and TCP/IP, 72
Berners-Lee, Tim, 6, 125, 182–183, 185,
    200, 244–245
Biro, Ross, 73–74, 77
Boich, Michael, 268
Bolzern, Mark, 96–97, 101,
    103–105
Boot and root disks, 87
Bostic, Keith, 149

Brooks, Fred, 14, 77, 148, 151
Browsers, 129–130
  and Netscape, 187
  open source, 182–183
  wars, 187–191
Bugs, 58–60, 83, 249

Caccamo, Wayne, 220–222, 248–249
Caldera (company), 99–100
  and corporate customers, 228–230
  and proprietary software, 229–230
  Network Desktop (CND), 99
  OpenLinux, 99–100
  support for GNU/Linux, 113, 114
Carr, Eric, 269
Case, Steve, 201–202
Cathedral and the Bazaar, The, 148, 150,
  165, 190
C (computer program), 21–22
  and the Amsterdam Compiler Kit
    (ACK), 21–22
  and the GNU C Compiler (GCC), 24,
    37, 237–240
CD-ROMs, 94–95
Charles, Philippe, 211–212
China, 317
Chowdhry Pankaj, 281–282
Clark, Jim, 186, 199
Clustering, 233
Cobalt Networks, 298
Code-forking, 75, 171, 305–306
Code Morphing Software, 164
ColdStorage (website), 250–251
Collabra (company), 189, 198
Commodore Vic–20 microcomputer, 8–9
Communicator (computer program)
  see Netscape Communications
Compaq Computer Corporation, 223,
  293–294
Computer Associates, 213
Computerworld, 170
Concurrent Version System (CVS), 173
Connolly, Dan, 182–183
Content Scramble System (CSS), 303
Control Data Corporation, 121
Convex (company), 183
Copyright
  and free software, 302–303
  and Linux, 44, 48–49, 112

and Mozilla Public License (MPL),
  197–198
and Netscape Public License (NPL),
  197–198
and open source code, 196–198
and Open Source Definition, 167–168
and Sendmail, Inc., 243–244
and the GNU Emacs General Public
  License, 26–29, 49, 79
and University of California at Berkeley,
  124
and X license, 63
mixed free and proprietary, 259–260
Cox, Alan, 72, 75–77, 80–82, 85, 103,
  179, 263, 308, 321
  and Apple computers, 296–297
  and multiprocessor support for Linux,
    114
Crusoe processor, 162, 298
Cryptozilla, 199–200
Currie, Peter, 189
Cutler, Dave, 6
Cygnus Solutions, 237–241, 299–300,
  306–307

Daemon, 125, 233
Dawes, David, 63
D'Cruze, Patrick, 103
Debian (computer program), 89–94,
  167–168
de Icaza, Miguel, 260–268, 298, 323
DeCSS, 303
Delivermail (computer program), 121–123
Dell, 222, 249, 298
Demetriou, Chris, 84
de Raadt, Theo, 84
Digital (company), 6, 13, 107
Ditzel, Dave, 162, 164
Document Object Model (DOM), 200
Domain Name System (DNS), 124–125
Dougan, Cort, 173
Duck Pond, the, 8, 10, 181
Duval, Gaël, 308
DVDs, 303
Dyroff, Roland, 234–235

Eazel (company), 268
Eckhardt, Drew, 47, 56, 61–62, 66
eCos, 300

EGCS, 307
Eich, Brendan, 200
Ellison, Larry, 215
Emacs (Editing Macros), 16–17, 22–23,
    171–172, 184, 237, 305
E-mail, 121–124, 150
    see also Sendmail
Eng, Eirik, 257–258
Ericsson (company), 298–299
Espinosa, Arturo, 318
Ettrich, Matthias, 255–260, 316
European Center for Nuclear Research, 6
Evans, Bruce, 37, 39, 68–69
Ewel, Jim, 278, 281
Ewing, Larry, 112
Ewing, Marc, 97–98, 223, 225–226
eXtensible Markup Language (XML), 199,
    246

File Transfer Protocol (FTP), 41
    and development of Linux, 69
Filo, Dave, 101–102
Finland, 6–7, 68
Fintronic, 101–102
Flagship (computer program), 96
Forbes, 170
Foresight Institute, 167
Forking
    see Code-forking
Freax, 42
FreeBSD, 84, 214–215, 295
Freely Redistributable Software
    Conference, 148
Freenet, 303–304
Free Software Foundation (FSF), 24, 91,
    92, 148, 149, 302, 312–313
Free software, 97–98, 145
    and code-forking, 171
    and DVDs, 303–304
    and IBM, 206
    and Netscape, 187
    and networking, 272
    and Open Source Definition, 167–168
    and proprietary software, 259–260
    and Slashdot.org, 302
    and Trolltech (company), 258
    Apache, 127–130
    Eric Allman and, 121–122, 160–161
    finding coders of, 316

image manipulation, 252–255
making money from, 237–251,
    315–316
Netscape Communications and,
    166–167, 182
Sendmail, 123, 182
    see also Shareware
Freeware Summit, 171, 199
Freshmeat (Web site), 250
Future of Linux Meeting, 215, 287

Gardner, Ray, 147
Garloff, Kurt, 174–175
Gates, Bill, 5, 188
    see also Microsoft
Gateway computers, 223, 298
Gecko, 200
General Image Manipulation Program
    (GIMP), 252–255
Germany, 234
Ghostscript, 233
Gilmore, John, 239
GNU Image Manipulation Program,
    252–255
GNU/Linux
    adaptations of, to different applications,
        60–61
    advantages over other operating
        systems, 65–67
    advantages over Windows, 58, 269–270
    after Linus Torvalds, 321–322
    and Alan Cox, 75–77, 80–82, 85
    and Caldera (company), 99–100
    and CD-ROMs, 94–95
    and code-forking, 75, 305–306
    and embedded systems, 299–301
    and Hewlett-Packard (HP), 220–223
    and IBM, 222–223, 289–290
    and image manipulation, 253–254
    and networking, 74–75, 80
    and Oracle, 213–216
    and proprietary software, 229–230
    and Red Hat (company), 97–98,
        217–219, 220–223, 228
    and Samba, 270–275
    and Ted Ts'o, 82–84
    and the Internet, 68–70, 71–72
    and Virtual Memory (VM), 47
    and Wine (computer program), 286

and XFree86, 64
and X Window system, 61–63, 73
boot and root disks, 87
bug fixes, 58–60, 83, 249
business services, 225–226, 234–235,
247–248
commercial ventures, 237–251, 284,
305, 309
competition with Berkeley Systems
Distribution (BSD), 65–67
competition with Minix, 53–54,
55–56
contributions to, by other hackers,
46–47, 56–58, 74, 80–81
control of, 84
control of, by Torvalds, 79–80
copyright, 44, 48–49, 79
corporate applications, 100–101
cost of operating, 285
customers, 247–248
distribution by Manchester Computing
Centre (MCC), 88
Documentation Project, 72
document processor, 255–256
early development of, 40–42, 111–112
Eric Raymond on, 150
flexibility of, 298–299
fragmentation of and problems with,
305–306
growth in applications and distribution
of, 88–89
growth of, 118–119, 289–295
High Availability, 301
in Germany, 234
in India, 317–318
in Japan, 232–233
in Mexico, 318–319
installation instructions, 48
integration with Debian, 92–93
integration with Minix, 57–58
International, 103–105
kernel development, 111–112
Kernel Version History, 67
Kongress, 165
logo and mascot, 112–113
making money from, 309
management of, 178–181, 285
Mandrake 5.1, 309
marketing, 104, 225–226

Matthias Ettrich on, 256–257
Mobile, 163–164, 298
multiarchitecture support, 113–114
multiprocessor support, 113–114
myths, 284–286
Network File System (NFS), 59–60
networking code, 77
Networking-Howto, 72, 74–75
patches, 173–181
portability of, 107–108, 113–114, 115,
286
Pro, 96–97
Redundant Array of Inexpensive Discs
(RAID) code, 261
release frequency, 67–68, 85
security, 285
Softlanding Linux System (SLS)
releases of, 88
software availability, 285
Standard Base (LSB), 310–311
technical support, 247–248
testing against Windows, 282–284
Torvalds's plan for, 46–47, 57
Turbo, 233
upgrades, 97
users, 119, 224–225, 247–248
version 0.01, 42–44
version 0.02, 45
version 0.10, 46
version 0.11, 46
version 0.12, 47
version 0.95, 55
version 1.0, 85
version 1.2, 112
version 2.0, 112
version 2.2, 274
Video and DVD Project (LiViD), 303
GNU Network Object Model Environment
(GNOME), 262–267, 295
GNU project, 20–30
and commercial software, 237–241
and Cygnus, 237–241
and GNUPro, 240
and Miguel de Icaza, 261
and Netscape Public License (NPL),
197
and open source code, 212–215
and the GNU Emacs General Public
License, 26–29, 49, 301, 312–313

Hurd, 45–46, 149
  integration with Linux, 57–58
Gnutella, 303–304
Google, 284, 301
Gophers, 126
Graphical user interfaces, 254, 258, 262
Greenblatt, Richard, 17–18
Gtk+ toolkit, 254–255, 262

Hackers, 3, 15–16, 17, 155, 315–316
  and code-forking, 171–172
  and DVDs, 303
  and Helix Code (company), 267–268
  and Initial Public Offerings (IPOs),
    235–236
  and Linux source code, 58
  and Mindcraft (company), 279
  and proprietary software, 229–230, 243
  and source code, 250–251
  and SourceXchange, 249
  and VA Linux, 250–251
  contributions to Linux by, 56–58, 74,
    80–81
  employment of, 248, 250–251
  management of, 320–321
Hackers (the book), 16
Hahn, Eric, 189–191, 194–195, 201, 205
Hall, Jon, 107, 116, 167
Harnois, Michael, 172
Hecker, Frank, 192–194, 200–201, 249
Helix Code (company), 267–268
Helsinki (Finland), 6–7
Henkel-Wallace, David, 239
Hertzfeld, Andy, 268
Hewlett-Packard (HP), 220–223, 248, 249
Hohndel, Dirk, 62
Homer, Mike, 189, 194
Homesteading the Noosphere, 155
HotBot (Web site), 301
HotWired magazine, 126–127, 130
Hubbard, Jordan, 84
Hurd (computer program), 45–46, 149
HyperText Markup Language (HTML),
    126
  and Emacs, 184–185
  early development of, 147–148
  tags, 185
HyperText Transport Protocol (HTTP),
    128

HyperText Transport Protocol daemon
    (HTTPd), 125

IA–64 processor, 287–288
IBM, 205–219
  and Linux, 222–223, 289–290, 311
  OS/2 Warp operating system, 257
  S/390 mainframes, 289–290
Image manipulation, 252–255
India, 317–318
Informix, 213
Infoworld, 213, 226
Initial Public Offerings (IPOs), 228
  and Caldera (company), 230
  hackers and, 235–236
  and Pacific HiTech, 233
  and Red Hat, 228
  and SuSE, 234–235
  and VA Linux, 235
  see also Venture capital
Intel
  80386 processor, 35–36, 162–163
  and development of Linux, 42–44, 50,
    64
  and Red Hat (company), 227–228
  Itanium chip (IA–64), 287–288
Internet
  and Sendmail, Inc., 242
  and source code, 250
  and TurboLinux, 233
Internet Engineering Task Force (IETF),
    128, 311
Internet Explorer, 188, 189
Internet, the, 6, 102
  and Domain Name System (DNS),
    124–125
  and free software, 182
  and HyperText Transport Protocol
    (HTTP), 125
  and Internet Engineering Task Force
    (IETF), 128
  and Requests for Comments (RFCs),
    128
  and the development of Linux, 71–72
  and the success of Linux, 68–70
  development of, 120–124

Jakarta (computer program), 289
Japan, 231–233

Jargon File, 146
Java (computer program), 6, 189–190,
    193, 211–212
Jeeves (computer program), 124
Jikes (computer program), 211–212, 289
Jobs, Steve, 183, 297
Johnson, Michael, 103
Jolitz, Bill, 65, 66
Jolitz, Lynne, 65
Journalism, open, 301–302
Joy, Bill, 124, 243
Julliard, Alexandre, 286
Junius, Martin, 88

Katz, Roberta, 194
K Desktop Environment (KDE), 258–262,
    308–309
    and KDE Free Qt Foundation, 264
Kerbango Radio, 298
Kerberos, 311–312
Kernels, 41, 44
    design, 50
    Linux, 111–112
    monolithic versus micro, 52
Kimball, Spencer, 252–255
Kirch, Olaf, 71, 103
Kleiner Perkins, 247
Knuth, Donald, 155–161, 255, 317

Lai, Glenn, 63
Le Duke, Dave, 247
Le Marois, Jacques, 309
Lemmke, Ari, 41, 42, 69, 183
Levy, Steven, 16, 17
Licenses
    see Copyright
Lieber, Derek, 55–56
LiGNUx, 92, 99
Lineo (company), 299
Linux
    see GNU/Linux
    see also VA Linux
Linuxcare (company), 246–248, 270
Linux Journal, 89, 94, 102, 103
Linux Kernel Version History, 67
Linux Network Administrator's Guide, 71,
    103
Linux News, 35
Linux Today, 277

Lisp (List Processing) Machine
    Incorporated (LMI), 17–19
Literate Programming, 156
Lonnroth, Magnus, 214
Love, Ransom, 229–231, 264
Lu, H.J., 88
Lycos Web site, 301
LyX (computer program), 255–257

MacDonald, Peter, 88, 234
Macmillan Publishing, 309
Mailing lists, electronic
    Apache, 127–128
    Linux-kernel, 172
    WWW-Talk, 126–127
Malda, Rob, 302
Manchester Computing Centre (MCC),
    88
MandrakeSoft (company), 309–310
Mares, Martin, 174, 175
Massachusetts Institute of Technology
    (MIT), 145
    and X license, 63
    see also Stallman, Richard
Mattis, Peter, 252–255, 262
McCool, Robert, 125
McNealy, Scott, 141
McVoy, Larry, 140–144, 178–181, 240,
    261, 298, 313–315
Media attention, 170
Metzenthen, Bill, 66
Mexico, 318–319
Microsoft, 5–6, 94
    ActiveX, 262
    and Kerberos, 311–312
    and Mindcraft (company), 275–284
    and Red Hat (company), 218–219
    and ResNova, 206
    and SMB protocol, 273–274
    and Transmeta, 162–163
    browsers, 188
    competition with Red Hat, 226–228
    Internet Information Server, 130
    myths about Linux, 284–286
    Office Suite, 217
    response to Hewlett-Packard support of
        Linux, 221–222
    security, 285
    success of, 194–195

support for World Wide Web
Consortium standards, 200
use of Linux by, 101
Windows emulators, 286
see also Windows
Miller, Cliff, 231–233
Miller, Dave, 108–110, 172, 174, 179–180,
261, 298, 308, 321–322
Mindcraft (company), 275–284
Miner, Allen, 214, 215–216, 223
Minix (computer program), 32–34,
36–40
and Linux version 0.02, 45–46
and the Intel 8086 chip, 64–65
competition with Linux, 49–50,
53–56
complaints about, by Linus Torvalds,
51
Mockapetris, Paul, 124–125
Moglen, Eben, 302, 312–313
Molnar, Ingo, 240, 282
Monni, Tove, 116
Mosaic (computer program), 183–184,
185, 245
Communications company, 186
Netscape browser, 186–187
see also National Center for
Supercomputing Applications
(NCSA)
Motif (computer program), 95–96, 185,
254, 262
Motorola, 108, 300–301
Mozilla, 192, 197-204, 205-206, 210, 211,
212, 214, 215, 227, 229
and America Online, 201–202
and distribution of Mozilla, 202–204
and Mozilla Stabilization Schedule,
200
party, 199
Mozilla Public License (MPL), 197–198
MS-DOS (operating system), 36
advantages of GNU/Linux over,
65–66
Multiarchitecture support, 113
Multiprocessor support, 113
Multisoft, 96
Murdock, Ian, 89–93
Murphy, Tim, 55
Mythical Man-Month, The, 14, 77

National Center for Supercomputing
Applications (NCSA), 125, 126–127,
183–184, 245
see also Mosaic (computer program)
Natural languages, 134–135
Navigator (computer program)
see Netscape Communications
NetBench, 270, 279
NetBSD, 84
Netscape Communications, 125, 127, 130,
219
and Caldera (company), 228–230
and distribution of Mozilla,
202–204
and IBM, 205
and Netscape Public License (NPL),
197–198
and the Open Directory, 301
browser source code, 166–167, 182,
190–191, 194–198, 205–206
Communicator, 205–206
Heresy documents, 189–190
Navigator browser, 187
support for World Wide Web
Consortium standards, 200
Network File System (NFS), 59–60
Networking
and electronic mail, 121–124
and Linux, 71, 74–75, 77, 80
and Windex program, 270–271
New Hacker's Dictionary, The,
146–147
Newsgroups, 36–39
and development of Linux, 63, 69
and Mindcraft (company), 276
and Perl, 136–137
New York Unix, 102
NeXT computer, 183
Next Generation Layout (NGL),
200
Noorda, Ray, 99
Nord, Haavard, 257–267
Novell, 99, 223. 229–231, 232, 249

Ockman, Sam, 167
Olson, Greg, 242–243
OpenBSD, 84
Open Directory, The, 301
OpenProjects (Web site), 250–251

Open source code, 167–168, 193–196, 212–217, 248, 265–266, 301–302, 312–313
  see also Source code
Open Source Solutions Operation (OSSO), 221
Operating Systems: Design and Implementation, 51
Oracle, 213–216, 223, 249
O'Reilly & Associates, 103, 139, 248–249
O'Reilly, Tim, 165–166, 169, 249
Ousterhout, John, 244–246

Pacific HiTech (company), 231–233
Palmisano, Sam, 291
Patch (computer program), 132
Patches, 173–181, 310
Pathworks, 271–272
Pauling, Linus, 7
PC Magazine, 281
PC Week, 281, 282
Penguin mascot, 113
PenguinRadio, 298
Perens, Bruce, 91–92, 166, 167–168, 264, 310
Perl (computer program), 135–139, 182, 319–320
Peterson, Christine, 167
Plattner, Hasso, 216–217
Posix standards, 40–41
Prince of Persia (computer game), 35–36
Programming
  as an art form, 156
  employment, 248–249
  Eric Raymond on, 151
  philosophies, 151–152
  profitability of, 315–316
  Unix, 153–154
Python (computer program), 319–320

Qt (computer program), 257–260, 264
Quarter Century of Unix, A, 13
Quasar Technologies, 257–258

Raymond, Eric, 144–155, 165, 177, 199, 235–236, 264
Red Hat (company), 96–98, 102, 217–219
  and Compaq Computer Corporation, 293–294

and embedded systems, 300
and GNU Network Object Model Environment (GNOME), 263
and Hewlett-Packard (HP), 220–223
and MandrakeSoft, 310
and open source code, 241
and proprietary software, 228–230
competition with Microsoft, 226–228
employment of hackers by, 248
growth of, 226–228
initial public offering, 228, 241
profitability of, 314–315
promotion of GNU/Linux by, 307–309
software marketing by, 225–226
Reisler, Kurt, 107
Requests for Comments (RFCs), 128
ResNova (company), 206
Richter, Adam, 95, 239
Ritchie, Dennis, 13–14
rn newsreader, 132–133
Roell, Thomas, 63
Running Linux, 57, 103
Rutgers University, 172

Safford, Dave, 88
Salus, Peter, 13, 148
Salzenberg, Chip, 137
Samba (computer program), 270–275, 293
San Francisco Gate, 170
Santa Cruz Operation, The (SCO), 140, 295, 296
SAP (company), 216–218, 223
Schneier, Bruce, 285
SCO (company), 295–296
Screen Phone, The, 298
Scriptics (company), 246
Security, computer, 285
Sendmail (computer program), 123, 182
  and proprietary software, 241–244
  early development of, 242
  marketing, 243
Sequoia Capital, 235
Server Message Block (SMB), 271
SGI, 109, 223, 242, 261, 277, 279, 280, 284, 287, 288, 293, 297, 315
Shan, Yen-Ping, 207–211
Shareware, 44–45, 256
Shearer, Dan, 272
Shields, David, 211–212

Sifry, Dave, 246–248
Silicon Graphics, Inc., 186, 223, 293
Silicon Valley Linux User Group, 167,
    169–170
Simputer, 318
Sinclair QL microcomputer, 9–10
Sinclair, Sir Clive, 9
Slackware, 93–94, 234
Sladkey, Rich, 56–60, 65
Slashdot.org, 301–302, 312
Sm@rt Reseller, 269, 274
Softbank Comdex, 104
Softlanding Linux System (SLS), 88–89
Software AG (company), 100
Software, proprietary
    and business-to-business e-commerce
        (B2B), 246
    and free software, 259–260
    and GNU Network Object Model
        Environment (GNOME), 267
    and Red Hat (company), 228–230
    and Sendmail, Inc., 241–244
    and the GNU project, 238–239
    hackers and, 229–230, 243
    in Japan, 232–233
    outside the West, 317
Solaris, 141, 294, 295
Soundblaster, 72
Source code, 58, 87, 88
    and distribution of Mozilla, 202–204
    and Freshmeat (Web site), 250
    and Mosaic, 186
    and Netscape, 187–188, 194–198,
        205–206
    and Open Source Solutions Operation
        (OSSO), 221
    and Red Hat (company), 225–228
    and SAP, 216–218
    and SourceForge (website), 251
    and VA Linux, 250–251
    see also Open source code
SourceForge (Web site), 251
SourceXchange, 249
Sparks, Bryan, 99–100, 119, 230–231,
    299, 300
Spyglass (company), 186
Stallman, Richard, 14–30, 145, 323
    and code-forking, 171–172
    and Cygnus, 307

and Open Source Definition,
    168–169
and profitability of free software,
    237–238
and the Artificial Intelligence (AI)
    Laboratory, 15–17
and the C compiler, 23–24
and the Debian program, 90–92
and the Freeware Summit, 166
and the GNU Emacs General Public
    License, 26–29
and the GNU project, 20–30
and Trolltech (company), 261
and Tcl, 245
and Unix, 19–20
coding method of, 23–24
see also Massachusetts Institute of
    Technology (MIT)
Sun Microsystems, 6, 140–141, 239, 249,
    294–295
    and Tcl (computer program), 245–246
    use of GNU/Linux by, 108
SunOS (operating system), 41
SunScript (company), 245–246
Sun World, 170
SuSE (company), 234–235, 289, 294
Sustained Development Networking
    Programme (SDNP), 317
Symbolics, 18–19
Symmetric Multi-Processor (SMP), 114
Systems Development Corporation (SDC),
    132–133

Tanenbaum, Andrew, 22, 32–34
    and Linus Torvalds, 50–53
    on control of Linux, 78–79
    on the Internet, 71
Tcl (computer program), 244–246
TCP/IP, 72, 124, 270–271
    and deployment platforms, 292
    Pathworks program for, 271–272
TECO (Text Editor and Corrector), 16
Texas A&M University, 88
T$_E$X (computer program), 157, 255
Thompson, Ken, 13–14, 52
386BSD, 65-67, 72, 76, 84, 85
Tiemann, Michael, 237–241, 300,
    306–307
Time, 170

TiVo, 298
Torvalds, Linus Benedict
  and Andrew Tanenbaum, 50–53
  and early PCs, 35–39
  and the Commodore Vic–24
    microcomputer, 8–9
  and the Sinclair QL microcomputer,
    9–10
  army service, 11–12
  college career, 10–11, 114–115
  complaints about Minix, 51
  early years, 7–9
  employment with Transmeta, 117–118,
    163-164
  first work on Linux, 40–42
  involvement with business activities,
    106–107
  leadership of Linux, 321–322
  master's thesis, 114–115
  media attention to, 170–171
  move to United States, 116–118
  newsgroup postings by, 36–39
  on GNU Network Object Model
    Environment (GNOME), 265–266
  on K Desktop Environment (KDE),
    265–266
  on the Internet, 71
  on Vger, 173–178
  plan for Linux, 46–47
  teaching experience, 114–115
Torvalds, Patricia Miranda, 116
Transmeta (company), 117–118, 162–165,
  298
Tribble, Bud, 268
Tridgell, Andrew, 113, 270–284
Troan, Erik, 165, 261
Trolltech (company), 257–267, 298,
  308–309
Tsillas, Jim, 63
Ts'o, Ted, 46–47, 56, 82–84, 175–176, 321
TurboLinux, 233, 249, 289
Tweedie, Stephen, 84, 321
Tyde, Arthur, 247

UltraSparc achitecture, 294
Ultrix (operating system), 13
UniForum, 104
Unix (operating system), 6, 107, 254
  and electronic mail, 124–125

and image manipulation, 253–254
and Novell, 99
and Posix standards, 40–41
and Samba (computer program), 293
and X license, 63
at University of California at Berkeley,
  121
development of, 13–14
fragmentation of and problems with,
  142–144, 296
newsletters, 224
programming, 153–154
Sun Microsystems and, 140–141
version 7, 32–33
Uytterhoeven, Geert, 172, 173

VA Linux, 235–236, 287–288
  and ColdStorage (website), 250–251
  and Intel Itanium chip (IA–64),
    287–288
  and OpenProjects (website), 250–251
  and Slashdot.org, 302
  and SourceForge (website), 251
  employment of hackers by, 248,
    250–251
  see also VA Research
Valloppillil, Vinod, 311
van Kempen, Fred, 74–75, 77, 80
van Rossum, Guido, 319–320
VA Research, 101, 102, 167, 170, 235
  see also VA Linux
Vaughan-Nichols, Steven J., 269, 276
Venture capital, 247, 310
  see also Initial Public Offerings (IPOs)
Vera, James, 102
Vger, 172–173
Virtual Memory (VM), 47
Visix (computer program), 229
Visual Basic, 5
Vixie, Paul, 125
Volkerding, Patrick, 94

Wall, Larry, 130–139, 161, 165, 319–320
Walnut Creek (software company), 94,
  295
Weaving the Web, 125
WebBench, 270
WebSphere Application Server, 205
Weiner, Bruce, 275–284

Welsh, Matt, 57, 103
Wexelblatt, David, 63
Whitinger, Dave, 275
Widgets, 254, 258
Williams, Riley, 67
Windex (computer program), 270–271
Windows (computer program), 5–6, 217
  advantages of GNU/Linux over, 58,
    269–270
  and Wine (computer program), 286
  browsers, 188
  competition with Red Hat, 218–219,
    226–228
  emulators, 286
  Matthias Ettrich on, 256–257
  networking, 273
  NT, 142–143, 273–275, 286–287
  portability of, 286
  web server, 206
  see also Microsoft
Wine (computer program), 286
Wired magazine, 126
Wirzenius, Lars, 10–12, 31–32, 69, 87, 92
Wladawsky-Berger, Irving, 290, 311
World Wide Web, 6, 125, 126–127,
    182–183, 244–245

and Freshmeat (Web site), 250
and HyperText Transport Protocol
    (HTTP), 125
and Mozilla, 199–201
Consortium (W3C), 200
WWW-Talk mailing list, 126–127, 182,
    184–185

Xanadu project, 147–148
X Consortium, 63
Xenix (operating system), 33
XFree86, 64
X Window system, 61–63, 73, 182–183,
    270
  and image manipulation, 254

Yacktman, Don, 297
Yahoo, 102, 130, 138, 235
Yang, Jerry, 101–102
Yggdrasil Computing, 95, 148, 239
Young, Bob, 102, 103, 223–230, 314

Zawinski, Jamie, 171, 191–192, 193, 197,
    199, 201–204
Zborowski, Orest, 62, 73
Ziff-Davis, 269–270